D1192231

A SHORT HISTORY OF AMERICAN
INDUSTRIAL POLICIES

A Short History of American Industrial Policies

William R. Nester
Professor of Political Science
St. John's University
New York

First published in Great Britain 1998 by
MACMILLAN PRESS LTD
Houndmills, Basingstoke, Hampshire RG21 6XS and London
Companies and representatives throughout the world

A catalogue record for this book is available from the British Library.

ISBN 0–333–72090–3

 First published in the United States of America 1998 by
ST. MARTIN'S PRESS, INC.,
Scholarly and Reference Division,
175 Fifth Avenue, New York, N.Y. 10010

ISBN 0–312–21102–3

Library of Congress Cataloging-in-Publication Data
Nester, William R., 1956–
A short history of American industrial policies / William R.
Nester.
p. cm.
Includes bibliographical references (p.   ) and index.
ISBN 0–312–21102–3 (cloth)
1. Industrial policy—United States—History. I. Title.
HD3616.U46N38 1998
338.973—dc21   97–36090
                                              CIP

This book is printed on paper suitable for recycling and made from fully managed and
sustained forest sources.

10   9   8   7   6   5   4   3   2   1
07 06 05 04 03 02 01 00 99 98

Printed in Great Britain by
The Ipswich Book Company Ltd
Ipswich, Suffolk

Contents

Introduction: The Industrial Policy Debate – Jefferson versus Hamilton

For nearly four centuries, Americans have debated the government's proper role in developing the economy. Most Americans would agree in principle with Thomas Jefferson's maxim that "the government that governs least, governs best."[1] Jeffersonians champion a radical individualism in which the government is restricted to guarding law, order, and, especially, private property. The government's sole role in the economy is to leave it alone. Markets should be completely free. The "free market," paradoxically, is not anarchical; the natural laws of supply and demand determine outcomes. Consumers desire something. Entrepreneurs supply it. "Greed is good" because in striving to serve one's own needs through work, innovation, buying, and selling, one inadvertently serves others. Thus does the "invisible hand" of the market solve all of society's problems and desires.

To the free market god, Jefferson was quite prepared to sacrifice any possibility of the United States developing its own industries. He dismissed the mercantilism of European monarchs who tried to nurture domestic industries to enhance the wealth and power of their respective kingdoms: "The political economists of Europe have established it as a principle that every state should endeavor to manufacture for itself." To that end, each state deployed duties, subsidies, workshops, navies, and armies to nurture domestic industries at the expense of foreign rivals. Even if those states proved that industrial policies worked, weighed against Jefferson's ideals, they were wrong to pursue them.

Jefferson shunned mercantilism for liberalism – the market rather than the state should decide each nation's economic fate. America would forever be a reaper of crops, sawer of lumber, and digger of metals for Europe's industrial powers: "such is our attachment to agriculture, and such our preference for foreign manufactures, that be it wise or unwise, our people will certainly [hew to] raising raw materials, and exchanging them for finer manufactures than

1

they are able to execute themselves. . . . While we have land to labour then, let us never wish to see our citizens occupied at a workbench . . . but, for the general operations of manufacture, let our work-shops remain in Europe. It is better to carry provisions and materials to workmen there."

The inveterate tinkerer and University of Virginia founder thought it folly for Americans to try to diversify and expand the nation's wealth by investing in manufactures. The Declaration of Independence's author not only saw nothing dangerous in America's dependence on European finished goods, he celebrated it: "Those who labor in the earth are the chosen people of God, if ever he had a chosen people, whose breasts he has made his peculiar deposit for substantial and genuine virtue."

For America to remain a "naturally" agrarian nation enjoyed the backing of no less an authority than Adam Smith, the father of liberal economics: "In North America . . . the purchase and improvement of uncultivated land is . . . the most profitable employment of the smallest as well as the greatest capitals. . . . Were the Americas . . . to stop the importation of British manufactures, and, by thus giving a monopoly to such of their own countrymen as could manufacture the like goods, divert any considerable part of their capital into this employment, they would retard instead of accelerating the further increase in the value of their annual produce, and would obstruct instead of promoting [their] progress . . . towards real wealth and greatness. This would be still more the case, were they to attempt . . . to monopolize their whole exportation trade."[2]

In a concept that would later be called "comparative advantage," Smith believed that all nations, like all individuals, possess certain natural endowments in whose production they should specialize and then trade that product for all others. Free markets led to specialization and the subsequent "invisible hand" that allows individuals and nations alike to fulfill their material needs and dreams. America's natural endowments were arable land and seemingly endless forests. Nature had thus destined America to provide the world with crops and lumber. Manufacturing would have been "unnatural" and thus to be avoided at all costs. History, of course, would prove those two great thinkers, Jefferson and Smith, profoundly wrong over America's ability to industrialize, and the overwhelming boost in wealth and power such a course provided the nation.

Not everyone agreed that free markets were the answer to all the nation's problems. Alexander Hamilton was Jefferson's political and philosophical nemesis. From his early manhood, Hamilton had displayed a genius for political economy that blossomed during his tenure as America's first Treasury Secretary. Through such brilliantly argued works as "Continentalist Number Five," "Report on a National Bank," and "Report on Manufactures" Hamilton demolished the "sage" of Monticello's flimsy sentiments and sophisms.[3] Throughout his works, Hamilton argued that policies which nurtured industries and the general economy were not only essential for enhancing American prosperity and power, they were solidly rooted in America's constitution and sovereignty.

Hamilton dismissed as utter nonsense the belief that "private interest will, if left to itself, infallibly find its own way to the most profitable employment.... To leave industry to itself, therefore, is ... the soundest as well as simplest policy." The result in America's case would be no industry arising at all, something Jefferson acclaimed and Hamilton deplored. The Treasury Secretary proceeded to argue that the more diversified a nation's economy, the greater its prosperity and power. Industry is the nation's engine of development and security. For a nation to allow its development to be shaped by market whims is to ultimately deliver it to the mercantilist policies of rival states. Free markets do not exist in the real world; far-sighted governments manage markets to advantage their own respective nation's industries. The greater America's dependence on the products of other states, the more it is potentially in their power: "the United States cannot exchange with Europe on equal terms; and the want of reciprocity would render them the victim of a system which should induce them to confine their views to Agriculture and refrain from Manufactures. A constant and increasing necessity ... for the commodities of Europe, and only a partial and occasional demand for their own ... could not but expose them to a state of impoverishment.... The importations of manufactured supplies seem invariably to drain the merely Agricultural people of their wealth." Even if foreign nations do not use America's economic dependence to force it to follow their own interests, America's undiversified economy leaves it vulnerable to economic disruptions: "the Nation which can bring to Market but few articles is likely to be more quickly ... affected by such stagnations."

Hamilton clearly understood the relationship between prosperity and power: "Not only the wealth, but the independence and security of a Country, appear to be materially connected with the prosperity of manufactures. Every nation, with a view to those great objects, ought to endeavor to possess within itself all the essentials of national supply."

How can America break its foreign dependence and stunted development? Hamilton argued forcefully that the United States should emulate the mercantilism of its rivals – "to secure such a market there is no other expedient than to promote manufacturing establishments." In a mercantilist world, the Federal government must work with its entrepreneurs to develop the economy: "certain nations grant bounties on the exportation of particular commodities, to enable their own workmen to undersell and supplant all competitors, in the countries to which those commodities are sent. Hence the undertakers of a new manufacture have to contend not only with the natural disadvantages of a new undertaking, but with the gratuities and remunerations which other governnments bestow. To be enabled to contend with success, it is evident, that the interference and aid of their own government are indispensible." By promoting industry, the government can stimulate a virtuous cycle of development in which "the multiplication of manufactories not only furnishes a Market for those articles . . . but it likewise creates a demand for such as were either unknown or produced in inconsiderable quantities . . . it is the interest of nations to diversify the industrious pursuits of the individuals who compose them."

American sovereignty, national interests, and the Constitution allow "the United States to consider by what means they can render themselves least dependent." To those who argue that the government cannot pick winners and losers, Hamilton replied: "Congress can easily possess all the information necessary to impose the duties with judgment, and the collection can without difficulty be made by their own officers."

The judicious use of tariffs would nurture American industries. Hamilton displayed a highly sophisticated understanding of how to wield that industrial policy weapon: "moderate duties are more productive than high ones. When they are low, a nation can trade abroad on better terms – its imports and exports will be larger – the duties will be regularly paid, and arising on a greater quantity of commodities, will yield more in the aggregate, than when they are so high as to operate either as a prohibition, or as an inducement to evade them by illicit practices." Hamilton went on to argue that competition would keep prices low for consumers; producers would not dare to pass the tariff on to their customers for fear of losing business to a rival.

Such policies would incur short-term costs and induce long-term benefits for the United States. Prices would initially rise as tariffs nurtured American industries but would fall steadily as competition with one another forced domestic entrepreneurs to perfect their manufacturing techniques. Thus "a temporary enhancement of price must always be well compensated by a permanent reduction of it."

Irony pervades America's industrial policy debate. To Hamilton's volumes of writings on political economy, Jefferson contributed no more than a handful of pages. While Hamilton joined the debate at the Constitutional Convention at Philadelphia in 1787 and defended the Constitution through his Federalist essays, Jefferson was on the Atlantic Ocean's far side as American ambassador to Versailles. It was Hamilton rather than Jefferson who was the genuine expert on the Constitution and political economy. Yet, to most Americans, Jefferson rather than Hamilton epitomizes the nation's laws and values, best captured by the slogan that "the government that governs best governs least."

The grave ended the duel between Jefferson and Hamilton. It did not end their philosophical and policy debate. Ever since then each generation has refought their battles. Two centuries later, Ronald Reagan repeatedly echoed Jefferson's ideas with the slogan, "government is not the solution, it is the problem." Bill Clinton's attempts to "reinvent government" so that it solves the nation's problems more efficiently is the latest assertion of Hamilton's philosophy.

While most Americans view Jefferson's principles as truisms, in practice they have come to depend on Hamilton's assertion that governments are necessary because markets are imperfect. Contrary to the Jeffersonian faith, Hamiltonians argue that the freer a market, the more likely that firms will impede and distort rather than advance the nation's development. Why is that so?

The fiercer the competition, the more short-term the outlooks of producers. Acting on the logic of economies of scale, firms race to produce as much as possible in hopes of bringing down per-unit production costs. The result is markets flooded with inexpensive goods. Consumers enjoy a buying frenzy and raise their living standards with ever more goods and services. Producers, meanwhile, fight for their business lives. The more everyone tries to undersell everyone else, the greater the number of bankruptcies and the thinner the profits for survivers. Obsessed with moment-to-moment battles, producers have little time or money to invest in long-term research and development for their own products, let alone invest in expensive, time-consuming projects with limited financial returns, such as dredging a port or digging a canal, that serve humanity. Inevitably, products are made for a "quick buck." Product obsolescence does not need to be planned. The lack of money to invest in quality control ensures that the product will fall apart sooner rather than later. The key is pushing that product to consumers before one's rivals. Slick marketing becomes essential for business success. Sales staffs should be able to sell refrigerators to Eskimos.

This market logic is magnified if the nation is wide open to foreign rivals, especially if they are promoted by their governments through such policies as subsidies, cartels, technology pirating, import barriers, export incentives, and the like. What happens then is the free market economy's development is warped and stunted by the policies of other states.

The long-term consequence of free markets are even grimmer. A Darwinian market where all war against all often ends with the survival of one fittest who rules all. Free markets and unbridled greed may provide an array of goods in the short term, but lead to stagnation, shoddy goods, inflated prices, and even the tyranny of domestic or foreign monopolies over time. By the late nineteenth century, a monopoly or oligopoly controlled virtually every industry and "market" in the United States.

It took the "visible hand" of the state to free American consumers from the tyranny imposed by private corporations. During that era, President Theodore Roosevelt was the most outspoken advocate of the Federal government using the "big stick" of antitrust laws and ethics to break up the monopolies and promote national interests. In doing so, he and other Hamiltonians rescued the United States from the destruction caused by unbridled Jeffersonianism. His cousin, President Franklin Roosevelt, would do so again during the 1930s as once more market Darwinism destroyed American wealth and power, this time with the Great Depression. Roosevelt's New Deal followed by the nation's mobilization for war succeeded where markets failed in promoting American prosperity and power. Most recently, President Bill Clinton has tried to trim the fat and expand the muscle of government so that it more efficiently regulates markets and thus promotes national development.

Time after time, the "visible hand" of public regulation is vital when the "invisible hand" of private greed and "free" markets fails to prevent the takeover by monopolies or to provide public goods that entrepreneurs lack the finance, time, and profit-motive to provide themselves. Hamiltonians insist that government should act as a partner with business in working toward the common goal of developing the economy. More specifically, the government can and should develop the nation's wealth and power by: nurturing leading industries behind tariff walls from foreign rivals; by building infrastructure such as ports, roads, and canals; by providing public education; by patronizing inventors, artisans, and artists; and by establishing a central bank, private banking system, and sound currency. The government can skilfully guide economic development by stressing cooperation or competition as appropriate, can help businesses distribute as well as create wealth, provide goods and services for individuals and society alike, and continually invest in the most dynamic, cutting-edge industries and technologies that can reap power and prosperity for the nation from the global economy. With government's far-sighted economic management, all this can be achieved far more efficiently, rapidly, and less expensively than if firms tried to do so alone, under the unlikely assumption they could do so at all.

The policies that Hamilton proposed would today be called industrial policies. What exactly are industrial policies? A lively debate swirls around the definition. Aaron Wildavsky argues that any policy designed to develop the nation is an industrial policy; it is synomous with "economic policy; its purpose is prosperity."[4] Thomas McCraw takes a narrower view of industrial policies as the means governments use to create a comparative advantage for their nation's industries. He informs us that the term "industrial policy" was used at least as early as 1876 when James Swank's book, *The Industrial Policies of Great Britain and the United States*, appeared. McCraw notes that the "book anticipated with uncanny accuracy the terms of today's debate: promotion of selected domestic industries, subsidies to exports, discouragement of imports. . . . The only difference is the two major players and their roles. In 1876 the protectionist upstart United States threatened the supremacy of free trade Britain. Today protectionist Japan threatens free trade America."[5]

A minority argue that there is no such thing as industrial policy. Mancur Olson explains that "industrial policy means different things to different people. Those . . . advocating industrial policy are . . . relatively vague. Some are so vague that they invite the reaction that industrial policy is neither a good idea nor a bad idea, but no idea at all; that it is the grin without the cat."[6] Robert Reich described industrial policy as "one of those rare ideas that has moved swiftly from obscurity to meaninglessness without any intervening period of coherence."[7]

Of these views, Wildavesky's is probably the most accurate. Industrial policies have come to mean any strategy by which a government attempts to develop the economy. Economists like to distinguish macroeconomic policies that serve the entire nation from microeconomic or industrial policies that target specific industries, technologies, regions, or firms. Actually, the effects of the two are so thoroughly entwined that it is impossible to distinguish their boundary.

Regardless of how one defines industrial policy, an even fiercer debate involves whether or not government should pursue them.[8] Even after two centuries, the idea that the Federal government should assist the nation's economic development is nearly as anathematized today as when Hamilton first proposed it. Industrial policies conflict with America's cherished myth of the rugged individual who, through hard work and inspiration, rises from "rags to riches." The Jeffersonian faith in markets remains as unshakeable as it is popular. At a June 1992 news conference, President George Bush was asked whether Washington should help American industries that were being bashed by foreign competition. Bush replied: "I don't think we ought to have industrial planning. I don't believe in targeting.... I do not want to see the Government pick winners and losers."[9] Supply and demand of unfettered markets should determine what mix of industrial winners and losers emerge from the Darwinian maelstrom. As Michael Boskin, President Reagan's chief economic advisor, was quoted as saying, it matters not if the economy produces "computer chips or potato chips."

Yet the centuries-long debate between Jeffersonians and Hamiltonians is quite sterile. The irony is that, since it was first instituted, the Federal government has picked winners and losers, favoring some industries, firms, regions, cities, and technologies, and neglecting others; the reforms of Theodore Roosevelt, Franklin Roosevelt, and Bill Clinton are only the most prominent examples of these activities. Nonetheless, despite the great number of industrial policies it has implemented, Washington has never realized Hamilton's idea of a grand development plan. Politics and pressure groups, rather than strategic planning, determine America's mix of industrial policies. Throughout the nation's history, an industry's relative lobbying power rather than its importance to the nation's economic development and security usually determined whether or not it was nurtured.

Today, whether they admit it or not, almost everyone, in practice if not principle, is a Hamiltonian. Why? Hamilton's industrial policies work far better in developing the economy and nurturing national power than Jefferson's zealous faith in markets. Jefferson himself eventually realized this. Ironically, he turned Hamiltonian in his second presidential term in 1806 when he asked Congress for a public works program not unlike much of what Hamilton had requested fifteen years earlier, and the following year imposed a trade embargo that boosted the nation's industries.

The fact is that Jeffersonian principles have some significant problems of consistency. Jeffersonians claim that the market will cure all society's ills and provide all of its wants. The reality, of course, is that when producers are not forced to, say, reduce pollution or improve efficiency, they will not. Regulations exist because free markets fail to provide all of the product quality, health, safety, and esthetic needs and desires of humans.

Nor does the Jeffersonian claim that "the freer the markets the faster the growth" bear close scrutiny. Washington's role in and impact on the economy have varied considerably over time. Before 1933, when America's economy was largely unregulated, the economy grew slower and more inequitably than since then, when Washington began to significantly guide development. Roosevelt's New Deal policies of the 1930s were the policy watershed that split a largely hands-off from a largely hands-on the economic tiller outlook. That more explicitly Hamiltonian approach has been successful. Overall, economic growth has not only been faster than before, but recessions are relatively brief and shallow compared to the frequent and prolonged "Panics" that dragged the economy into economic troughs. Thus can the central Jeffersonian claim be turned on its head – the more carefully Washington has managed markets, the stronger the economy. In all, free markets are a theoretical abstraction that do not exist in the contemporary world. Given their flaws, few would want them even if they could exist.

Jeffersonians celebrate "private property" rights above all else. Unfortunately, gross hypocrisy characterizes most of those waving the "property rights" banner. While arguing that they should be free to do with their land as they will, polluters do not hesitate to spew their waste on the private and public land of others, thereby diminishing – stealing if you will – the value of that land. Ideally, the polluter pays; in reality taxpayers bear the burden.

Despite the reverence with which many Americans view private property, there are limits to what one can do with one's land. The US Constitution grants the government the right of "eminent domain" in which it can seize private property under certain circumstances. The old adage, "your right to swing your fist stops an inch from my nose," captures the contradictions of those who believe private property rights should be unrestricted. Someone who burns tires or heaps sewage on his own property obviously diminishes the property values and thus rights of his neighbors. If there is no absolute legal or philosophical right to property, where do Americans draw the line of restrictions? Jeffersonians cannot answer such questions.

Jeffersonians are powerful across America, nowhere more so than in the seventeen Western states. There are significant ironies in the West being the ultimate Jeffersonian stronghold. While Jeffersonians decry "big government" and "welfare," no region of the United States is more heavily dependent on federal subsidies and handouts of various kinds, "welfare" if you will, than the West. For over a century, Western ranching, mining, farming, logging, and other special interests have reaped vast riches from the public domain and periodically emerged to shrilly denounce any attempts by Washington to regulate their businesses or cut back their generous government subsidies. The most recent "rebellion" among Western special interests appeared in the late 1970s and has gained political strength ever since. The self-proclaimed "sagebrush rebels" do not hesitate to speak of damming the Grand Canyon or grazing cattle in Yellowstone meadows. They wave the banner of "equal footing" to justify their demand for a massive federal land handout to their respective states, based on the idea that Western states should control as much of the land within their boundaries as Eastern states. Their claim conveniently overlooks the reality that the Western lands were bought and paid for by America's taxpayers for all Americans, and thus are public property owned by all Americans.

Because of all these contradictions, paradoxes, and failings, few contemporary Jeffersonians are pure market Darwinists. Most now admit to "market imperfections" that government has a duty to iron out. The government's role is to act as the impartial referee over the market to ensure the competition remains fair and no one takes undue advantage. Regulations impose standards for product safety and content. Antitrust laws and the Fair Trade Commission manage competition to prevent "imperfections" such as monopolies or cartels from arising and destroying the market. Ever-stricter pollution controls impose costs on business to provide benefits for all Americans. Medicare, social security, medicaid, and various welfare programs protect the sick, the poor, and the elderly from being victims of market Darwinism. Over the course of more than 120 years, Washington has created a succession of national battlefields, monuments, forests, parks, wildlife refuges, and wildernesses that celebrate America's natural, cultural, and historic heritage by carving them from public lands or buying them from private owners to save them from market exploitation. Washington underwrites much of the nation's research and development bill through tax incentives for private efforts, grants to universities and other research institutes, and through its own array of laboratories. Federal money underwrites highways, ports, railroads, bridges, airports, telecommunications, satellites, and other infrastructure essential for a modern economy. As the world becomes ever-more interdependent, Washington increasingly intervenes to protect domestic industries from "unfair" foreign competition such as dumping, cartels, and subsidies, and to pressure foreign governments to open their own carefully managed markets.

Thus, if the real rather than theoretical world is examined, it soon becomes apparent that the Jeffersonian claims are delusions. In reality, all governments, including that of the United States, conduct industrial policies which profoundly affect their respective nations' economic development. Genuinely free markets have never existed in America; instead, over time they have been more extensively managed. The supposedly golden age of free markets before Franklin Roosevelt's New Deal is a popular myth: "Big government ... begins with the founding of this country. Almost from the very first budget the federal government has grown faster than the economy."[10] Increasing numbers of Americans recognize this political economic reality. Summarizing the economic issues of the 1990s, Laura Tyson, President Clinton's Council of Economic Advisors' Chair, concluded that "the debate in Washington has shifted from whether the nation has a competetiveness problem to what should be done about it."[11]

While all governments may try to develop their national economies, the values underlining those policies, the processes by which the policies are conceived and implemented, and the scope and methods of those policies vary greatly from one country to the next. "Industrial policy" remains a dirty word in America's political and academic worlds. Like any other government, Washington conducts industrial policies, but they are shaped far more by politics than grand strategy. As a result, Washington ends up subsidizing with various means such relatively unimportant industries as textiles, logging, ranching, tobacco-growing, mining, and so on, while largely neglecting such strategic industries as microelectronics, automobiles, machine tools, and steel, to name a few.

This tendency for politics rather than strategy to shape America's industrial policies is built into its political system. No democratic nation has a more deliberately fragmented political system than the United States. The Founders satisfied diverse political forces and philosophical perspectives by agreeing to decentralize power in the Federal government among the executive, legislative, and judicial branches, and then further diluting that federal power by sharing it with state and local governments. The result is a system which emphasizes limited power at the expense of efficiency.

Policymaking thus does not reside in any particular branch of government, but in a complex, dynamic relationship among the executive, legislative, and judicial branches at the federal, state, and local levels. Over time, that system has become ever-more complex as the role and power of government have expanded to meet an ever-greater array of interrelated problems and expectations. When George Washington took office in 1789, he presided over a mere five cabinets which altogether employed around 4000 civilians. There were no executive agencies or independent and emergency agencies. Meanwhile Congress mustered 200 members and the Supreme Court had not even been organized. In 1990, the number of departments had reached fourteen, executive agencies fourteen, and independent or emergency agencies 101. The executive branch employed 3.067 million, Congress 38 000, and the judicial system 22 000. To that must be added the fifty state, 3042 county, 19 200 municipal, 16 691 township and town, 14 721 school district, and 29 532 special district governments, for a total of 83 237 governments employing millions in the United States.[12]

Within this elaborate federalist system, most policies change incrementally. Dramatic policy shifts are rare; they usually occur only during crises when the president and legislators feel compelled to do something. The system encourages politicians and bureaucrats to tinker with existing programs rather than establish new ones. This incrementalism can provide policies with stability and predictability. But it can also stifle innovation and allow chronic problems to worsen into crises. Most harmfully, the fragmented system enables powerful interest groups to armtwist politicians and bureaucrats into providing them with unwarranted subsidies or stymie reform that damages broader American interests.

How does this happen? The government, of course, does not make policy in a vacuum. Thousands of lobby groups compete to assert their different and often conflicting interests. America's political system allows those interest groups many ways in which to pursue their ambitions. Theoretically, the system is based on James Madison's goal of using interest groups, or "factions," as he called them, to check "ambition against ambition." In reality, interest groups vary enormously in their relative financial, membership, organizational, motivational, and thus lobbying power; generally speaking, the more money and voters an interest group can muster, the greater its ability to assert its goals within the political system. Although, overall, the policymaking system is highly pluralistic and decentralized, specific industrial policies tend to be shaped by "iron triangles" of affected interest groups, bureaucracies, and politicians. Not surprisingly, Hamilton's vision of a grand strategy to develop America's economy disappears in this Darwinian political marketplace, where policies are shaped by power rather than national interests.

The United States is unlikely to abandon its *ad hoc*, heavily politicized industrial policymaking system any time soon. The system is rooted deeply in American values and institutions of decentralized political power, radical individualism, and get-rich-quick dreams. Most policies will continue to be shaped by the most powerful, whose power is enhanced by the ability to get government to implement policies that favor them. America's economic development is both negatively and positively shaped by scores of huge industrial complexes that feed off this cycle of political and economic wealth and power.

Yet despite these realities, Jefferson's dream lives on. In no country have the abstract ideals of Jeffersonians taken a firmer hold on the popular imagination than in the United States. Most democratic industrial nations have developed ways to balance individual rights and social needs. In the United States the balance is tipped decisively toward the values of decentralization, private ownership, free enterprise, and markets, over the needs of the poor, the sick, the environment, or the entire nation. Radical individualism or Social Darwinism lies at the root of most American values, behaviors, and institutions.

Why is Jefferson's concept of a minimal state deeply imbedded in the United States? In contrast to the European experience, democratic values and institutions developed in what is now the United States from the very first settlements. In the United States, corporate bureaucracies emerged before governmental ones; in Europe, Japan, and elsewhere, the opposite occurred. John Ikenberry explains that,

> Variations in the sequencing and timing of political and economic development and the state-building responses to economic depression and war powerfully affect the centralization and capacities of the representative and bureaucratic institutions of the state. Many European nations, for example, constructed powerful administrative organizations in advance of the spread of democratic institutions, which served to strengthen the role that executive officials could play in subsequent periods of economic and political development. War and geopolitical conflict from the early modern period onward also had centralizing effects on European state bureaucracies; they also created incentives for developing extensive capacities for economic intervention and extraction.[13]

Popular culture reinforces this historical experience. The Horatio Alger "rags to riches" myth is central to America's national psyche. Of course, few Americans have ever had the product, ambition, business skills, and luck to be successful entrepreneurs. In fact, nine of ten new businesses in the United States fail within five years of their inception. While some of those would-be entrepreneurs keep plugging away with new businesses, most will simply go to work for someone else, while others end up on welfare. Those businesses which are the most dynamic are usually those which enjoy the most government largess. But that hard fact prevents few Americans from trying, and even less from believing, that with a little extra work and luck they will become millionaires some day – and that government can only hinder them from doing so.

A Short History of American Industrial Policies will analyze the ideological, political, and industrial policy struggle between Jeffersonians and Hamiltonians from the colonial era to the 1990s. To give a complete understanding, both the chronology and process of America's industrial policymaking and policies will be explored in depth throughout.

1 For Better or for Worse: Policymaking

Policies are the broad outlines within which governments view and often act on a situation. They are implemented with specific laws, programs, regulations, and other actions. A policy can be as much what a government does not do as what it does. Some policies may simply be statements of principle that leaders have no intention of following. Deciding not to decide is a decision too. When a government refuses to do or say anything it is following a policy. As Hugh Heclo put it, a policy is "a course of action or inaction rather than a specific decision or action."[1] But, mostly, policies are concrete actions that a government takes toward a problem.

How are policies made? The popular image is that of experts sitting around a table rationally debating the reason for a problem and various remedies for solving it. After careful deliberation they reach a decision.

The process is rarely that neat. Policymaking is not about rationally debating, choosing, and implementing solutions to problems; it is about narrow political, bureaucratic, and other interests asserting themselves – policy results from the subsequent multi-stranded tug of war. As Graham Allison put it, "What happens is not chosen as a solution to a problem, but rather results from compromise, conflict, and confusion among officials with diverse interests and unequal influence."[2]

Those who study policymaking have yet to devise a model which encompasses all these forces. Instead, they analyze policymaking from one of the following: a "state-centered approach" that emphasizes the role of officials, congressmen, and bureaucratic politics; a "society-centered approach" that explores the demands made on government by interest groups, public opinion, cultural values, and historic precedences; or, if the issue involves international relations, a "system-centered approach" that explores the relative power balance among those countries involved with the issue.[3]

In discussing the ways in which American industrial policies are formulated and implemented, the following discussion will incorporate elements of the state, international system, and society approaches where appropriate.

THE NATURE OF THE SYSTEM

Perhaps no nation has a more complex policymaking system than the United States. The American Constitution's architects designed it to check power, not promote efficiency. The Founders were primarily concerned with creating a system that prevented any individuals, groups, or institutions from dominating. To this end, they split power among the legislative, executive, and judicial branches of the Federal Government, and among the Federal, state, and local governments. The result is a perennial struggle among and within these different realms, as each tries to assert its respective power and interests.

What explains this emphasis on restraint rather than efficacy? The answer is rooted deep in American culture. Culture is the systematic way in which a group perceives, values, and expresses itself and the world. Cultures provide their members with traditions, ceremonies, arts, systems of right and wrong, histories, aspirations, taboos, and institutions which uphold all of that. By definition, any group with shared characteristics has a culture, however rudimentary or complex. In the contemporary world, culture is most commonly used to analyze the shared characteristics of nations.

How does culture affect policy? Political culture is that aspect of culture which shapes the way people manage conflicts. Economic culture is composed of the values and behaviors that govern production and exchange. Aaron Wildavesky goes so far as to argue that "when individuals make important decisions, these choices are simultaneously choices of political culture."[4]

Political, economic, and social liberalism forms the core of American culture.[5] From the time the first English settlers landed in what would become the United States, the inhabitants have developed liberal, democratic ideals and institutions more powerful than those of any other country. For most early Americans, not only the Crown but even their colonial legislatures were far away and often irrelevant to their needs. From the beginning, American governments were limited mostly to maintaining public order. Isolated not only from England but from each other, each colony fiercely guarded its own representative system.

Yet not all of America's inhabitants shared equally in the treasured ideal of liberty. Slavery existed in all the colonies, although most pervasively in the South. Women were little better off than slaves; few colonies allowed them to own property, none allowed them a political life. In most colonies only property owers – those who paid more than a certain tax or owned more than a certain acreage – could vote. Even stricter property standards determined who was eligible for public office. Opportunities for advancement up the socioeconomic ladder varied considerably from one locale to the next.

Several centuries of bitter civil rights conflicts punctuated by a Civil War bloodbath have gradually enlarged the opportunities for greater numbers and types of Americans. Yet the socioeconomic and political playing field remains anything but level. In all, Americans treasure liberty much more than equality. The United States surpasses any other liberal democratic country in extremes of wealth and poverty, a reality that most American shrug off as "natural." American culture celebrates the "rags-to-riches" myth in which the wealthy by definition have worked hard and honestly to enjoy what they have. Most Americans seem unconcerned about the possibility of rule by a wealthy aristocracy rather than the "people." Both in its ideals and execution, the system seems to give every individual ample opportunity for political expression and economic enrichment.

The delegates to the Constitutional Convention of 1787 essentially nationalized 150 years of previous political development. Given the mutual animosities and ambitions among and within the states, the decentralized Federal system to which the Founders finally agreed was all but inevitable. Hugh Heclo decribes America's constitutional tradition as, "not a set of answers but an invitation to struggle over problems of order and diversity, authority and accountability."[6]

While the Constitution is effective in promoting individual rights and dispersing power, it has created an inefficient policymaking system. In America's decentralized system, those responsible for addressing issues rarely have enough power to act decisively. With power diffused so broadly, there are numerous positions or "veto points" which can derail proposed or enacted laws, budget cuts, regulations, and so on. Other politicians, bureaucrats, special interest groups, laws, regulations, limited budgets, personnel, and policy priorities all can inhibit decisive action.

The popular view of policymaking revolves around the president and his advisors rationally discussing problems, devising solutions, and issuing orders. While the "buck" on many if not most industrial policy issues may well stop with the president, his decision is shaped and constrained by a host of other forces. The president is only one link in a multi-stranded tug-of-war which can also include his advisors, bureaucracies, politicians at the congressional, state, and local levels, interest groups, public opinion, the existing policy toward the issue, cultural values, the issue's relative importance to other issues, and foreign governments and their respective policies, which in turn are often shaped by a similar struggle. The bottom line of any political struggle is the relative power balance among the participants. In all, there are as many policymaking processes as there are issues. Each issue has its own cast of actors whose power and roles may well shift over time.

Nonetheless, no matter what the power of various interest groups, public opinion, and the mass media, policies are ultimately decided by those in charge. The trouble lies in determining just where the proverbial "buck" stops. In the executive branch alone, a half-dozen institutions play a major role in shaping economic policy: the Council of Economic Advisors (CEA), the Office of Management and Budget (OMB), the Treasury Department, the Commerce Department, the United States Trade Representative (USTR), and the Federal Reserve. Depending on the issue, all other departments and agencies can assert their interests and duties in shaping economic policy. Other prominent agencies include the Securities and Exchange Commission (SEC), the Federal Trade Commission (FTC), the Interstate Commerce Commission (ICC), the National Labor Relations Board, the Federal Energy Regulatory Commission, the Federal Deposit Insurance Corporation (FDIC), the Environmental Protection Agency (EPA), and the Occupational Safety and Health Administration (OSHA).

No one agency coordinates this array of departments, agencies, and bureaus. The executive branch's collection of economic policymaking institutions evolved over time, starting with the Treasury Department's founding in 1789. Most historians agree that the modern presidency began with Franklin Roosevelt. With the 1934 Reciprocal Trade Act, Congress tipped the power balance over trade policy toward the presidency, where it has stayed ever since. That power, however, was not enough for Roosevelt. Six years after taking office and beginning his war against the Great Depression, the president finally recognized that he needed a formal institution to aid economic policymaking. In 1939, he created the Executive Office of the President which included representatives of various agencies and the Bureau of the Budget taken from the Treasury Department.

Subsequent presidents added new institutions and policymaking arrangements. The 1946 Employment Act further boosted the institutional expertise available to the president by creating within the White House the CEA. Although the CEA is supposed to give the president "objective" advice over economic policy, the field is divided into various schools which bitterly disagree. For example, the University of Chicago school promotes an extreme *laissez faire* view; the Massachusetts Institute of Technology (MIT) a more centrist economic perspective. Presidents tend to appoint economists who echo their own views.[7]

Few presidents have been content to rely on the CEA alone; many outright ignored it. President Ford created an Economic Policy Board, President Carter an Economic Policy Group, and President Reagan a Cabinet Council on Economic Affairs, all in attempts to centralize policymaking. In 1993, President Clinton established a National Economic Council to forge and coordinate geoeconomic policies as a counterpart to the National Security Council which does the same for geopolitical policies. But none of these new institutions proved capable of asserting control over the entrenched powers and interests of the other economic bureaucracies.

Each administration makes its own adjustments to the policymaking system. No matter what institutions and arrangements it chooses, every administration finds it takes years before a satisfactory policymaking arrangement emerges, if at all. The arrival of a new president results in the wholesale firing of over 4000 officials at the top ranks of government departments and agencies, and their replacement with 4000 new, largely inexperienced people. No other democratic industrial country allows non-professionals such easy access to government's top echelons and fires them so readily just as they have begun to acquire some expertise in their duties.

In such a system, the president can at best focus on formulating policy on a half-dozen critical issues and delegate the rest to the bureaucracy. Even then, the president risks being overwhelmed by the endless information and myriad of interest groups shaping those issues. And even when the president makes a decision, he may not be able to implement it. Presidential power is mostly the power to persuade other politicians, bureaucrats, interest groups, the public, and the media that his policies should be implemented. As President Truman once said, "I sit here all day trying to persuade people to do the things they ought to have sense enough to do without my persuading them. . . . That's all the powers of the President amount to."[8]

What gives the bureaucracies so much power? After all, is it not the duty of politicians to determine and bureaucrats to implement policy? In reality, the bureaucrats are as influential as the interest groups and politicians in shaping policy. In fact, bureaucracies themselves are interest groups. Perhaps no groups in society are more resistent to change than bureaucracies. After all, they are in charge of formulating, implementing, and maintaining policies. Thus, in any political system, those in bureaucracies do anything they can to preserve themselves and, if possible, expand their duties, power, status, and other perks. Like policies, bureaucracies often outlive their usefulness but "are likely to persist even when the social forces and circumstances that forged those institutions have gradually changed."[9]

Bureaucrats "control the personnel, money, rewards, materials, and legal powers of government.... And it is they who receive most of the implementation directives from executive, legislative, or judicial decision makers."[10] In sheer numbers, the bureaucrats far outweigh the politicians. The federal bureaucracy includes 13 departments, 52 independent agencies, and five regulatory commissions, run by an army of 2.8 million people. Each segment of this vast bureaucracy, from the largest department to smallest section, is an interest group itself. And like other interest groups, it fights fiercely to enhance its power, prestige, budget, personnel, and other privileges. Invariably, jurisdictions overlap. Bureaucracies thus either fight like pitbulls or cooperate to transcend the boundary dispute.

There is considerable overlap in duties and powers among the various bureaucracies. In many issues, two or more bureaucracies could potentially be in charge of implementing a policy. The result are bitter battles over policy "turf." The ever greater diffusion of power and duties makes bureaucratic battles ever-more intractable. While any given industrial policy may more or less ineffectively address its targeted problems, in seeding money, personnel, and power across hundreds of public and private institutions it creates powerful entrenched political forces. Once a bureaucracy captures a program, it will fight fiercely to retain it no matter how obsolete or unnecessary it has become. What happens is that, "Dependents readily become constituencies, quick to protect and promote their programs. Programs may prove almost impossible to terminate, or may be reformed only after protracted political battles, because the constituencies have a material or ideological stake in the status quo."[11]

The bureaucracies are anything but omnipotent once they have won the battle for implementing a policy. Although their duties have grown, departments and agencies increasingly lack the personnel, money, and expertise to do their jobs. As a result, underfunded and understaffed bureaucracies must rely on the very industries they are supposedly regulating to supply vital information and even write the rules. Attached to the bureaucracies are over a thousand advisory committees composed of representatives of special interest groups. These advisory committees do things like help officials write up regulations. The result is more than a little like having foxes guard chicken coops. Conflicts of interest proliferate in such a system. For example, bureaucrats are often unable or reluctant to enforce the tough penalties that Congress writes into environmental laws. Instead, often to avoid lengthy and expensive court battles, officials bargain with the violating industry, city, or state over their degree of compliance and sanctions. Like their politician counterparts, bureaucrats may have greater powers to obstruct than to implement.

If economic policymaking just involved the executive branch it would be complex enough. But, theoretically, the power to regulate the economy actually lies in Congress. The Constitution's Article I empowers Congress, "To lay and collect Taxes, Duties, Imposts and Excises, to pay the Debts and provide for the common Defense and general Welfare of the United States.... To borrow Money on the credit of the United States.... To coin Money [and] regulate the Value thereof.... No Money shall be drawn from the Treasury, but in Consequence of Appropriations made by Law." Through laws, investigations, resolutions, filibusters, and appropriations, Congress sets the policy parameters within which the president can operate; wielding those same powers, it can redo policies the president has already done. Congressional policymaking is criticized on several grounds.

Congress does most of its work not on the floor but in a maze of committees and subcommittees with the powers to investigate and formulate policies in their respective issue areas. Unfortunately, as with the bureaucracies, many committee and subcommittee duties and powers overlap. And, like the bureaucracies, rather than providing forums for debates on the issues, committees and subcommittees often become captives of special interests as politicians rely on affected interest groups to formulate the policies for them. Senators and representatives tend to join those committees and subcommittees whose decisions affect the interest groups that put them in office. The committee and subcommittee system tends to fragment policies and give interest groups too many pressure or veto points to realize their goals. Thus, in Congress, special interests tend to prevail over national interests.

As in the White House, policies that emerge from Congress tend to be compromises of conflicting interests and thus often too weak to address adequately that issue. Laws frequently are often riddled with ambiguities, contradictions, and unrealistic deadlines. Congress often fails to appropriate funds for the programs it creates. Sometimes the laws Congress passes are too detailed, and thus give officials little flexibility to respond creatively to changing and differing situations; at other times they are so vague that their implementation is blocked through law-suits by adversely affected groups.

In America's political system, short-term needs almost invariably elbow aside those of the long term. The system channels the actions of politicians (no matter how far-sighted some would like to be) in the White House and Congress alike to think in two- and four-year reelection limits. Presidents and their staffs shape their policy priorities to fulfill campaign promises in hopes they will carry the next election. So, of course, do the members of Congress.

Every two years, all 435 representatives and one of three senators face reelection. Unfortunately, elections are increasingly won by negative campaigns. To smear one's opponent with half-truths is the best way to cut him or her down in the polls. The opponent inevitably retaliates and the public is subjected to barrages of vitriolic accusations. Public cynicism rises; faith in the system falls. Each election campaign seems more vicious than the previous. During the 1994 mid-term elections, surveys revealed new levels of disgust among voters and non-voters alike toward Washington's policy gridlock, porkbarrel politics, and the *status quo*.

Whether newly elected or reelected, the representative or senator will largely act as either the delegate or trustee of his district's or state's interests. Delegates represent the demands of the prevailing interest groups; trustees attempt to find a public interest that encompasses all demands and needs. Not surprisingly, delegates tend to be reelected more frequently than trustees. Thus, representatives tend to be delegates. It is frequently said that "all politics is local." Representatives are beholden to the special interest groups that mobilized the votes and money to put them in power. Once in Congress, representatives will "logroll" in voting each other legislative "pork" to carry home to voters. To win reelection, the representative must cart back enough largess to his or her district to satisfy political patrons and the general public alike. Representatives win one election and then immediately begin focusing on the next less than two years away. Many policies thus tend to reflect the short-term outlook of House elections. Although with six-year terms, senators can take a broader perspective, they too are often the mouthpieces of the handful of well-organized and financed interest groups that helped elect them. Worried constantly about winning the next election, representatives and senators alike tend to do what is popular rather than right. Hyprocrisy is rampant; the same politician who decries the pork-barrel politics of others does not hesitate to shovel as much of it as possible to his own constituents.

A major impediment to confronting worsening problems at every level of government is the "not in my term of office" (NIMTOO) dilemma. Myopic beyond the next election, politicians often find that the costs of confronting such problems as, say, medicare's looming bankruptcy, the proliferation of leaking toxic wastedumps, and so on are often financially and politically exorbitant. Powerful business interests enriching themselves from the *status quo* demand that it remain unchanged, no matter what the cost to the public. Hefty campaign contributions pour into the coffers of politicians who support the *status quo*; those who challenge it are often financially strapped. Few elected officials want to rile special interests with tougher regulations or the public with higher taxes. The costs of addressing worsening socioeconomic problems bite businesses and taxpayers hard in the short term, while such long-term benefits as reduced health care costs, higher quality of life, a more efficient economy, and more jobs remain abstract for most.

Although the committee system is supposed to transform its members into policy experts, that rarely happens. In 1997, 56 of 100 senators and 40 percent of the representatives were lawyers, most others were businessmen. Congress rarely has the expertise among its representatives or advisors to understand and act on the increasingly complex technical and scientific issues it must confront in industrial policy issues. Despite their often long committee and subcommittee tenures, where they are exposed to daily briefings and investigations, few senators or representatives acquire an understanding of complex problems. They lack the time and sometimes the inclination or ability to do so. Not only are they often members of other completely unrelated committees and subcommittees, but their time is consumed with struggling toward reelection, fund-raising, placating powerful interest groups, and bringing home the "pork" to their districts or states. John Moore, a former EPA deputy director, succinctly captured the dilemma: "You've got 1 or 2 Congressmen who truly know [science]; there are 400 others that are going to vote on it."[12] The result is "an assembly of scientific amateurs enacting programs of great technical complexity to ameliorate scientifically complicated ... ills most legislators but dimly understand."[13]

The judicial system has become an increasingly powerful player in shaping industrial policies. The Supreme Court at times has played a decisive role in making or breaking laws and regulations affecting entire industries. More recent decisions have enhanced government's power to regulate the economy. However, for its first 150 years through the 1940s, the Supreme Court tended to interpret the Constitution very narrowly and literally. It ruled illegal dozens of laws that increased the government's ability to manage the economy and specific sectors. In contrast, the Warren and Burger Courts of the 1950s through the 1970s were criticized for "judicial legislation" or making policy rather than simply ruling on whether or not an existing law was constitutional.

Perhaps the Supreme Court's most important contribution to enhancing the judicial system's own role in industrial policy is to expand the concept of legal "standing" – or those who have the right to sue. Until a quarter century ago, laws limited the ability to sue to those directly affected. Starting with the 1970 Clean Air Act, most environmental laws include provisions that allow "any person" to sue those who violate the law. Since then, court decisions have not only accepted but reinforced that legislative expansion of "standing". Now anyone or any group can sue, say, a factory for polluting or a development for destroying endangered species, regardless of whether or not they are directly affected. This allows environmental groups to champion those who might lack the funds, time, determination, and ability to do so themselves, whether the victims are human or not. In rendering judgements on environmental suits, the courts often force reluctant bureaucracies to enforce their own laws or reluctant corporations to obey the laws that supposedly govern them. Since then, lawsuits against businesses of all kinds have proliferated like so many mushrooms after a rain.

Businesses fight back by issuing a "strategic lawsuit against public participation" or SLAPP. SLAPPs claim the shaky legal ground that any protest or legal challenge to a business devalues and sometimes destroys its property rights. A related legal strategy involves suits against "takings" or regulations which restrict property rights and thus cause a loss of value or income. Developers claim the Constitution requires that government compensate them for such losses. The Reagan and Bush administration packed the courts with conservatives who have ruled in favor of those claiming "takings".[14]

Anti-developers counter that they are simply exercising their First Amendment right to freedom of speech; if a business's property value drops from the subsequent publicity and regulations, then that is only just and may deter others from polluting. They further claim that industrial pollution is not a right and, indeed, destroys the property that is downstream or downwind of it.

The participants' endurance rather than the relative strength of a case often determines who wins in a lawsuit. And endurance largely depends on who can expend more money, time, energy, and expertise on slugging it out in the courts. Although courts have ruled in favor of defendants in SLAPPs 80 percent of the time, the suits can debilitate environmental groups. Through 1991, over 400 had been filed and the average case lasted three years. The business goal is not so much legal victory as it is the intimidation of citizen groups from addressing their concerns.[15] Yet, SLAPPs are becoming a less effective strategy for developers. Environmentalists have retaliated with "SLAPP Backs" by suing developers with malicious prosecution suits. To date, three states – New York, California, and Washington – have enacted anti-SLAPP laws that place a greater burden of proof on those who file them and imposes penalties for frivolous suits. A national anti-SLAPP law may eventually be passed, although not as long as the Republican Party controls Congress. Regardless, the courts will play a important role in shaping some industrial policies for the forseeable future.

As if federal industrial policies were not shaped by a diverse enough range of participants, each of the fifty states and most local city, county, or town governments pursue their own industrial policies. Even the smallest government can promote or hinder industries by adjusting various property and income tax rates, pollution, labor, zoning, and safety laws, infrastructure, and the education system. States compete fiercely to attract new industries. Bidding wars erupt among states to attract, say, a Japanese automobile plant by offering its developers tax holidays for years on end and massive public investments in roads, ports, railroads, sewage, and so on. State and local governments can also pursue policies that discourage certain industries.[16]

The competence, laws, and interests among state and local governments in industrial policies vary enormously from one jurisdiction to the next. Several factors shape the response of state and local governments to developmental questions. As elsewhere, the judicious use by state and local governments of existing wealth and power can create yet more wealth and power. The more populous industrial states often have much more money and expertise to promote yet more development. States with professional legislatures have more skills and time to confront complex industrial questions than those with part-time legislatures. Yet, even states with fewer resources with which to attract new or transform established industries can use such low-cost policies as rewritten regulations, tax adjustments, and so on to advance their goals. These same factors apply to local governments as well, though obviously on a much smaller scale.

Twenty-one states allow citizens to participate in the drafting of laws and regulations affecting them; sixteen states require environmental impact studies which include citizen input. Most of the referendums that appear on ballots will become laws that either promote or hinder industry, and often pit business against environmental interests. As at the federal level, industrialists use such standard political tactics as lobbying, campaign contributions, litigation, and public relations to promote their interests at the state and local levels. They are usually more effective in using these tactics than their opponents because they have much more money and thus can buy more politicians and media. For example, industrialists spent $6 million, or five times more than their opponents, to defeat "Big Green" Proposition 128 on the November 1990 California ballot. The initiative would have banned clear-cutting, new offshore oil drilling, and carcinogenic pesticides, and reduced carbon dioxide emissions from utility plants. Surveys indicated that nearly two-thirds of Californians favored "Big Green" when it was first approved for the ballot. Yet, by barraging voters over a half year with an elaborate and often misleading mass-media campaign, the industrialists succeeded in getting voters to defeat Proposition 128 by a two to one margin.

Recently, industrialists have not just successfully defeated environmental referendums, but initiated their own. "Trojan Horse initiatives" are written to protect industrial profits and practices but are titled and sold to the public as strict environmental laws. The average uninformed citizen concerned with environmental issues might well have voted "yes" for such seemingly progressive measures as the Global Warming and Clear-Cutting Reduction, Consumer Pesticide Enforcement, and Wildlife Protection and Reforestation acts which appeared on various state ballots. All of these actually protected industrial rather than environmental interests.

Though industrial interests usually far outgun environmentalists in financial and political clout, they do not always win, especially at the local level. Industrial versus environmental battles have proliferated at the state and local level, in part because of NIMBYism ("Not in my backyardism") – the attitude and often actions of those who believe that they have a right to a healthy, safe, and valuable home and neighborhood. NIMBYism is shared by people across the political spectrum, including many of those tireless defenders of private property who would otherwise shrug at a dam across the Grand Canyon. To protect their quality of life, NIMBYists attend local hearings, negotiate with representatives of offending interests in "environmental dispute resolutions" (EDRs), and sue. Local groups have been espcially effective in repelling proposed hazardous waste sites. Between 1979 and 1986, of 179 attempts to locate waste dumps, about 25 percent were rejected, 53 percent were still being fought, and only 22 percent were allowed.[17]

NIMBYists are generally more affluent and white. When one community resists a hazardous waste dump, another and usually less affluent and often minority community will invariably receive it. Those communities least politically united or financially viable are usually the most adversely affected by hazardous waste sites. Race plays a definite role in just where a government will site an industrial development or hazardous waste dump. A 1992 study found that regulators were much more likely to protect white than black neighborhoods from environmental problems, and imposed 46 percent higher penalties for violations of environmental laws and 500 percent higher penalties for violations of toxic waste laws if they took place in a white community.[18]

Since many NIMBYists lack an understanding or empathy with larger environmental concerns, NIMBYists prove to be ephemeral environmental allies. The commitment of NIMBYists is to the specific problem affecting them: "They fight fiercely and then, win or lose, they vanish."[19] However, a few citizens have carried the environmental fight beyond their local concern. For example, former Love Canal resident Lois Gibbs founded the Clearing House for Hazardous Waste in 1981 to coordinate a nationwide effort among local groups battling hazardous waste dumps.

As on the federal level, the abilities of state and local governments to initiate industrial policies are restrained by an array of political, legal, financial, and cultural forces. Sometimes the most powerful restraint on the ability of state and local governments to act is the Federal government itself. Congress has passed dozens of health, safety, and environmental laws that state and local governments are supposed to abide by. The Federal government outright owns more than half of Alaska, Idaho, Nevada, Oregon, Utah, and Wyoming, and more than one-third of Arizona, California, Colorado, and New Mexico. The decisions Washington's politicians or bureaucrats make in developing or preserving those public lands can enrich or deplete that state's economic and environmental health. Yet, state and local governments are anything but powerless before Washington. Bargaining among the federal, state, and local governments over policy and law is incessant. The enforcement of federal law is flexible and sometimes discarded altogether.

Whether an industrial policy issue arises first at the federal, state, or local level, it will inevitably attract a constellation of bitterly opposed interest groups. As acrimonious as such conflicts can become, most would that agree with Founder James Madison that the success of American liberal democracy depends on the initiative of its citizens and the pitting of "interest against interest" and "ambition against ambition." In such a system, the only way for an individual to assert his or her interests is to form an alliance with like-minded people. The better organized, financed, and membered the group, the greater the chance it has to influence policy. Theodore Lowi agreed with Madison that, with respect to interest group politics, it is, "both necessary and good that the policy agenda and the public interest be defined in terms of the organized interests of society."[20]

However, like individuals, not all interest groups are created equal; some are naturally more advantaged than others in terms of money, organization, connections, and skills. Unsurprisingly, business groups almost invariably outgun all other interests in policy conflicts. Interest groups are composed of individuals. Sometimes an interest group is so powerful that it can get most politicians to reject public opinion on an issue. The National Rifle Association (NRA), for example, regularly shoots down most laws regulating guns despite the fact that 70–80 percent of Americans polled favor varying forms of gun control.

Though everyone is free to join a group that promotes their respective interests, just who is more likely to exercise that right? Here again, the more wealth and power someone has, the more likely he or she will be an active interest group member. The greater one's affluence and education, the greater one's tendency to assert one's interests. Why is there such a difference? Poorer, less-educated people may be quite aware when their interests are threatened by those of other groups, yet lack the time, money, organizational, and connection advantages to assert themselves. Weak power often becomes powerlessness when the holder discards any possibility of fighting back with an apathetic shrug.

Interest groups have proliferated in the United States, from fewer than 500 registered in Washington in 1960 to 6083 in 1992. Virtually every interest group has a political arm or "political action committee" (PAC) with which to raise money, shape elections, and prowl the corridors of power in Washington and elsewhere to influence policy. The only constraints on interest groups and their PACs are other interest groups and their respective PACs. The 1946 Federal Regulation of Lobbying Act and the 1971 Federal Election Campaign Act and its 1974 amendment have failed to curb PAC power.

Indeed, PACs have proliferated for several reasons, the most important of which is that elections have steadily become more expensive and, paradoxically, the 1974 law that limited individual and group donations to a candidate to $1000 and $5000, respectively, actually stimulated PAC power. Politicians must tap into many more PACs than before, which gives interest groups a powerful incentive to create a PAC to fill that need. The level playing field imposed by the campaign finance laws certainly made it more competitive. Those laws, however, are easily skirted. While direct contributions to individual politicians ("hard" money) are regulated, there are no limits on donations that individuals or groups can make to political parties or simply in advertising campaigns or voter registration drives ("soft" money).[21]

The largest interest groups are the nation's two major parties – the Republicans and the Democrats – which are composed of loose coalitions of more narrow interest groups for whose allegiance they compete fiercely. Like other interest groups, political parties achieve and hold power by mobilizing a virtuous cycle of money, voters, organization, and popular images, slogans, and policies. Yet the parties lack the cohesion of most interest groups. There is no party discipline. Politicians do not hesitate to cross the aisle to vote with the other party when it suits their purposes.

Business interest groups tend to be the most powerful. The most prominent business groups are the National Association of Manufacturing (NAM) which has been shaping policies since it was founded in 1895, the Chamber of Commerce since 1912, and the Business Roundtable since 1972. More specific industrial groups, however, have a greater policy impact. Every industry has its own lobby group, such as American Medical Association (AMA), the Independent Insurance Agents of America, or the American Bar Association (ABA). In addition to lobbying through its industrial association, every corporation invests a significant portion of its budget in pressuring government on its own. Size and power are related. The Fortune 500 largest corporations can generally twist enough congressional arms more easily than smaller firms. When, say, a GM, ATT, or IBM talks in Congress, everyone listens.

Business groups give more to the Republicans than to the Democrats, since the former are more devoted to favoring special interests than the latter who support a wider array of policies including business, civil rights, the environment, and so on. The 1996 campaign was the most expensive ever, with the Republican Party raising $398 million and the Democratic Party $242 million, up 63 percent and 71 percent, respectively, from the 1992 campaign.

Congressional votes are clearly for sale to the highest bidder, as a study of fourteen issues not surprisingly revealed.[22] In 1991, the sugar industry funneled an average $13 473 into the pockets of 61 senators and $5994 to 217 representatives who voted for a bill that cost consumers an extra 50¢ for a five-pound bag of sugar; senate opponents received only $1461, and representatives $853. The timber industry fattened the coffers of 54 senators by an average $19 503 and 211 representatives by $2675 in 1996 to allow loggers to clear-cut "dead" or "diseased" trees in formerly protected national forests; the 42 senators and 209 representatives who voted against the bill received a mere $2415 and $542, respectively. Northrop spent an average $2100 buying the votes from representatives for $493 million more in corporate welfare for the B-2, a manned bomber that has no strategic rationale and does not even work; the 210 representatives courageous enough to vote against the outrageous boondoggle that has so far cost taxpayers over $40 billion received a mere $100 each.

Sugar, trees, and B-2 bombers are three examples of hundreds of industries and corporations that yearly buy congressional votes that shower them with tens of billions of dollars in corporate welfare. There is nothing strategic about sugar, trees, or B-2 bombers. Of the three, the B-2 is by far the most wasteful, diverting $40 billion from strategic civilian industries or from weapon systems that do have a strategic rationale and do work. Hypocrisy, of course, fattens the corruption. How many of those same senators and representatives do not hesitate to laddle out the pork to huge corporations that pad their campaign funds, while simultaneously waving the Jeffersonian banner that "government is not the solution, it is the problem," or decry unwed teenage mothers on welfare?

With some exceptions, nearly all non-business groups are outgunned in finance, numbers, and organization when they square off with an industry or industries. The nation's largest labor organizations, the American Federation of Labour – Congress of Industrial Organization (AFL – CIO) and the Teamsters, peaked in power, finance, and members in the 1960s and have declined ever since. Yet their efforts helped promote laws and regulations that improved safety, hours, and compensation for workers. Likewise the National Association for the Advancement of Colored People (NAACP) was influential in forcing the White House and Congress to enact civil rights laws in 1964 and 1965 that promoted political and legal equality, but has since faded in importance. The voices of watchdog human rights groups such as the American Civil Liberties Union (ACLU) or Common Cause are usually drowned out by entrenched interest groups.

Some non-business groups have become more powerful in asserting their interests. Environmental groups have proliferated and have scored important victories in curbing the worst excesses of market Darwinism and promoting sustainable development. The American Association of Retired Persons (AARP) has been instrumental in blocking efforts to reform such middle- and upper-class welfare programs as social security and medicare. But perhaps the most powerful interest groups of all have been conservative religious groups such as the Moral Majority and Christian Coalition. They have been successful not so much in winning specific issues on abortion, prayer in public schools, or public financing of private religious schools, but in electing officials who promote their views at the national, state, and local levels; the Moral Majority is widely credited with getting Ronald Reagan elected in 1980 and the Christian Coalition with electing a Republican majority to Congress in 1992 and 1996.

In a system dominated by interest groups, what role does public opinion play in shaping industrial policies? Ideally, the "public" is the sum of every citizen, each of whom is well-educated, reflective, and open-minded. America's public may have never come close to realizing that ideal. As the world becomes ever-more complex and its problems ever-more interrelated, people become less capable of comprehending it all, no matter how much they try. The ever-swelling ocean of available information and the manifold problems it reveals, seem to overwhelm most people rather than liberate them from ignorance. No matter how well-educated an individual is, he or she must inevitably paper over vast realms of ignorance with "I just don't know" or, more likely, more or less inaccurate images. In the world views of most people, what is important is not so much what really is out there, but what they believe is out there. People act on their beliefs, no matter how ill-founded those beliefs may be. Many Americans hold such contradictory beliefs as that the budget should be balanced, taxes cut, and social spending increased. With popular expectations that the president is primarily responsible for economic prosperity, presidential races hinge on the economy's performance.

Most people may express outrage or delight over particular issues, politicians, parties, or ideologies, yet only about half of all eligible Americans bother to vote. Few who enter the polling booth have a firm grasp of the current issues and the respective positions of the contending politicians. As Walter Lippman put it, the American voter "lives in a world which he ... does not understand and is unable to direct ... his sovereignty is a fiction. He reigns in theory, but in fact he does not govern."[23] At best, public opinion serves "as a system of dykes which channel public action or which fix a range of discretion within which government may act or within which debate at official levels may proceed."[24]

The education system is supposed to create "good citizens." But America's school system, which seems to put as much emphasis on football and proms as on studies, or on feelings as on thinking, is certainly partly reponsible for public ignorance. Yet the school system only reflects popular American culture's prevailing values. From the nation's beginning, Americans have distrusted intellectuals, relying instead on "common sense." Alas, what often passes for common sense is simply common prejudice or ignorance.

Special interest groups have tapped into these prejudices by mobilizing segments of the public through mass mailings and telephone calls, "hate radio," church pulpits and television stations to write their representatives and senators on specific issues. These well-orchestrated campaigns aside, the "public" is incapable on its own of playing a significant role in national industrial policies. Public opinion polls survey a cross-sampling of Americans on general issues, and rarely address more specific industrial policy questions such as whether the federal government should give a loan to Chrysler, protect the semiconductor industry from Japanese dumping, or impose tougher clean air or water regulations. The most important impact the public makes on policy is through elections. But only about half the public even bothers to vote.

And what of the mass media's role in industrial policy? The mass media are supposed to play as important a role as the schools in educating the public and acting as the watchdog of government. The mass media are often called the government's "fourth branch" which checks the power of the other branches by revealing mistakes and corruption. How well do the mass media fulfill these roles? Generally the mass media have a limited effect on industrial policy. Investigative reports by muckraking newspapers, magazines, and television programs can highlight such problems as misappropriated funds, subsidies to obsolete industries, severe pollution problems, corruption of the system by special interests, and so forth. If the revelations spark a mass public outcry then politicians may be forced to act – usually symbolically, sometimes substantially.

Perhaps the most powerful impact the mass media can have on industrial policy is indirect, through identifying festering environmental problems spawned by unbridled industrialization. Politicians are well aware of the public's growing environmental awareness and increasingly respond to it. Over the past several decades, environmental regulations on business have proliferated, reducing severe pollution problems at a considerable cost to producers, which of course is passed on to consumers. A crisis can jolt a lethargic or gridlocked system into action. For example, public outrage at revelations of the Love Canal toxic waste dump prompted Congress to pass the "Superfund" toxic cleanup law less than a year later. But such decisive action is the exception rather than the rule.

LEGACY

Given America's vastly complex political system, just where do industrial policies originate? The answer is just about anywhere. While the White House may decide many policies, the debate over what to do about a problem can be initiated from many sources – politicians, bureaucrats, interest groups, the mass media, private citizens, foreign governments or corporations, or international organizations – to name the more prominent. A "policy entrepreneur" identifies an issue, proposes a solution, elbows aside other policy entrepreneurs on other issues, and musters the political forces necessary to convert a proposal into policy. Half the battle for policy entrepreneurs is getting their issue to the top of the policy agenda where those with power can debate it. As policies evolve, they draw in different mixes of public and private groups with a stake in the issue, which in turn shape that policy, sometimes subtly, sometimes decisively.

Many policy initiatives do come from those at the top. In a liberal democracy, leadership involves setting a clear agenda with a few priorities and then fighting like hell for them. The reason is simple. Governments are capable of addressing only a few problems at once. Meanwhile, countless other major and minor problems fester.

Theoretically, policies can emerge anywhere in the political system. In practice most policies are shaped by "iron triangles," sometimes called "policy clusters" or "subgovernments," composed of relevant congressional committees and subcommittees, interest groups, and bureaucracies which share and fiercely defend a common interest. A classic iron triangle is the "military–industrial complex" among the allied Pentagon, military industries, and politicians, whose districts or states have military bases or factories; the military–industrial complex is politically invincible nearly all the time. The result is the proliferation of weapons systems, bases, and perks for the military that annually cost taxpayers tens of billions of dollars and often have little or no strategic rationale.

Regardless of whether an iron triangle dominates the issue or not, every industrial policy is fought over and shaped by dozens of Congressional committees and subcommittees, special interest groups, bureaucratic rivalries and inertia, perennial reelection campaigns, budget limitations, popular apathy and ignorance that sometimes flares into passion, porkbarrel politics, financial contributions, disinformation, direct mailing campaigns, and demagogery.

Constitutionally strapped together in a three-legged policy race, the president and both Congress houses must cooperate to move forward. Unfortunately this cooperation is increasingly fleeting. Cooperation becomes ever-more imperative and difficult as lobbyists grow ever-more powerful in numbers, organization, and influence. Of course, the more dominant the special interests, the greater the tendency for each senator and representative to become a party unto him- or herself, representing the interests that can provide or deny the most financial and media support.

The inevitable result is compromise. Those in power are continually frustrated by its limits: "At any given time, there will be differences between what policy makers want and what they can accomplish, between what they are compelled to do and what they would prefer to do, between what is feasible and what is not."[25] Policies are rarely comprehensive in addressing problems. New policies often contradict older policies. More often than not, policies result in greater bureaucratic inefficiency, fragmentation, redtape, and often outright deadlock in dealing with an issue.

Regardless of their origins, policy proposals are far easier to derail than promote. Those with a stake in the *status quo* enjoy too many veto points throughout the system. But once a policy is implemented, it is relatively easy to retain and difficult to change. The longer a policy and its institutional bearers have existed, the more entrenched become those with economic, social, and political stakes in the *status quo* and the more adept they become at leeching benefits from the system. Even if a particular policy is not governed by an iron triangle, change is unlikely. Humans tend to stick to what has worked, however inadequately, in the past over what might work better in the future. And that tendency is reinforced by the constellation of interest groups which both shape and are empowered by that policy. Opportunities, or "windows," to promote policy shifts are fleeting.[26]

Change, when it occurs, is usually in response to a crisis in which existing policies and institutions prove inadequate and there is a widespread consensus on the need to try something new. For example, President Franklin Roosevelt would have had trouble enacting any of his New Deal initiatives without the Great Depression. Policymakers are continually trying to catch up to the crises of the moment, and thus lurch from one seemingly compelling issue to another, with little ability to achieve an overall perspective or comprehensive response. Yet, even then, when a policy shift occurs at all, those responsible generally prefer to act incrementally rather than decisively: "incrementalism favors reliance on past experience as a guide for new policies, careful deliberation before policy changes, and a rejection of rapid or comprehensive policy innovation.... But incrementalism can also become a prison to the imagination by inhibiting policy innovation and stifling new solutions to issues."[27]

While the interrelationship among all economic problems and need to address those issues comprehensively is increasingly recognized, policymaking and implementation remains fragmented among dozens of departments and agencies which battle each other savagely for status, power, and finance in a multistranded tug-of-war. Within the federal bureaucracy, the industrial policy duties are fragmented and squabbled over by virtually all the departments and agencies. Added to the policymaking system are 435 representatives and 100 senators, each with his or her own special set of constituents that must be satisfied. To further complicate the process, hundreds of special and public interest groups battle each other for the ears, votes, appropriation, and other handouts of politicians and bureaucrats. For the past quarter-century, the courts have increasingly shaped industrial policy as the judicial concept of standing has expanded to include anyone with an interest in an issue, whether or not they are immediately affected by it. Judges shape policy by interpreting often ambiguous statutes and forcing often reluctant officials to implement their own laws. Duplicate versions of this at fifty state and thousands of local levels, mesh it with the federal system, and you have America's industrial policymaking system.

So who serves the "public interest" in this special interest system? In the minds of most politicians, bureaucrats, and lobbyists, the public interest is synonomous with their own interest – or at least that is how they try to sell their interest to the public. If James Madison is correct, the public interest is whatever momentary imbalance of power teeters among countless special interest groups. In other words, power rather than enlightened reflection determines the nation's policies; public interest is a relative and political rather than abstract and philosophical phenomenon.

Alas, in such a system, politics rather than strategy determines America's industrial policies. Corporate welfare and strategic investments are diametrically opposed; the former fritters away American wealth and power while the latter enhances it. The more that scarce money and other perks are wasted on corporate welfare, the less money is available to invest in the strategic industries, corporations, and technologies that stimulate the nation's development.

In American politics, victories are rarely absolute; compromise is inevitable; gridlock is common; the more powerful special interests are amply benefited; the weaker interests are neglected. It is the American way.

2 For Better or for Worse: the Policies

Over time, Jeffersonians have joined with Hamiltonians in believing that government should manage the economy. Adherents of the two philosophies, however, bitterly dispute the degrees, types, and purposes of government management.

Jeffersonians believe that the federal government has only two economic roles. Washington's primary role is to act as the economy's impartial referee which protects the free market from forces that would destroy it, such as monopolies, insider trading, patent infringement, and the like. If markets operate freely and fairly, all of society's needs and desires will be granted. Then there is a secondary role that Jeffersonians allow government to pursue. As long as the government does not play favorites, it can also use macroeconomic policies to create a better business climate. Governments can use policies that "tack against the wind" to keep the economy moving forward, such as raising or lowering the federal budget, interest, tax, and currency rates to stimulate the economy when it is depressed and dampen it when it is overheated. But in doing so policymakers should never lose sight of the central Jeffersonian belief that the freer the markets, the greater the economic growth.

Hamiltonians point out that a world of difference separates "growth" and "development." Economic growth is measured purely by more dollars – if the dollar value of goods and services exchanged increases, the economy is growing. It matters not how the dollars are made or who gets the dollars. When speculators bubble up stock or real estate markets, when corporate raiders buy out a dynamic industrial group and sell off the companies for a huge profit, when the rich get richer faster than the poor and middle class get poorer, when investors chose to put their money into potato chips rather than computer chips, when forests are clear-cut, factory smokestacks and drains foul streams and air, hallowed battlefields are converted to suburbs – all is well – the market is working its "magic." In other words, growth is solely a quantitative measure.

While Jeffersonians are content with growth, Hamiltonians push for development. Development is not just more but better. An

38

economy is developing when it not only creates but distributes more wealth so that everyone enjoys a larger portion; when jobs and industries are increasingly diversified; when the nation achieves trade and payment surpluses with its key rivals; when research, development, and productivity rise ever higher; when people enjoy ever-better levels of education, leisure, and security; when production enhances rather than destroys the nation's cultural, natural, and historic heritage.

For related political and economic reasons, the key to development is to expand the middle class in number, real income, and as a percentage of the population. The larger a nation's middle class, the greater its buying power and political stability, which are essential for its further expansion. And the key to broadening and deeping the middle class is for government and business to work together to spawn as many "strategic industries" for the economy as possible.

What is a "strategic" or "winner" industry? Industries differ in the wealth they can create for an economy. Hamiltonians argue that $1 billion worth of computer chips are far more valuable to an economy than $1 billion worth of potato chips. Computer chips are the hub for the microelectronics industry. That billion dollars worth of computer chips may well stimulate tens or even hundreds of billions of dollars worth of related industries and their high-paying jobs. In contrast, potato chips are junk food that demand few refinement steps from field to package. A billion dollars worth of potato chips contributes little in income, skills, related industries, and new technologies – in other words, in development – to the economy. Computer chips, thus, are a "strategic industry;" potato chips are not. A developed economy and its consumers are as dependent on computer chips as they can do without potato chips. Yet, given the vast difference in start-up and maintenance costs between the two industries, investors would be far more inclined to try making money from potato chips than computer chips.

Hamiltonians insist that Washington should provide the strategic vision that businesses cannot afford in cut-throat markets. Strategic industries such as computer chips can and should be developed by government and business working together. Washington can contribute by, say, granting the computer chip industry tax reductions to encourage research and development, relaxing antitrust rules that allow firms to cooperate, using tariff and non-tariff barriers creatively to permit just enough foreign competition that forces domestic firms to work harder to expand their market shares, to pressure foreign governments to allow domestic chip producers access, to match any subsidies given by foreign governments to their own industry, and to gather and share information about technology, markets, and foreign strategies with domestic firms. All that, of course, is heresy to Jeffersonians.

Development goes beyond targeting for development strategic industries that continually create and distribute ever-more wealth. It also includes the promotion of esoteric values that are impossible to measure with dollar signs. Just how much are such values as safe products or cities, cleaner air, national parks or wildernesses, tree-lined streets, an ever-healthier or more literate population, or the artistic or scientific creativity of its citizens, to name a few, worth? Hamiltonians would argue that the government can play a role in fostering all of these priceless values that create a richer America.

What follows explores the ways in which Jeffersonians and Hamiltonians agree or differ over the government's role in the economy, and how the power to assert specific policies has changed over time.

MACROECONOMIC POLICY

As the name implies, macroeconomic policies are supposed to affect the entire economy, as opposed to industrial policies that target a specific sector. In reality, there is tremendous overlap between macroeconomic and industrial policies, to the point where it is difficult to determine just where the effects of one begin and the other end. For example, although a "macroeconomic policy" decision like raising interest rates is supposed to slow down the entire economy, the action may well benefit some economic sectors and firms and harm others. Likewise, an "industrial policy" decision to impose tariffs on automobile imports to protect the domestic industry will ripple across the entire economy, launching some industrial boats and swamping others. Nonetheless, macroeconomic and industrial policies can be separated by intention if not effect.

Washington has four broad macroeconomic tools with which to guide economic development – spending, taxes, interest rates, and the dollar's value. Each of these can be used either to stimulate or to dampen the economy. Ideally they are used in tandem; more commonly, they contradict each other. Yet even when those specific macroeconomic tools work together, they are often used to attempt to achieve simultaneously goals that may well contradict each other, such as economic growth, full employment, stable prices, and a positive payments balance.

Of the government's macroeconomic tools, none has a greater industrial policy effect than fiscal or budget policy. The Federal government is the world's largest buyer of goods and services. Every budget item potentially can help or hinder the economy. For example, when the government borrows to finance a deficit, it competes with the private sector for money to the detriment of them both in higher interest rates. More positively, it is estimated that every $1 billion spent on public works generates 25 000 construction jobs and 15 000 spillover jobs throughout the economy. The Federal highway program is the government's biggest job maker. In 1992, the $20 billion spent on Federal highway construction generated 800 000 jobs across the nation, often in communities that had few other sources of income.[1]

Fiscal policy's essence lies in the fight over shaping and implementing the federal budget.[2] The president, House, and Senate prepare, squabble over, and eventually reconcile three different budgets. Although the president is the first to propose a budget, until recently, the power to shape the budget had resided largely in the two congressional houses. The Federal government can only spend money if Congress decrees it can do so with authorization bills and specifies the exact funds with appropriation bills, which in turn are largely shaped by the political fighting in the Senate and House Appropriation Committees. Until the president received a line-item veto in January 1997, he had either to accept or reject the entire budget presented to him by Congress. For political reasons, presidents tended to grit their teeth and sign the budget bill that appeared on their desk, no matter how much it differed from their original proposal. A veto would start the whole laborious process over again, with higher and worsening animosities within and between Congress and the president. The public, meanwhile, would boil in anger against both the White House and Capitol Hill as cherished programs ran out of money. Voters could vent their frustration in the next election on the party deemed most responsible for the gridlock.

President Clinton's decision to veto not one but two Republican budgets in late 1995 before signing a compromise budget was a bold gamble that eventually paid off. Most voters perceived that the Republican Party, led by its radical wing, was largely responsible for the gridlock. That perception was an important reason why, in the November 1996 election, the Republican Party lost House seats and the White House to the Democratic Party, although they did gain in the Senate and retained control of both Houses. Although President Clinton was able to use the line-item veto in 1997, it is too early to tell how much its use has tilted budget power toward the Oval Office.

Such budget battles are relatively new to American politics. Until the Bureau of the Budget (BOB) was created and attached to the Treasury Department in 1921, the final budget resulted from departments and agencies separately submitting their individual budgets to Congress for approval. The result was a budget shaped purely by politics rather than strategic vision. This did not change under the Budget Bureau; the White House usually just went along with the balance of congressional power. In 1939, President Roosevelt attempted to assert more control over the process by transferring the BOB from the Treasury Department to the White House to provide him with even greater control over budget making. Politics not only prevailed, it intensified as the president more actively joined the fray.

Big changes in budget making occurred again during the Nixon administration. In 1970, President Nixon renamed BOB the Office of Management and Budget (OMB) and expanded its powers. The OMB's primary duties are to prepare the federal budget for the next year and monitor the budget's execution for the current fiscal year, which runs from 1 October to 30 September. In 1973, President Nixon provoked a fight with Congress when he refused to spend authorized funds. Congress responded with the Congressional Budget and Impoundment Control Act of 1974, which forced the president to spend authorized funds, and created the Congressional Budget Office (CBO) within the legislature to help it devise and implement federal budgets.

Theoretically, to work well, fiscal policy should expand the budget when the economy slows down and reduce the budget when the economy picks up. In practice, the government has run deficits nearly every year from the 1930s through today. Those deficits have grown greater over time. The eight years of Presidents Nixon and Ford added $193.9 billion to the national debt, Carter's four years $226.8 billion, Reagan's eight years $1.338 trillion, and Bush's four years $930.0 billion. The Clinton administration reversed this trend by sharply reducing the deficit each year for four straight years. In 1995, both Clinton and the Republican Party agreed to balance the budget by the year 2002, although as of 1997 they have failed to agreed on the specifics of doing so.

The reasons for the persistent budget deficits are simple – they result from the difference between what Americans demand from the government and their willingness to pay for what they demand. The budget is filled with direct and indirect subsidies to different industries. Entitlements such as social security, medicare, medicaid, and other programs are a major reason for the growing budget. Another growing budget item is the interest paid on the national debt. The biggest single item, however, is military spending.

Monetary policy, or those actions affecting the cost of money, clearly has an enormous impact on consumption.[3] When interest rates rise, people are less inclined to borrow money to buy a car, house, or some other expensive good, and become more inclined to do so when interest rates fall. Many political, economic, and social forces shape interest rates. The Federal Reserve's role is to harness those forces and manipulate interest rates in a way which ideally promotes growth and stable prices.

It took nearly 150 years before Washington adopted all the instruments of monetary policy it wields today.[4] A nascent monetary policy goes back to Alexander Hamilton, the first Treasurer, and his attempts to "monetarize" the national debt by issuing government securities and bonds to creditors. The First (1791–1811) and Second (1816–36) Banks of the United States performed such central bank roles as regulating the national money supply through issuing currency and limiting the states' banks notes. The Bank directors followed a tight monetary policy which limited credit and kept inflation low and the banking system sound. However, many Americans complained that high interest rates squelched economic opportunity and burdened debtors. Capitilizing on these complaints, President Andrew Jackson succeeded in killing the Bank in 1836 by distributing its funds to chartered state banks. Lacking its own funds, the Bank withered and eventually died. Jackson unleashed a period of "easy money," in which the number of state banks soared from 329 in 1829 to 1500 in 1860 which together issued about 9000 different types of bank notes.[5] The United States lacked a national currency throughout this era. Only gold and silver held consistent value, and there was not enough of those metals to supply more than a fraction of the need.

It took the carnage and crisis of the Civil War to force Washington to reform the system. Congress passed the National Banking Act of 1863, which allowed the government to sell bonds to finance the war and taxed state bank notes to inhibit their use. Yet, despite the reassertion of Federal control, the Treasury Department still did not manipulate interest rates to regulate economic growth – the heart of monetary policy. Whether credit was tight or easy, America's economy was wracked by a series of prolonged depressions starting in 1837, 1847, 1857, 1864, 1873, 1883, 1893, and 1907, which the government was incapable of alleviating. Economic growth throughout the nineteenth century was only about 1 percent annually.

Following the Panic of 1907, Congress created a National Monetary Commission to propose ways to smooth out the business cycle. Congress acted on the Commission's recommendations by passing the 1913 Federal Reserve Act which established a Federal Reserve Board in Washington, designated 12 regional affiliated banks, and created the Federal Open Market Committee which sells and buys government securities. When an opening on the seven-member Board arises, the president appoints a successor and can designate a chair, both subject to senate approval.

Although the Federal Reserve theoretically has had full monetary power since its inception in 1913, until 1935 it largely presided over the independent policies of the twelve regional banks and the Treasury Department's borrowing needs. The 1935 Banking Act broke the regional banks' power by renaming the Federal Reserve Board the Board of Governors of the Federal Reserve System, and making it responsible for, among other things, the appointment of the regional bank presidents. National and regional policies became more closely aligned as men of similar mind became presidents. In 1951, the rising cost of financing the national debt prompted President Truman and Congress to forge the Federal Reserve–Treasury Accord which removed the Federal Reserve's duty to maintain stable interest rates. Thus empowered, the Federal Reserve has more actively manipulated interest rates to manage the economy. The Federal Reserve's power was further enhanced by passage of the 1980 Monetary Control Act, that extends reserve requirements to non-member banks and gives them equal access to Federal funds at the prevailing discount rate. That same bill authorized Board terms to run for 14 years, while chairs and vice-chairs serve for four-year terms; a member's term expires in an even numbered year, and they serve only one full term; the same seven people sit on both the Federal Reserve's Board of Governors and the Federal Open Market Committee.

To prevent politics from determining policy, Congress made the Federal Reserve an independent agency and the twelve regional banks privately owned. Profits from fees charged for services and interest earned on security holdings provide the operating costs for the Federal Reserve and the regional banks. Although only about one-third of the nation's 12 000 banks have chosen to become Federal Reserve members, they hold 70 percent of the commercial bank reserves and 65 percent of the deposits in all other 15 000 lending institutions.

The Federal Reserve's purpose is to regulate the money supply so that growth remains steady and inflation low. It does so through three means. The Federal Reserve can increase or decrease the amount of money in circulation by adjusting: (1) the reserve requirements for member banks; (2) the discount rate; and (3) open market operations. In 1980, Congress set reserve requirements for members and nonmembers alike of 3 percent for the first $25 million and 12 percent for transactions beyond that. But the Federal Reserve can adjust these requirements as it sees fit. Members and non-members alike can borrow money from the Fed at an interest rate called the discount rate. By raising or lowering the discount rate, the Fed indirectly affects all interest rates, most importantly the prime rate charged by member banks to their mostly credit-worthy business customers. The Federal Open Market Commission operates through the Federal Reserve Bank in New York. When the Fed buys a security it increases the amount of money in circulation, and when it sells one it decreases it.[6]

Interest rates are surely important, but how important? The monetarist school, popularized by Milton Friedman at the University of Chicago, believes that the relative supply and cost of money is the primary force shaping the economy. In contrast, mainstream economists believe that monetary policy is only one of several vital factors including budget, tax, and currency forces.

"Supply siders" disagree with both the monetarist and mainstream economists, and instead fervently believe that tax rates have the most important effect on the economy, with the higher the tax rate, the lower the economic growth, and vice versa. This theory is very popular. Few people enjoy paying taxes, whether or not they agree with Supreme Court Justice Oliver Wendell Holmes that, "Taxes are what we pay for civilized society." Most Americans instead might well agree with the sentiments of John Marshall, an earlier Supreme Court Justice, in McCulloch v. Maryland (1819) that, "The power to tax involves the power to destroy." Yet, few wealthy Americans would be as honest as Leona Helmsley, who declared: "We don't pay taxes. Only the little people pay taxes."[7]

Such attitudes are understandable. After all, American independence was rooted in a tax revolt. Since then, politicians who promise tax cuts have generally done well at election time, no matter what the effect of those cuts on the national debt. One reason a majority of voters sent Ronald Reagan twice to the White House was his promise to cut taxes and get government off the backs of the people. As Reagan put it, the "American taxing structure, the purpose of which was to serve the people, began instead to serve the insatiable appetite of government." He then embraced the proposed Kemp Roth Bill, which cut taxes by 25 percent over three years. Alas, reality did not accord with the simple theory. Supply-side Reaganomics resulted in America's growth rate during the 1980s dropping to the lowest since the 1930s, the tripling of the national debt, and the conversion of the United States from the world's greatest creditor to its worst debtor nation – all during Reagan's eight years in office. Since then, most Americans have recognized that "supply-side" Reaganomics was an abject failure, perhaps the most important reason why Republican candidates George Bush and Bob Dole lost the presidential elections of 1992 and 1996 with their respective promises to, "Read my lips, no new taxes," and to cut income taxes to 15 percent and halve the capital gains tax.

How effective have tax cuts been in developing the economy? President Kennedy's tax cuts are largely applauded for developing the economy, while President Reagan's are mostly maligned for helping triple the national debt while having no discernible effect on growth during his eight years in office. In fact, there appears to be no relationship between high taxes and low growth rates, or vice versa. Until recently, most other democratic industrial countries enjoyed growth rates that exceeded those of the United States, despite their higher tax rates. As always, Mancur Olson put it well:

Even most economists who were strongly identified with right-wing ideology agreed that supply-side economics was not consistent with the quantitative evidence about the supply of labor and saving. Yet the Reagan tax cuts were nonetheless passed, and the nation is now burdened with a huge and very harmful structural deficit.

Experience has now confirmed that supply-side economics was
as baseless as almost all economists had said it was, yet it even
now retains some journalistic and political support.[8]

The American obsession with taxes is puzzling to most foreigners
who envy the relatively low tax rates. America's tax system does
have its quirks – it is relatively inequitable and encourages consumption rather than production. Like the Federal budget, politics
rather than strategy shapes the tax system, a system that does indeed pick winners and losers. The US tax code seems largely to
have been shaped by special interests. Washington offers tax deductions and credits for a bewildering range of economic activities, including equipment purchases and depreciation, home
mortgages, depletion allowances for energy, and so on. Tax codes
in most other democratic industrial countries tend to be less inequitable. Another anomaly is that the United States is one of the few
democratic industrial nations that does not have a value added tax
(VAT) or sales tax on all retail and wholesale purchases. As a result, America's tax system encourages consumption and discour-
ages savings.

Mancur Olson is among those who would emphasize tax equity
rather than cuts as a means to develop the economy:

> the best way to reduce the inefficiencies arising from our tax
> system is by eliminating tax loopholes and taxing essentially all
> forms of income impartially. If the tax code were simple and
> straightforward, all of the legal and accounting talent that is now
> devoted to the complexities of the tax code could be used in-
> stead for the production of goods and services. More important,
> firms and individuals would no longer distort their pattern of
> activity to make use of tax advantages that pertain to certain
> types of revenue and expenditure, and the economy would surely
> be more efficient. If the loopholes or special provisions of the
> tax code were eliminated, the same amount of revenue could be
> collected with lower tax rates, further increasing efficiency.[9]

Finally, Washington can enormously affect the economy by ma-
nipulating the dollar's value. When the dollar is relatively strong,
it lowers the prices for foreign goods in the United States and
raises the prices for American goods at home and abroad. As a
result, American consumers enjoy cheaper prices and American

industries lose business, wealth flows overseas, and people lose their jobs. A relatively undervalued currency has the opposite effect.

How can Washington affect the dollar's value? The Federal Reserve's interest rate policy is the most powerful tool. When interest rates are high, foreign and domestic investors alike are more inclined to buy US Treasury bills. The demand for dollars raises its value. When the Federal Reserve lowers interest rates, the dollar generally declines as well. The Treasury Department can manipulate the dollar's value by selling it to weaken it or buying it to strengthen it. This policy is more effective when it is done in concert with other industrial countries. The White House can talk up or down the dollar's value simply by threatening to use interest rates or trade currencies.

Washington's powers over the dollar's value diminish as the world's financial markets become ever-more integrated and active. Over $1 trillion daily flows through global financial markets. Of that, government money represents less than 5 percent. Thus, when governments buy or sell currencies they can at best affect the psychology of the marketplace. The amounts that government trade are too small to affect directly currency values.

Fiscal, monetary, tax, and currency policies are supposed to affect the national economy without playing favorites. In reality, those "macroeconomic" policies either singly or jointly do indeed help some industries, regions, firms, and individuals, and hurt others. Jeffersonians and Hamitonians, of course, differ sharply over whether government should favor some parties over others.

INDUSTRIAL POLICY

Industrial policies are the means by which a government assists economic development by favoring some industries, regions, or firms over others. Should the government pick winners and losers? Jeffersonians argue that markets are always superior to governments in developing the economy. Thus government should not pick winners and losers because it cannot. Hamiltonians counter that the relative efficacy of markets or governments in economic development depends on the situation; many times, government can provide the strategic vision, direction, and investments lost to business in a Darwinian market where the imperative is simply to survive. Thus, because government can pick winners and losers it should do so.

There is no question that experts who devote their professional lives to studying the real rather than imagined world can, indeed, point out industries and technologies that will be dynamic power-houses of future economic development. For example, in November 1990, the White House Office of Science and Technology head, Alan Bromley, called for a comprehensive high technology policy.[10] In March 1991, he released a list of 22 technologies critical to America's national security and prosperity. Later that year, the Defense Department announced its own list very similar to Bromley's.

Pointing out strategic technologies and industries is easy. The hard part is elbowing aside the array of powerful pork-barrel interests in order to target those strategic industries and technologies with sensible policies that develop them into global champions. And it is this that Washington remains largely incapable of doing.

What are the means by which government policies can develop an industry? As has been seen, the tax code and budget items can confer enormous benefits on specific industries or firms. Another effective industrial policy involves the Federal underwriting of the research and development of select technologies. Among the most effective of these policies is to organize "cooperative research and development agreements (cradas)" between government laboratories and private businesses. The number of cradas has been growing for several years. For example, the Energy Department's cradas rose from virtually none to over 300 between 1990 and 1992, although they remained only $201 million of the $6 billion research budget. The Energy Department's largest crada was the $130 million it invested over four years into the Advanced Battery Consortium to develop a battery for an electric car. Outright government subsidies to industry, however, are relatively small as a GDP percentage: about 0.5 percent in the United States, 1.0 percent in Japan, and 3.0 percent in the European Union.[11] Also uncommon are government direct or guaranteed loans to industries, such as the Federal bailouts of Lockheed in 1971, New York City in 1975 and 1978, Chrysler in 1979, and the savings and loan industry from 1989, which have been enormously expensive. The cost to taxpayers and the economy of the savings and loan bailout alone may cost over $500 billion.

Washington has frequently played the referee role in preventing industry from abusing consumers or laborers. The 1890 Sherman and 1911 Clayton antitrust acts were supposed to break up consumer-gouging monopolies. However, the Justice Department's antitrust division has been very selective about which industries to punish. In addition, the Federal government will offer to mediate prolonged and economically disrupting strikes from the coal strikes of Theodore Roosevelt's administration to the baseball strike of Bill Clinton's. At times, the White House has actually intervened in favor of management as in the steel strikes of 1949 and 1951.

The Federal government indirectly subsidizes industries through a variety of means. Washington freely provides literally thousands of publications to businesses which provide information about virtually anything remotely related to economics. This taxpayer-provided service is an enormous saving to businesses which otherwise would have to search and pay for that information on their own. The Trade Adjustment Assistance program compensated workers who lost their jobs from import competition. In 1982, the Job Training Partnership Act provided additional subsidies and training, thus saving those targeted industries the enormous training costs. With the Cold War's end, Washington has been sharing out the peace dividend in the form of lower defense spending and the conversion of many military bases to civilian use. Disaster relief flows to specific regions devastated by floods, earthquakes, hurricanes, droughts and the like.

Meanwhile, every state and many local governments conduct their own macroeconomic, industrial, and trade policies. For example, states get in bidding wars to attract factories and businesses by offering arrays of tax holidays, infrastructure, and other benefits. Ironically, the largest public works project in the nation is being implemented not by Washington or one of the states, but by Los Angeles. By the year 2020, Los Angeles hopes to complete a $150 billion 300-mile subway system. Los Angeles also made headlines by attempting its own industrial policy. On 22 January 1992, Los Angeles County canceled a $122 million deal by which a Japanese firm would supply subway cars to its new system. Instead, the county promised to build a $49 million factory within Los Angeles which it hoped could build as many as 600 rail cars and 6000 buses over the next three decades, which would create 740 jobs in Los Angeles and 4445 jobs elsewhere in the United States. After building the factory, Los Angeles would lease it to manufacturers to actually build the cars. This industrial policy followed the immense controversy that followed Los Angeles' decision on 18 December 1991 to choose Sumitomo over a $5 million lower bid from Morrison Knudsen, America's last rail-car maker. American corporate and labor leaders fiercely lobbied Los Angeles County to reverse its decision.[12]

Virtually every Federal department and agency has its own range of industrial "clients" which it nurtures with a variety of means. Few bureaucracies have developed a wider spectrum of economic sectors than the Pentagon. No Pentagon institution has been a more effective industrial policy leader than the Defense Advanced Research Projects Agency (DARPA), which was founded in 1958. DARPA lacks its own laboratories, scientists, and factories, and employs only 150 staff. Its purpose is to investigate and subsidize promising technologies. The assumption behind DARPA is that national security rests on a diversified, dynamic industrial and technological foundation. Among DARPA's greatest successes were the development of packet switching which breaks down computer data and sends it through networks, lasers that helped inspire the Star Wars scheme, radar absorbent materials for stealth jets and bombers, advanced computer chips, and composite materials. All of these technologies have both civilian and military uses. One important reason DARPA has been successful is its ability to bypass the Pentagon's ossified bureaucracy and directly identify and develop promising technologies.

DARPA's successes deeply embarrassed classical economists. Such policies were supposedly doomed to failure. Rather than change their mindsets, the ideologues with the Reagan White House instead tried to destroy DARPA. They failed. Concerned with America's eroding economic power, a majority in Congress not only restored money cut by the Reagan White House from DARPA's budget, but mandated research in X-ray lithography, superconductivity, and high definition television (HDTV). The Bush administration's ideologues were more successful. OMB Director Richard Darman and Chief of Staff John Sununu called for sharp cutbacks in DARPA's funding and programs, especially its support for Sematech, the highly successful microelectronics research consortium, and the HDTV program. Commerce Secretary Robert Mosbacher and Science Advisor Allan Bromley joined with DARPA's director, Dr Craig Fields in protesting the cuts in the overall budget and specific programs. President Bush overruled them. The cuts went through. In May 1990, Bush fired Fields when he continued to protest.

The controversy over DARPA reflected a broader national debate over just what industrial policies were appropriate for developing technologies, and which technologies should be targeted. For example, President Reagan's penchant for expensive, glitzy, and, well, Hollywoodish science projects like Star Wars, the supercollider, the Hubble space telescope, and the space station set off a fierce industrial policy debate. Those four projects alone if completed and maintained would cost the United States hundreds of billions of dollars. The White House argued that all four projects were essential to American national security. Critics countered that Reagan's huge projects drained money that could be invested in smaller-scale and less expensive projects that had a greater potential to create wealth, and improve America's competitiveness and the quality of human life, as well bolster the nation's already formidable military–industrial complex. Debaters argued whether Washington should invest in "big" or "small" and "basic" or "applied" science, or whether it should invest at all.

In the postwar era, Washington has tended to spend ever more on "big science" projects. Adjusted for inflation, the number of big science projects in the 1950s numbered nine which cost collectively $260 million, while in the 1980s there were 34 worth $6.7 billion. Meanwhile, overall Federal spending on science has been relatively constant. In 1967, the tab came to $46 billion and in 1990 $48.2 billion.[13]

Pork-barrel politics are often the primary motivation for those legistators who approve the big science projects. The larger the project, the wider the procurements can be spread among congressional districts. Costs for the big science projects tend to shoot figuratively into the stratosphere. The space station was originally priced at $8 billion; it may eventually cost $70 billion. The Hubble space telescope cost $3.5 billion when it was finished and still did not work properly. Astronauts were dispatched on a special space shuttle mission to put a corrective lens over the telescope's eye. The cost – another $2.5 billion.

Perhaps none of the Reagan era's big science projects was more wasteful than the supercollider. The White House's endorsement of a supercollider set off a lobbying war among a half-dozen states that wanted to host it. Republicans and Democrats joined hands in lobbying the White House for the project. With an eye to the next election, the White House finally bowed to the fierce lobbying of Democratic Senator Lloyd Bensten and Republican Senator Phil Gramm to bring it to Texas. The supercollidor was to be a 54-mile-long elliptical ring within which particle beams would be shot through 11 000 huge superconducting magnets. It was hoped that the reactions of the particles as they were beamed would provide insights into yet undiscovered realms of physics. The price tag for any revelations would be vast – $8.3 billion just for the supercollider's construction. In 1990, to help pay for the project, the Bush administration offered Japan a major role in managing the supercollider in return for a $1 billion investment.

As the supercollider's cost soared to $11 billion, reports of gross mismanagement and misallocation of funds emerged. In 1992, the Energy Department's Inspector General found that $203 million or 40 percent of the funds which had been spent until then could not be accounted for. It did find that $51 000 was spent on office plants and $16 000 for a party. Supercollidor supporters argued that technology leadership rather than political pork was at stake. To run, the supercollidor requires enormous inputs of superconductors and thus could have helped establish economies-of-scale production and technological advances for that nascent industry. But, in June 1993, Congress finally pulled the supercollider's plug, thus preventing the squandering of billions of additional taxpayer dollars. Although contractors made fortunes, the supercollider fiasco left the nation worse off.[14]

Meanwhile, smaller projects with great applicability and payback are starved for cash. During the 1980s, of ten Nobel Prizes in physics, one was in pure theory, three in big projects, and six in small projects. Almost all Nobel Prizes for chemistry and physiology were based on small-scale projects. Private corporations and laboratories find it increasingly difficult to fund their own research. In February 1992, the National Science Foundation reported that industrial research and development investments had begun to contract after decades of expansion. Adjusted for inflation, those investments peaked at $79 billion in 1989 and have since diminished. The drop among domestic firms may be even steeper, since the total includes investments by foreign rivals in their American laboratories. The proportion of foreign research and development to the total in the United States rose from 6 percent in 1980 to 13 percent, worth $10.3 billion in 1989. Among the reasons for the decline in American corporate research and development were the immense corporate debts amassed during the 1980s from the merger and acquisitions craze and America's relative economic decline.[15]

University laboratories have been at the cutting edge of basic science research. Yet the universities too are feeling the financial pinch and cutting back their scientic research. Most of their money comes from Washington. In 1992, $10 billion of the $17 billion universities spent on scientific research were Federal funds. As big science projects consumed an ever-larger portion of Federal largess, universities have increasingly turned to private – and increasingly foreign – corporations for help. In 1991, private firms funneled $1.2 billion into university laboratories. These private funds often come with strings attached. For relatively small investments, the corporations get to tap into America's best scientific minds and laboratories, and enjoy exclusive rights to exploit patents held by the schools. Many of those universities are public schools supported by taxpayers. In 1988, 41 universities allowed 2848 American and 496 foreign corporations into their laboratories. Of the foreign firms, 76 percent invested in just three universities – MIT, the University of California at Berkeley, and Texas A & M. In 1989, MIT's industrial liason service had 291 members, of which 130 were foreign and 161 American who paid annual $50 000 fees. Among the foreign firms were 56 Japanese, 13 French, and 13 Italian companies. The universities have little control over the corporate activities in their midst. In 1988, for example, Japan's Hitachi Corporation leased 2.7 acres of land from the University of California at Irvine and built there a $16.5 million laboratory, the top two floors of which are closed to all but Hitachi employees.[16]

In contrast and reaction to the Reagan years, the Clinton administration asserted a sharp break in industrial policy. Rather than continue the heavily politicized, *ad hoc*, and often contradictory industrial policies of the past, President Clinton advocated a comprehensive set of policies which would systematically develop America's economy. To do so, Clinton proposed shifting an ever-greater amount of Federal research funds from military to civilian ends. The president argued that,

> America cannot continue to rely on trickle-down technology from the military. Civilian industry, not the military, is the driving force behind advanced technology today. Only by strengthening our civilian technology base can we solve the twin problems of national security and economic competitiveness.[17]

A vital part of Clinton's new industrial policy orientation involved reordering the priorities of the government's high technology policies. In 1993, Clinton inherited a Federal budget of $73 billion for various research and development projects, of which military projects consumed 80 percent. By 1998, civilian projects would take half of the budget, up from 41 percent when Clinton took office. Applied research would receive equal weight with basic research. Federal laboratories would be required to devote one-fifth, or $5 billion of their annual $25 billion budget to joint ventures with private industry, up from a mere 5 percent in 1993. DARPA would invest a greater part of its $1.4 billion research budget in dual-use technologies. The Energy Department's complex of laboratories would shift much of their $4.1 billion in spending from research on weapons to commercial projects. Consortiums rather than single firms would characterize most government joint ventures. Sematech would be the model for the government–business partnerships. The president boosted the Commerce Department's research role by raising its National Institute for Standards and Techology budget from $117 million to $1.3 billion by 1997. As John Gibbons, White House Office of Science and Technology director, put it, "The point is not to get on the back of business. The point is to help some of them get off their backs.[18]

As vital as Clinton's policy shift is to the nation's economic future, the transition away from the military–industrial complex to the research and development of commercial projects has not been painless. Unused to a commercial environment, some laboratories have had trouble picking the right projects and firms. Once a consortium forms, difficulties often arise between the labs geared to basic research and the businesses concerned with applied research and a quick payoff.

Not surprisedly, the Commerce Department's industrial policies have been implemented the most smoothly. To choose which technologies to develop, the Commerce Department studied over 550 White Papers submitted by industry. Among those projects chosen were: to develop DNA diagnostic equipment; manufacturing techniques for advanced composite materials; modular software programs that can be connected like building blocks; electronic information networks for health care, and computer-guided systems for electronic manufacturing.[19]

Clinton has not hesitated to target specific industries for revival. In October 1993, he announced his intention to revitalize America's shipbuilding industry through a combination of government guaranteed, low-interest loans, negotiations with foreign governments to end their shipbuiding subsidies, the infusion of new technology, streamlining regulations, and boosting foreign sales. Clinton followed up this commitment on 2 August 1994 when he announced $1 billion of guaranteed loans to buyers of American ships or investors in American shipyards. Among the loan guarantees were: $726 million for the purchase of 30 container ships by the Swiss-based Saracen Ltd, to be built by McDermott Shipbuilding in Morgan City, Louisiana; $133 million for the purchase of four tankers for the Greek-based Fleve Shipping Corporation to be built by Newport News Shipping in Virginia; and $115 million for two oceangoing barges for Coastal Shipping, to be built by Trinity Marine Group at Gulfport, Mississippi.

TRADE POLICY

Industrial policies can be asserted through many means. In the United States, where admitting the reality of industrial policy is politically incorrect, trade policy often provides a mask for promoting industries. From the nation's founding, the Federal government has made trade policy an essential part of its industrial policies.[20] Over the last two centuries, foreign trade policy has been shaped by four different phases.

From Independence through the Civil War, trade policy was a compromise between northern interests which wanted a high tariff to protect their nascent industries from foreign competition, and agrarian southern and western interests which wanted no tariffs on the foreign goods they desired. The relatively low tariffs during this era reflected the reality that most Americans still farmed or made things in their homes.

The northern victory in the Civil War and accelerating industrialization resolved that conflict. Between 1865 and 1934, the United States maintained high tariffs to protect American industry, while Washington and business alike increasingly pushed American exports to relieve overcapacity at home and garner more wealth. The rates, however, varied considerably. For two generations following the Civil War, American foreign economic policy centered on a high tariff to protect American industries and supply revenue to the government. In 1887, President Grover Cleveland proposed a policy of tariff protection from European imports and free trade on certain items with Latin America in order to promote exports there. The debate raged until 1894 when Congress passed a tariff which differentiated sharply between European industrial goods and most Latin American commodities. The step toward freer trade was short-lived. Growing pressure from various economic interests prompted Congress to pass the protectionist Dingley Tariff of 1897 and the Payne–Aldrich Act of 1909.

Without a national tax, the Federal government had depended on tariffs to supply most of its revenues. The implementation of the 1914 Constitutional amendment allowing the income tax gave Washington unprecedented flexibility in foreign economic policy. Anticipating the passage of the income tax amendment, President Woodrow Wilson and his Democratic Congress succeeded in 1913 in passing the Underwood Tariff Act which lowered tariffs on both commodity and industrial goods in order to spur domestic competition and bring down prices. Tariffs were reduced from 41.0 percent to 26.8 percent on competitive goods and from 20.0 percent to 8.0 percent on all other goods, the lowest rate between the Civil War and World War II. In justifying the tariff reductions, Wilson argued that,

> You can't sell everything and buy nothing. You can't establish any commercial relationships that aren't two-sided. And if America is to insist upon selling everything and buying nothing, she will find that the rest of the world stands very cold and indifferent to her enterprise.[21]

Wilson's liberal rates were short-lived. During the 1920s, Republican presidents Harding, Coolidge, and Hoover each raised tariffs. This policy of tariff escalation to protect domestic industries culminated with the Smoot–Hawley Act of 1930 which boosted tariffs by an average 50 percent and helped topple the global trade system.[22]

The fourth phase began with the 1934 Reciprocal Trade Act, by which Congress bestowed upon the president the power to negotiate trade treaties with other nations. The Act decisively shifted the power to shape and implement foreign economic policy from Congress to the president where it has resided ever since.[23] By this time, President Roosevelt and a congressional majority understood that American prosperity depended on access to a dynamic, expanding global trade system. With Britain too economically enfeebled to uphold the system with the gold standard and free trade policies, only the United States had the economic power to revive world trade. Throughout the 1930s, the Roosevelt administration negotiated a series of bilateral deals in which both sides agreed to reduce trade barriers.

Despite these efforts, world trade still foundered. Much more sweeping measures were still needed. In 1944, amidst World War II, the United States hosted a conference at Bretton Woods, New Hampshire, attended by representatives of 44 countries. At this conference, the United States agreed henceforth to act as the global trade system's financier and free market. The dollar was placed on the gold standard of $35 an ounce, and other currencies were tied to the dollar. Two institutions were created to bolster the system – the International Monetary Fund (IMF) and International Bank for Reconstruction and Development (IBRD, World Bank) – both of which acted as lenders to its members. The IMF extended loans to countries having trouble maintaining a trade balance and currency value in hopes that the money would be invested in ways that boosted the economy. Governments used the money they borrowed from the World Bank to reconstruct their war-shattered countries or develop their economies.

The national consensus on America's new-founded commitment to open markets and free trade took a while to forge. In 1947, representatives created the third great organization which undergirds global trade, the General Agreement on Trade and Tariffs (GATT). The GATT was originally supposed to be a temporary institution which would be replaced by the International Trade Organization in 1948. But the US Senate voted down the treaty so, until recently, the multilateral reduction of trade barriers occurred through GATT. Trade relations for GATT members operate on the "most favored nation" principle in which a trade advantage that a state gives another state must be extended to all.

In addition to guiding the creation of these institutions, Washington extended $14 billion in aid to Europe through the Marshall Plan and $2.2 billion to Japan, and from the 1950s gave away tens of billions of dollars to other needy countries around the world. Although the institutions bound the signatories to free trade, Washington allowed the other countries to delay compliance with these treaty obligations. Immediately following World War II, most countries were too devastated and poverty-stricken to survive free trade. Inexpensive, high-quality American goods would have wiped out their industries; only high trade barriers could save them. Meanwhile, the United States kept its own markets open to foreign goods and services. Washington also encouraged the European states to reduce their economic barriers and form a common market. In 1951, six countries – France, West Germany, Italy, Belgium, the Netherlands, and Luxembourg – agreed to unite their coal and steel industries; in 1957, they formed the European Economic Community (EEC). By the late 1950s, American efforts at reviving the global trade and investment system had proved successful.

But by the early 1970s, increasing numbers of Americans questioned whether the costs of upholding the global trade system exceeded its benefits. The biggest problem in the immediate postwar world was a lack of money. Foreign countries needed to import equipment with which to rebuild their factories, and often food, fuel, and clothing simply to survive, but could not afford them. The United States filled this "dollar gap" with foreign aid. But by the late 1950s, what had been a dollar gap had become a "dollar glut" as Europe, Japan, other regions and countries rapidly expanded their economies.

Gold ultimately backed the fixed currency system. Foreign governments could use dollars to buy gold. The problem was that the value of dollars circulating around the world eventually exceeded the value of gold in the United States. In 1952, the United States held 50 percent of all international reserves of gold and tradable currencies while no other country held more than 5 percent; by 1972, America's total had dropped to 8.2 percent, surpassed by West Germany's 14.9 percent and Japan's 11.5 percent. America's payments surplus of $2.3 billion in 1970 became a deficit of $1.4 billion in 1971 and $5.8 billion in 1972. If all those governments holding dollars demanded gold, the trade system would collapse. Clearly the dollar had become grossly overvalued.

On 15 August 1971, President Nixon announced his New Economic Policy whereby the United States would no longer convert dollars into gold, would imposed a temporary 10 percent surcharge on imports, and imposed a 90 day freeze on prices and wages. Under the December 1971 Smithsonian Agreement, the dollar was devalued 10 percent against the other major currencies. In March 1973, Nixon abandoned the fixed currency system for a floating system in which the values of currencies were determined by markets rather than government *fiat*. Nixon's policies temporarily worked. The international account balance swung to a $7.1 billion surplus in 1973 and the surpluses continued through 1976.

Another important policy change was for Washington to work together with the other leading industrial countries to manage the global economy. Starting in 1975, the United States joined with Japan, West Germany, France, Britain, Italy, and Canada, known as the Group of Seven, to convene an annual summit to discuss global geopolitical and geoeconomic issues. At times the Group of Five – the United States, Japan, Germany, France, and Britain – have intervened in currency markets to manipulate the dollar's value. In 1985, the Group of Five devalued the dollar and in 1987 stabilized its value.

As America's geoeconomic power declined relative to its rivals, Washington has played an increasingly important role in using trade policies to supplement its industrial policies. Trade policies are asserted through diverse means. And, like the broader set of industrial policies of which they are an integral part, trade policies are just as controversial. Neoclassical economists argue that free trade is essential to economic development, and go so far as to insist that the United States should keep its markets open even if others close their markets. Political economists or strategic trade theorists counter that trade relations should allow reciprocal benefits, and that to achieve reciprocity governments can employ a range of retaliatory measures. Fair trade or reciprocity is essential for industrial survival in an ever-more competitive, interdependent global economy where increasing numbers of governments are following Japan's lead in skilfully conducting neomercantilist policies.[24]

Just as over time Washington established a widening range of institutions to regulate the economy, it likewise created agencies and laws to regulate trade. Governments can boost their nation's exports by directly subsidizing them or encouraging industries to dump their goods overseas. As foreign export subsidies and dumping took an increasing toll of American firms, industries, and wealth, Washington has created a broader array of laws and institutions with which to retaliate. American attempts to deter foreign subsidies first emerged with congressional laws in 1909 and 1913 authorizing the Treasury Department to impose duties equal to the foreign subsidy. A series of trade laws have empowered the victims of foreign dumping with the means to retaliate. The first antidumping law appeared in the 1916 Revenue Act, and was strengthened by another law in 1921. In all of its trade treaties since 1947, Washington has included an "escape clause" in which it could suspend treaty obligations for industries damaged by unfair foreign trade practices. The 1974 and 1988 Trade Acts included Section 301 and Super 301, respectively, each of which conferred unprecedented power upon the president to retaliate.[25] In order to remove the politics from determining unfair trade allegations, Congress founded the

International Trade Commission (ITC) to judge disputes from petitioners.

These laws empowered presidents to retaliate against predatory foreign trade strategies. But it became increasingly clear that much more was needed to promote American trade. In 1963, the office of the United States Trade Representative (USTR) was created to lead America's bilateral and multilateral trade negotiations. With a small staff of 150, the USTR can only concentrate on the worst current problems, rather than promote a long-term, comprehensive trade strategy. Yet, the USTR has been vital in opening closed foreign markets and deterring foreign dumping in the United States.

Just how effectively has Washington wielded its range of retaliatory trade weapons? Once the White House finally decides to intervene, the trade negotiators, holding to free-trade rhetoric, generally emphasize rules over results. Washington has refrained from retaliating against predatory foreign trade tactics, preferring instead to negotiate. Unfortunately, this outlook has hurt American geoeconomic interests. Without the threat of retaliation, the foreign power has little incentive to negotiate sincerely, conclude negotiations quickly, or implement any promises it eventually makes.

Deterrence has become as important to economic competition as it was to the nuclear arms race. Undeterred, states will shamelessly purse neomercantilist policies. Deterrence includes three essential components: (1) the clear communication to the other side of what is considered unacceptable behavior; (2) the power to inflict unacceptable damage to the other side when it transgresses those limits; and (3) the swift and decisive retaliation against aggressors. Once a government establishes a reputation for retaliation, it will usually succeed in deterring aggression. Successful retaliation depends on the power to hurt the other side worse than it can hurt one's own side.

Successful retaliation thus depends on two interrelated components, the speed with which it is imposed and the damage to the offending firms. If a penalty is imposed quickly but becomes a mere slap on the wrist to the offender, it may well encourage rather than deter future neomercantilism. Likewise, if the penalty is harsh but imposed too late, the domestic industry may have suffered irreparable harm. American retaliation against Japanese and other foreign predatory traders has often been deficient on both counts.

The United States has not deterred Japanese and other foreign economic aggression. Certainly, the United States has the power to retaliate and inflict enormous damage on Japan. With Japan's selling $65 billion more worth of goods and services in the United States than it buys, it is extremely vulnerable to retaliation. About 60 percent of Japan's trade surplus involves automobiles or automobile parts, many of which are made in the United States. True, some American industries have become dependent on highly sophisticated components that are no longer made in the United States, largely as a result of past Japanese dumping. But if an all-out trade war resulted, in which bilateral trade dropped to zero, Japan would be devastated while America's economy might well actually expand. In all, while the United States has the power, it lacks both the will and a consensus on what degree of damage it will not tolerate to deter foreign economic aggression effectively.

Deterrence and reciprocity promote rather than undermine free trade. Countries like the United States which tolerate neomercantilism in the short term may end up exploding against it in the long term. Deterrence prevents the damage inflicted by predatory traders from reaching unacceptable levels which could provoke a full-scale trade war.

Deterrence and retaliation also depend on those affected firms uniting and pressuring their government to act against the aggressors. "Strategic groups" are those firms which "resemble each other closely and, therefore, are more likely to respond in the same way to disturbances, to recognize their mutual dependence quite closely, and to be able to anticipate each other's reaction quite accurately."[26] America's "Big Three" automobile makers exemplify such a strategic group. Generally, they supported each other in the face of Japan's automobile invasion, although getting Washington's attention proved to be difficult.

The more diversified an industry, the less likely it will forge a common stand against foreign aggression: "In highly segmented industries, some firms may be unaffected in the short term by a foreign competitive threat. They may not perceive the foreign threat in a similar way to other firms, or they may not respond to that threat similarly."[27] America's steel industry of the 1970s was not a strategic group because there were so many producers of various scales, efficiencies, and products. Yet, largely because foreign dumping of steel hurt that industry earlier, Washington protected steel sooner than it did automobiles. Other highly segmented industries that failed to respond in time to Japanese dumping were televisions and machine tools.

Politics rather than grand strategy seems largely to determine when the White House intervenes. As America's most immense trade surplus became an ever-growing deficit after 1971, pressure built on Washington to retaliate against foreign dumping and other neomercantilist practices. Washington did impose "voluntary export restraints" (VERs) in textiles and steel during the 1970s, and in automobiles in 1981, which may well have saved those industries from complete bankruptcy. But Washington stood by as Japanese dumping destroyed America's television producers during the 1960s and 1970s, and machine tools in the 1980s.

The pressure on Washington to wield the VER weapon more widely increased during the 1980s with America's ever-deepening trade and budget deficits and the blatant neomercantilist practices of Japan and other states. Increasing numbers of prominent Americans demanded that the United States abandon its one-sided "free trade" policies and instead insist on "fair" or "reciprocal" trade with its partners. While the Reagan administration maintained its free trade rhetoric, it negotiated a series of VERs and market-opening agreements with Japan and other states. With Tokyo alone, the White House sought VERs in automobiles, motorcycles, and semiconductors and got Tokyo to promise to open its construction, baseball bat, beef, orange, and other markets. The semiconductor deal was particularly sweeping. Under it, Tokyo not only agreed to stop dumping chips and maintain a price floor in the United States and third markets, but to give American chip-makers a 20 percent market share in Japan by 1991. In all, Tokyo presented Washington with ten "market-opening packages" throughout the 1980s. Yet, like Hercules battling the hydra, two more Japanese non-tariff barriers (NTBs) appeared for every one that America's exasperated negotiators seemed to loop off. By 1995, Japan's trade surplus with the United States reached $70 billion.

VERs are an ineffective and sometimes self-defeating means of retaliation. If a VER is imposed too late after dumping begins and allows the dumper too high a market share, those hurt will be consumers while domestic and foreign producers alike may reap windfall profits. The Reagan administration's VER with Tokyo over automobiles backfired. By agreeing to allow the import of 1.6 million Japanese vehicles, the White House conceded a 20 percent market share which the Japanese expanded by later raising the quota to 2.3 million imported vehicles on top of an ever-growing number of Japanese automobiles built in "screwdriver assembly" plants in the

United States. Although American automobile makers did gain a respite from Japan's onslaught, protectionism's costs were imposed on American consumers rather than Japanese producers. A much more sensible policy would have been to impose high tariffs on any foreign automobile maker selling more than, say, 100 000 vehicles in the United States. Thus, the enormous profits reaped by the Japanese under the VER would have gone to the United States Treasury instead. By imposing higher tariffs, America would have been stronger and Japan correspondingly weaker.[28]

Retaliation with higher tariffs is much more difficult to achieve, since it must first be approved by the ITC. ITC rulings reveal some strange priorities over which American industries are to be protected and which are to be exposed to unfair foreign competition. For example, in 1992, the ITC ruled that Japan's dumping of minivans was not harming America's automobile producers, despite the fact that Japan's market share had risen from nothing to about 12 percent of the market and American producers often had to sell at a loss to prevent a further market erosion. That same year, the ITC imposed a 6.51 percent duty on the wood products of Canadian firms after it claimed that sales in the United States harmed America's logging industry, despite the fact that the two countries have a free trade pact, the wood was not being dumped at a loss, and America's logging industry is far healthier than its automobile industry. In 1992, while Japanese vehicle and auto parts exports to the United States amounted to $41 billion, Canadian wood products exports were only $2.7 billion. When Section 301 and Super 301 are used, they work. A recent study showed that two-thirds of the suits filed under those trade laws resulted in at least a partial opening of the foreign market.[29]

Washington protects its own industries with tariffs and quotas. Tariffs have diminished in importance; today, they average only 3.5 percent. Quotas, however, have become increasingly important in protecting certain industries. All told, the United States has 3600 quotas on mostly agricultural and textile products. Foreign peanuts and dairy products are allowed no more than a 7 percent domestic market share. Only 1.2 million foreign-made men's heavy and worsted wool suits are allowed into the country each year. These are anything but strategic industries. Politics explains the protection.

These import barriers cost American consumers plenty – $75 billion in 1991 in higher prices, or nearly one-sixth of that year's $490 billion import bill. The sugar quota, for example, effectively doubles the price Americans pay for sugar. The net cost of protecting 21 industries with sales of $1 billion or more and 1.8 million jobs cost the nation an average $54 000 and consumers $170 000 per employer; for the 7500 jobs in the luggage industry, $115 000 and $934 000; for the 871 000 jobs in the apparel industry, $51 000 and $170 000; for the 8100 jobs in the ceramic tile industry, $6000 and $400 000; and for the 1500 jobs in the corn broom industry, $4000 and $100 000. The average tariff for those 21 industries was 34.5 percent; while for the luggage industry it was 16.5 percent; for apparel, 48.0 percent; for ceramic tiles, 19.0 percent; and for corn brooms, 32.0 percent. These statistics, however, do not include the benefits that the United States enjoys from those tariffs in the form of savings in worker dislocation, unemployment compensation, lower economic growth and wealth, lower tax revenues, and higher socioeconomic costs such as crime if that protection did not exist.[30]

Overall, only about 5 percent of America's manufacturing workforce and 10 percent of those who actually work in factories are protected from foreign competition. What is notable about these protected products is their absolute absence of strategic economic value. The quotas are just another form of pork-barrel politics. A representative who gains a quota for a sensitive industry in his or her district is most likely guaranteed to be reelected. And with a trade deficit that tops $100 billion, the United States can certainly not be labeled a protectionist country. Politics rather than grand strategy shapes America's industrial policies.[31]

Another way in which Washington conducts trade policies is to encourage exports. Unlike its competitors, Washington does not heavily subsidize American exports. In 1991, export subsidies amounted to only $114.2 million. At times, the United States will offer another government a loan guarantee to buy American products. In addition to these benefits, Washington has special tax and credit programs to expand exports. The 1982 Export Trading Act built upon the Webb–Pomerence Act of 1920 which encouraged small businesses to form export-trading firms which banks can partly or wholly own and are free from antitrust laws.

Unfortunately, special rather than national interests shape Washington's export assistance program. Most of those subsidies and loan guarantees go to boosting American food products. Altogether, agricultural products accounted for only one-tenth of the nation's exports, but gobbled up 75 percent of America's $2.66 billion in subsidies and loan guarantees. Altogether, the United States spend

$50 in export assistance for every $1000 of agricultural products and a miserly 93 cents for every $1000 of other exports, in comparison to Britain's $1.91 and France's $1.81 for every $1000 of non-agricultural exports. As West Virginia Senator John D. Rockefeller pointed out, "If we could do for manufacturing what we do for agriculture, you could see in time a real reduction in our deficit."

Aside from the Agriculture Department, the missions of several other bureaucracies include export promotion. Most prominent of these is the State Department's Agency for International Development (AID) which mostly works with Third-World countries. The US Trade and Development Program spends $37 million to study export opportunities. The Overseas Private Investment Corporation insures companies against foreign expropriation. Like the Agriculture Department, the Energy Department and Small Business Administration promote exports from the industries in their charge. The Export–Import Bank provides loans and loan guarantees for exporters. The Commerce Department is partly organized to oversee select industries, including their relative effectiveness in penetrating foreign markets. Even NASA and the Interior Department have small sections which promote exports.

There is no coordination among the various bureaucracies that push exports. Politics rather than strategy determines which industries are promoted and which languish. Even when a firm can find a Federal program which offers loans or loan guarantees to export its product, the paperwork and filing fee often discourage its use. The staff of all the bureaucracies, including the Export–Import Bank, have been criticized for lacking the knowledge about international marketing vital needed to properly advise those who apply for assistance.

Until recently, Washington's Cold War obsessions meant that American exports or foreign investments received little concern from US embassies. For example, in 1990, there were 3233 American business executives in Japan, compared to 999 Britons, 446 Germans, 313 French, 276 Canadians, and 90 Italians. Yet, despite the small army of American executives, the embassy provided only one commercial official for every 62.17 executives, while Britain's embassy provided one for every 21.26, Germany one for every 9.30, France one for every 5.80, Canada one for every 6.73, and Italy one for every 2.31 of its business executives in Japan.[32]

Recently, the Justice Department has become more involved in trade policy. In April 1990, it announced that henceforth it would assert a jurisdiction over foreign markets in which collusion resulted in lost exports for American firms. Foreign governments, particularly Japan's, protested the policy, arguing that it violated their sovereignty. Undeterred, in March 1992, the Justice Department brought a suit against C. Itoh & Co., a Japanese conglomerate, which it accused of fixing prices to buy American shellfish at below market prices. Although the price fixing occurred in Tokyo, the Justice Department claimed jurisdiction because the adverse effects were on America's economy.

Most governments tie some or most of their foreign aid to the recipient's purchases of their respective nation's goods and services. In effect, foreign aid becomes an export subsidy. Faced with a severe balance of payment's problem, in July 1963 President Kennedy first linked foreign aid with purchases of American products. On 15 May 1990, the Bush administration announced that it would commit $500 million in export credits to existing foreign aid programs to four countries – Indonesia, the Philippines, Thailand, and Pakistan. The policy was intended to counter the mixed credit and aid programs of Japan and other governments that have undercut American exports. The White House selected those four countries because Japan's tied aid to them amounts to $2 billion a year. Meanwhile, the White House promised it would seek an agreement among the OECD (Organization for Economic Cooperation and Development) countries to end that very practice. This represented a sharp reversal of the White House policy of indifference towards American firms which lost sales to the mixed credit and aid policies of other countries.

The control over foreign investments within the United States has become an increasingly important policy area. Economists and labor unions alike once believed that if foreign corporations would only set up shop in the United States, the trade deficit would drop and employment would rise. Instead, contrary to neoclassical expectations, most foreign corporations which have set up factories in the United States have acted like "Trojan horses" by importing most of their components, exporting capital, and bankrupting domestic firms. In 1989, US affiliates of foreign corporations (with at least 10 percent foreign ownership) accounted for an astonishing 78 percent of the merchandise trade deficit. Four industries alone – autos, chemicals, steel, and electronics – made up 42 percent of the trade deficit. Foreign firms buy twice the value of imports per worker compared to American firms – Japanese firms import four times more.[33]

Both domestic and foreign corporations avoid paying taxes through the illegal practice of transfer pricing, in which they overcharge for products supplied by their subsidiaries to assembly plants in the United States, and thus show losses on their books. Foreign firms are particularly notorious for transfer pricing. In 1988, foreign firms which had invested in the United States sold $825.6 billion of goods and services, but paid only $5.8 billion in taxes. Estimates of how much the foreign firms really owe range up to $30 billion in Federal and $3 billion in state taxes a year.[34] Although during the 1992 election campaign, Bill Clinton promised to eliminate these loopholes, he has yet to do so.

Next to the complexity of the policymaking and implementation system, the power of foreign lobbyists is the most important reason why Washington fails to enact comprehensive trade policies. There is a revolving door between the Federal government and foreign corporations. The law currently bars senior officials from representing, aiding, or advising a foreign firm or power for a mere one year after they leave office, and the US Trade Representative for three years. There have been recent attempts to stiffen these restrictions. On 15 March 1992, the Justice Department ruled that registered foreign lobbyists could not serve on the Federal government's over 1000 advisory panels that work with the bureaucracies to forge policy. American trade officials share often secret information with trade advisory groups. The previous practice of allowing foreign lobbyists on those advisory groups effectively gave America's rivals knowledge of its negotiating strategies. In 1993 and 1994, President Clinton tried to get Congress to pass a tough law that would have barred senior non-career employees from lobbying their former departments for five years if they joined a domestic firm, and for their entire lives if they worked for a foreign firm. Republican Senators filibustered the bill to death.

The power of foreign lobbyists to assert their interests in the United States remains largely unhindered. No foreign power has a larger lobbying army in the United States than Japan. In 1992, Japan's lobbyists officially spent $60.434 million influencing American policies. The next biggest lobbyist, Canada, spent $22.710 million, followed by Germany with $13.140 million, France with $12.857 million, and Mexico with $11.046 million. By one estimate, the amount that Japan's government and businesses spend on influencing American policy may be as high as $400 million a year.[35]

Japan's power essentially to buy favorable policies from America's political system was spotlighted during the Toshiba scandal of 1987. Toshiba Machine had sold the Soviet Union a technology which allowed its submarines to run more quietly. In order to keep tracking the Soviet submarines, the United States would have had to invest an estimated $40 billion. When the sell-out was publicized, many in Congress angrily called for sanctions. A bill was introduced which would have cut off the entire Toshiba group's sales in the United States for three years. The Japanese lobby spent millions of dollars successfully to defeat that bill. Recently, Japanese have used their investments in American firms and communities indirectly to influence policy. By pulling their economic levers behind the scenes, the Japanese still assert their interests while avoiding the public eye.

A final aspect of Washington's trade policies involves attempting to open foreign markets. To do so, Washington uses both multilateral negotiations through such international organizations as General Agreement on Tariffs and Trade (GATT), World Trade Organization (WTO), the North American Free Trade Association (NAFTA), and Asia Pacific Economic Commission (APEC), along with bilateral negotiations with individual countries. No country's trade barriers have proven more impregnable or have had a more adverse effect on American geoeconomic interests than Japan's. Any comprehensive, objective analysis of Japan's political economy cannot help but conclude that: "The invisible hand is at work in Japan, but it is not Adam Smith's invisible hand – it is the invisible hand of the government working with Japanese industry."[36] By one estimate, Japan's non-tariff barriers are the equivalent of 25 percent tariff walls. Without them, American exports to Japan would increase by 30 percent.[37]

Getting the Japanese to promise to open their markets is a prolonged, frustrating experience for American negotiators that can drag on for months and even years. Getting the Japanese to fulfill their promises is nearly impossible. To the Japanese, trade negotiations are simply another means of promoting industry. They drag out the talks usually until Washington threatens relations, make a few symbolic concessions, and then declare that Japan's market is the world's most open and if foreign firms cannot sell there, their goods are inferior and they are not trying hard enough. The strategic core of Japan's negotiating strategy is to buy enough time and divert enough attention for their corporations to devastate their foreign rivals. In one industry after another, Washington has spent months and often years negotiating access with Tokyo, only to find that after the Japanese promised to open their markets, American sales there remained stagnant.

LEGACY

So what combination of macroeconomic, industrial, and trade policies have the most positive effects on developing the economy and which the worst? A comparative study of each four-year term of presidents from Truman through Bush analysed economic performance according to five criteria – unemployment, inflation, economic growth, current account balance, and productivity – concluded that the best overall economic managers were Democrats rather than Republicans, with the Truman, the Kennedy–Johnson, and Johnson terms the best. Only the Carter term ranked among the bottom five, although his term ranked higher than the two Reagan terms or the Bush term, which was last in economic performance. A systematic comparison of those presidents' respective policies would reveal just what the best performers did right and what the worst did wrong.[38]

What is the government's proper role in the economy? Americans have debated the question for over 380 years. Few would disagree with Stuart Bruchey that "given other favorable conditions, incentives to invest one's time, effort, and capital, to work to the best of one's ability, and to improve one's situation – in short, a determination to get ahead – may well be the most important factor in economic growth."[39] The controversy arises over what are the "favorable conditions" which best stimulate the human desire for self-improvement. Genuine free markets would mean absolutely no government; free markets are synonymous with anarchy. No serious economist advocates the complete dismantlement of government. Nonetheless, while economists agree that some government is necessary for economic development, they are split over how much. Jeffersonians have maintained that the less government, the better; they reject the notion that bureaucrats can be more prescient about the nation's economic future than businessmen. Hamiltonians counter that government policies can assist the private sector in developing the economy, and that government experts are often better able to understand the big economic picture and long-term possibilities and pitfalls than businessmen obsessed with quarterly profits or just survival.

Just because industrial policies can develop the economy does not mean they necessarily do. How do we determine when an industrial policy works or fails? Unfortunately, all we have is what history records. Lacking God's omniscience, we can never truly know whether different policies or decisions under the same circumstances would have produced better or worse results.

Yet, some decisions are easier to evaluate than others. The supercollider, B-1 bomber, B-2 stealth bomber, and Strategic Defense Initiative (SDI) together directly wasted over $150 billion and indirectly hundreds of billions of dollars more by diverting key financial, scientific, manufacturing, and technological resources away from productive projects or weapons systems that not only worked but had a strategic rationale. Those industrial policies clearly failed. More positively, it is fairly certain that Lockheed and Chrysler would have gone out of business had not Washington bailed them out. Today, Lockheed and Chrysler are dynamic wealth-, technology-, and job-creating corporations – strategic corporations. America is better off with Lockheed and Chrysler than without them. The industrial policies that saved those corporations were clearly successful in practical if not theoretical terms.

What, if anything, can Washington do to embrace constructive and reject destructive industrial policies? The recommendations are endless. Laura D'Andrea Tyson argues persuasively that "we must devise macroeconomic, trade, and industrial policies that promote our own high-technology industries while continuing to lobby for a more liberal trading system."[40] She goes on to offer specifics:

> the government and the business community should share their costs to ensure serious industry participation and to guide projects into commercially promising areas; projects should be initiated and designed by private firms and should be funded only after they have been competitively reviewed by an independent panel of experts; and the institutions responsible for administering such programs should be insulated as much as possible from continuing budgetary and political pressures."

The semiconductor research consortium Sematech is often held up as a model for a successful government–business partnership.

Starting first in the 1980s among "New" or "Atari" Democrats, increasing numbers of moderate politicians in both parties have advocated rational industrial policies. Bill Clinton's election to the

White House in 1992 represented the triumph of Hamiltonians. That triumph was short lived. While conservative Republicans continue to reject the idea, moderate Republicans increasingly embrace it. The trouble is that moderate Republicans are becoming an endangered species within the Grand Old Party. Since the 1994 Republican takeover of Congress, the power balance has tipped decisively from Hamiltonians to Jeffersonians, who have stymied most of Clinton's industrial policy initiatives. Whether Jeffersonian rule continues or their efforts succeed remains to be seen. The industrial policy debate, however, will never end.

3 The Roots of Industrialization, 1607–1860

From the time the first settlers arrived on America's east coast, government has shaped and often led the nation's economic development. Although the economy remained largely agrarian throughout the two and a half centuries from Jamestown's settlement to the Civil War's eve, the colonial and later federal governments imposed an array of measures that usually promoted and sometimes impeded entrepreneurship.[1] Then as today, the government developed the economy by, among other strategies, issuing corporate charters, imposing laws, collecting taxes, procuring goods and services, and protecting industries from foreign trade.

Both the colonial and early republic governments were more sympathetic to manufacturing than is popularly believed. To varying extents, London and each colonial assembly passed laws to promote the manufacture of certain products. Following 1776, although the Confederal and Federal governments officially embraced the Jeffersonian ideal of an agrarian republic, they issued a range of remedies which either directly or indirectly promoted manufacturing. The government subsidized the building or improvement of roads, ports, canals, and eventually railroads. Textile and iron industries developed in the early nineteenth century, aided considerably by Jefferson's 1807 trade embargo and a succession of tariffs. By the time Confederate batteries fired on Fort Sumter, the United States enjoyed a powerful, diverse manufacturing sector, albeit mostly concentrated in the northeast. And the Federal government could take pride in having borne a considerable weight in developing those industries.

THE COLONIAL ERA

America's colonization in the early seventeenth century sprang from interrelated intellectual, commercial, political, and technological

73

changes in Europe over the preceding centuries that undermined and eventually destroyed a millenium-old feudal order.[2] Most of these changes first occurred in northern Italian city-states which became to the commercial revolution of the fourteenth and fifteenth centuries what England was to the industrial revolution of the eighteenth and nineteenth centuries. Commerce flourished following the Italian inventions of bills of exchange and double-entry bookkeeping, two very basic business practices taken for granted today. The techniques soon spread across Europe.[3]

The commercial revolution sweeping across Europe stimulated the exploration and often outright conquest of overseas lands, particularly in the western hemisphere. Starting in the fifteenth century merchants, soldiers, and missionaries rapidly knit the world into what became one vast trade and colonial system. Why did the commercial revolution and colonialism develop together? A vital reason was technology. Advances in ship design (caravels, galleons), sails (lanteen), and navigation (compass) enabled kings and corporations alike to dispatch trade and colonial expeditions to the world's far corners.

But just because merchants had the ability to sail around the world did not mean that they necessarily would. Shifts in the continent's power balance provided the motivation to do so. Europe's nobility and burghers had become dependent on an array of exotic spices which came all the way from South-east Asia. When disrupted trade routes across the Middle East resulted in higher prices and smaller supplies, enterpreneurs looked for alternate routes. At first, sailing around Africa seemed the only viable alternative, a route Portugal and Spain were best poised to exploit. Then in 1492 Columbus tried sailing dead west across the Atlantic toward the spice islands. About one-third of the way there he "encountered" America.

Colonies demanded settlers. Aside from enterpreneurs, the American colonies were populated from two sources – the displaced at home and African slaves. Between 1450 and 1600, Europe's population swelled from about 50 or 60 million to 80 million. "Enclosure" exacerbated the population pressures. Landowners in Spain and England, in particular, chased tenants off their land so that sheep could graze there. In desperate search of subsistence, the peasants drifted to towns and cities, and some eventually ventured overseas to the new colonies. These immigrants were not always numerous or willing enough to work the plantations and mines.

Slaves bought from African kingdoms made up the difference.

Yet another reason was the embrace by European monarchs of the strategy of mercantilism, which assumes a virtuous circle between economic and military power. The more wealth a state garnered, the more was available to build up a powerful fleet and army with which to defend an ever-expanding realm. In a mercantilist world, free trade is dangerous for a state's economic and military security. States that become dependent on foreign sources of raw materials may lose that source during a war. Trade surpluses thus enhance national power, while trade deficits undermine it. States promote their realm's industries through trade barriers; they expand markets and increase availability of raw materials for those industries through conquest. Imperialism became a vital aspect of mercantilism. While colonies may have been expensive to take and administer, states captured foreign lands to exploit their wealth through mines, commerce, and plantations.

Yet it was corporations rather than kings that conquered "new worlds." Enterprising titled and moneyed aristocrats, alike, pooled their wealth to form corporations to exploit potential overseas riches. They would then apply to the Crown for a charter granting them monopoly rights for a specific trade route or foreign land. In return, the crown would receive a cut of the profits (the "King's Fifth").

In the sixteenth century, England joined the imperial race. As in Spain, Portugal, France, and Holland, the English Crown at first abstained from directly seizing foreign lands. Instead, it chartered a series of corporations such as the Muscovy (1555), Levant (1581), and East India (1600) companies and empowered them with trade monopolies over distant lands. Joint stock companies would eventually found six of the nine first English settlements in North America. Like its rival kingdoms, England's colonial policy was based on mercantilism, perhaps most succinctly expressed by the 1549 "Discourse on the Commonweal of This Realm of England": "We must always take heed that we buy no more of strangers than we do sell them; for so we should impoverish ourselves and enrich them."[4]

The Crown also licensed privateers like Francis Drake and John Hawkins who looted Spanish treasure ships in the Atlantic, Caribbean, and even the Pacific, and brought back vast wealth to England. Drake's three-year circumnavigation of the world (1577–80), for example, had cost only £5000 to equip but brought back Spanish treasure worth £1 500 000! Elizabeth enjoyed a cut of £250 000 pounds and other investors made 4600 percent profits.[5]

The wealth and glory brought back by England's trading companies and "sea dogs" alike stimulated numerous imitators. Yet, while English companies could reap wealth from trade and privateers could harass Spanish fleets, few entrepreneurs were bold enough to consider planting a colony on faraway shores. It was feared that any colony would become prey to native peoples or Spanish warships. Nonetheless, in 1584, Sir Walter Raleigh and his associates set aside these fears to finance a colonial expedition to what is now North Carolina. When a relief ship arrived three years later, no survivors were found.

It would be two more decades before entrepreneurs would try again to carve settlements from America's wilderness. Peace was the prerequisite. Two generations of war between England and Spain ended with the Treaty of London in 1604. While James I recognized Spain's existing new-world colonies, he asserted that any unoccupied regions of the Americas remained open to conquest.

While peace allowed colonists to establish a foothold in the new world without constantly fearing a Spanish attack, other forces contributed to English colonialism. By the late sixteenth century, England faced both a population explosion and a growing natural resource shortage. The population had nearly doubled over the preceding century, while the enclosure movement forced hundreds of thousands into ever-more-crowded towns and cities. Meanwhile, between 1550 and 1650, the cost of lumber from Britain's diminishing forests rose fivefold.[6] The shipbuilders, iron smelters, and constructors who depended on forest products had to buy abroad what could not be produced at home. Increasing numbers of prominent Englishmen disparaged the British fleet's growing dependence on the lumber, hemp, tar, and wax from the Baltic region. Why not take North America, they argued, and thus at once expand and protect a vital source of wealth and power?

In April 1607, three ships disembarked 105 colonists at a point on the James River in Virginia which they would call Jamestown. Jamestown was not only America's first English-speaking town, it was America's first company town. Everyone was an employee of the Virginia Company which financed, organized, and dispatched colonial expeditions. Communalism rather than free enterprise shaped Virginia's first decade. All the land was owned by the Virginia Company, which only loosely supervised its employees. The Virginia Company fed and clothed its charges according to their needs rather than work. With no incentive to work, few did. At first, most searched vainly for gold and silver lodes like those found in Peru and Mexico under Spanish rule. Eventually, most became sullen idlers in the new land. Lacking food and hygiene, nine of every ten colonists eventually succumbed to starvation and disease. After three years and several boatloads of new arrivals, only 60 of over 600 people who left England survived.

In 1617, the Virginia Company trustees finally realized the folly of communalism. They decreed that, henceforth, land would be distributed and tilled by its private owners. Aside from simply selling off its holdings, the Virginia Company dispatched land through the Headright system whereby anyone who payed the transatlantic fare of himself or others received 50 acres for each person brought over. As peasant tenants became independent farmers, Virginia's economy began to develop from bare subsistence into wealth and diversification. Captain John Smith noted the effect of these policies on production: "when our people were fed out of the common store and laboured jointly together, glad was he who could slip from his labour, or slumber over his taske, he cared not how; say, the most honest among them would hardly take so much true paines in a week, as now for themselves they will do in a day." By the time the Virginia Company disolved in 1624, the population had achieved relative security and prosperity.

Meanwhile, in 1620, settlers founded Plymouth in today's Massachusetts. As in Virginia, communalism governed the first Massachusetts settlers before eventually giving way to private land ownership and enterprise. Throughout the American colonies, but particularly in New England, entire congregations or neighborhoods would transport themselves to the new settlements. Communalism continued longer in spirit than wealth. As land was distributed and opportunities opened, some people naturally made more wealth than others. While maintaining a tight control over the social order, the colonial and village leaders justified in Biblical terms the growing economic disparities. As John Winthrop put it, "God Almightie in his most holy and wise providence, hath soe disposed of the Condition of mankinde, as in all times some must be rich, and some poore, some highe and eminent in power and dignitie; others meane and in subjection."[7]

Over the next century, thirteen separate colonies would emerge along the east coast. The population soared from 100 in 1607 to 250 000 in 1700, to 2 354 000 in 1774 at the American Revolution's eve. Despite this population explosion, there always seemed to be too few rather than too many people as the demand for labor exceeded its supply. Wages thus were from 30–100 percent higher than in England, which also attracted new settlers. With relatively free access to land and riches wrought from their own ingenuity, Americans quickly surpassed in individual wealth those they had left behind in England and other realms. By 1775, the average household head enjoyed a net worth of £243, the equivalent of $13 000 in 1978.[8]

What led those first and subsequent immigrants to abandon their homes in England and elsewhere for America's far away shores and wilderness? The British Register for Emigration asked 2532 people who were accompanied by 1926 dependents just why they were leaving for America. All those surveyed had paid their own passage to America. More than half replied that they were

> seeking to better themselves, or planning to 'plant' themselves on American soil, or hoping to establish a 'settlement' for their families there, or expecting to join relatives with whom they had been in communication, or assuming that they would be able to engage abroad in crafts and trades for which they had been trained.[9]

Every immigrant had his or her own particular reasons. But surely nearly all of them were motivated by the quest for greater freedom, whether it was of land, marriage, trade, religion, or just the ability to roam. Freedom, of course, is relative to one's circumstances. A village in Delaware or North Carolina could be just as socially suffocating as one back in England, even if it were easier to be a landowner and accumulate wealth in the former than the latter. And, ironically, many willed themselves into temporary servitude to gain future freedom. From Bristol alone from 1654 to 1686, 10 600 people sailed as indentured servants.[10]

And, of course, hundreds of thousands of humans beings were dragged in chains to America. Slavery alleviated the labor shortage and gradually replaced indentured servitude. As the slave trade developed, it became cheaper to own rather than temporarily rent a human being. One by one, the colonial legislatures legalized and codified slavery. Every colony had slavery, although the proportion of slaves to the general population varied from as little as 3 percent in New England to 60 percent in South Carolina in 1720. As for the total number of slaves, the records are sketchy. There were anywhere from 5000 to 20 000 slaves in America by 1700. Between then and 1790, over 275 000 slaves were brought to America. The influx of slaves combined with reproduction resulted in a black population numbering 675 000 or 20 percent of the total in 1790, the year of the first national census.[11]

Land and crops were the primary sources of wealth. Although few of the early settlers would have probably admitted it, and few that followed were probably aware of it, the ultimate success of early American agriculture depended on borrowing heavily from native crops and techniques. European grains were either supplemented or replaced by native maize, pumpkins, beans, squash, and melons. Settlers adopted not just foods from the Indians but methods of clearing, tilling, and harvesting crops. Within years of the first settlement, most communities were producing an agricultural surplus which was shipped abroad with other raw materials such as lumber, pitch, furs, dried fish, hides, and iron to pay for imported manufactured and luxury goods. Tobacco became the primary cash crop for most of the colonies as addiction spread on either side of the Atlantic. By the Revolution, the colonies produced over 100 million pounds of tobacco. Grain was the primary cash crop for northern farmers while rice, indigo, and sea island cotton swelled the incomes of southern plantations.[12]

American farmers were hard on the land. With land cheap and seemingly endless, it was easier to use up a patch and then move west rather than carefully nurture the soil through crop rotation and erosion control. The reason for the waste was simple. As Thomas Jefferson put it, "We can buy an acre of new land cheaper than we can manure an old one."[13] Colonist Jared Eliot condemned American farming techniques in his various essays between 1748 and 1762:

> when our fore-fathers settled here ... here, they entered a land which probably had never been Ploughed since the creation ... when they had worn out one piece they cleared another, without any concern to amend their land, except a little helped by the Fold and Cart-dung. . . . Seduced by the fertility of the soil on first settling, the farmers think only of exhausting it as soon as possible, without attending to their own interest in a future day.[14]

Some colonial governments did attempt to stem the devastation. Not everyone could simply pull up stakes and move west after they had ruined their land. Those left behind were stuck with the legacy of destruction. Among the first economic measures passed by colonial governments were those designed to conserve dwindling resources. As early as 1626, Plymouth Colony passed laws regulating the cutting and sale of timber; eight years later it forbade the setting of forest fires to clear land. In 1639, Newport, Rhode Island outlawed deer hunting for six months to allow local herds to replenish. William Penn, Pennsylvania's Proprietor, decreed in 1681 that one acre of forest must remain untouched for every five clear-cut.[15] In 1691 and 1711, Parliament passed laws preserving trees over a certain size for ship masts. In 1718, Massachusetts outlawed deer hunting for four years. In 1739, Connecticut prohibited deer hunting for a season. In 1772, New York closed a season on quail and partridge hunting. Enforcement of these few laws on public lands was nearly impossible. And once someone acquired property rights, they were free to do whatever they wanted with it. In all, these conservation laws were the exception rather than the rule, and even then limited to certain places and practices.

English mercantilism did not just attempt to regulate trade to the nation's advantage, it also encouraged the development of manufacturing through what we know today as "industrial policies." London offered various financial inducements to encourage the mining, growing, and manufacture of those products in the thirteen colonies which it could not fully supply from within Britain. However, it was the colonial assemblies which provided the biggest boost to local manufacturing. Various assemblies offered bounties, subsidies, patents, monopolies, and low interest loans to those who manufactured not only "strategic" goods such as hemp for rope, canvas for sail, and flax for textiles, but targeted virtually any product including glass, guns, lumber, barrels, boats, salt, wagons, carriages, paper, potash, linseed oil, pearl ash, and soap, along with those who erected forges, gristmills, sawmills, and watermills. Patents to inventors became increasingly widespread. In 1646, Joseph Jenks enjoyed the honor of receiving the first patent issued to an American. Massachusetts awarded Jenks a patent for his improved sawmills and scythes. All of these various colonial-assembly industrial policies had first to be approved by Parliament's Board of Trade. Of the 8563 total laws submitted by the various assemblies during the colonial era, the Board of Trade rejected only 469 or 5.5 percent.[16]

During the colonial era, only two American industries achieved large-scale production. Several of the American colonies had abundant iron ore resources. The 1750 Iron Act encouraged iron ore mining and smelting by eliminating tariffs on its import to Britain.

By the Revolution, America's iron production was one-seventh of global production. London, however, forbade the refining of the pig iron into steel, thus retaining the most value-added and strategically important process for British manufacturers. America's largest industry was shipbuilding, most of which was located in the New England states with their accessible hardwood forests. Virtually all of America's merchant fleet and about one-third of Britain's was built in the colonies.[17]

Despite these industrial policies, manufacturing remained largely a household or shop craft. Although Americans take for granted their right to form corporations, London discouraged the practice during the colonial era. Parliament did not begin to regulate corporations closely until after the South Sea Bubble speculative scheme burst in 1720 and ruined many fortunes. Parliament ruled that, henceforth, all corporations were illegal without an official license. Licenses were difficult to obtain. During the American colonial era, only two corporations were licensed during the seventeenth century and four in the eighteenth century.[18]

Trade was considerable, not just between the colonies and England but among the Americans. From 1768 to 1772, about 25 percent of the thirteen colonies' trade was with each other. The regions differed greatly in their participation in this trade. Economically diversified New England exported as much as 60 percent of its goods to other colonies, the middle colonies about 40 percent, and the southern colonies minimal amounts. Most of this coastal trade was conducted by American merchants in American built and owned ships.[19]

What commercial and manufacturing incentives London provided were often discouraged by other policies. Starting with the Trade and Navigation Act of 1651, Parliament issued a series of laws which formed the essence of British mercantilism. The Navigation Acts severely limited the trade opportunities of the American colonies in three broad ways. Firstly, goods could be shipped to or from the American colonies only in the hulls of British or American owned ships, of which the captain and three-quarters of the crew had to be English subjects. Secondly, each Act expanded the list of "enumerated" goods, or those goods that could only be exported to Britain. Thirdly, some of the acts restricted trade among the colonies themselves. The 1699 Woolens Act and 1732 Hat Act forbade trade in woolen textiles or beaver hats from one colony to another. The Navigation Acts strengthened Britain at the expense of its Dutch,

French, and Spanish rivals. Without international competition the merchant fleets of both Britain and the colonies expanded rapidly. Wealth accrued to the British Empire that would have flowed to other states with free trade.

Mercantilism, however, was not without its costs. The British and Americans alike paid higher prices for goods than they would have if free trade had prevailed. Many American products were reexported from Britain to third countries. English middlemen thus enjoyed profits at the expense of American producers and merchants. A scarcity of capital in the colonies cramped American entrepreneurship. Had the colonies been allowed to manufacture and trade freely, their development would have far exceeded the historic rate.

Every region of colonial America experienced the "development of underdevelopment" because of Britain's trade restrictions, none more so than the South. During the colonial era, tobacco rather than cotton was "king" in the South. London named tobacco an "enumerated" good as early as 1660. Slaves were imported to work the fields. The tobacco was wagoned down from the scattered plantations to small landings and then shipped to Britain. Much of the tobacco was consumed in Britain, much more was transshipped elsewhere. By enumerating tobacco, the Crown reserved vast wealth for British merchants, shippers, and itself that would have otherwise gone to their American counterparts. British government policy prevented those commercial counterparts in the South from emerging until after the Revolution.[20]

Stuart Bruchey nicely captures the reasons why the South underdeveloped as it did:

> All three factors then – geography, legislation, and the market – must be taken into account if we are to understand the convergence of policy and interest, colonial as well as British, that supplied the South with the capital it needed in the form of slaves, the shipping required to move the staples to market, and the numerous services needed in the marketplace itself. The region's dependence on Great Britain for these requirements weakened the urbanizing effects that domestically located entrepreneurial headquarters might have exerted. At bottom though, it is British policy and interest that are the decisive factors.[21]

Towns and wealth developed wherever unenumerated products were grown or manufactured. Britain not only did not enumerate wheat and livestock, it encouraged northern farmers to export those products elsewhere around the world so that they would not compete with those grown at home. Consequently, it was American merchants and ships that handled the wheat and livestock trade. Boston, Newport, New York, Philadelphia, and Baltimore grew into bustling entrepôts by handling those and other unenumerated products. Bruchey points out that "most northern products were usually unwanted in the mother country. Indeed, in the five year period 1768–1772, they accounted for only 14 percent of the value of colonial exports to Great Britain."[22] About 92 percent of New England's trade with Britain and the Caribbean and 82 percent of the middle colonies was in American built and owned ships. The result was a much more diversified, egalitarian, and dynamic economy along the northern than southern coasts. The political, economic, and social consequences of that unequal regional development has haunted America ever since.[23]

In the South, Charleston appeared to be the exception to the rule that towns failed to develop where goods where enumerated. Charleston's population rose steadily in the eighteenth century, from 4500 in 1730 to 12 000 by 1775. On the Revolution's eve, Charleston's port handled more business than New York's. However, the merchant class was largely British rather than American, and few products were manufactured there. Thus, all the decisions and wealth were "made in England, capital was raised there, ships were built or chartered there and outfitted there, [and] insurance was made there – all for the South Carolina trade."[24]

How much did British mercantilism hold back America's economic development? British policies trapped the American colonies into a vicious cycle of economic underdevelopment. By restricting America's ability to trade freely, London distorted and stunted America's economic development. Industries, skills, technologies, and wealth that might have developed in America, largely did not. Americans had to import what, under different circumstances, they could have made at home. The result was a huge annual trade deficit with Britain and Ireland – an average £1 331 000 annually between 1768 and 1772. America also suffered annual trade deficits with the West Indes and Africa. It was only with southern Europe that the American colonies enjoyed a small surplus – £412 000 a year during the same period. Overall, however, the net costs of mercantilism were low, from a mere 41¢ per person or less than 1 percent of income in 1770 to three times as much.[25]

With its economy governed by a strict mercantilism, London allowed no gold or silver coins to underwrite trade even with its American colonies. The colonists lacked gold and silver mines from which they could mint their own coins. The Navigation Acts cramped the colonies' development, and led to an enormous annual outflow of money because of persistent trade deficits. Given America's annual trade deficits with Britain and surpluses with southern Europe, it was Spanish silver *reals* (pieces of eight) and Portugese gold *johannes* rather than English pounds that circulated most abundantly in the colonial period. In 1786, Congress made the Spanish silver dollar the basis of America's monetary system.

The thirteen colonies suffered severe shortages of coin throughout the century and a half of English rule. Colonial American merchants tried to supplement their meager coinage with commercial paper like promissory notes and bills of exchange, a development one scholar has called "the distinctive contribution of the American colonies to financial and monetary practice."[26] But these notes were not enough to satisfy the demand for capital. Most trade in the hinterlands was through barter. Without capital, prospective entrepreneurs could not become capitalists. The colonial assemblies were just as chronically underfunded:

> given the relatively small tax base, the scarcity of specie, the lack of liquidity in property, the nonexistence of commercial banks and business corporations, and the urgency of need, especially in wartime, the colonies found themselves unable to depend on taxation or borrowing.[27]

Eventually the colonial assemblies began paying off some of their bills by having their colonial loan offices issue bills of credit. Using their land as collateral, citizens could borrow from the loan offices (which became known as "land banks") as well, securing loans for 8–10 years during which they paid annual interest. These loan banks, which were

> not banks in the modern sense, but rather batches of paper money resting on the security of land – provided individuals with the long-term credit needed to expand their agricultural activities, government with a source of revenue in the form of interest payments, and the public at large with an increased supply of money.[28]

The interest payments were large enough in the middle colonies to cover administrative costs, so that there were no local taxes.

The land banks actually conducted monetary policy by lowering interest rates and easing credit during recessions. The colonies differed in how effectively they wielded monetary policy. Generally, the middle colonies followed a conservative monetary policy, while New England and the southern colonies issued excessive credit, with the appropriate results. Much of New England and South Carolina's excessive credit was issued to underwrite their participation in the frequent wars against the French and Indians throughout the eighteenth century. The trouble was that the flood of paper money depreciated rapidly and few merchants wanted to handle it. No colony administered its monetary policy more effectively than Pennsylvania, which was so prudent that real prices remained stable for 50 years and the economy steadily expanded before the Revolution. Rhode Island, on the other hand, recklessly issued credit, thus stimulating inflation and defaults. In response, in 1751 Parliament issued the first of several regulations of the commercial paper business.[29]

Ironically, jealous of ceding more than minimal powers, the states would not allow the new Republic to conduct monetary policy as they themselves had done during the colonial era. Thus was the art of monetary policy lost for nearly a century and a half after Independence. Monetary policy had stimulated colonial development. Its lack hampered the United States' development.

INDEPENDENCE AND REVOLUTION

The American Revolution broke out in 1775 because of a range of interrelated long- and short-term socioeconomic and political reasons.[30] Perhaps the most important was the development of American nationalism. For over 150 years, the people who settled the thirteen colonies developed an identity increasingly distinct from that of their English brethren across the Atlantic. In many respects, the American Revolution asserted an independence of values, institutions, identity, and spirit which had long existed.

Then, in the decade preceding the Declaration of Independence, London provoked American nationalism by issuing a series of heavy-handed laws that not only further restricted entrepreneurship and trade, but, more importantly, struck at the heart of American values and institutions of freedom. The thirteen colonies were developed by people courageous enough to abandon England in search of something better. The freedom to head west and succeed or fail on one's own merits became a central American value. In search of fresh farmland, hunting grounds, or "elbow room", at least one-tenth of the population searched out lands along the frontier between civilization and wilderness.

The Proclamation of 1763 forbade any new American land grants west of the Appalachian Mountain crest. To Parliament, the law made perfect sense. To a great extent, Britain had won its war with France over North America by forging an alliance with most Indian tribes along the frontier. In return, the British promised the Indians many things, the most important of which was a ban on any further encroachments of Americans on their lands. In 1774, Parliament reinforced the 1763 Proclamation with the Quebec Act which invalidated any outstanding land claims north of the Ohio River and incorporated that region into Quebec Province. Both acts prompted bitter protests from the assemblies and peoples in all thirteen colonies. Most of the colonies claimed lands beyond the Appalachian divide. The acts particularly incensed Massachusetts, Connecticut, and Virginia which had extensive claims north of the Ohio River.

As if the restrictions on westward settlement were not an affront enough to American sentiments and ambitions, London also restricted the financial freedom of the colonies. In 1751, the fiscal irresponsibility of several New England colonial assemblies had prompted Parliament to revoke their power to issue paper money. The Currency Act of 1764 extended the restriction to all the colonies. Unable to finance their operations with paper money, the colonial assemblies faced the unsavory choice either of increasing taxes or cutting back expenditures. London turned a deaf ear to the subsequent protests.

In winning its seven-year war with France and other enemies, Parliament incurred an enormous debt. It seemed only fair to most Members of Parliament that their colonists help pay down the debt with higher taxes. Afterall, London had eliminated a French threat which had periodically brought devastation and atrocities along the frontier for almost a century. And, compared to the average Englishman, Americans paid an extraordinarily low rate of taxation to the Crown. With the average English tax burden indexed at 100, Pennsylvania, Maryland, and Massachusetts paid four, New York three, and Connecticut and Virginia two.[31]

The Sugar Act of 1764 actually reduced the existing duty on rum to six pence per gallon. But it established a new vice-admiralty court at Halifax, Nova Scotia to administer the law and collect fees. This was a deep affront to liberties Americans had long taken for granted. Previous offenders were tried in common courts before a jury of their peers who seldom issued a conviction. The vice-admiralty court had no jury, just a judge whose duty was to gather as many revenues as possible and make harsh examples of evaders. Parliament followed the Sugar Act with a series of other laws designed to raise revenue. The Stamp and Quartering Act of 1765, Townsend Acts of 1767, and Tea Act of 1773 expanded the range of taxable goods.

Parliament imposed these higher taxes and restrictions at a time when the colonies suffered recession, land shortages, and growing discrepancies between the rich elite and mass poor. Increasing numbers of American leaders and the populace alike reacted against Parliament's series of acts with cries of "down with tyranny" and "no taxation without representation." Although Parliament repealed the Sugar Act in 1766 and Townsend Act in 1770 in response to such protests, the colonists still complained bitterly about those remaining.

The worsening relations broke down into warfare between the colonies and England in April 1775, with the Declaration of Independence being made in July 1776. After seven long years of war, Britain and the United States ratified the Treaty of Paris in 1783 which accepted American independence.

Economic and political revolution accompanied and followed independence. During the 1770s and 1780s, the United States briefly became more economically egalitarian. One by one, the states abolished such vestiges of feudal order as primogeniture and entail. Tens of thousands of loyalists fled the United States, after which the states confiscated and distributed their properties. The wartime inflation had been a boom to debtors and bane to creditors. The destruction, debts, and confiscations during the war sapped the wealth of most of America's socioeconomic elite. Alexander Hamilton pointed out that the war had "destroyed a large proportion of the monied and mercantile capital of the country, and of personal property generally."[32] Most would regain it within a generation; many would not. As the war and its aftermath brought down many from the established wealthy class, it provided enormous opportunities for the rise of a new class of contractors, privateers, and speculators.

The first government to unite the new states was simply a

confederation of the thirteen sovereign states. This government was codified in the Articles of Confederation ratified in 1781. In debating and drawing the Articles of Confederation, the states fiercely guarded their own economic and political privileges. In doing so, the states may have hurt themselves and the country. Article 2 asserted each state's sovereignty and independence. The power to tax and negotiate trade treaties resided in the states.

Throughout the war, Congress' most important and difficult task had been to finance the American army and navy. Lacking the power to tax, Congress simply printed money – $241.5 million between May 1775 and November 1779 alone. To cover their own expenses, the states too printed money. By 1781, the continental dollar was worth less than 1 percent of its printed value. The United States also attempted to cover its expenses through borrowing. By 1787, the total amount of debts accumulated by the Confederation and individual states to foreign and domestic creditors amounted to $27 million. The Confederation was impotent to pay its own debts, let alone conduct commercial treaties. In 1786, the Confederation's income was less than one-third of the interest due on its debts![33]

Debt bedeviled not only Congress; to survive the inflation most people went deeply into debt. After the war the attempts by creditors to collect their debts led to scattered violence, particularly in western Massachusetts. In 1786, Shay's Rebellion broke out when debtors refused higher taxes and debt collection. Although troops dispersed the rebellion, state and national leaders alike trod even more gingerly around issues of debt and revenue.

No matter how large the state, all lacked the power to negotiate commercial agreements with Britain and other countries. In the years following Independence, foreign governments played the states off against each other to gain the best advantages for their own merchants and squeeze American merchants. In order to gain access to another country, states competed with each other to lower their duties on imports. Manufactured imports bankrupted one American cottage industry after another. Revenues fell so states had little with which to pay their enormous debts, let alone address contemporary problems. Although Americans were now free to trade with whomever they wished, the old trade patterns forged by a century of British mercantilism proved difficult to change. Britain still depended on American raw materials and thus kept duties low or nonexistent for those products. Parliament did, however, shut the British West Indies to American merchants.

Foreign governments had no incentive to negotiate a commercial treaty with the United States when they could so easily armtwist the individual states into granting unreciprocated privileges. In a parliamentary debate over trade policy toward the new American government, Lord Sheffield succinctly captured Britain's advantage: "No treaty can be made with the American States that can be binding on the whole of them.... It will not be an easy matter to bring the American States to act as a nation; they are not to be feared as such by us."[34]

America's trade deficit soared after the Revolution, as those who could afford it unleashed a pent-up demand for foreign-made luxuries and necessities alike. The result was a loss of scarce specie to foreign merchants and governments at a time when America most needed it for reconstruction. James Madison explained that

> another unhappy effect of a continuance of the present anarchy of commerce will be a continuance of the unfavorable balance on it, which, by draining us of our metals, furnishes pretexts for the pernicious substitution of paper money, for indulgences to debtors, for postponement of taxes. In fact, most of our political evils may be traced to our commercial ones.[35]

Alexander Hamilton also wrote eloquently about this problem, as asking his countrymen to consider if

> we had a government in America capable of excluding Great Britain, (with whom we have at present no treaty of commerce) from all our ports, what would be the probable operation of this step upon her politics? Would it not enable us to negotiate with the fairest prospect of success for commercial privileges of the most valuable and extensive kind in the dominion of that kingdom?[36]

It was clear to increasing numbers of Americans that the United States would never be a true government asserting national interests unless it shared with the states the power to tax, and received exclusive rights to negotiate international treaties, coin money, and eliminate internal trade barriers. It was to overcome the Confederation's weaknesses that delegates from all the states except Rhode Island gathered in Philadelphia between May and September 1787 to debate and draw up what became the United States Constitution.[37]

The Constitution replaced the Confederacy of sovereign states with a Federal system in which sovereignty was transferred to the national government. Power, however, was decentralized at the national level among the executive, legislative, and judicial branches, and throughout the country among the national, state, and local governments. A Bill of Rights attached to the Constitution granted Americans full freedoms of speech, press, religion, and assembly, as well as freedom from arbitrary arrest and imprisonment. Under the Constitution, the United States enjoyed full sovereign powers, including the right to regulate both foreign and domestic trade. The new Federal government assumed responsibility for all previous state and Confederation war debts. In doing so, the framers at once attempted to bring the nation's finances in order, while paying a huge price for the states' acceptance of the Constitution's sweeping transfer of powers. With their financial slates wiped clean, the states would henceforth be responsible for whatever debts they incurred.

THE AGRARIAN REPUBLIC

The new constitution and government provided America's leaders with a more effective means of dealing with a vast array of socio-economic problems. While most congressmen recognized that American power and prosperity depended in part on sound economic policies, they were bitterly divided over how far the government should go in developing the economy. At the debate's heart were conflicting visions of democracy and power.

Most adopted a *laissez-faire* attitude that government should play a minimal role in the economy. Jefferson argued that national liberty and prosperity depended on yeomen farmers and decentralized governmental powers. A minority shared Hamilton's view that the government could and should assist the nation's economic development, and that industry and central authority were the best means of creating and protecting wealth. Thus different political philosophies shaped the debate over every issue addressed by the new government after it convened in 1789.

The nation's most pressing economic problems remained the interrelated needs to establish a secure currency and pay down America's debts. Only three commercial banks existed in the entire country – the Bank of North America chartered by the Continental Congress in 1781, and the state banks of Massachusetts and New York. Fiscal conservatives favored a national bank which could supply productive ventures with capital while curbing inflation and paying off the national debt. Proponents argued that without the discipline and guidance provided by a national bank, private banks would proliferate, issuing a flood of commercial paper and setting off uncontrollable inflation. Jefferson and others opposed such a bank, fearing that

a government burdened by deficits and debt would undermine its republican and constitutional foundations while promoting widespread social and economic inequality. This inequality would emerge through two simultaneously occurring events. First, speculators, bankers, and the moneyed aristocracy could gain the financial leverage and profits derived from financing the national debt. Second, the government itself would spread its added revenues by promoting an industrialized economy through Hamiltonian policies resembling those of mercantilist and corrupted England. Once again England served as the model to be avoided, for just as its government was corrupted in no small way due to its enormous debt, English society and its moral values were also corrupted by a system of manufacturing and industry that created vast social and economic inequities.[38]

The incisive and eloquent arguments of Treasury Secretary Hamilton's 1790 "Report on a National Bank" convinced a majority in Congress that a national bank was essential to getting the new republic on a sound financial and economic footing.[39] In January 1790, Congress chartered the First Bank of the United States. With its headquarters in New York, the First Bank eventually had eight branches, which gave it an enormous advantage over state-chartered banks. The Federal government owned one-fifth of the First Bank's $10 million of stock, and private investors the rest.

Through the National Bank, Hamilton attacked the national debt by floating loans on foreign money exchanges, setting a low domestic interest rate of 4 percent, paying off debts and loans alike in hard coin rather than paper money, lending money to other banks and buying their notes at discounts, and increasing import duties – which supplied 90 percent of Federal revenues. The Coinage Act of 1792 reinforced these sound money policies by requiring the U.S. dollar to consist of 24.75 g of pure gold and 371.25 g of pure silver. It also allowed foreign as well as domestic coins to be legal tender.

Although Hamilton effectively used the Bank of North America to attack the national debt, his successors were not as effective. The First Bank devoted most of its resources to financing the Federal government's expeditures and debts, along with collecting customs bonds and foreign exchange. Yet, overall, the First Bank's policy strangled rather than kept a tight rein on economic expansion. Private ventures lacked access to low-priced capital. The demand for credit grew with America's population and commerce. Between 1791 and 1811, when Congress allowed the First Bank's charter to expire, the number of state-chartered banks soared from five to 117, and their combined capital stock from $4 600 000 to $66 290 000. Without the First Bank's conservative credit policies, the number of banks doubled in numbers and capital over the next six years. The subsequent tide of credit worsened an already virulent inflation stimulated first by the embargo, followed by war with Britain, and then an explosion of pent-up demand after the war and poor harvests in Europe.[40]

Faced with this economic morass, the congressional balance swung back toward fiscal conservatism. In 1816, Congress chartered the Second Bank of the United States with $35 million in stock, of which the government again owned 20 percent. Unfortunately, under its initial head, Langdon Cheves, it proved no more capable than the First Bank in curbing rampant inflation and speculation. By 1819, the inflationary bubble popped with a drop in international prices for grains as Europe's farmers enjoyed their first good harvest in years. Exports dropped from $73 854 437 in 1818 to $50 976 838 in 1819. A panic in American financial circles ensued. Investments plummeted. Financiers vainly recalled their loans. Scores of banks went under, dragging down with them legions of faithful investors and depositors. Of the 215 banks around the country in late 1818, only 125 survived by the summer of 1819.[41] The only financial bright spot was the Supreme Court's decision in McCulloch *v.* Maryland (1819) to strike down Maryland's attempt to tax notes issued by the Second Bank.

Throughout this era, America had no national financial system, only pockets of ambitious investors and trusting depositors. Even after the 1819 shakeout, there were still many banks but they lacked the information and transaction network within which to invest. Information about investment possibilities and pitfalls alike was fragmented, sketchy; capital itself wedded mostly to local concerns. Banking was concentrated in the north-east and along the Atlantic coast. The rapidly expanding economy west of the Appalachians was starved for capital. Countless opportunities for making wealth disappeared for want of money to develop them.

Manufacturing, meanwhile, suffered its own share of advances and reverses, largely because of conflicting and weak government policies. Hamilton had argued that fiscal responsibility was only the first step to the nation's economic development. The state could and should do much more. In his 1791 "Report on Manufactures," he argued for Federal policies tc assist entrepreneurs in developing America's industries.[42] Hamilton was concerned that too much of the nation's scarce capital was chasing "get-rich-quick" speculative schemes rather than being invested in manufacturing enterprises. Central to his ideas was the establishment of a Society for Establishing Useful Manufactures (SEUM). Congress rejected Hamilton's vision for a comprehensive industrial policy to develop the national economy.

America's industrial revolution would not take off for another half century. Meanwhile, merchants rather than industrialists were the engine of American growth. American merchants reaped fortunes by selling to all sides in the series of wars that had raged across Europe since the French Revolution broke out in 1789. With European manufacturers preoccupied with supplying their nation's armies, American producers captured vacant markets. The United States shipped not only raw materials, but also textiles to the belligerents. With British warships ruling the waves, France relied on neutral American shipping to carry goods, services, and messages. In 1793, Paris opened its West Indies colonies to American merchants. Spain followed suit in 1797, and Britain shortly thereafter. America's first millionaires emerged during the Napoleonic wars; by 1815 there may have been a half-dozen. And that wealth trickled down through much of the economy. International trade contributed to wealth not just with the actual goods carried, but by requiring banks, insurance, ships, lumber, rope, tar, metal fittings, food, and so forth.[43] Lucrative as this carrying trade was, it was not risk-free for American merchants. Both the British and French navies would board and seize American ships if they deemed the supplies were bound to or from an enemy port.

What was the Federal government's role in promoting and protecting this trade? President Washington's Farewell Address captured the essence of American national interests and the proper policy to protect and enhance those interests:

The great rule of conduct for us in regard to foreign nations is, in extending our commercial relations, to have with them as little political connection as possible.... Europe has a set of primary interests which to us have none or a very remote relation. Hence she must be engaged in frequent controversies, the cause of which are essentially foreign to our concerns. Hence ... it must be unwise in us to implicate ourselves by artificial ties in the ordinary vicissitudes of her politics, or the ordinary combinations and collisions of her friendships or enmities. Our detached and distant situation invites and enables us to pursue a different course.[44]

The center of American manufacturing proceeded from home, to shop, to factory. Early Americans made at home most of their goods – candles, clothing, shoes, spirits, food, brooms, furniture, and so forth. Gradually, entrepreneurs opened gristmills, cobblers, tanneries, breweries, brickyards, lumbermills, hatters, tailors, coopers, blacksmiths, weavers, paper mills, ironworks, and glass blowers. Specialization brought cheaper prices and an easier lifestyle for households. According to Bruchey, "household manufacturing appears to have reached a peak in 1815, after which decline was so rapid that the transfer from homemade to shop- and factory-made goods was generally complete by 1830."[45]

Foreign mercantilism threatened to destroy America's nascent manufacturers. The European powers not only excluded American manufactured goods from their home markets, but encouraged their industries to dump products in the United States to bankrupt domestic producers. In words reminiscent of contemporary complaints about Japan, Treasury Secretary Albert Gallatin noted the disadvantages American industrialists faced in competing with Britain: "The only powerful obstacle against which American manufacturers have to struggle arises from the vastly superior capital of Great Britain which enables her merchants to give very long term credits, to sell on small profits, and to make occasional sacrifices."[46]

Congress protected American manufacturers with a series of tariffs, 24 alone between 1794 and 1816. Tariffs not only nurtured America's industrialization, but supplied 80 percent of the Federal revenues up through the Civil War. Tariffs were essential to protect American factories from British mercantilism, which encouraged its firms to dump goods in the United States to destroy their rivals. In 1816, the British Chancellor of the Exchequer declared that the dumping of British goods would "glut, to stifle in the cradle these risky manufacturers in the United States, which the war had forced into existence contrary to the natural cause of things."[47]

Trade expanded rapidly during the 1790s, with the volume 30 percent higher than before the Revolution. Flour and cotton edged aside tobacco as the nation's largest exports. Eli Whitney's 1793 invention of the cotton gin enabled the United States to take full advantage of the series of wars across Europe, from the French Revolution in 1789 to Waterloo in 1815. American merchants sold to all sides in the conflicts and captured markets necessarily abandoned by competitors. Between 1792 and 1807, the earnings of American shippers rose from $7.4 million to $42.1 million, while exports increased fivefold.[48]

As secretary of state and later president, Jefferson enthusiastically embraced the policy: "Commerce with all nations, alliance with none, should be our motto."[49] Yet, during his White House years Jefferson faced a growing crisis with Britain and other belligerents in the Napoleonic wars who seized American ships, thus threatening the idea of commerce with all, alliance with none. With his Embargo Act of December 1807, Jefferson attempted to maintain American neutrality by cutting off all trade with all belligerents.

Although James Madison abandoned the embargo after taking office in March 1809, the damage to American exports had been done. Trade plummeted and bankruptcies proliferated among American merchants and shipbuilders. Yet, although the losses to American merchants were severe, the embargo was not a complete loss to the American economy. Merchants invested their idle capital in manufacturing and infrastructure such as canals and turnpikes. Between 1807 and 1815, 418 new factories opened. Between the 1815 Treaty of Ghent and the 1819 Panic, only 56 factories opened, while most of the newly established factories went bankrupt.[50]

A central pillar of Hamilton's vision for America's development involved tying the nation together in a web of roads, canals, and ports. President Jefferson and a swelling number of congressmen and merchants rallied around the idea. In 1802, Congress created the US Corps of Engineers to improve navigation in the nation's ports and rivers. In 1806, Congress authorized appropriations for a National Road from Cumberland, Maryland to the Mississippi River, the first strand in what would become the vast web of America's interstate highway system.

Jefferson proposed doing much more. While Jefferson preferred an America of farmers, he also wanted a properous, unified, and educated nation. In 1806, he asked Congress to devote surplus revenues to

> the improvement of roads, canals, rivers, education, and other great foundations of prosperity and union, under the powers which Congress may already possess, or such amendment of the constitution as may be approved by the states.

A majority in Congress agreed. The Senate authorized Treasury Secretary Albert Gallatin to submit a plan for the "opening of roads and making canals, together with a statement of the undertakings of that nature, which, as objects of public improvement, may require and deserve the aid of Government." In his 1808 "Report on Roads and Canals," Gallatin argued that

> goods roads and canals will shorten distances, and unite, by a still more intimate community of interests, the most remote quarters of the United States. No single operation, within the power of Government, can more effectively tend to strengthen and perpetuate that Union which secures external independence, domestic peace, and internal liberty.[51]

After justifying a Federal effort to bind the nation, Gallatin then proposed a national turnpike along the Atlantic coast from Maine to Georgia linking all the main seaports. A hundred miles of canal would be dug through four necks of land to facilitate sea transport. Gallatin not only sought to bind north and south, but also east and west by linking with roads and canals the Susquehanna and the Allegheny, the Potomac and the Monongahela, the James and the Kanawha, and the Santee and the Tennessee. Gallatin even proposed linking the Hudson River with Lake Ontario by what would become the Erie Canal.

Although Gallatin's vision had such prominent backers as John C. Calhoun and Henry Clay, Congress and most subsequent presidents felt the plan was too ambitious and probably unconstitutional. Although the Constitution clearly granted the Federal government the power to regulate interstate commerce, Presidents James Madison and James Monroe feared that such projects were an unwarranted Federal intrusion into realms best left to the private sector. Madison vetoed a Calhoun-sponsored bill that would have diverted some

National Bank profits to internal improvements. Monroe vetoed a bill that would have maintained the National Road with tolls. In 1824, Monroe seems to have shifted his views, signing one bill authorizing a national survey of all possible canal and road sites, and another which was the first in a series of harbor and river improvement bills. Finally, on his last day in office, he agreed to a Federal stake in the Chesapeake and Delaware Canal. President John Quincy Adams was an unabashed supporter, signing bills authorizing a Federal subscription toward three canals – the Louisville & Portland, Dismal Swamp, and Chesapeake & Ohio. In the end, only a few projects were approved; progress on those targeted was slow. Approved in 1806, the National Road did not reach Wheeling, Ohio until 1818 and Vandalia, Illinois until 1850! President Andrew Jackson gave away all finished sections of the National Road to the appropriate states.

Perhaps no Federal policy had a greater impact on America's economic development than its land policy. Although Jeffersonian practices and attitudes did not change after Independence, one of the ironies of American history is that the government of the nation which worships free enterprise and private property is the largest landowner. But as soon as the Federal government got the land, it tried to get rid of it. For over a century after Independence, the government's policies involved giving the land away to homesteaders and speculators alike, rather than exploiting or conserving it for all the people.

During the Revolutionary War, men were induced to enlist in return for land in the western territories – privates were promised 100 acres, colonels 500 acres. The trouble with these promises was that the Continental Congress first had to take the land before it could begin giving it away – it did not yet hold any rights to the western lands. By signing the 1783 Treaty of Paris, Britain not only granted independence to the United States but all of its lands west of the thirteen states to the Mississippi River. Seven of the thirteen states – Massachusetts, Connecticut, New York, Virginia, North Carolina, South Carolina, and Georgia – asserted claims to 233 415 680 acres of those western lands, and in some cases beyond the Mississippi River all the way to the Pacific Ocean! Maryland led the protests of those states lacking such claims, and refused to sign the Articles of Confederation until the others renounced their claims. On 1 March 1781, New York was the first to do so, but only if all other claimants followed suit. Congress passed a resolution calling on the other states to cede their claims to the national government which would hold them in trust until new states could be formed from them. When that resolution was passed, Maryland ratified the Articles of Confederation that same day. Although most of the states claiming western lands granted them to Congress by 1785, the last concession did not occur until 1802.

Thus did the United States government, so mired in debt and militarily weak, begin to amass a vast empire which eventually stretched to the Pacific Ocean. The Federal government expanded its holdings through purchases from other countries – the 523 446 400 acre Louisiana Purchase (1803) from France; the 43 342 720 Florida Purchase (1819) from Spain; the 180 644 480 acre Oregon Compromise (1846) with Britain, the 344 479 360 acre cession by Mexico through the Treaty of Guadalupe Hidalgo (1848); and the 18 961 920 acre Gadsden Purchase (1853) from Mexico. By the Civil War, the Federal government had taken title to three of every four acres in the nation.[52] Of the negotiations leading to those purchases, only the Guadalupe Hidalgo Treaty was preceded by war. After acquiring international recognition of its ownership of those lands, the United States then had to conquer and impose treaties on the native peoples who actually lived there.

The land was a godsend, both for the government which could sell it for revenue and those who wished to settle and exploit it. On this, virtually all Americans agreed. Until the Civil War, the central question was not whether public lands should be converted first into territories and later, as the population expanded, into states, but whether or not slavery should be allowed there. Another controversial question was whether to set the land sale terms at rate which encouraged speculators or small farmers.

At first Congress favored speculators. Under the Land Ordinance of 1785, Federal land would be surveyed and divided into townships of 36 square miles, which in turn would be subdivided into 36 sections of one square mile each. The land would be sold in minimum allotments of 640 acres for $1 an acre in cash – requirements only the very rich could meet. These measures were included in the Northwest Ordinance of 1787 which also forbade slavery in the territory and reserved one square mile of each township for public education. Subsequent natural resource and public land laws simply reinforced or elaborated those first two laws.

The Constitution's ratification in 1787 settled once and for all the question over whether the Federal government had the right to own, manage, and dispose of public lands. Under Article IV, Section 3, "The Congress shall have Power to dispose of and make all needful Rules and Regulations respecting the Territory or other Property belonging to the United States."

The new Federal government continued to favor speculators. A 1796 bill offered public lands at a minimum of 640 acres for $2 an acre, with 5 percent down, half the price due in 30 days and the rest within a year. Only wealthy land owners could afford such terms. Sales did not take off sharply as anticipated. In 1800, Congress reduced the minimum allotment to 320 acres and extended payments over four years. Four years later, the minimum purchase was dropped to 160 acres.

The political see-saw swung the other way in 1820 when Congress cut the price to $1.25 an acre but again required cash for purchases. Speculation and land companies increased, along with farm tenancy. Small farmers who had benefited from the earlier laws were squeezed by the 1820 law. Many farmers lost their land when they reneged on repaying the government. These problems were somewhat alleviated by laws in 1830, 1838, and 1840 that allowed pre-emption rights for those already living on public lands. The 1854 Graduation Act allowed the price of lands unsold for 30 years to be reduced to a mininum of 12.5¢ an acre. Each concession stimulated more emigration. In 1790, only 3 percent of 3.5 million Americans lived west of the Appalachian Mountains; in 1810, 15 percent of 7.2 million or 1.0 million people did; in 1820, the West's population had doubled to 2 million people, or 23 percent of the nation's 9 million.[53]

Washington not only sold land to speculators and families, but gave it away to the new states carved from the western territories. Once a territory's population exceeded 20 000, its white male adult inhabitants could vote for statehood. Washington then ceded enormous amounts of land to the new state. In all, the new states received huge realms of federal land – 400 million acres. These give-aways to states often had strings attached.

Stymied from directly unifying the nation with roads and canals, Hamiltonians indirectly underwrote the development of national infrastructure by tying it to land grants to the states. Under the 1802 Ohio Enabling Act, Congress agreed to give away 5 percent of its land sales to Ohio if that state's legislature agreed to devote it to road construction. Congress wrote similar strictures into the enabling bills for other states. Most state land grant recipients enthusiastically used them for development. The 1841 Internal Improvements Act granted each state 500 000 acres whose sale had to be used for developing roads and canals. Under the 1848, 1850, and 1860 Swamplands Acts, Washington gave away 65 million acres of Federal wetlands to the states, which in turn usually sold them to private corporations to be drained and exploited. Between 1823 and 1866, Washington gave away to the states 4.5 million acres to build canals, 3.5 million acres for roads, and 1.7 million for river improvements. Washington also targeted education for development. Initially, states had to designate one square mile of every 36 for schools; the ratio was eventually raised to four out of 36. Over 77 million acres of Federal lands were turned over to the states to fund secondary education and an additional 21 million acres for universities and technical schools. Smaller amounts were donated if the states earmarked the land for penitentiaries, fish hatcheries, mental hospitals, and other institutions. The states dispersed much of their holdings to private interests. For example, when California became a state in 1850 it received 8.8 million acres. In the 140 years since, Sacramento sold off over 8 million of those acres to private businesses and households. Environmental historian Bernard Shanks points out that if, "California had rented the 8 million acres instead of selling them, it would reap huge benefits today and in the future."[54]

Whether they received land grants or not, it was the states rather than the Federal government which built most of the nation's infrastructure. By 1860, the states, with Federal backing, had built 4254 miles of canals. The difference in transportation costs between wagons and canal barges was astonishing – while wagons cost about 20¢ a ton per mile, barges cost a mere 2¢ per ton per mile. The canals not only helped to create a national market, they also boosted employment and spread wealth. At the height of canal building around 1840, the projects accounted for about 10 percent of the value of all national construction and employed 5.5 percent of the total non-agricultural labor force. The projects injected a huge amount of capital along the routes, which of course multiplied as dollars changed hands.[55]

Who paid for the canals? Of the estimated $188 million cost of all canal contruction, state and local governments contributed about $136.5 million or 75 percent and the rest came from private investors. Rather than raise taxes to finance their contribution, the states borrowed $127 million, mostly from foreign sources. The cost would have been far greater had not Washington contributed the land which could be sold for state revenues or used for routes.[56]

The states chartered either public or private corporations to build canals, roads, and other projects, and, as incentives, granted them monopoly privileges, tax exemptions, eminent domain, lotteries, and other benefits. In return, the states supervised the corporations through their boards of directors. Bank charters included restrictions on interest rate levels, reserves, and dividends. Through these public chartered corporations, the states were able to develop their realms without raising taxes. These corporations were a largely progressive marriage of public and private interests. Between 1787 and 1801 alone, the states formed over 300 public corporations to develop various infrastructure and other projects. Of the 300, two-thirds developed roads, toll bridges, and river navigation, while 32 underwrote insurance policies for foreign traders. Between 1808 and 1815 alone, New York chartered 165 joint stock companies in manufacturing and 164 in public utilities. Lacking Federal land grants, New York financed the $7 million Erie Canal solely with its own money. Pennsylvania was just as enthusiastic a supporter of enterprises; Between 1790 and 1860, it chartered 2333 corporations, of which 64.17 percent were in transport, 11.14 percent in insurance, 7.72 percent in manufacturing, 7.2 percent in banking, 3.21 percent in gas production, 2.79 percent in water supply, and 3.77 percent in other fields. Pennsylvania devoted $100 million to railroad and canal construction.[57]

This enthusiastic burst of state guided development in the late eighteenth and early nineteenth centuries waned by mid-century for several reasons. The Panic of 1837 bankrupted many state chartered corporations. Afterward, states curbed or even outlawed their creation. As important was the hostility of Supreme Court Justice Roger B. Taney. Taney adopted a strict constructionist interpretation of the constitution which included an aversion to any government-sponsored enterprises. Taney asserted his views shortly after taking office in a 1836 case involving banks chartered by the District of Columbia. After pointing out the exclusive rights and privileges a charter bestows upon a corporation, Taney argued that the

only inquiry which the constituted authorities can properly make on such an application, is whether the charter applied for is likely to produce any real benefit to the community, and whether that benefit is sufficient to justify the grant. In other words, any corporations chartered by public authorities must be for the public good.[58]

Such rulings inhibited state initiatives throughout and long after Taney's tenure as Chief Justice from 1836 to 1862.

Yet, there were ways around Taney's rulings. If states could not form a public corporation to assist development, they could at least charter private corporations. The states competed with each other to encourage incorporation. As a result, over three hundred corporations received state charters from 1789 to 1800 alone. More than two-thirds of those corporations formed to build vital infrastructure like bridges and turnpikes.[59]

Here again, the Supreme Court shaped public policy. While John Marshall was the Chief Justice, the Supreme Court favored the rights of established over subsequent state laws. In Fletcher v. Perk (1810), Marshall ruled that a state could not rescind any rights it conferred upon a corporation, a ruling reinforced by the Dartmouth College case (1819). The Taney court further expanded the rights of private corporations. In his Charles River Bridge (1837) and Richmond Railroad v. Louisiana Railroad (1851) cases, Taney ruled against the monopolistic claims of older chartered corporations, making the practical argument that to do otherwise would impede development. In Bank of Augusta v. Earle (1839), he allowed for corporations to operate in states even if their charter was from elsewhere. In Louisville, Cincinnati and the Charleston Railroad v. Letson, he ruled that corporations be allowed a legal fiction of citizenship. In Woodruff v. Trapnall (1851) and Curran v. Arkansas (1853), the Supreme Court ruled that states and banks had to fulfill their legal obligations to corporations.

Stuart Bruchey sees this philosophical shift between the Marshall and Taney courts as the most important boost the Federal government gave to development during the early Republic era. He characterizes the shift as the abandonment of "an earlier principle of strict liability and its associated principle of just compensation in favor of a negligence doctrine which held both governments and their chartered offspring not liable for damages unless caused by carelessness." The result was the

leading means by which the dynamic and growing forces in American society were able to challenge and eventually overwhelm the weak and relatively powerless segments of the American economy. After 1840 the principle that one could not be held liable for socially useful activity exercised with due care became a commonplace of American law. In the process, the conception of property gradually changed from the eighteenth century view that dominion over land above all conferred the power to prevent others from interfering with one's quiet enjoyment of property to the nineteenth century assumption that the essential attribute of property ownership was the power to develop one's property regardless of the injurious consequences to others.[60]

THE INDUSTRIAL TAKEOFF

Two generations after Hamilton and Jefferson squared off over industrial policy, Whig Henry Clay and Democrat Andrew Jackson fought over the same different visions for American economic development. Clay coined the term "American System" in an 1824 speech supporting the tariff:

> We must speedily adopt a genuine American policy. Still cherishing the foreign market, let us create also a home market, to give further scope to the consumption of the produce of American industry. Let us counteract the policy of foreigners, and withdraw the support which we now give to their industry, and stimulate that of our own country.

In words that echo today's arguments for industrial policy, Clay argued that

> in a new country, the condition of society may be ripe for public works long before there is, in the hands of individuals, the necessary capital to effect them ... the aggregate benefit resulting to the whole society, from a public improvement, may be such as to justify the investment of capital in its execution.[61]

Jackson dismissed any Federal initiatives to develop the economy. During the 1828 election campaign he promised that his primary objective in the White House would be to eliminate the national debt and, after taking office, swore he would do likewise to the Second National Bank in order "to prevent a monied aristocracy from growing up around our administration that must bend it to its views, and ultimately destroy the liberty of our country."[62] Jackson eventually accomplished both objectives.

Although Jackson's policies prevailed, they probably only slightly dampened the nation's economic development. By the time Jackson took office, an industrial revolution was transforming American life. What was the industrial revolution? It involved an interrelated series of technological and productivity advances which swept away the reliance on specialized craft production, animal- or human-drawn transportation, and the use of wood for fuel that characterized most agrarian societies. Instead, the early stage of industrialization involved steam power, highly purified iron and steel, mass production, interchangeable parts, machine tools, and the use of coke for fuel. British inventors and entrepreneurs began to create and apply these innovations in the late eighteenth century. Precision in producing things once came from the eyes and fingers of skilled craftsmen; it now came from machines. Sailing ships and ox carts gradually gave way to steam ships and railroads. Iron replaced wood for bridges and the girders of buildings.

The United States did not begin to industrialize until well into the early nineteenth century. While America's natural resources were abundant, its labor and capital were scarce and thus highly priced. If scarcity is a primary stimulus to innovation, America's abundance of raw materials actually delayed the need for manufacturers to adopt substitutes such as coke for charcoal in blast furnaces. This occurred only after America's iron and steel producers had laid to waste all the adjacent forests and discovered massive anthracite coal deposits in Pennsylvania. The iron industry took off during the 1840s after manufacturing began using anthracite coal rather than charcoal to smelt it. Yet, even as late as 1860 only 13 percent of all pig iron in the United States was smelted with coke.[63]

Yet, despite its tardy start, America's industrialization was propelled by its own brilliant inventors and entrepreneurs. The average annual number of patents increased from 535 during the 1820s to 646 during the 1840s and 2525 during the 1850s. As in Britain, an agricultural revolution preceded an industrial revolution – greater farm productivity freed the labor and created capital to invest in manufacturing. Agricultural production climbed through the introduction of Eli Whitney's cotton gin (1797), Charles Newhold's single-piece cast plow (1797), Jethro Wood's iron plow (1819), Jim Manning's mowing machine (1831), Cyrus McCormick's reapers (1833, 1834), Hiram and John Pitt's grain-threshing machine (1836), and John Deere's steel edge plow (1837). The introduction of seed drillers in the 1840s and threshing machines in the 1850s further boosted farm production. These innovations spurred huge productivity advances: "a man with a sickle could cut one-half to three-quarters of an acre of wheat in a day; with a cradle, he could cut two to three acres a day; and with a self-rake reaper he could cut ten to twelve acres a day."[64]

Just one of these inventions alone – Whitney's cotton gin – revolutionized cotton production in the south by allowing the planting of short-staple green seed cotton, whose use previously languished because it was so time-consuming to remove the seeds. The number of cotton bales increased from 100 000 in 1800 to 5.4 million in 1859. Cotton became an important export commodity. In 1791, America's cotton production was only 0.05 percent of world production; in 1840, it had soared to 62.6 percent of all cotton produced around the world.[65]

Innovation and information spread quickly because most Americans could read and write. Schools, however, were the responsibility of local and state governments rather than Washington. In 1860, education composed 1.5 percent of America's economy.[66]

Americans not only innovated in agriculture but in all fields of production. America's labor shortage stimulated a range of labor-saving devices, many not only encouraged but imagined by the workers themselves. Worker attitudes toward machines were quite different in Britain with its labor surplus. The American locksmith Alfred Hobbs recounted those differences:

> In America [the workers] might set to work to invent a machine, and all the workmen in the establishment would, if possible, lend a helping hand. If they saw any error they would mention it, and in every possible way they would aid in carrying out the idea. But in England it was quite the reverse. If the workmen could do anything to make a machine go wrong, they would do it.[67]

The fruits of American innovation were amply displayed at the 1851 Crystal Palace Exhibition in London. America's corner presented machines that allowed the mass production of scores of products. Sam Colt's pistol, for example, was entirely made from interchangeable parts. The application of that technology to other weapons would worsen the carnage of America's Civil War and countless other wars since. But the principle of interchangeable parts pushed industrialization into ever higher stages.

As in Britain, textiles were America's first mass-production industry.

Capitalizing on British textile inventions and production techniques, American entrepreneurs rapidly expanded their production in the early nineteenth century. In 1807, the cotton textile industry had only about 15 or 20 mills employing 8000 spindles; by 1811, the number of mills had risen to 87 and spindles to 80 000; there were 191 000 spindles in operation in 1820 and in 1831 1.25 million! In New England, cotton cloth production rose from about 4 million yards in 1817 to 323 million in 1840! There were similar production advances in wool and linen textiles. More than half or 561 of the 1071 textile mills operating in 1850 were in New England and only 161 in all of the South. Bruchy attributes this textile revolution to "better textile machinery (which cut wage costs), a fall in the price of raw cotton, and growth in the number of skilled technicians."[68] To these three factors we can add Federal tariffs, which combined with entrepreneurship to make this extraordinary growth possible – with merely one without the other, the textile revolution would have never taken place.

As American industry became more competitive and land sales increased Federal revenues, Congress gradually reduced the protective tariff rates. In 1828 the tariff rate peaked at 50 percent of an import's value. In 1833, rates dropped to a uniform 20 percent. At the Civil War's eve, tariffs averaged about 5 percent. Tariffs on cotton textiles, however, came down much more slowly.[69]

Communications and transportation revolutions occurred together and provided the skeleton upon which America's industrial muscle could expand. The telegraph revolutionized communications as thoroughly in the mid-nineteenth century as the telephone did in the late nineteenth century and satellites have recently. While Samuel Morse invented the telegraph, it was Washington which got the industry off the ground. Congress appropriated $30 000 in 1844 to build an experimental line between Washington and Baltimore. Its success encouraged entrepreneurs to begin stringing telegraph wire across the nation, thus allowing buyers and sellers to communicate their desires to each other within minutes. The telegraph allowed the Chicago Board of Trade to open and flourish in the wholesale trade as early as 1848. By 1852, there were 23 000 miles of telegraph wires binding the nation.[70]

Meanwhile, steam engines revolutionized transportation and eventually united all of the states. By the mid-nineteenth century, the United States finally achieved a national market as steamboats and railroads speedily conveyed bulk shipments across the country at ever lower costs. Only 17 steamboats churned western rivers in 1817; by 1855, there were 727 steamboats with 727 000 tons of capacity. Transportation costs plummeted. In 1815, it cost $100 to ship a ton from New Orleans to Louisville; by the 1850s, it was only $5 a ton by steamboat.[71]

What role did the Federal government play in developing the steamboat and railroad industries? Aside from enjoying the benefits of the Army Corps of Engineers' dredging rivers and ports, the steamboat industry largely developed from private initiatives. Federal policies, however, were decisive in developing the railroads. Between 1824 and 1838, Federal survey teams explored the viability of possible routes. Congress then saved the railroads an estimated $6 million between 1830 and 1843 by lowering the tariff on iron, although in 1843, domestic iron makers succeeded in regaining higher tariffs to protect their industry. Starting with the 1850 Illinois Central Land Grant Act, the Federal government underwrote the development of many of the nation's most important railroads. Between 1850, when it made its first large grant to a railroad, and 1860, Washington handed out 27.8 million acres to railroads. The land grant extended 200 feet on either side of the tracks, plus alternate sections of one square mile in a checkerboard fashion six miles on either side of the railroad. Railroads were the nation's steel skeleton which united the United States not only economically, but politically and socially as well. As importantly, the railroad industry drove the economy throughout the mid-nineteenth century, much as the automobile industry did during the mid-twentieth century. By 1860, the railroads demanded 40 percent of all iron produced in the country.[72]

Dramatic as were the trains chugging through the countryside on their steel tracks and steamboats plying the nation's rivers, steampower remained a relatively limited form of power at mid-century. In 1850, America's factories generated only about 181 000 horsepower from steam compared to 2.5 million from inanimate sources and 8.5 million from all sources including human.[73]

The interrelated agricultural, manufacturing, and transportation revolutions would not have been possible without abundant and inexpensive finance. The Panic of 1819 had destroyed half of America's banks. Then, between the Panics of 1819 and 1837, American banking expanded steadily in numbers, assets, and geography. By mid-century, banks had begun to catch up to the demands of western migration. Between 1819 and 1837, the capital stock of New England and Atlantic coast banks dropped from 64.1 percent to 49.6 percent of the nation's total, while that of the west and south rose from 35.9 percent to 50.4 percent. To protect the public, one by one the states began to regulate banking. In 1842, Louisiana became the first state to require minimum bank reserves against deposits.[74]

In most states, banking was completely unregulated. Anyone could set up a bank, take deposits, print bank notes and sell them for hard currency, pay himself any salary or fees, and then declare bankruptcy and skip town. The free market for banks may have been a boom for economic theorists but a disaster for thousands of people who often lost their life savings in them. Bank failures, however, were uncommon. Altogether, the free banking market cost investors only $1.851 million before the Civil War. Some states did require that any notes issued be backed with securities deposited with the state government. Under this system, when a bank failed, the state could reimburse the noteholders. By the Civil War, the more than 1600 state-chartered banks had issued more than 9000 kinds of bank notes![75]

What role did the Second Bank of the United States play in that expansion? Nicholas Biddle, Second Bank President in 1819, surveyed the damage and proposed a shift in policy: "of banking in the interior, we have been almost destroyed by it. It is time to concentrate our business – to bank where there is some use and profit in it ... to make at present the large commercial cities the principal scene of our operations." Like Hamilton, Biddle had a comprehensive plan to develop American wealth and power, the heart of which involved dampening speculation and encouraging investments in solid enterprises that created rather than simply shifted wealth. He proposed not just fiscal conservatism but investments in infrastructure such as ports, canals, and turnpikes, and strategic industries such as steel and railroads in order more rapidly to expand and diversify America's economy. Biddle did not confine his efforts to the Second Bank. In 1824, he and financier Matthew Carey joined to create the Pennsylvania Society for Promotion of Internal Improvements. Throughout Biddle's decade-long tenure as president, the Second Bank devoted two-thirds of its loans to "the direct encouragement and extension of agriculture and the mechanic arts, the promotion of internal improvements, and the erection of all sorts of buildings." Biddle understood how America's perennial international trade and payments deficits drained away the nation's wealth and dynamism. He long advocated capital controls to inhibit imports and higher tariffs behind which to nurture America's infant industries. After blasting the "evil... and ruinous consequences" of the import flood sweeping away American enterprises, Biddle asserted: "Against these it is the business of the Bank of the U. States to guard. It has accordingly placed itself in an attitude of security & strength, so as to interpose whenever it may be necessary to protect the community."[76]

Unfortunately, Biddle's Hamiltonianism eventually clashed with President Andrew Jackson's Jeffersonianism. The idea of developing the "community" through strategic investments, curbing speculation, and erecting tariff walls was anathema to Jackson and all those then or since who idealize "free markets" and minimal government. For Jacksonians, the Bank was the "Monster," the symbol of eastern elitism and greed which sucked out what little hard-earned coin the west could garner. Land rather than industry and commerce was and should remain the west's economic core. Selling land to thousands of yearly emigrants demanded easy credit. In 1834, referring to himself in the third person, Jackson swore that he

"yets lives to put his foot upon the head of the monster and crush him to the dust.... Andrew Jackson would never recharter that monster of corruption. Sooner than live in a country where such a power prevailed, he would seek an asylum in the wilds of Arabia."[77]

From where did Jackson's virulent hatred of the Bank come? Sectional jealousies certainly played a powerful role. Jackson was the first western and populist president. He had campaigned as the champion of the farmers and laborers who were exploited by eastern bankers, merchants, and industrialists, the very people Biddle was trying to help. Jackson was an angry and vengeful man, had killed two men in duels and painfully carried the slug from another duel in his shoulder. Although Jackson espoused mass democracy, as a former general he demanded unquestioning obedience from those below him. Some find in Biddle a significant reason for the subsequent Bank War, using many of the same words to describe him as others have Jackson – "abuse of power; vanity and absense of self-criticism; excessive fluency; and errors of judgement, temper, and calculation."[78]

All of these factors contributed to the possibility of a clash between him and Biddle. Yet, the Bank itself was not an issue in the 1828 campaign. What became an issue was the unfounded rumor that the Louisville and Lexington branches had denied loans to Jackson supporters during the campaign. Kentucky's delegates to the new Congress demanded that Biddle appoint Jackson supporters to those and other branches. Biddle was aghast: "There is no one principle better understood by every officer in the Bank than we must abstain from politics." His prompt investigation found no wrongdoing at the Kentucky branches or, later, in charges against the New Orleans branch. All along he adamantly refused to accept any political appointees to the Bank, defiantly declaring that

> I will not give way one inch in what concerns the independence of the Bank, to please all the administrations, past, present, or future. The bigots of the past reproached me with not being for them, the bigots of the present will be annoyed that the Bank will not support them. Be it so, I care nothing for either class of partisans and mean to disregard both.[79]

The controversy might have blown over had it not triggered within Jackson's tormented mind a paranoid obsession with the Bank as a "hydra of corruption" that "is trying to kill me but I will kill it."[80] Ironically, unlike those among his most fervent supporters who demanded the Bank be abolished because its credit policies were too tight, Jackson hated the Bank because it issued any credit and paper money at all. Old Hickory believed only in hard coin, and rejected any notion of paper money or credit. Going back to his own debts and perceived ill-treatment by creditors of his early entrepreneurial days, Jackson hated all banks, particularly the biggest of them all. In 1833, Jackson wrote that "everyone who knows me does know that I have always been opposed to the United States Bank, nay all banks."[81]

Jackson declared war on the Bank shortly after taking office in 1829, saying that if he had his way its charter would not be renewed when it expired in 1836. Biddle attempted to thwart Jackson's efforts to curb his investments in infrastructure and industry. When Jackson vetoed the Maysville Road Bill in 1830, Biddle tried to fund the project through the relevant states and private firms. As for the Bank's rechartering, Biddle waited until 1832 before acting. That year he got congressional supporters to sponsor a bill authorizing the Bank's rechartering. Biddle gambled that a Jackson veto would cost him the election, bringing to power Bank supporter Henry Clay. Biddle lost. The bill passed; Jackson vetoed it, but he won reelection by a overwhelming margin. The Bank bill was the campaign's most important issue. Jackon's victory was interpreted as a popular mandate on the Bank's fate. Then, rather than simply wait for the Bank's charter to expire, Jackson attacked it immediately by depositing all new issues in state banks favorable to him and the Democratic Party. After the Second Bank's charter expired in 1836, Pennsylvania rechartered it as a state bank. The Bank finally failed in 1841. The United States would not have another central bank until the Federal Reserve was created in 1911.

Biddle had accomplished much as Second Bank President. He anchored the nation's currency and finances upon a strict fiscal conservatism. The Second Bank worked carefully with the state banks to discourage their issuance of excessive credit. By raising and lowering its demand for repayments in hard coin, the Second Bank carefully regulated the state banks. Biddle's policies brilliantly balanced monetary expansion and restraint. Between 1819 and 1859, the nation's money supply increased sevenfold from $80 million to $580 million. Meanwhile, wholesale prices actually fell from an index of 131.0 between 1790 and 1819 to 96.0 between 1820 and 1850. Real income rose considerably at the cost of not supplying all the demand for credit. Much of that demand, however, was for speculation in land and stock schemes of dubious value.[82] Biddle curbed speculation and encouraged sound investments. He did this directly through Second Bank investments in infrastructure and industry, and indirectly encouraged economic development by tight monetary policies and protection against excessive imports. Although Biddle attempted to concentrate banking in the eastern cities, his strict monetary policies made it more likely that those that did arise anywhere would be soundly managed. In 1832, for the first and last time in American history to date, the Federal government actually settled all outstanding claims against it. Ironically, Jackson took credit for an accomplishment that would not have been possible without the Second Bank.

Without the Bank's restraining hand, once again speculation and credit skyrocketed. The number of banks leapt from 506 in 1834 to 901 in 1840. Jackson responded by issuing an executive order in late 1836 forbidding the use of banknotes to purchase land, thus bursting the speculative bubble. With the subsequent Panic of 1837, the economy plunged into a deep depression that took years to overcome.

Yet another way in which the Federal government affected the nation's economic development was its continued toleration of slavery. The South's white population in 1860 was 1 516 000 families, of whom only 385 000 owned slaves. Nearly 90 percent of those who did own slaves had less than 20. There were about 1 million blacks in the south, virtually all of whom were slaves. These were the descendants of about 661 000 Africans who survived the Atlantic crossing between 1617 and 1808 when Congress outlawed the importation of slaves. Even after 1808, smugglers spirited in at least a thousand Africans a year until 1860. Slavery continued not just because it was vastly profitable to the holder – the "average slaveowner was more than five times as wealthy as the average Northerner, more than ten times as wealthy as the average nonslaveholding Southern farmer" but from its integration into southern culture in which the "slaveholding psychology, habit of command, race pride, rural lordship, aristocratic pretensions, political domination, and economic strength mitigated in favor of the status quo."[83]

Prohibitionists had little choice in tolerating slavery. The Constitution legalized slavery, counting slaves for voting apportion purposes as three-fifths of a human being. Slavery restrained national expansion as politicians attempted to preserve a balance between free and slave states. When the Republic of Texas voted in 1836 to join the United States, President Jackson clearly would have liked to comply had it not been for northern protests that the inclusion would tip the precarious power balance toward slave interests. Compromises over the expansion of slavery in 1820 and 1850 defused national crises that threatened to erupt in civil war. Would slavery have eventually died out on its own without civil war? Historians continue to debate the question. But the election of anti-slavery Abraham Lincoln as president in November 1860 stimulated eventually eleven slave states to secede from the United States. The firing on Federal Fort Sumter in Charleston harbor in April 1861 sparked what would become a four-year Civil War.

LEGACY

By the Civil War's eve, the United States had achieved considerable economic development. Most Americans lived comfortable, middle-class lives. A network of roads, ports, railroads, and canals had created a truly national economy. A range of industries textiles, steel, railroads, armaments, and others were rapidly developing. About 150 millionaires presided over the economy.

These accomplishments capped two and a half centuries of economic development. The American colonies prospered despite British restrictions. Between the mid-seventeenth century and the Revolution, the average income of Americans doubled.[84] The United States grew rapidly following American independence. From 1799 to 1838, per-capita income rose between 1.0 and 1.5 percent annually; from 1839 to 1854 it rose 1.7 percent annually. America's economic development from the Revolution to the Civil War was shaped by three periods of expansion broken by years of painful contraction. According to Bruchey, the

> first surge occurred during the years 1793–1806 and is associated with the expansion of shipping and trade made possible by American neutrality during the wars of the French Revolution and Napoleon. The second lasted from the early 1820s to about 1834 and appears to have been connected with early manufacturing development. The surge in the third growth cycle, also apparently associated with continuing industrialization, commenced in the latter half of the 1840s and ran its course before the firing on Fort Sumter.[85]

Each period of expansion left the nation more economically dynamic and diversified than before.

Industrialization was not an unmitigated blessing for the United States. Factories bankrupted thousands of shops. Teenage daughters went to work in the mills which had made their homes' looms and spinning wheels obsolete. Conditions in the factories were as exploitive, dangerous, and mind-numbingly dull in America as they were in Dickens' England. Some tried vainly to improve these conditions. Strikes occurred among female textile workers in the 1820s and 1830s. The "Ten Hour" movement arose and died in Boston in 1825, and for the next few decades periodically was resurrected among factory workers in the north-east. In the 1830s, working men's parties emerged in many of the nation's largests cities. All these efforts came mostly to naught. Owners simply fired the dissenters and replaced them from among the flood of Irish and other immigrants of that time. There were, however, some limited successes. In 1835, Philadelphia became the first city to mandate a ten-hour working day. President Martin Van Buren signed an executive order instituting the same for all Federal employees. For the Federal government to extend that protection to all workers would have been unthinkable at the time.

The era between the Revolution and Civil War was the closest America ever came to achieving Adam Smith's ideal of minimal government and unrestricted entrepreneurship. During the early 1790s, Jefferson's agrarianism resoundingly defeated Hamilton's assertion that government and business should be partners in economic development, and that industrialization was the engine of economic growth and national power. Instead, the Federal government's role in the economy was confined largely to selling off western lands, registering patents, and imposing small tariffs on imports – all three more for the sake of government revenue than economic development. Industrialization was left largely to market whims.

The Federal government's minimal efforts to develop the economy both reflected and reinforced deeply ingrained cultural attitudes. Entrepreneurs colonized and developed America. Most people came to America to escape stifling social, economic, and political laws and conventions. Colonial government played a minuscule role in most people's lives. Although Henry Clay is said to have coined the phrase, the "Self-made Man," the sentiment had been a part of American life from the very beginning. The belief was and remains that character and will rather than broader circumstance determine one's destiny. Anyone can transform himself from "rags to riches" if he only tries hard enough. Government should be confined to maintaining public order and protecting the nation from foreign aggression.

The desire among most people to improve their lives, and the opportunity for most to do so, were present from the very first settlements. As American culture evolved, it developed a very deep materialism. The central economic issue from the planting of the first colonies to the Civil War was what to do with all that land which, by 1860, stretched all the way to the Pacific Ocean.

For the nation's first three centuries, Americans believed that natural resources are endless and are there to be exploited for humanity's material needs. This attitude was reinforced by the continent's seemingly endless riches, but did not originate there. Among the foundations of Western civilization is the belief that there is an eternal struggle between Man and Nature in which Man must either conquer or be conquered by Nature. The religions and civilizations of the Jews, Greeks, Romans, and Christians all propounded versions of this attitude. The Bible admonishes humans not only to "Multiply and Subdue the Earth," but condemns wilderness as the abode of evil. Sinners were cast into the wilderness, either to perish or prove the purity of their faith. God forced Moses and his people to wander the wilderness for 40 years in atonement for their sins before allowing them to reach the promised land; Jesus spent 40 days and nights in the wilderness resisting an array of evil temptations before he returned to preach his path to salvation.

The first Puritans to settle in America brought with them this attitude that Nature was there to be exploited by and for Man. Puritanism was and remains as much about Man's relation to the land as to God. To the Puritans, wilderness – nature wild and unfettered – was the abode of savages, beasts, and perhaps Satan himself. What is Man to do in the face of such evil? "Multiply and Subdue the Earth" the Bible commands. To glorify and obey God, Man must attack and transform nature into tilled fields, country lanes, and tidy villages. Nature was something alien, forbidding, corrupting; its only worth was what it could be made into. Nature's value was measured by the market price of logs cut, tons of ore extracted, or harvest yielded from carefully plowed fields. But nature represented more than just a means of enhancing one's livelihood. Nature, and the "savages" that roamed it, became the national scapegoat. People projected onto wilderness all their own most perverse or destructive impulses. In tranforming wilderness, people either sublimated or fulfilled their vilest inner demons. These pioneer attitudes are understandable given their intellectual tradition and vulnerability to the dangers of Nature and native peoples. The wilderness and its resources seemed endless; the pioneers' tools and skills fragile. Nearly everyone believed that what the country needed was more people eager to transform Nature into civilization.

A puritanical belief in hard work, frugality, family, God, and making money pervades American culture, although the practice has loosened somewhat recently. These values were constantly reinforced during America's early era by stern protestant clergy from Cotton Mather to Henry Ward Beecher, along with thousands of other preachers from pulpits and revival meetings across the country.

Of these related values, the most powerful and persistent has been materialism. That was true of New York in 1748 when someone observed that the "only principle of Life propagated among the young People is to get Money, and men are only esteemed according to what they are worth – that is, the Money they are possessed of."[86] In the various editions of his *Poor Richard's Almanac*, Benjamin Franklin celebrated the maxim "Time is Money." At least one social scientist has argued that that simple phase "probably exerted as much practical influence on Americans as the combined teachings of all the formal philosophers."[87]

This already powerful biblical materialism was reinforced in the late eighteenth century with the propogation of Adam Smith's teachings that human ingenunity combined with free markets would forever ensure everyone's material needs. Yet, religion rather than philosophy remained the primary justification for American materialism. Reverend Thomas Hunt's 1836 interpretation of the Bible was summarized in his book's title, *The Book of Wealth: In Which It Is Proved from the Bible That It is the Duty of Every Man to Become Rich.*[88] Public and private schools alike, particularly through the McGuffey readers, also preached the virtue of devoting one's life to making money. Alexis de Tocqueville captured the American attitude toward nature:

> in Europe people talk a great deal of the wilds of America, but the Americans themselves never think about them; they are insensible to the wonders of inanimate nature and they may be said not to perceive the mighty forests that surround them till they fall beneath the hatchet. The eyes are filled upon another sight . . . the march across theses wild, draining swamps, turning the course of rivers, peopling solitudes, and subduing nature : . . the rapacity with which the American rushes forward to secure this immense booty that fortune proffers to him. . . . Before him lies a boundless continent, and he urges onward as if time pressed and he was afraid of finding no room for his exertions."[89]

Jeffersonianism prevailed. The stump was as much the symbol of progress for early Americans as the factory smokestack was for later generations. Freedom to exploit and even destroy the land was almost unlimited.

Yet, even from the earliest days of American settlement, there were alternative visions for the relationship between humans and Nature. From Western civilization, there were the exceptional examples of John the Baptist and St Francis who lived in harmony with Nature. While no religious faith which settled in America built its

beliefs around those two mystics, there were certainly more immediate examples for the pioneers to ponder and perhaps emulate.
Native Americans had a completely different relationship with the
earth than the newcomers:

> We did not think of the great open plains, the beautiful rolling
> hills and the winding streams with tangled growth as "wild". Only
> to the white man was nature a "wilderness" and ... the land
> "infested" with "wild" animals and "savage" peoples.[90]

There was no Indian word for wilderness. Nature was simply home.

Of course, even Native Americans transformed the land. Prai-
ries and forests were burned regularly to provide new forage for
grazing animals, fields were tilled and often exhausted, game driven
off and streams fished out. But their technology and small numbers were not powerful enough to destroy more than tiny portions
of the vast continent. And most importantly, the native peoples
viewed themselves an integral part of Nature, and thus should nurture rather than destroy it.

Not all Americans were indifferent to Nature's sublime beauties.
Many early American explorers expressed mixed feelings about
wilderness and its eventual exploitation that they were helping bring
about. The journals of Meriwhether Lewis and William Clark across
the west to the Pacific Ocean and back are filled with delight at
the magnificient landscapes through which they journeyed – as well
as complaints about its cruelties. In his "Autobiography", the fron-
tiersman Daniel Boone describes himself in both cornucopian and
naturalist terms, as "an instrument ordained to settle wilderness"
and someone who "resigned my domestic happiness for a time ...
to wander through the wilderness of America."[91]

Some Americans saw in Nature and their relationship toward it
elements that distinguished their civilization from Europe's. A growing
American nationalism made the country's vast wilderness a source
of pride and inspiration. Wilderness had value not just for its material rewards but for the virtues it wrought from the American
civilization grinding against it. In a 1784 letter from Paris to a friend
back in the United States, Abigail Adams wrote, "do you know
that European birds have not half the melody of ours? Nor is their
fruit half so sweet, nor their flowers half so fragrant, nor their
manners half so pure, nor their people half so virtuous." New York
Governor DeWitt Clinton asked rhetorically if there could

be a country in the world better calculated than ours to exercise and to exault the imagination – to call into activity the creative powers of the mind, and to afford just views of the beautiful, the wonderful, and the sublime? . . . here Nature has conducted her operations on a magnificent scale. The wild, romantic, and awful scenery is calculated to produce a correspondent impression in the imagination – to elevate all the faculties of the mind and to exault all the feelings of the heart.[92]

And a few Americans went beyond those patriotic sentiments. In the early nineteenth century, a number of prominent novelists, poets, and painters expounded a very different use of Nature by Man. Transcendentalists believed that Nature manifested God rather than evil. Wilderness, thus, was the true temple; to know God, man must seek spiritual union with Nature. As the minister Thaddeus Harris put it in 1805: "There is something which impresses the mind with awe in the shade and silence of these vast forests. In the deep solitude alone with nature, we converse with God." Echoing Harris' thoughts, Estwick Evans wrote in 1818: "How great are the advantages of solitude! – How sublime is the silence of nature's ever active energies! There is something in the very name of wilderness, which charms the ear, and soothes the spirit of man. There is religion in it."[93]

Ironically, this new attitude developed not on the frontier whose inhabitants were too busy trying to survive and would have scoffed at such sentiments. Transcendentalism emerged in the drawing rooms and studios of Boston, Concord, and New York. Its proponents reacted against an increasingly urbanized, industrialized, materialistic America that seemed to have abandoned Jefferson's ideal of an agrarian republic.

Transcendentalism was influenced by the earlier philosophical and cultural movements of deism and romanticism. Deism removed the biblical God from religion. In their "clockmaker theory," deists believed that the universe was created by an impersonal divine spirit which then settled back and let things run on their own. In a deistic world, Nature was neither good nor evil; it simply existed for its own sake as the Creator's work. Most of the American Revolutionary leaders subscribed to variations of deism. When such a prominent group of Americans popularized the idea that there was no Devil in Nature, they prepared the way for the transcendentalist belief that God was eminent in Nature.

The romantics celebrated Nature for its sublime attributes or as a refuge for man's wildest passions. Jean-Jacques Rousseau popularized the idea of a "noble savage" whose virtues far surpassed those of peoples from more "civilized" lands. François-René de Châteaubriand set his novels in an America where the heros plunge into wilderness to realize their higher nature. As Byron put it: "There is a pleasure in the pathless wood, / There is a rapture on the lonely shore. / There is a society where none intrudes.... / I love not man the less, but nature more."[94]

For transcendentalists, the wilderness is as much within as around man. According to Ralph Waldo Emerson, "the whole of nature is a metaphor of the human mind."[95] In his five Leatherstocking novels, James Fenimore Cooper explores the experiences of the quintessential American hero, Nathaniel Bumpo, who can flourish in white and Indian culture alike or in untrammeled wilderness. Through poetry, William Cullen Bryant explored the interdependence of humanity and nature. In Nathaniel Hawthorne's *The Scarlet Letter* (1850), Hester Pryne finds in the wilderness a refuge from society's oppression and hyprocrisy. The Hudson River school of painting put these thoughts to canvas. As that school's founder Thomas Cole put it, "We are still in Eden; the wall that shuts us out of the garden is our own ignorance and folly."[96]

None among the transcendentalists explored the relationship between humans and Nature more clearly or thoroughly than Henry David Thoreau:

> I wish to speak a word for Nature, for absolute freedom and wildness, as contrasted with a freedom and culture merely civil – to regard man as an inhabitant, or a part and parcel of Nature, rather than a member of society.... [I]n Wildness is the preservation of the World.[97]

He based his philosophy on his direct experiences with nature. "I went to the wood," Thoreau wrote, "because I wished to live deliberately." In Nature, Thoreau found "some grand, serene, immortal, infinitely encouraging, although invisible companion, and walked with him."[98]

This swelling movement had virtually no impact on America's industrial policies up through the Civil War. The transcendentalists' importance was to lay the philosophical foundations upon which the related movements of conservationism and environmentalism could build mass support and industrial policies in the late nineteenth century. They would create an expanded version of Hamiltonianism that acted on the understanding that economic power and prosperity depended as much on the government promoting conservation and preserving priceless national historic, cultural, and natural treasures as it was on developing industries and infrastructure.

Meanwhile, the much more limited Hamiltonianism prevailed to battle Jeffersonianism. Aside from Biddle's efforts at the Second Bank, what role did the Federal government play in America's industrial revolution? Its direct role was modest, at best. Taking up Hamilton's long-fallen banner of industrial policy, Henry Clay proposed creating an "American System" by building infrastructure and tariff protection for budding industries. Most southerners vociferously opposed Clay's "system" because they feared it would develop the north-east and mid-west at their economic and political expense. Clay's scheme never became law.

Several new government agencies quietly developed important economic sectors. Since its founding in 1802, the US Army Corps of Engineers aided navigation by widening and deepening river channels, and erecting lighthouses along the coast. From 1836 through 1862, Washington's Patent Commissioner aided technological advances by gathering information on similar innovations in machines, factories, and crops from Europe and disseminating it to American entrepreneurs and inventors.

The Federal government's most important contribution in developing the economy lay in binding the nation with infrastructure. The Federal and state governments spurred competition by investing in turnpikes, railroads, and canals. From 1800 to 1819, the rate charged on the turnpike between New York and Buffalo ranged from 0.19¢ to 0.30¢ a ton; with the Erie Canal's completion, the rate dropped to 0.02¢ between 1830 and 1850.[99] These lower rates united local with national markets, developed the economy, created wealth, and raised incomes. And these lower rates would not have been possible if the Federal and state governments left the "free market" alone. Merchants, farmers, and manufacturers would have been at the mercy of any private corporation which provided local transportation. Middlemen rather than producers would have reaped most of the profits. The higher the freight charges, the higher the inflation and lower the economic growth. By 1850, one canal and four railroads had breached the Appalachian Mountain barrier – the Erie Canal, the New York Central, the Baltimore &

Ohio, the Erie, and the Pennsylvania railroads. All of these projects had been built either solely or substantially with public finance. If the government had not underwritten this development,

> the settlement of the interior would have been delayed, and the chances are that the Midwest in the 1850s would not have contained a large enough population to have induced private entrepreneurs to construct railroads with public funds. . . . [E]conomic development in fact got under way sooner than it would otherwise have done. Spatially separated markets were extended and integrated, commercialized agriculture made greater inroads on the subsistence sector, land values rose, and prices of commodities shipped over long distances declined along with freight costs. In all probability, savings increased, interest rates went down, and capital was formed in the major sectors more quickly.[100]

Washington's early industrial policies – limited as they were – advanced America's economic development by at least a generation. Would America have industrialized a generation or so sooner if Hamilton's comprehensive industrial policy vision had been embraced and systematically implemented? Would the United States have been more prosperous and powerful sooner, as America's first Treasury Secretary claimed would happen? Any answer to these questions, of course, is unprovable. Nonetheless, Jeffersonians would answer no; Hamiltonians yes.

4 Industrialization Unbound, 1860–1932

America's industrialization expanded steadily between the Civil War and World War I. During this era, manufacturing surpassed agriculture as a source of national wealth; manufacturing's proportion rose from 43 percent to 65 percent while agriculture's dropped from 57 percent to 35 percent. Of the total economy, the percentage of workers in manufacturing rose from 19.1 percent to 22.2 percent between 1870 and 1910, while agriculture's fell from 52.5 percent to 31.4 percent. Most people profited by the expansion of national wealth. From 1840 to 1860, per-capita income rose an average 1.4 percent yearly; from 1870 to 1910, it rose 2.1 percent yearly. With the general prosperity, American households and businesses alike could afford to save more. The national savings rate hovered between 18 percent and 20 percent throughout the era, thus keeping interest rates relatively low and encouraging investments.[1]

By 1894, the United States had become the world's greatest industrial power, and 20 years later in 1914 American industrial production was greater than that of Britain, France, and Germany combined! From 1870 to 1913, America's share of factory production rose from 23.3 percent to 35.8 percent of the world's total. The United States had suffered trade deficits throughout its early history up through the late nineteenth century. Then, between 1874 and 1914, America enjoyed trade surpluses every year but three. In 1895, America's international account became positive and stayed that way for another half-century. Seeming paradoxes accompanied this trade success. As America's economy became more properous and diversified, and its population swelled, the proportion of production that the United States exported declined from around 20–30 percent of GNP between 1710 and 1720, to 10–20 percent between 1790 and 1800, to around 6 percent between 1830 and 1914. While America's export power grew, its merchant fleet power declined. Throughout this era, Americans increasingly conducted their foreign trade in ships registered under other national flags. The proportion of cargo shipped in by America's merchant marine dropped from 38 percent in 1870 to 26 percent in 1914. The United States emerged from World War I as the world's greatest creditor nation. Between 1914 and 1920, America was transformed from a net international debtor of $3.7 billion into a net creditor of $12.6 billion.[2]

Americans invested as well as traded abroad. Of the total investments made by Americans, the percentage going overseas rose from about 1 percent in 1869 to nearly 7 percent by 1914. When World War I broke out in August 1914, Americans had invested over $3.5 billion overseas, 75 percent of which was in the form of direct investments and 25 percent as portfolio investments. As in recent times, American businessmen invested abroad for a variety of reasons, including to capture foreign markets and supplies of raw materials. Like the United States, other countries erected import barriers to nurture domestic industries. American firms such as Kodak Camera, Singer Sewing Machine, McCormick, Standard Oil and Ford built plants overseas during this era. Other American firms and individuals invested in mines and plantations around the world.[3]

What was Washington's role in the transformation of the United States from a small agrarian republic into the world's greatest industrial power? The Federal government gave away vast realms of public land to railroads, speculators, and genuine homesteaders alike, thus spreading development across the country. Antitrust laws at the century's turn helped restrain the industrial monopolies and oligopolies whose price-gouging had sapped the middle class and poor. Laws against restraint of trade unified the states into one vast and ever-growing market. Meanwhile, Federal protection from foreign competition had developed many American industries into global champions. As William McKinley put it, America leads "all nations in agriculture, we lead all nations in mining, we lead all nations in manufacturing. These are the trophies which we bring after twenty-nine years of a protective tariff."[4] Increasingly, Washington also protected American trade and investments overseas. Between 1860 and 1918, American soldiers marched into Mexico, various Caribbean islands and Central American countries, the Philippines, and finally France.

Perhaps even more important to the nation's long-term prosperity and quality of life were new types of industrial policies that conserved natural resources and preserved America's wilderness and historical treasures. In the nineteenth century, two related but distinct philosophies arose to challenge the get-rich-quick materialism that pervaded American life. As the United States became more prosperous, powerful, and populated, increasing numbers of Americans feared that industrialization was destroying vital essences of both the nation's heritage and future. Environmentalists urged Washington to protect regions of unique and inspiring beauty before they were logged, dammed, plowed, or poisoned by industrial waste. Conservationists warned that the free markets for logging, mining, grazing, hunting, fishing, and producing were destroying the nation's natural resources for short-term profits, the equivalent of Americans eating their seed corn. Conservationism and environmentalism represented an expanded version of Hamiltonianism, ideas that Alexander and his early followers did not anticipate but probably would have supported. By the century's turn, these two movements had garnered enough popular and political support to get Congress to pass laws that created a range of national parks, forests, monuments, and wildlife refuges and tried to curtail the most rapacious industrial practices.

By 1914, the Hamiltonian concept of development had acquired a new meaning and thus a new set of policies to promote it. Development meant not just promoting higher material living standards but a better quality of cultural life as well. If development, however defined, was the Hamiltonians' highest value, free markets remained the Jeffersonian holy grail. The Hamiltonian vision seemed to increasingly overshadow Jeffersonianism. The United States had become not just an industrial giant but an increasingly sophisticated society that sought to preserve and enhance its cultural and natural heritage.

World War I further boosted American economic development and sustained it until the Great Depression. American exporters sold to both sides during the war's first three years. Fortuitously, the United States shed itself of foreign investments as the belligerents sold off their American holdings to finance their war effort. After Congress declared war in April 1917, Washington asserted an unprecendented level of management over the economy. The economy grew 18 percent during America's year and a half participation in World War I, the fastest rate in the nation's history. Within weeks of the armistice, Washington had dismantled its extraordinary economic powers. Aside from a recession in 1920–1, the economy expanded for another decade until the October 1929 stock market crash announced the Great Depression.

This half-century of assertive Federal industrial policies, underwritten at times with American marines, mostly ended after World

War I and the Senate's rejection of the Versailles Treaty. Jeffersonian policies prevailed during a dozen years of Republican Party rule from 1921 through 1933 as the White House tried to cut back government economic initiatives at home and abroad. Accompanying a decade of relative prosperity during the 1920s were such memorable if puzzling slogans as President Warren Harding's "return to normalcy" and President Calvin Coolidge's "the business of America is business."

Yet all along, insidious economic cancers were eating away at the apparent prosperity. The October 1929 stock market crash followed by an intractable and devastating depression discredited the giddy *laissez-faire* creed that unfettered markets were the key to economic development. President Herbert Hoover lacked the institutional and cultural power to put people back to work. One of four people would remain jobless and the economy moribund until President Franklin Roosevelt began his bold experiments in 1933.

INDUSTRIALIZATION FROM THE CIVIL WAR TO WORLD WAR I

The Civil War was the greatest of American history's turning points: slavery was outlawed, the political power balance shifted decisively away from the south, and three new constitutional amendments strengthened American civil rights.

But what impact did the Civil War have on America's industrialization? Did the demands of the northern armies for the machinery and sustenance of war stimulate the takeoff of America's industrial development? Traditionally, scholars answered yes, maintaining that the Civil War was a "second revolution" in which America's latent industrial potential was realized.[5] To adherents this was self-evident. After all, modern war has an insatiable demand for industrial production. America emerged from each world war of the twentieth century with a vastly expanded economy. Were not the same forces at work for northern factories during the Civil War?

Recently, analysts have taken a second look at the evidence.[6] To the surprise of scholars and laymen alike, they found that economic growth actually faltered during the 1860s. Production of pig iron alone had increased by 24 percent between 1850 and 1855, 17 percent between 1855 and 1860, and 100 percent from 1865 to 1870, but only 1 percent between 1860 and 1865! New railroad tracks increased by 11 627 miles between 1850 and 1855, 8721 miles from 1855 to 1860, and only 4076 miles during the Civil War. Commodity production increased 4.6 percent annually in the 20 years before the firing on Fort Sumter, 4.4 percent from 1870 to 1890, and only 2 percent during the 1860s. Manufacturing expanded at an annual rate of 7.8 percent between 1840 and 1860, 6 percent between 1870 and 1890, and only 2.3 percent during the 1860s.[7] In other words, the Civil War interrupted rather than spurred on America's industrialization.

How do we explain this gap between what actually occurred and popular imagination? There is little question that the diversion of millions of men – as many as one of five – and their manifold enterprise and energies from productive pursuits into armies dampened economic growth. Incomes and thus spending dropped as yankee and rebel soldiers for years received only a private's pay of $13 a month. Inflation ravished North and South alike. In the North, prices nearly doubled from an index of 100 in 1860 to 196 in 1865; prices in the South increased 1000 percent. Wages lagged far behind inflation. And as for production, all those rifle and cannon barrels, ironclad steamships, and bayonets demanded only 1 percent of total iron production throughout the four years of war. Contracts to supply the armies barely made up for the losses textile and shoe manufacturers suffered from the plummeting civilian demand. North and South lost each other's markets; the northern blockade eventually destroyed southern exports. Contractors made fortunes; almost everyone else was left worse off. During the war's latter years, Union armies rampaged through the South, destroying as much as $1.5 billion worth of factories, homes, businesses, railroads, and other property. In 1860, most of the South's wealth was invested in $2.7 billion worth of slaves. This wealth disappeared when Lincoln issued the Emancipation Proclamation. The Civil War's total cost may have been as high as $6.6 billion. Four years of war destroyed not only property but at least 650 000 lives and crippled another 500 000 able-bodied men. The real figures may be billions of dollars and hundreds of thousands of lives higher.[8]

To finance their respective crusades, both Washington and Richmond raised taxes, borrowed heavily, printed ever-more money, raised tariffs, and confiscated goods and services. Federal spending alone rose from $66.5 million in 1861 to $1.3 billion in 1865, while the national debt soared from $65 million to $2.7 billion. To help finance the swelling budget and debt, on 1 January 1862 Congress inauguarated the nation's first income tax. The tax was progressive, with the rate initially 3 percent on incomes higher than $800, and later 3 percent on incomes between $600 and $10 000 and 5 percent on incomes beyond $10 000. The tax was difficult to enforce. By 1865, the income tax accounted for only 18 percent of the budget. Additional revenues came from higher tariffs which averaged 47 percent by 1865 but contributed only 25 percent of the budget. Throughout the war, most money was raised through sales of interest-bearing bonds. Washington's insatiable demand for money raised interest rates and crowded out private investment.[9]

Despite the overwhelming need to finance, supply, and direct the war, the Lincoln administration initiated several important industrial policies that would significantly advance America's economy. On 20 May 1862, President Lincoln signed the Homestead Act which allowed anyone to acquire up to 160 acres of land by either paying $1.25 an acre for it or farming it a minimum of five years and paying a $10 registration fee. Homesteaders claimed over 1.5 million acres between 1863 and 1900.

Promising as it seemed, the Homestead Act did little to promote the interests of small farmers. Most of the acres were bought up by speculators and land companies making fraudulent claims, or ended up being owned and then sold off by banks. Land prices and mortgages rose throughout the nineteenth century, leading to tens of thousands of foreclosures. By the early twentieth century, about one of every four farmers was a tenant on someone else's land. Farm prices dropped steadily as more land was plowed, production was mechanized, and railroads brought more to market. From the early 1870s to the late 1880s, corn prices fell by 50 percent, wheat by 30 percent, and cotton by 25 percent. The result was an increasingly politicized farm population. In 1867, Oliver Kelly tapped into growing dissatisfaction among farmers by forming the Grange movement; by 1875, the Grange had 850 000 members. Other farm organizations like the Greenbackers and Alliance arose to protest mortgage and railroad transportation prices. These in turn inspired the Populist movement of the 1890s. However numerous and vociferous these movements were, none directly influenced public policy in their favor; indirectly, they joined the chorus for antitrust laws which were enacted in 1890 and 1914.[10]

Not just Federal financing but the nation's entire financial system needed an overhaul. In 1863, Congress passed the National

Banking Act which regulated the banking system. In return for a Federal charter, banks had to agree to forgo real estate loans, limit any loan to no more than 10 percent of deposits, and maintain minimal reserves of $50 000 in towns of fewer than 5000 people, $100 000 for towns with 5000–50 000 people, and $200 000 for cities with 50 000 or more people. The designated "central reserve city banks" in New York, and later after 1887 in Chicago and St Louis had to maintain reserves of 25 percent of deposits. To curb the issuance of state banknotes, Congress in 1865 imposed a 10 percent tax. By 1866, over 1600 banks accepted these guidelines. Thus arose a Federal banking system to compete with those of each state. Despite the competition, state banks eventually outnumbered Federal banks by the end of the century; entrepreneurs preferred the often looser requirements of state-chartered banks. In 1910, Federal banks represented only 29.1 percent of the nation's 24 513 banks.[11] Although the 1863 National Banking Law and subsequent reforms improved America's financial system, they did not go far enough. America's banking system before 1913 lacked a central reserve which could regulate the money supply and thus smooth out business cycles.

The existing regulations, however, did promote greater efficiencies and trust in banks. Money circulated more freely among regions. The north-east was consistently a net exporter and the south, midwest, and west net importers of capital. After banks, life insurance companies became a leading source of capital. Between 1869 and 1914, the life insurance industry's assets increased by twenty times. Following the Civil War, the government helped set the nation's finances on solid ground again by cutting spending and paying down its debts. Banker Jay Cooke's financial innovations helped marry those seeking investments with those who had it. Finally, a massive influx of foreign investments further enlarged the nation's capital pool. From 1870 to 1895, foreign investments in the United States yearly averaged $1.5 billion. This combined with high domestic savings allowed banks to keep interest rates low. Industrialists thus had ample and relatively low-priced investment funds.[12]

Technological advances were as important as ample finance in fueling American industry. When did America's industrialization really gather steam? If steam power is considered the essence of the early industrial revolution, then America's occurred after the Civil War. By 1870, steam-generated horsepower had surpassed water-generated horsepower in importance for American factories. That year, American industries were run by 1 215 711 steam-generated horsepower and 1 330 431 water-generated horsepower. Although obviously it cost more to run machinery from coal than from free-flowing streams, steam-power could be generated anywhere.[13]

If iron was the core product of industrialization's first phase, steel was for the second. Production innovations by Henry Bessemer in 1856 and Thomas Gilchrist and Sidney Thomas in 1878 led to higher-quality steel. More than anyone else, Andrew Carnegie capitalized on these innovations. In 1866, he obtained the patent to the Bessemer process of blowing air through iron to produce steel. Between then and 1901 when he sold out to J.P. Morgan, the Carnegie Steel Company grew steadily into an industrial empire that eventually accounted for one-quarter of all American steel production. Steel formed the skeletons of railroads, ships, and later skyscrapers. In 1870, about 70 000 gross tons of steel were produced in the United States; by 1910, the total had risen to 26 095 000 tons.[14]

Yet another sign of a deepening industrial age was the growing importance of machine tools, or machines that make machines by

turning, boring, drilling, milling, planing, grinding, polishing, etc. Moreover, all machines performing such operations confront a similar collection of technical problems, dealing with such matters as power transmission (gearing, belting, shafting), control devices, feed mechanisms, friction reduction, and a broad array of problems connected with the properties of metals (such as ability to withstand stresses and heat resistance). It is because these processes and problems became common to the production of a wide range of disparate commodities that industries which were apparently unrelated ... and uses of the final product became very closely related (technologically convergent) on a technological basis – for example, firearms, sewing machines, and bicycles.[15]

The greater a machine tool's precision, the more sophisticated the interchangeable parts and thus final product it can make. High-quality steel coupled with countless innovations made machine tools possible.

After the Civil War, every industry eventually adopted assembly-line production, interchangeable parts, machine tools, and scientific management and accounting. As for this last item, no one was more important than Frederick W. Taylor. He developed his ideas as the chief engineer for the Midvale Steel Co. in the 1880s, and later published them as the *Principles of Scientific Management* in 1911. A Taylor Society was formed to propagate his ideas. By the 1920s, Taylor's ideas were widely incorporated into virtually all industries.[16]

In May 1869, the presidents of the Central Pacific and Union Pacific railroads took turns hammering in a golden spike which completed their transcontinental railroad, thus literally and symbolically uniting the east and west coasts. Other transcontinental railroads and hundreds of branch lines would be completed in the coming decades, knitting the states into one vast national market. Across the west, the railroads mostly preceded settlement. In many places, however, businessmen and families bought up land ahead of the tracks in hope of future profit and comfort.[17]

A series of innovations spurred the efficiency and growth of the railroad industry, including the use of steel (which lasted eight times as long) rather than iron rails, bigger and better steam engines, air brakes, and automatic couplers. Engines expanded in power and size from ten tons in the 1830s to 70 tons around 1900. The invention of the refrigerated railroad car in 1881 allowed the food demands of city dwellers to be met by crops and livestock raised in ever-more remote regions of the country. Transportation costs dropped, thus generating enormous savings and incentives throughout the economy. In 1870, it cost about $1.65 to send a ton of freight a mile; in 1910, it cost only $0.75.[18]

The railroad industry was the economy's growth engine throughout the late nineteenth century. From 1860 to 1890, America's miles of track expanded from 40 000 to 170 000. From 1860 to 1900, the percentage of America's workforce directly employed in the railroad industry rose from 1 to 5 percent, while the gross capital formation of railroads rose from 15 to 18 percent of total investments. Between 1880 and 1910, train engines devoured nearly one of every five tons of coal consumed in the United States and around 30 percent of all iron and steel production. By 1910, the railroads directly or indirectly accounted for one-sixth of the economy.[19]

Washington led the creation of this network by donating 131 million acres either directly to the railroad companies or to them via state governments. Texas, which joined the United States without transferring any land to Washington, handed over an additional 27 million acres. The land was granted in alternating checkerboard sections usually six miles but sometimes as far as 40 miles wide. These 158 million acres of free land underwrote about 5 percent of the railroad's construction costs between 1850 and 1880.[20]

The Federal government also helped create a genuinely national market by several Supreme Court rulings. Well into the late nineteenth century, many states and localities still protected local businesses from national competition. For example, Missouri enacted a law in the 1840s which required those who sold goods manufactured outside the state to buy an expensive and hard to obtain license. In 1873, the Singer Company sued Missouri, charging that its law violated the Constitution. In 1876, the Supreme Court ruled in favor of Singer in Welton v. Missouri, with Justice Stephen Fielding asserting that "inter-state commerce shall be free and untrammelled." This ruling was reinforced by Webber v. Virginia (1880) and Minnesota v. Barber (1890). Bruchey summarized the significance of these rulings:

> Had state legislation succeeded in balkanizing the American continent, had it prevented the emergence of the great American common market of the nineteenth century, the scale on which goods were produced, distributed, and consumed would have been abridged by higher unit costs and prices. Thus economies of scale and lowered transportation costs depended on the constitutional allocation of power over interstate commerce to the Congress, on the willingness of the Supreme Court to defend that allocation in the interests of free trade, and on the emergence of firms with sufficient financial resources and interests to press for improvements in the efficiency of the legal system.[21]

Most Federal industrial policies involved settling the public lands of the west. In addition to giving away land to railroad corporations and homesteaders alike, the Federal government aided the private takeover of public lands in several ways. First, it deployed the US army to round up defiant and passive Indian tribes alike, impose treaties on them in which they ceded their territory, and herd them onto mostly barren lands no Americans then wanted. Maintaining military posts and reservations, and embarking on the occasional campaign was a very expensive subsidy for all settlers across the west, whether they were farmers, merchants, ranchers, miners, or loggers.

Washington also aided the west's exploitation by ignoring its own laws. An 1880 report fatalistically concluded that the, "people of those regions have to a certain extent framed customs which take the place of laws. In other words they are a law unto themselves."[22] In no economic sector was the government more blind to violations of Federal law than mining.

Many motives lured the first English settlers to America's shores. Perhaps none was greater than the dream of finding gold mines as rich as those of Mexico and Peru. In this, they were disappointed. The first gold strikes would not occur until the late eighteenth century in North Carolina and the early nineteenth century in northern Georgia. Federal law required miners to pay a royalty.

The modest yields of the first gold rushes did not prepare the nation for the 1848 gold strike in California. In 1852 alone, miners panned or dug $81 million from the Sierra Mountain foothills, and $70 million each of the following two years; by the 1860s, the annual yield dropped to $15–20 million and $11 million thereafter for the rest of the century. In 1859, the frenzy shifted to Nevada and Colorado where vast gold and silver deposits were struck. Later strikes unleashed floods of fortune-seekers on the Rocky Mountains of Montana and Idaho, South Dakota's Black Hills, and Arizona's high desert. In all of these strikes, the lone prospector with his pan and burro was soon shoved aside by huge corporations that could systematically and literally move mountains to gain the ore within. New inventions spurred the ability to do so – water cannons washed away hillsides, crushers powdered boulders, pumps drained flooded mines.

The western strikes all occurred on public lands and thus were public wealth. A 1785 law explicitly stated that the Federal government would "retain title to public mineral lands in order to extract rents from them for 'public purpose.'" This law was reinforced by a similar 1841 law. Public lands containing minerals could be leased but not sold. Royalties on the minerals extracted went to the national treasury. Although laws in 1846 and 1847 allowed for the sale of lands containing copper and lead in the midwest, the public lands elsewhere remained subject to the earlier laws.

Unfortunately for the American people, the Federal government did not attempt to uphold these laws in any of the great mineral strikes of the far west. Federal authorities were overwhelmed by the flood of miners and others converging on those strikes and watched helplessly as the public wealth was carted away for private gain. In classic American fashion, the inhabitants of the mining camps organized and ruled themselves. Ordinances were established to determine claims and publish criminals. In 1865 and 1866, Washington acquiesced to the reality, and recognized the claims. Jeffersonianism had triumphed![23]

The Federal government also turned a blind eye to the "cattle barons" who seized vast realms of public grasslands across the west. Before the Civil War, the Great Plains were still largely inhabited by buffalo herds and scattered nomadic Indian tribes. Only in Texas had ranchers killed off enough buffalo and Indians so that they could raise cattle. By 1860, there were over 3.5 million cattle ranging across the Texas plains. Following the Civil War, several ranchers acted on the idea of driving herds north across the plains to railheads creeping west across Kansas. From there, the cattle could be transported to eastern markets. Over 5 million cattle were driven north from Texas to Kansas cowtowns from 1866 to 1880. Eventually, as the buffalo were slaughtered and Indians imprisoned on small reservations across the plains, some ranchers drove herds north not to sell immediately but to breed. Throughout this era, the cattlemen faced a more formidable opponent than buffalo and Indians for the public range – sheepmen. Bloody wars between cattlemen and sheepmen over grasslands broke out across the west. By the century's end, cattle and sheep ranches covered not only most of the high plains from the Rio Grande to the Canadian border, but virtually every grassland across the west to the Pacific coast.

Cattle from the Great Plains composed an ever-larger proportion of the nation's beef. In 1860, of 14 779 373 cattle across the United States, only 107 086 were on the plains north of Texas. By 1890, 7 791 285 cattle ranged the plains of 33 734 128 across the entire nation. By 1890, there were about 10 million sheep across the Great Plains, 3 million more than cattle. By 1900, western ranches supplied 50 percent of America's cattle, 56 percent of its sheep, and 25 percent of its hogs. Despite this rapid increase in numbers, the nation's cattle and sheep barely kept up with the demands of an ever-burgeoning population. By allowing the unregulated use of America's public grasslands, Washington aided the supply of meat, hides, and wool to keep up with national demand, but at the expense of lost revenues from leasing and sales. Here again, Jeffersonian values prevailed.[24]

As with farming and mining, technology aided the spread of ranching across the west. In 1874, Joseph Gidden invented barbed wire. Rather than let their cattle or sheep roam free, ranchers could now fence off immense tracts of land for themselves, thus reducing the depredations of nature and rustlers. Gustavus Swift invented the refrigerator car in 1881, thus allowing livestock to be slaughtered far closer to the range than before. Ranchers and consumers were spared the feed and transport costs of shipping livestock to distant cities. With their livelihoods threatened, the National Butchers Protective Association convinced many state legislatures to protect them with laws forbidding the sale of any meat uninspected by officials 24 hours after slaughter. In Minnesota *v.* Barber (1890), the Supreme Court struck down these laws as a restraint of interstate commerce.

Across most of the west, farmers trailed behind miners, ranchers, loggers, soldiers, and railroads. New technologies helped farmers settle the Great Plains and the west's other wide open, arid but fertile lands. The invention of a new steel plow in the 1860s enabled farmers to gouge through the tough prairie grasses to the rich soil below. Barbed wire aided farmers just as it did ranchers, permitting farmers in largely treeless regions to protect their crops from wandering beasts. Grain elevators allowed farmers to store huge amounts of grains safe from Nature until they were needed. Despite these innovations, to survive, farmers had to sell their surplus to others such as the local army post or mining camp. Railroads connected farmers with national markets. Yet, even with access to markets, western farmers faced heartbreaking challenges of often biblical proportions – droughts, floods, locusts, and disease.[25] Mostly, though, they suffered from the financial Panics that devastated the economy.

America's remarkable economic growth did not suspend the standard business cycle. The economy was wracked by deep contractions during 1873–9, 1881–3, 1887–8, 1893–7, and 1907–8. The absence of any Federal management prolonged these depressions. Lacking monetary or fiscal tools, the Treasury Department could only shrug at such free market whims. Factory owners were faced with a terrible dilemma. When prices dropped for their goods, they naturally tended to produce more, hoping to squeeze out more profits from the greater volume. This, of course, simply flooded markets and dropped prices further. Yet, factory owners continued to step up production for fear of losing market share to their competitors and because the costs of shutting down production were often greater than selling at a loss.

Industrialists attempted to curb this ruinous free market competition through collusion, setting price floors and production ceilings, or dividing markets like they were the spoils of war – which of course they were. As Andrew Carnegie put it,

> Combinations, syndicates, trusts, they are willing to try anything. The manufacturers are in the position of patients that have tried in vain every doctor of the regular school for years, and are now liable to become the victim of any quack that appears.[26]

It was through a series of trusts that John D. Rockefeller was able eventually to control 90 percent of the oil refining industry. Holding companies held the stocks and securities of different corporations. Several state legislatures actually legalized the creation of holding companies because they profited so greatly from the incorporation fees.

By the early twentienth century, virtually every industry was managed by some kind of collusion, whether it was through monopolies, pools, syndicates, trusts, or holding companies. In 1904, 318 corporations controlled 40 percent of all manufacturing in the United States. Between 1895 and 1904, an average of 301 corporations disappeared as they were consolidated or acquired by corporate groups; the peak year was 1899 when 1028 firms were merged. Holding companies were responsible for 86 percent of these mergers. By 1904, one corporation held 60 percent or more of the market in over fifty industries. Firms like Dupont, Westinghouse, Pullman, General Electric, and American Tobacco actually enjoyed over 80 percent market shares. According to the 1900 census,

> 185 industrial combinations, making up less than one-half of 1 percent of the manufacturing establishments in the country, owned 15 percent of the industrial capital, employed 8 percent of the industrial labor force, and produced 14 percent of industrial output of the United States. In 1914, it was estimated that 318 mergers had involved 5,300 plants across America and an investment well in excess of $7 billion.[27]

None of the era's "robber barons" had greater power than J.P. Morgan who, with his partners,

> held 721 directorships in 112 of the country's largest financial, transportation, industrial, and public utility companies. About half of the firm's total deposits of $162.5 million belonged to

seventy-eight interstate corporations, and of these thirty-two included one or more Morgan men on their boards. Between 1902 and 1912 Morgan & Co.'s public security offerings reached a total of $1.95 billion.[28]

One of Morgan's partners, George W. Perkins, succinctly captured the mentality of the era: "The old idea that we were raised under, that competition is the life of trade, is exploded. Competition is no longer the life of trade, it is cooperation."[29] Jeffersonianism had led not to its promised free market Utopia but to the tyranny of monopoly.

Perhaps none of the huge monopolies that arose in the late nineteenth century was more rapacious than the railroads which charged exorbitant rates for even the shortest of hauls. Like most other industries, the railroads consolidated into a few hands during the late nineteenth century. Depression during the 1880s ravished the railroads, bankrupting 279 companies between 1882 and 1891. Those lines were quickly gobbled up by the larger, more resilient railroad corporations, most of which were controlled directly or indirectly by J.P. Morgan.[30]

With their bulk shipments, farmers and ranchers bore the brunt of high transportation and storage fees. It was largely to combat the' railroad monopolies that farmers organized the Grange in 1867 and Farmers Alliances in the 1870s. These organizations lobbied state governments for relief and cast their votes for the Greenback and Populist parties. They also formed cooperatives to give themselves more bargaining power with the banks and railroads, build their own grain elevators, and share equipment.[31]

One by one, the states began regulating the railroad and warehouse industries. Those industries fought back, claiming that government could not infringe on their "free markets." In Munn v. Illinois (1876), the Supreme Court ruled that the states had the right to regulate business, arguing: "When private property is devoted to a public use, it is subject to public regulation." This triumph for farmers, ranchers, and others was short-lived. The Court reversed itself in Chicago, Milwaukee, and St. Paul Railway Company v. Minnesota (1890), asserting the power of the courts rather than legislatures to determine a fair rate and thus striking down state laws.

Pressured by powerful constituents outraged by the price-gouging, Congress passed the Interstate Commerce Act of 1887 which forbade any price or passenger discrimination by transportation corporations, and set up a five-man commission to investigate claims of wrongdoing. The Interstate Commerce Commission's powers to regulate the transportation industry, including the imposition of price ceilings, were reinforced by the Elkins Act of 1903 and Hepburn Act of 1906.

Congress took an even larger leap toward regulating business in 1890 when it passed the Sherman Antitrust Act which forbade monopolies. Whatever the Congressmen may have privately thought of the bill, they overwhelming supported it in the Senate (52–1) and House (242–0). In practice, the Sherman Antitrust Act was more a statement of principle than anything else – it was hardly enforced. The Department of Justice was entrusted with upholding the law, but was not given the financial, personnel, or moral authority to do so. The trust-busters came from private firms or individuals assailing monopolies through the courts. From 1890 to 1903, only eighteen antitrust cases went to court.

The Supreme Court interpreted the antitrust law very creatively. In 1895, the Supreme Court ruled in United States *v*. F.C. Knight Company that the American Sugar Refining Company, which owned 98 percent of America's sugar refining capacity, was not guilty of monopoly practices. In its 1899 Addyston Pipe & Steel *v*. United States, the Supreme Court did declare illegal a pool arrangement. With these two cases, the Supreme Court seemed to be saying that a trust like American Sugar was legal and a pool like Addyston Pipe was illegal under the Sherman Antitrust Act. But the underlying distinction the Supreme Court made was between "good" trusts that did not skewer the public and "bad" trusts that did. In this the Court was in accord with the presidents and most congressmen of that era. In other words, most Americans realized that "free trade" was an impossible dream; the best that the nation could achieve was "fair trade," and only then if government served as a diligent and fierce watchdog. The Supreme Court made this distinction in two landmark 1911 cases. Standard Oil Company owned 91 percent of America's oil refining capacity, and used that near monopoly to gouge the public. American Tobacco Company produced 50–90 percent of all tobacco products except cigars, and charged exorbitant prices to tobacco addicts. The Court ordered both trusts broken up.[32] In 1914, Congress reinforced the existing body of antitrust law with the Clayton Act and the Federal Trade Commission Act which, respectively, widened the range of illegal trade practices and set up a watchdog bureaucracy to enforce it.

America's workforce swelled with its industrial power. Between 1870 and 1910, the official army of employed rose from 12 505 900 to 38 167 300.[33] Where did these new workers come from? Greater life expectancy and immigration stimulated a population explosion in late nineteenth century America with the population doubling between 1870 and 1910. During those four decades, 20 million immigrants poured into the United States, transforming forever most of America's cities. America's rural population during those years dropped from three (74.3 percent) of every four people to one (54.3 percent) of two.[34]

Millions of immigrants continued to pour into the United States, and encouraged the relatives and friends they left behind to follow, because the often wretched life of squalor and overwork they had entered was an improvement over what they had fled. During this era, Congress tried to stem the immigrant tide only against Asians streaming into the west coast. Chinese were barred for ten years after 1882, and permanently after 1902. In 1906, President Roosevelt made a "gentlemen's agreement" with Japan's government in which it would limit its immigration to the United States – Japan refused to honor the agreement.

Whether they were native born or not, millions of women and children made up an increasing percentage of the workforce. More and more women left the home for work – 1 836 300 in 1870; 8 075 800 in 1910. Women comprised most workers in a few fields such as textiles and secondary education. Children too were an important part of the workforce – 13 percent of the total in 1900.[35]

Work conditions in the factories were at best harsh. By one estimate "from 1880 to 1900, 35 000 workers were killed annually and another 536 000 were injured."[36] Increasing numbers of workers united in protest against the harsh conditions and low pay. Of the trade unions which arose, the largest were the Knights of St Crispin of shoemakers, the Sons of Vulcan of iron and steelmakers, and the Workingmen's Benevolent Association of miners. In 1869, Uriah Stephens founded the Noble and Holy Order of the Knights of Labor to unite all the unions into one national movement. By 1885, the Knights of Labor had 110 000 members. That year, they struck against Jay Gould's railroads. Inspired by their defiance, new members swelled the Knights' ranks to 700 000. In early 1886, they struck against Gould's south-western system. The strikes reached a climax in May when police fired into a riot in Haymarket Square in Chicago. The strikes failed and the Knights' strength quickly withered.[37]

The Haymarket riot proved a watershed in the labor movement. Within months of Haymarket, the craft unions withdrew from the Knights to form the American Federation of Labor (ALF). Samuel Gompers headed the AFL's first 30 years, and established the tradition of a tough pragmatism for American labor. Strikes were frequent, averaging 1000 with 380 000 total participants every year. The goals generally were higher wages, shorter hours, and better safety. Gompers helped organize other unions including the Teamsters, Building Laborers, Electrical Workers, and Musicians. Between the AFL's founding in 1886 and 1914, the membership soared from 140 000 to 2 020 000. Despite this accomplishment, only 8 percent of the labor force were in unions in 1914.[38]

Those who attacked labor unions did so on many grounds. The most philosophical objection was that the labor market should be as free as any other market. In this spirit, the 1887 Interstate Commerce Act and 1890 Sherman Antitrust Act worked against rather than for laborers. Throughout the late nineteenth and into the twentieth centuries, the courts treated strikes as illegal restraints of trade, and ordered the leaders jailed. It was not until the 1914 Clayton Act that Congress explicitly stated that trade unions were not subject to antitrust laws. The Supreme Court, however, struck down this assertion in two 1921 cases, Duplex Printing Press Co. *v.* Deering and American Steel Foundries *v.* Tri-City Central Trades Council.

Whether caused by the labor movement or not, work conditions improved overall. While immigration, female, and child labor undoubtedly depressed wages for native-born men, the average real wage improved nearly 50 percent between 1860 and 1914. The average working week declined from 65 hours in 1860 to 56.6 in 1910, while the factory working day likewise declined from ten and a half hours to eight and a half hours.[39]

Generally speaking, there is a dynamic relationship between education and productivity. The government helped develop America's economy by helping develop its citizen's minds. Public secondary education rose steadily as a percentage of the total, from 57 percent in 1860 to 79 percent in 1900. Public vocational schools which taught a trade became increasingly common in the late nineteenth century. The number of medical and basic science schools expanded from 75 to 131 between 1870 and 1910, with their graduates soaring from 7988 to 39 997. In nursing, the expansion was even faster, from 15 to 1129 schools and 157 to 8140 graduates during those same years. During those same years, public education expenditures rose from $19.9 million to $229.6 million.[40]

Although public education was primarily the duty and expense of state and local government, the Federal government aided its expansion in several ways. In 1862, Congress passed the Morril Act by which the Federal government granted land to the states to be sold or developed to establish agricultural colleges. Child labor laws helped expand secondary school ranks. The 1917 Smith–Hughes Act provided Federal aid to schools which offered vocational training to those over 14 years old.

Throughout this era, most people enjoyed longer, more affluent lives because of the advances in public health. Although water pollution had been identified as a severe hazard from the colonial days, the problem was little understood and even less could be done about it. In the 1880s, scientists proved what had long been suspected – that many diseases were waterborne. The discovery set off the sanitation movement in the United States. In 1886, Congress first acted against water pollution by banning the dumping of wastes in New York harbor, but only then because those waters involved interstate and international commerce. In 1893, Congress passed the Interstate Quarantine Act which allowed the Surgeon General to regulate the bacteria levels of interstate waters. The law lacked any enforcement power. Although the 1899 Refuse Act forbade the dumping of wastes into commercial streams, it too failed to deter polluters. In 1912, Congress authorized the formation of the US Public Health Service which, among other duties, was authorized to monitor pollution. Two years later in 1914, the Public Health Service issued national drinking water standards to curtail diseases. As a result of these Federal and local policies, the number of city inhabitants enjoying filtered water rose from 30 000 in 1875 to 10 million by 1910. By 1910, virtually every big city had a sewage system. As a result, the infant mortality rate dropped and life expectancy soared.

Despite all of these advances in living standards and quality of life for most people, millions failed to enjoy these advantages. Pockets of mass poverty scarred the burgeoning cities and countryside alike. Nowhere was poverty more common or ingrained than in the South. Most of what little industry the South had developed before 1861 was destroyed during the Civil War. Wartime inflation was followed by a severe depression in which farmland lost half its value. The South was enmeshed in a vicious cycle of underdevelopment. Mass poverty kept consumption, savings, and investments low. Northern industries supplied southern demands for goods. One in three southerners was black. The status of most blacks simply changed from slave to sharecropper, with little more incentive or opportunity to improve their lot. Those who struggled to get ahead had to contend with the Black Codes, Ku Klux Klan, and Jim Crow laws. With labor a farmer's most abundant resource, they had little incentive to abandon old methods of tilling, sowing, and reaping their land. Farm productivity stagnated. Despite the doubling of America's population during the era, crop and livestock prices remained low because of the opening of western lands to agriculture and ranching. The Civil War broke the backbone of the South's economy, cotton, as the North, Britain, and other textile producers found alternative supplies in India, Egypt, and elsewhere. Cotton prices remained depressed thereafter. Coins had been scarce before the war and dried up during and long after it. Credit was limited and exorbitant. Both reinforcing and reflecting all these problems was the South's neocolonization after the Civil War, first fleetingly by a flood of carpetbaggers and then substantially, by northern industrialists who sucked profits from the region through "branch plants, branch banks, captive mines, and chain stores."[41]

The South was not the only region invaded by American merchants, industrialists, and investors. The United States was a belated participant in the second great wave of western imperialism. During the late nineteenth century, steam power, rapid firing rifles and cannon, medicines to combat tropical diseases, industrialization, the telegraph, and modern finance gave the Europeans the ability to project economic and military power virtually anywhere in the world. American merchants had first traded with China in the late eighteenth century, and in the 1820s through Latin America as Spain's empire over the much of the Western Hemisphere crumbled. By the late nineteenth century, American entrepreneurs were selling or investing all around the world.

American businesses were inevitably affected by the volatile politics in many of those foreign countries, and, in turn, attempted to manipulate local politics in their favor through bribes and, as a last resort, a request to the president for US marines. American multinational corporations were often among the best organized political and economic forces in many countries in the Caribbean, Latin America, and across the Pacific. American plantation owners in Hawaii blatantly tried to orchestrate politics there for a generation before the United States annexed the islands in 1893. In 1898, American business interests and jingoism pressured Washington into a war with Spain which netted the United States colonies in Puerto Rico, Guam, and the Philippines, and a protectorate over Cuba. From the Civil War through to today, the Caribbean basin has been an American sea. Even before World War I, American marines landed in the Dominican Republic, Nicaragua, Mexico, Haiti, and Guatemala. Between 1911 and 1916, the United States almost went to war with Mexico to protect American investments, particularly those of Standard Oil. Every administration did what it could to aid American trade and investments. Perhaps none did so more vigorously than President William Howard Taft, whose "dollar diplomacy" was based on "lending all proper support to legitimate and beneficial American enterprise in foreign countries." Taft reorganized the State Department to "make it a thoroughly efficient instrument in the furtherance of foreign trade and of American interests."[42] Yet, important as this trade and investment with the tropics was for certain American firms and industries, as today, most American trade was with other industrialized countries rather than with the poorer countries.

Despite the antitrust laws and supportive public opinion, Congress and the Supreme Court battled continuously over the government's proper role in the economy. A majority in Congress recognized that the government could and should regulate the economy when markets failed. The Supreme Court consistently ruled in favor of a "laissez faire constitutionalism" in which any restrictions on free enterprise were unconstitutional. Although by 1911, the Supreme Court and Congress seemed to reach a consensus over "good" versus "bad" trusts, the justices continued to rule against trade unions long after the congressmen gave their lukewarm approval.

Meanwhile, the problem with the nation's financial system was not too few but too many. Despite the Federal attempts to regulate banking markets through the 1864 National Banking Act, the 1873 Coinage Act, the 1875 Resumption Act, the 1890 Sherman Silver Purchase Act, and the 1900 Gold Standard Act, banks proliferated in the late nineteenth century. Between 1860 and 1914, the ratio of banks dropped from one to every 10 000 people to one to every 3500 people. By 1895, state banks again outnumbered national banks. In the competition between Washington and the states to charter banks, regulations were dropped until they were largely meaningless. Allowed to regulate itself, the banking industry failed miserably to fulfill that Jeffersonian ideal. Throughout the late nineteenth century, groups of banks formed clearinghouses to handle a variety of transactions; by 1913, the number of clearinghouses reached 162 with total transactions of $170 billion. Yet neither the competition or collusion prevented the financial panics of 1873, 1877, 1883, 1888, and 1907, and subsequent prolonged depressions. They did, however, make most of the owners extremely rich. The rise of stock markets, trusts, and insurance companies further worsened the nation's financial instability and speculation.

Having won the antitrust battle, progressives targeted banks for regulation. In 1908, Congress passed the Aldrich–Vreeland Act which allowed groups of ten national banks to form national currency associations, and authorized the creation of a National Monetary Commission to investigate the financial system and propose reforms. After a year of study, the Commission proposed the creation of a central bank. The Republicans controlled Congress and President William Taft shelved the report. But Democrats captured the House in 1910 and the Senate and White House in 1912. In 1913, President Woodrow Wilson signed into law the Federal Reserve Act creating the Federal Reserve System. The Federal Reserve presided over 12 regional districts with each led by a district bank which oversaw their respective members. All national banks were required to join the Federal Reserve, while state banks which met the requirements could join. Members had to maintain reserves equal to 10 percent of their assets and buy Federal Reserve stock equal to 3 percent of their assets. In turn, members could borrow and sell commercial paper and government securities.

By the century's turn, Washington was experiencing increasing difficulties in raising enough money to finance its expanding responsibilities. The McKinley Tariff of 1888 raised the rate to an average 48 percent on imports. Yet, the additional revenues could not keep up with Federal expenses. In 1911, the United States adopted a national income tax. Although Jeffersonians howled at this latest affront to the free market ideal, Hamiltonians prevailed in their argument that the tax was not only vital for financing Federal programs that fueled and channeled economic development, but was just since it skimmed from those who benefited the most from the system.

NEW KINDS OF INDUSTRIAL POLICIES:
ENVIRONMENTALISM AND CONSERVATIONISM

Not all Americans were prisoners of the national obsession with getting rich at all costs and to all ends. By the late nineteenth century, a growing number of Americans sought to preserve or conserve some rather than destroy all of Nature in the pursuit of wealth. The new policies that emerged from the environmental and conservation movements would eventually affect all industries by restricting how they used the land or treated pollution.

Around mid-century, the transcendentalists' sentiments were reinforced by hard scientific analysis. In his *Man and Nature: Physical Geography as Modified by Human Action* (1864), George Perkins Marsh explored the relationship between the rise and fall of civilizations and Nature, noting numerous examples of great empires which had collapsed when their human activities exhausted the natural resources upon which they were based. All living and non-living entities are interdependent; when humans ravish links in that vast web, the entire system which supports humans can collapse. The solution, according to Marsh, is simple – humans must conserve rather than destroy the land; for humans to do otherwise, as the ruins of numerous past civilizations reveal, is to do so at their ultimate peril. Yet Marsh knew that humans are too mired in wasteful practices to make any transformation toward conservation easily. To restore lands ravished by former destructive practices would require "great political and moral revolutions in the governments and peoples by whom those regions are now possessed."[43]

In 1878, another seminal ecological study appeared which further shifted how influential people viewed land-use policies. John Wesley Powell's *Report on the Lands of the Arid Region of the United States* was based on observations from his descent of the Colorado River in 1869. Powell argued that American land-use policies that had been devised in the eastern United States of abundant rainfall, rich soils, and hardwood forests had no relevance in the arid western lands. The west could support only a small population, mostly in those lands adjacent to rivers where irrigation was possible. Powell recommended that for the arid lands, the homestead laws be amended to allow 2500 acres per person.[44]

These ideas were embraced by new professional scientific groups such as the American Forestry Association. In the late nineteenth century, magazines such as *American Sportsman* (1871), *Forest and*

Stream (1873), *Field and Stream* (1874), and *American Angler* (1881) emerged to push for conservation. Theodore Roosevelt was a leading conservationist. In 1887, he and other concerned sportsmen formed the Boone and Crockett Club which pressured the state governments to conserve threatened hunting and fishing grounds from destruction by commercial hunters and fishermen. Men of leisure thus battled men who hunted and fished for their livelihood.

At first, conservationism was largely a hobby of enlightened rich industrialists who recognized that the failure to conserve threatened their traditional pursuits of hunting, fishing, and camping. But increasingly it became a comprehensive outlook and set of policies to manage the nation's natural resources. Conservationism thus emerged from the braiding of two major strands – scientific studies of biology, forestry, geology, hydrology, agronomy, and anthropology, and the political power of wealthy outdoorsmen. Conservation was not "a science like ecology but a reform movement using political and legal methods to obtain what Theodore Roosevelt called 'wise use' of resources."[45]

The results were policies designed to develop the nation's natural resources on a long-term, sustainable basis. Markets with their emphasis on immediate profits were eschewed in favor of long-term planning and management of resources. Conservationism caught on quickly in the United States because rich, influential men championed it with the utilitarian terms that other businessmen and politicians could understand. "Conserve today or lose money tomorrow," was conservation's essential message. Increasing numbers of America's industrial leaders understood that the failure to conserve might well mean the eventual failure of America's economic and political system.

The conservation movement, in turn, was part of the "progressive era" which spanned the late nineteenth and early twentieth centuries. The collection of antitrust, labor, health, and conservation laws that fall under the "progressive" rubric, were reactions to the excesses of rapid industrialization, the frontier's elimination, massive immigration, and fears that something vital about American civilization was withering.

Historian Samuel Hays wrote that:

The lack of direction in American development appalled Roosevelt and his advisors. They rebelled against a belief in the automatic beneficience of unrestricted economic competition, which, they believed, created only waste, exploitation, and unproductive economic rivalry. To replace competition with economic planning, these new efficiency experts argued, would not only arrest the damage of the past, but could also create new heights of prosperity and material abundance for the future. The conservation movement did not involve a reaction against large-scale corporate business, but, in fact, shared its views in a mutual revulsion against unrestrained competition and undirected economic development. Both placed a premium on large-scale capital organization, technology, and industry-wide cooperation and planning to abolish the uncertainties and waste of competitive resource use."[46]

In the late nineteenth century, laws and policies began to crack the mentality that assumed public lands were there simply to be sold off or exploited. In 1872, Congress passed two laws which would symbolize the split between Jeffersonians and Hamiltonians. The Federal Mining Law allowed anyone to file a gold, silver, or copper mining claim on public lands for a minimal fee and mine it to its exhaustion without ever paying a single royalty or being required to clean up the resulting environmental mess. The Yellowstone Protection Act set aside two million acres in north-west Wyoming and fringes of Montana and Idaho to create the world's first national park.

In the decades since that 1872 balance between the Jeffersonian and Hamiltonian laws, the nation's policies and values seemed to shift toward the latter. Scores of other lands have been set aside as national parks, not just in the United States but around the globe. In 1886, Congress created the Division of Forestry and in 1891 passed the Forest Reserve Act empowering the president to set aside forest lands for management. From then until the end of President Roosevelt's White House tenure in 1908, more than 200 million acres of forest reserves had been created. Subsequent presidents have expanded the nation's forests even further.

But despite these successes, the Hamiltonian conservation movement itself eventually split between those who advocated managing the nation's resources for primarily economic reasons and those who wanted to protect the nation's natural splendors for cultural, historic, aesthetic, and even spiritual reasons. Those who rallied around the former values continued to be called conservationists while those who pressed for the latter values would eventually be known as environmentalists. On issue after issue, the lines between conservationists and environmentalists were drawn and fought as fiercely as between them and the Jeffersonians.

In the late nineteenth century, John Muir emerged as environmentalism's titan. Although his words were as eloquent, profound, and prolific as those of Thoreau, his political battles were far more important than the latter's few minor forays into the public arena. Throughout his adult life, Muir studied the transcendentalists and penned his own perspectives on Nature. Wilderness to Muir was a temple in which he achieved mystical union:

> you bathe in these spirit-beams, turning round and round, as if warming at a camp-fire. Presently you lose consciousness of your separate existence: you blend with the landscape, and become part and parcel of nature.[47]

Muir articulated a deep ecology perspective that has inspired adherents ever since. He saw man as not removed from Nature but an integral part of the vast web of life: "The universe would be incomplete without man; but it would also be incomplete without the smallest transmicroscopic creature that dwells beyond our conceitful eyes and knowledge."[48] Thus every creature of Nature has its own right to exist.

Muir corresponded with Emerson and actually guided him through Yosemite during the latter's visit in 1871. He was disappointed, however, when Emerson and his entourage chose to settle in the hotel rather than beneath the stars. Nonetheless, their correspondence continued long after Emerson returned to Concord. In a letter of 1872, Emerson urged Muir to join him at Concord and thus "bring to an early close your absolute contracts with any yet unvisited glaciers or volcanoes.... [Wilderness] is a sublime mistress, but an intolerable wife."[49] Muir refused.

Muir gradually attracted national attention and a small but growing following through a series of publications. In his 1876 essay, "God's First Temples: How Can We Preserve Our Forests?" he called for national forests that would be preserved from the bite of the axe. His effort inspired an abortive attempt by California assemblymen to create a state park in Kings Canyon. A similar attempt to protect Mt Shasta also died.

These controversies and Muir's growing reputation caused Robert Underwood Johnson, an associate editor of the monthly magazine *Century*, to solicit him as a guide through Yosemite in June 1889.

Muir complied. During their trip, Johnson was appalled by the destruction caused by logging and grazing. Together they planned a national campaign to designate Yosemite a national park with the same protection as Yellowstone. Muir wrote two essays for *Century* magazine which appeared in autumn 1890. Johnson meanwhile lobbied for Yosemite in Congress. A bill was introduced, passed Congress with little debate on 30 September 1890, and was signed by President Benjamin Harrison the next day. The following year, Congress passed a law as significant as that creating Yellowstone two decades earlier. The 1891 Forest Reserve Act allowed the Federal government to conserve forests on public lands so that future generations could benefit from them.

Elated by these successes, Muir and Johnson agreed that future battles could be more easily fought and won with an organization. On 4 June 1892 in San Francisco, John Muir and 26 associates formed the Sierra Club dedicated to preserving other beautiful and sensitive regions in California. Muir was named the first president and served in that post until his death 22 years later. In advocating nature's preservation, Muir argued that wilderness was essential for civilization:

> Thousands of tired, nerve-shaken, over-civilized people are beginning to find out that going to the mountains and reservations are useful not only as fountains of timber and irrigating river, but as fountains of life.[50]

Muir's philosophy soon found a mass appeal. By the early twentieth century, environmentalism had spread from small coteries of intellectuals to increasing numbers of citizens. In addition to Muir's eloquent appeals, the transformation was sparked by a set of socioeconomic, cultural, technological, and historic forces. The 1890 census announced that the frontier had ended, setting off a wave of nostalgia about the pioneer experience and anxiety that the nation would now become effete without the challenge of conquering Nature and Indians. Frederick Jackson Turner's 1893 essay, "The Significance of the Frontier in American History" and several successive essays gave those fears an intellectual foundation.[51] Turner argued that there was a dynamic relationship between the pioneers and wilderness, that each transformed the other into something different and superior. Man converted wilderness into farms, mines, logs, and countless industrial products; Europeans had become Americans through their struggle against and conquest of wilderness. The frontier experience was essentially democratic as small groups of individuals cooperated to overcome common problems.

Jackson's thesis crystallized a growing debate over the meaning of wilderness and the pioneer experience. Some writers celebrated America's wilderness experience such as Roosevelt's series on the "Winning of the West" while other works such as Helen Hunt Jackson's *Century of Dishonor* decried that very conquest. Jack London explored wilderness through many of his novels and short stories, perhaps none so symbolically as in *Call of the Wild* in which a dog lost in the wilderness gradually reasserts its primal instincts to survive. Edgar Rice Burroughs explored the same theme of reversion from domesticity to wildness in his "Tarzan of the Apes" series.

America was a very different country at the century's turn than it was a generation or more earlier. Industrialization had transformed the nation with new wealth, and in so doing had widened discrepancies between rich elites and the masses of urban and rural poor. Railroad and other industrial monopolies gouged consumers and depressed the economy. More people now lived in ever-more polluted and crime-ridden cities rather than the countryside. Millions of immigrants with foreign languages and values crowded into those cities and threatened to undermine traditional American culture.

Increasing numbers of people escaped from these travails through wilderness depicted in literature. A widening urban middle-class sought an outlet for its wealth and leisure through excursions to the countryside; the automobile gave it the means of getting there. Others joined groups which lobbied the government for more protection of the nation's natural wonders. Throughout the early twentieth century, the Sierra and Appalachian Mountain clubs were joined by several new national environmental groups such as the National Audubon Society (1905) and the National Parks Association (1916). Organizations such as the Boy Scouts, Boy Pioneers, Woodcraft Indians, and Sons of Daniel Boone attempted to reconnect boys with frontier skills and values. For three decades, only the Bible exceeded the *Boy Scout Handbook* in sales.

No one, including Muir, exemplified this movement to recapture the American pioneer experience more than Theodore Roosevelt. Throughout his public life and particularly as president, Roosevelt continually called on Americans to revive the nation by engaging in the "strenuous life." According to Roosevelt, the national paradox or dilemma was that, "as our nation's civilization grows older and more complex, we need a greater and not a less development of the frontier virtues."[52]

Roosevelt did more than talk about the importance of conserving the nation's resources and preserving its natural beauties. No president has done more to advance both the conservationist and preservationist agendas than Roosevelt. In 1900, Roosevelt became the nation's youngest serving president when, as vice-president, he took over after President McKinley was murdered. During his eight years in office, Roosevelt added nearly 150 million acres to the national forest reserve system, and created a score of national monuments, the wildlife refuge system, and the Bureau of Reclamation to provide irrigation to the west's farmers.

In 1903, Roosevelt traveled to Yellowstone and Yosemite, camping with reknowned naturalists John Burroughs in the former and John Muir in the latter. Roosevelt declared his wholehearted support for the nation's protected wild lands because, "no nation facing the unhealthy softening and relaxation of fibre that tends to accompany civilization can afford to neglect anything that will develop hardihood, resolution, and the scorn of discomfort and danger."[53]

Roosevelt was just as fervent a conservationist in some areas as he was an environmentalist in others. Roosevelt and his Forestry Service head and chief advisor, Gifford Pinchot, worked closely together to shape conservation policies. In 1908, the Roosevelt administration convened the Governor's Conference on the Conservation of Natural Resources at the White House. Pinchot succeeded in packing the conference with conservationists and excluding preservationists like Muir and Johnson. Nonetheless, Jeffersonians were not only excluded but blasted for devastating the nation's resources and long-term future. In Roosevelt's address to the gathering, he asserted that the American people

are coming to recognize as never before the right of the Nation to guard its own future in the essential matter of natural resources. In the past we have admitted the right of the individual to injure the future of the Republic for his own present profit. In fact there has been a good deal of a demand for unrestricted individualism, for the right of the individual to injure the future of all of us for his own temporary and immediate profit. The time has come for a change.[54]

Although the Sierra Club and other environmental groups across the country cheered Roosevelt's preservationist policies, they increasingly criticized his conservationist policies. This was the major reason why Pinchot excluded them from the 1908 conservation conference. The breaking point between the environmentalists and conservationists was over a proposed dam at Hetch Hetchy Valley, below Yosemite Valley. Pinchot pushed for the dam to channel water to San Francisco; the Sierra Club vigorously opposed it. The controversy lasted from 1906 until 1913 when President Wilson finally broke the impasse and authorized the dam's construction. Shortly thereafter, Muir broke bitterly with Pinchot. From then on, Muir would neither speak nor write of any compromise with conservationist perspectives – preservation was to be the only goal. On World War I's eve, Hamiltonians were split into two antagonistic camps.

FROM WORLD WAR TO WORLD DEPRESSION

World War I was a godsend for American economic power. American businessmen reaped enormous profits by selling to both sides throughout the war, particularly to the more accessible Allied Powers. Between 1914 and 1917, America's trade surplus to the Allies totaled $5.3 billion. To pay for their war effort, the belligerents liquidated much of their investments in the United States and borrowed heavily from American bankers. The United States became a creditor country during World War I.

Why then did not the United States continue to sit safely on the sidelines, selling goods and finance to the belligerents? Unrestricted German submarine warfare increasingly strained President Wilson's pledge to keep America out of the war. As German submarines sent more American merchant ships to the ocean's depths, the Wilson White House took steps to prepare the United States for war. In December 1916, Wilson created a Council of National Defense to advise his administration on the mobilization of industry. The Council was organized into over 100 advisory committees composed of industrial leaders in sectors such as iron and steel, transportation, oil, rubber, lumber, and so on. When this committee system proved to be too unwieldy and inefficient, Wilson reorganized it into the War Industries Board (WIB) in July 1917, and appointed Bernard Baruch to head it.

The WIB eventually formed over 300 war service committees to advise 57 commodity groups on the supplies, demands, and prices for their respective goods and services, along with the regulations and laws necessary to provide them. While the WIB mobilized production, other agencies were created to fulfill more specific tasks:

the War Trade Board licensed imports and exports; the Capital Issues Committee regulated investment; the War Finance Corporation lent funds to munitions industries; the Railroad Administration unified the nation's railroads; the Fuel Administration fixed the price of coal and imposed 'coal holidays' on eastern industry, and the Food Administration controlled the production and consumption of food.[55]

The war boards did more than simply set production goals. They recognized that war production could be enhanced through better housing, recreation, work conditions, health care, and sanitation for workers, and tried to pressure industry to enact such measures.

Upon what authority did these boards act? Although they were armed with sweeping laws and regulations, the WIB and other boards were able to mobilize America's economy for war largely with handshakes rather than lawsuits. Even when a corporation failed to comply with an initial WIB request, the government's threat to resort to tougher measures was almost always sufficient for ultimate compliance.

When Congress declared war on 6 April 1917, the United States was prepared. During World War I, the Federal government and business cooperated to an unprecedented extent. For the first time in American history, the Federal government systematically regulated and coordinated the economy and virtually all of its industries. Most of America's business associations date from World War I. America's war effort was expensive – the Federal budget rose from $1.34 billion in 1917 to $18.21 billion in 1919. By 1919, the war consumed nearly one-third of America's economy, and was financed largely through sales of "liberty bonds." World War I enormously boosted America's economy from $49.9 billion GNP in 1917 to $65.7 billion in 1919. America's economy would not expand as rapidly or hum as efficiently until Washington took even more sweeping measures to coordinate it during World War II. The United States emerged from war as the world's greatest economic power – it was now the global creditor, having converted a net debt of $3.686 billion in July 1914 to a net credit of $12.562 billion by December

1919. Britain and France owed more than 80 percent of the debt to the United States.[56]

The war induced profound social as well as economic changes. Between 1914 and 1919, America's labor force increased by 1 675 000, while its farm employment fell by 447 000. The overwhelming demand for workers boosted the power and legitimacy of labor unions. Wilson created the National War Labor Board in April 1918 to mobilize and keep labor quiescent. In return for largely keeping a promise not to strike, the unions were allowed to organize freely. By 1920, the unions had twice the membership of a decade earlier; 12 percent of the labor force was unionized. Women and black males also took a step higher on the socioeconomic ladder. As white men were conscripted and sent to France, women and blacks took their place on assembly lines. In 1920, there were 515 000 more blacks in the North than in 1910; most had moved there to fill factory jobs. However, all this economic and social expansion came at an enormous cost. World War I's short-term effects on the United States were harsh. Over 140 000 Americans were killed and a million wounded.[57]

Nonetheless, following World War I, the United States rapidly returned to near "normalcy," as promised by President Warren Harding. America's war boards and their economic controls were quickly dismantled. Four million men were stripped of their uniforms and shown the street; nearly three million people were fired from war industries. Although three million new jobs were created within a year of the war's end, nearly four million workers remained unemployed. Hundreds of millions of dollars worth of natural resources, equipment, factories, ships, and weapons were either warehoused or dumped on markets. As European farmers and workers returned to their jobs, the demand for American goods and services plummeted.[58]

The result of all these forces was a sharp depression between 1920 and 1921 in which prices dropped by 56 percent and about 10 percent of workers were unemployed. What was Washington's response? Unfortunately, Washington's policies exacerbated rather than alleviated the depression. The Federal government's budget deficit in 1919 was $13 billion, an amount that might have helped mitigate the depression's depth. But, eager to return to fiscal conservatism, the Treasury ran a $290 million surplus in 1920 and $500 million surplus in 1921 thus deflating the economy even further.[59]

Eventually American consumers dragged the economy out of that recession as they had previous ones. No product contributed more to the economy's expansion than the automobile. Between 1920 and 1929, the number of cars on the road jumped from 8.1 million to 23.1 million, and trucks from 1.2 million to 3.5 million. The demand for these vehicles spurred a range of related industries including oil, rubber, steel, glass, concrete, and machine tools. The number of miles of paved roads jumped from 369 000 to 662 000 between 1920 and 1929, of which the Federal, state, and local governments contributed $2 billion or about 2 percent of gross national product (GNP). By 1929, the automobile industry accounted for 12.7 percent of total manufacturing, 7.1 percent of factory labor, and 8.7 percent of factory wages. No one was more responsible for the automobile industry's expansion than Henry Ford who improved assembly line production. Over at General Motors, Alfred Sloan and Pierre Dupont innovated the multidivisional corporation. Similar advances elsewhere occurred in accounting and finance. These innovations spread throughout the corporate world, widening profits and production.[60]

Throughout the twentieth century's first decades, American industry steadily shifted from steam- to electricity-based energy. Between 1919 and 1929, the proportion of electricity to total power used by manufacturers rose from 55 percent to 82 percent. The electric power grid woven across the nation sparked a revolution in electrical appliances. During the 1920s, Americans filled their homes with a range of labor-saving electrical devices such as vacuum cleaners, washing machines, refrigerators, heaters, irons, stoves, and so on. By the decade's end, most homes had several of these products. This consumer boom was further stimulated by modern mass advertizing, which blossomed during the 1920s. People increasingly bought cleverly packaged rather than bulk products, and paid higher prices for the privilege.[61]

What was the government's role in a decade of prosperity popularly believed to have been driven by "marketplace magic?" Although its deflationary policy had deepened the 1921–2 recession, Washington's economic initiatives were considerable and largely positive. The industrial policies of the 1920s largely centered on promoting exports. The Webb–Pomerene Act of 1918 allowed exporters to operate free of antitrust laws, and thus encouraged them to collude to boost foreign sales. The Edge Act of 1919 offered incentives for creditors to lend money to foreigners to buy American products. Washington boosted America's industrialization by imposing ever-higher tariffs, such as the Emergency Tariff Act of 1921 and the Fordney–McCumber Act of 1922.

Between Teddy Roosevelt's last year in the White House in 1908 and Franklin Roosevelt's first year in 1933, all of the presidents pursued mostly Jeffersonian natural resource policies of giving away public wealth to private interests. They backed away from the careful management of the nation's forests and added little or nothing to the nation's parks, wildlife refuges, forests, or monuments. There were a few conservation victories. In 1916, Congress passed and Wilson signed a bill creating the National Park Service. The 1920 Mineral Leasing Act mandated that henceforth public land would be leased rather than sold to miners. Neither environmental or conservationist Hamiltonians had an impact on public policy during the dozen years of Republican rule from 1921 to 1933.

Hamiltonians mounted one major campaign. Water pollution can destroy the livelihood of commercial fishermen and the repose of the Sunday angler alike. The Izaak Walton League was the first environmental organization to protest the steady destruction of the nation's waterways. It sponsored an assessment which revealed that by the late 1920s, 85 percent of American streams were polluted and only 30 percent of all municipalities treated their waste. The League used its report to lobby Congress for tougher pollution regulations. Predictably, industry fought back. The American Iron and Steel Institute, Manufacturing Chemists Association, and American Petroleum Institute banded together to argue that the nation's streams were the nation's natural sewers to which all Americans deserved unrestricted access. The president and Congress agreed and rejected the League's recommendations.

Nonetheless, no Commerce Secretary who preceded him and perhaps none since has been as tireless a champion for American economic development and exports as Herbert Hoover. As Commerce Secretary between 1921 and 1928, Hoover reorganized the Commerce Department's Bureau of Foreign and Domestic Commerce along commodity lines, "staffing it with men from the export industries. The agency thus became an associational system for gathering and disseminating commercial intelligence and for dealing with foreign governments and cartels. A cooperating industrial committee worked in conjuncture with each commodity division in efforts to develop and expand markets." To boost commercial research and development, Hoover enacted similar reforms in the Bureau of Standards whose

Building and Housing Division became the nucleus of a network of cooperating committees and study groups, each of them tied to the major trade and professional associations in the housing field, each of them undertaking educational campaigns in an effort to overcome the bottlenecks blocking 'modernization' and 'rationalization.' The Census Bureau, the Bureau of Customs Statistics, the Inter-American High Commission (designed to promote trade in Latin America), the United States Coal Commission, the Federal Oil Conservation Board, the Northeastern Super Power Committee, and still other government agencies, including the Treasury and Labor departments, felt the guiding, transforming hand of the secretary of commerce. Essentially, Hoover made that department an 'economic general staff,' 'business correspondence school,' and national coordinator, all rolled into one. By implementing its plans through nearly four hundred coordinating committees and numerous private groups, and by appealing to science, community, and morality to bridge the gap between between public and private interests, the agency managed to avoid bureaucratic dictation and legal coercion and to preserve the essential of American individualism.[62]

All of these measures worked wonders with America's economic development and exports. Between 1923 and 1928, the trade surplus rose from $400 million to $1.09 billion.[63]

Other government initiatives contributed to the nation's development. As in previous eras, public spending on infrastructure was an unsung but essential aid to development. Federal funds for highway construction alone rose from $70 million in 1918 to $750 million in 1930. The government also invested more in education during this decade, with expenditures rising from 1.17 percent to 2.22 percent of GNP between 1920 and 1928. The percentage of high school graduates among seventeen-year-olds rose from 16.3 percent to 26.2 percent. The number of male undergraduates obtaining university degrees rose from 48 622 to 111 161, while females attaining degrees rose from 16 642 to 48 869. By 1928, 24 percent of the entire population was in school.[64]

Throughout the decade, Washington was hostile to labor unions and immigrants alike. The National Association of Manufacturing and American Farm Bureau Federation were the leading trade associations to pressure governments against enacting labor protection laws. Governments at all levels responded with hostility to organized labor. No branch of government was more hostile to union goals than the courts. In 1916, Congress enacted the nation's first child labor law; within a year, the Supreme Court ruled it unconstitutional in Hammer *v.* Dagenhart. In 1918, Congress passed a similar law only to have the Supreme Court strike it down in Bailey *v.* Drexel Furniture Company (1922). Although the 1914 Clayton Act specifically removed unions from antitrust laws, courts continued to rule that strikes blocked interstate commerce and were thus illegal. The Supreme Court ruled in Adkins *v.* Children's Hospital (1923) that minimum wage laws were illegal. As a result of such rulings, during the 1920s union membership declined from its peak of 5 million in 1920 to around 3–4 million in 1929. Nonetheless, labor did make some progress. By 1929, 11 states had enacted pension laws and 43 states had enacted workers' compensation laws.

Workers, in turn, helped pressure the government to curb immigration which was driving down the price of labor. Immigration dropped considerably during the decade as the 1924 National Origin Act cut those allowed in to one-fourth the prewar total. Wages thus rose for Americans and immigrants alike.

Several worsening problems clouded the economic expansion of the 1920s. Washington had trouble adjusting to America's new role as creditor for the global economy. The industrial countries were locked in a vicious debt circle. Britain, France, and other allies owed $9.6 billion to the United States, a value equal to one-sixth of America's economy, but tied their repayments to the $33 billion in reparations they demanded from Germany, payable at $375 million a year through 1925 and $900 million a year thereafter. Throughout the early 1920s, Germany suffered hyperinflation and depression, and thus could not fulfill its reparation payments. In an attempt to wring more payments from Germany, France occupied the industrial Ruhr valley in 1923. But the occupation only worsened Germany's economic crisis.

In 1924, the United States responded to the payments problem with the Dawes Plan, in which the industrial countries would lower their interest rates to stimulate growth and reduce the debt burden. In addition, the United States loaned Germany $800 million so that it could pay off some of its reparations. But even this was not enough to jumpstart Germany's economy. The entire world was suffering a liquidity crisis which only the United States was capable of easing. Between 1924 and 1929, the United States pumped over $6.4 billion into the global economy, with most funds going to Europe and Latin America.[65]

At home, although unemployment averaged only 5.1 percent

between 1923 and 1929, the growing prosperity was poorly distributed. The gap between rich and poor widened steadily throughout the decade. The income of the richest 1 percent of the population rose from 13 percent of GNP in 1920 to 19 percent in 1929.[66]

While most economic sectors revived in 1921, the farm economy fell into an ever-worsening depression which would drag on for another two decades. Several interrelated forces depressed farming. Between 1914 and 1919, farmers had responded to the increased global demand by expanding their production acreage by 38 million. Farm income doubled during those years from $649 million to $1.395 billion. Most farmers financed this expansion with debt – by 1920 farmers owed $8.4 billion. Once Europe's farms resumed peak production, the demand for American foodstuffs withered. As this occurred, American farmers expanded their production to boost their declining incomes. The result was an oversupply of food in the United States which further depressed land and commodity prices. To worsen matters, farm production mechanized rapidly with the number of tractors rising from 85 000 in 1918 to 827 000 by 1929. The productivity gains put tens of thousands of farm laborers and draft animals out of work. Fields that once produced oats and hay for animals were converted to other crops which further swelled the surplus and depressed prices. Regional blights such as the boll weevil for cotton, Texas Fever for cattle, and mosaic disease for sugar bedeviled those farmers throughout the decade. The development of nylon and rayon cut into natural fiber production. Many farmers worked other people's land; in the South, 55 percent of all farms were worked by tenants. Tenant farmers had little incentive or capital to improve their production. The depression chopped away 60 percent of farm income between 1919 and 1921. Farming declined rapidly as a percentage of the economy, from 18.5 percent in 1919 to 9.5 percent in 1928.[67]

Proposals to alleviate the depressed farm sector failed to become policy. Although Washington raised tariffs to protect American farmers from foreign competition, it failed to promote agricultural exports. In 1924 and 1928, Senator Charles McNary and Representative Gilbert Haugen succeeded in introducing and getting Congress to pass bills that would use price supports to restore "parity" between the prices received and paid by farmers. President Coolidge vetoed both bills.

Other sectors also declined during the decade. As automobiles and trucks became more numerous, railroads became less important in transportation. Railroad passengers dropped from 47 million in 1920 to 34 million in 1927. The lumber industry expanded during the 1920s with a housing boom. Unfortunately, constructors overbuilt. By the decade's end, there were more houses than buyers. Lumber products dropped in value from $311 million in 1928 to $173.2 million in 1929 on the Great Depression's eve. The automobile market was also saturated; production peaked at 622 000 in March 1929 then dropped to 416 000 in September, dragging down with it all related industries. The nation's overall industrial production dropped by 20 percent between August and October 1929, while prices fell 7.5 percent. Amidst this contraction, many American were deep in debt to banks and other creditors. As unemployment rose, increasing numbers of people stopped buying anything more than the essentials, thus exacerbating the depression.[68]

What might have been a recession became the Great Depression when a speculative bubble swelling on the New York stock market finally burst on 24 October 1929. Shares traded on the exchange had more than quadrupled during the 1920s, from 236 million in 1923 to 1.125 billion on 1 January 1929. Mergers drove much of this expansion, as new stocks were issued to pay for the purchases. Cross-holdings among corporations became increasingly common as corporate leaders sought to cement alliances and diversify risks. Brokers loaned investors the money at margin to play the market. With the stock market surging ever upward, with periodic minor corrections, the loans seemed like safe bets. Although in 1929, commercial banks only owned about 1 percent or $1.2 billion of outstanding shares, they had loaned out over $8.3 billion to speculators. By the summer of 1929, brokers' loans amounted to over $7 billion. About 1 million people or 8 percent of the population owned stocks; about 500 000 investors owned 75–85 percent of all stocks. As John Kenneth Galbraith put it, "the striking thing about the stock market speculation in 1929 was not the massiveness of the participation. Rather it was the way it became central to the culture."[69]

The stock market was clearly overvalued, with most of the nation's largest investors grossly overextended. The Federal Reserve could have dampened the speculation by raising the discount rate. Instead, in 1927, it lowered the discount rate from 4 to 3.5 percent and bought government securities, all to encourage Britain to stay on the gold standard. Over the next two years, the Fed assumed a strictly hands-off policy despite the ever-growing speculative bubble, relying solely on pressurizing its member banks to curb their loans. And even there it sent mixed messages. In February 1929, the board issued the *laissez-faire* statement that it had, "no disposition to assume authority to intervene with the loan practices of member banks."[70] When the Fed finally did raise the discount rate in August 1929, it helped convert many speculators from wariness to near panic that the bubble would soon burst.

The panic came two months later. On 24 October 1929, "Black Thursday," the stock market plunged. Altogether, between September 1929 and July 1932, the New York stock market's value declined from $89.668 billion to $15.663 billion and the industrial average from 452 to 58. In those three years, industrial production dropped by half, farm prices by 60 percent, and investments by 90 percent. One of four workers was unemployed. The most serious immediate effect was a domino effect of bank failures. Businesses and households dashed to their banks to withdraw their savings while the reserves held out. Within two months, 608 banks with $532 million in assets had failed. Banks and other creditors, in turn, recalled their loans. A chain reaction of bankruptcies spread across the country.[71]

What was the White House's response to the stock market crash and ever-deepening depression? Ironically, President Herbert Hoover was not the pure free marketeer he is commonly believed to have been. By all accounts, Hoover was a brilliant, dedicated humanitarian who espoused a "cooperative individualism" or "capitalism with a conscience" in which businesses would voluntarily work together to alleviate socioeconomic problems. According to Hoover, America's economy and society "was passing from a period of extremely individualistic action into a period of associational activities."[72]

Unfortunately, the man who had been such a dazzling Commerce Secretary proved to be a inadequate president. At first, he tried pressurizing corporate leaders into cutting back profits rather than wages or jobs with the moral argument that public and private interests must be equally served by those with economic power. Yet, he refused to back his moral assertions with power. Without the threat of governmental sanctions, corporate leaders saved their own skins rather than those of their fellow Americans. Hoover did cut taxes by 1 percent and boosted the public works budget from $2.4 billion in 1929 to $2.8 billion in 1930. However, these efforts were overwhelmed by the fall in construction from $9 billion to $6.3 billion. He also succeeded in getting Congress to create a

Reconstruction Finance Corporation (RFC) which could loan entrepreneurs money for developmental projects, the Farm Board to ease the farm crisis, and Home Loan Banks system to help people with mortgages. Washington's most important act was passage of the 1932 Glass–Steagall Act which separated the banking and securities industries.

Despite these efforts, Hoover and the economy remained prisoners of *laissez-faire* economic idealism. He undercut his mildly positive actions through a series of policies which deepened the depression. Not only did the Federal Reserve refuse to lower the discount rate to pump money into the economy, the Treasury actually insisted on preserving a balanced budget! Hoover succeeded in balancing the budget in each of his four years, and actually raised taxes in 1932 in order to do so. To this end, he vetoed the veteran's bonus bill which could have put more money in people's pockets. Hoover rejected direct relief to the unemployed, poor, homeless, and hungry because he believed it would undermine private aid efforts and individual responsibility.[73]

Perhaps most damaging was the Smoot–Hawley Act of 1930 which hiked the average tariff from 25 percent to 50 percent. Protectionism, however, could not isolate the United States from the global economy. Other countries retaliated by raising their own tariffs. Although the United States maintained a trade surplus, its exports dwindled. Britain abandoned the gold standard in September 1931. Anticipating that the United States would follow, investors converted their dollar holdings into gold. America's gold stock dropped by $725 million in six weeks during September and October. The Federal Reserve responded by raising the discount rate twice in October. This sparked an even worse wave of bank failures – 1860 banks with deposits of $414 million died between August 1931 and February 1932. Money and confidence plunged even further. Altogether, over 9000 banks worth $2.5 billion disappeared between 1929 and 1933. The Federal Reserve did not begin an expansionary policy until April 1932. By then, it was too little too late. Within three years, global trade had plummeted by two-thirds. Bank failures multiplied around the world. Foreigners defaulted on their loans from the United States, undermining yet more American banks.[74]

Was the Great Depression inevitable? As in other times, public policy held the key to economic prosperity or calamity. Most analysts would agree with Stuart Bruchey that had the Federal Reserve System prevented or moderated the large decline in the money supply between 1929 and 1933, it is reasonable to believe that both the severity and the duration of the Great Depression would have been reduced.[75]

All along, Hoover's deflationary policies overwhelmed his positive measures of pumping more money into the economy.

LEGACY

America's two worst traumas – the Civil War and Great Depression – bookend the 72 years from 1860 to 1932. During that time, America's economy rapidly grew, industrialized, and urbanized. The United States was transformed from a secondary player in the global economy into the world's greatest industrial, trade, and financial power.

Industrial policies largely aided and sometimes impeded this transformation. Washington's give-away of public lands helped bind the country with railroads, farms, mines, and ranches that might have otherwise never existed. Tariffs helped nurture American industries into global champions; without protection, inexpensive and better-quality imports would have wiped out those infant industries. Government's economic role expanded in response to market failures. An income tax was established in 1911 to help pay for increased commitments and fill the revenue gap as tariff rates fell. The Federal Reserve was established in 1913 to regulate the banking industry and smooth business cycles. As America's corporations began trading and investing in the world's far corners, the flag inevitably followed. Washington frequently sent in the marines to counter foreign threats to American economic interests. During World War I, Washington asserted unprecedented powers over the economy, and it never expanded as quickly or efficiently.

Yet from 1929 through 1932, all of these expanded powers and policies of government were incapable of preventing what could have been a recession from becoming the Great Depression. Economic management was neither an art nor science. Regardless, the Hoover White House performed it badly. It would take the "bold experimentation" of the subsequent Roosevelt administration before the modern presidency and its powers to manage the economy blossomed.

5 Industrialization Bound, 1933–80

The nearly half-century from 1932 through 1980 represented the triumph of Hamiltonianism. Throughout those decades the government's role in the economy expanded steadily to overcome challenges posed by the Great Depression; World War II; the Cold War; the persistence of poverty, ignorance, ill-health, and racism amidst plenty; environmental destruction; and the space, education, and science races, to name the more prominent.

Few questioned that expansion. President Franklin Roosevelt's policies to fight the Great Depression and World War II decisively shifted public expectations about the government's duty to maintain prosperity, help the disadvantaged, and defend the free world. Roosevelt's New Deal policies put millions of people back to work and transformed entire regions from economic backwardness to dynamism. America was never more productive than during World War II when Washington planned the economy and outright controlled entire industries.

When the guns finally fell silent in August 1945, Washington quickly demobilized its war machine. Within 18 months, however, it was recreating an ever-larger, financially voracious military – industrial complex to fight the Cold War. In tandem, Washington targeted for development or protection an ever-expanding realm of other economic sectors, regions, firms, classes, races, ecosystems, and sometimes even species. All of these industrial policies would have been unthinkable before Franklin Roosevelt took office. Of the presidents since then, none has built more upon Roosevelt's legacy than Lyndon Johnson with his Great Society welfare programs. Yet, whether the president was by inclination more a Hamiltonian or Jeffersonian, each from Roosevelt through Carter has been caught up in the new, prevailing American belief that government's central duty is to work with its citizens to fulfill an expanding agenda of national goals. Each president contributed his own industrial policies, institutions, and initiatives toward that Hamiltonian vision of government-nurtured national development.

However, each policy that involved greater government management of the economy, whether it meant fighting depressions, mobilizing for war, promoting civil rights, protecting the environment, ameliorating conditions among the poor, uneducated, and sick, stimulating the global economy, bailing out a Lockheed or Chrysler, and so on, was dogged by controversy and entrenched opposition by unconvinced Jeffersonians. The relative success or shortcomings of each program varied considerably. Costs mounted steadily. In 1932, the Federal budget accounted for only 3 percent of the economy; by 1980 it had soared to 25 percent. During the 1970s, the nation's development slowed from such forces as growing international competition and the quadrupling of oil prices. Socioeconomic problems such as crime, drugs, out-of-wedlock births, and crumbling cities and infrastructure worsened. No matter how much they may have personally benefited from various policies, increasing numbers of Americans saw government as the problem rather than the solution. The ideological tug-of-war between Hamiltonians and Jeffersonians began to tilt toward the latter.

THE NEW DEAL AND GLOBAL LEADERSHIP: 1933–45

Upon winning the presidency in November 1932, Franklin Roosevelt faced a national crisis that had sunk his predecessor's political fortunes – the Great Depression. The national economy was two-thirds and trade half the size it had been four years earlier; one in four workers was unemployed; millions of Americans were poverty-stricken. America was trapped in a vicious cycle of bankruptcies, mass unemployment, declining production, and limited business and household income and spending.

The reason why the economy remained mired in depression was clear. Free markets and the private sector had failed miserably to maintain prosperity. Indeed, the very logic of markets forced investors and consumers alike during the economic collapse to hoard rather than spend their money, thus deepening and prolonging the depression. The solution was for the very visible hand of government to do what the invisible hand of market magic refused to do – spend money.

During the 1932 election campaign, Roosevelt promised to return prosperity to America. A landslide victory in which he won 472 electoral votes to his rival's 59 certainly gave him the political mandate to rule. Like his distant cousin Teddy, Franklin deplored the fact that "many hard lessons have taught us the human waste that results from lack of planning." Within months of becoming president, Roosevelt pushed through Congress a set of new Federal policies and institutions known collectively as the New Deal and designed to pump money into the stalled economy and get Americans back to work. An alphabet soup of institutions – FDIC, RFC, AAA, TVA, CCC, WPA, SCS, etc. – was created either to provide direct relief for the poverty-stricken or jobs for the able-bodied.

How well did the New Deal fulfill its promise to restore prosperity and reform American capitalism's deep flaws? The depression did not get worse under Roosevelt. The economy steadily improved from 1933 until 1937 before it dropped again, when the government briefly tried to balance the budget, only to resume its slow plodding upward until America's participation in World War II brought full employment. Yet, the policy shift from Hoover to Roosevelt "was not from laissez faire to a managed economy, but rather from one attempt at management, that through informal business–government cooperation, to another more formal and coercive attempt."[1]

In fact, contrary to popular belief, when he entered the Oval Office Roosevelt had few ideas about how to combat the depression. Although Roosevelt's economic management certainly surpassed that of his predecessors, his understanding of how a modern economy worked was incomplete. For example, like his predecessors, Roosevelt wrongly assumed that the Federal budget deficit was the root of the nation's economic evils. During the 1932 campaign he had blasted Hoover for his relatively small Federal budget deficit. A week after taking office, Roosevelt declared that the 1933 $1.6 billion deficit "has contributed to the recent collapse of our banking structure. It has added to the ranks of the unemployed."[2] Like Hoover, Roosevelt believed the budget should be balanced even during a depression; fortunately, unlike Hoover, he mostly failed to do so. As Bruchey put it, "Roosevelt was a bold experimenter and a compassionate man, yet one who lacked a coherent program for economic recovery."[3] Roosevelt was certainly honest about his own ignorance. During the 1932 campaign, he called for "bold, persistent experimentation. It is common sense to take a method and try it. If it fails, admit it frankly and try another."[4]

He quickly acted on his inaugural declation that Americans had "nothing to fear but fear itself." It was clear that the economy would never rebound unless the nation's banking and financial system was restored to a sound foundation. On 6 March 1933, Roosevelt declared a bank holiday, using powers granted under the 1917 Trading with the Enemy Act to suspend banking and gold transactions. The Treasury Department would then examine each bank's books and grant a license to reopen only if it passed stringent requirements. Of the 17 800 banks operating when he imposed the holiday, he allowed only 12 000 to reopen when he revoked the suspension on 9 March. Eventually he allowed a further 3000 to resume business, but ended up shutting down 2800. He would later use the Reconstruction Finance Corporation (RFC) to lend $2 billion to 8500 endangered banks, and an additional $1 billion to purchase capital stocks in 6000 banks. In all, the government owned one-third of the banking system's assets by the end of 1933.[5] On 9 March, Congress passed and the president signed the Emergency Banking Act which authorized Roosevelt's declared bank holiday, and also allowed the RFC to buy the stock of shaky banks, the Federal Reserve to lend to non-member banks, and the requirement that banks could only open after they received a government license.

These measures were reinforced on 16 June 1933 when Congress strengthened the previous year's Glass–Steagall Banking Act by creating the Federal Deposit Insurance Corporation (FDIC) to which all Federal Reserve member banks were required to belong. The Act also allowed branch banking. By the summer of 1934, 97 percent of all commercial banks were insured. Glass–Steagall also separated the banking and securities industries, and required banks to specialize in either deposits or investments. The Federal Reserve and its dozen affliliates received enhanced powers to regulate the industry. The 1934 Securities Exchange Act established the Securities Exchange Commission to regulate the stock and bond industry.

In 1933, the president got Congress to establish the Reconstruction Finance Corporation (RFC) to oversee the mortgage industry. The RFC was perhaps the New Deal's most effective industrial policy tool. It lent more than $1.5 billion to farmers, $1 billion to 89 railroads, $848 million to 12 000 home-buyers, and $90 million to 133 insurance firms.[6]

Roosevelt also acted decisively to prevent the continued flight of gold from the United States. On 7 March, the Treasury Secretary announced that all member banks had to turn over all gold or gold certificates to the Federal Reserve. The next day, Roosevelt prohibited not only any export but even private ownership of gold. On 19 April 1933, the White House announced that the United States was abandoning the gold standard. The 1934 Gold Reserve Act raised the price of an ounce of gold from $20.67 to $35 and reduced the dollar's gold content by 40 percent. This encouraged other countries to sell gold to the United States, tripling the nation's gold stocks from $4.036 billion in 1933 to $12.700 billion in 1937. By devaluing the dollar, Roosevelt boosted exports and reduced competitive imports.

Roosevelt also tried to rescue the farm economy. On 12 May 1933, Congress passed the Agricultural Adjustment Act (AAA) to rescue beleaguered farmers. The AAA established price supports for a variety of crops. On 16 June 1933, the Farm Credit Act provided for short- and medium-term loans for farmers to invest in production and marketing, and long-term loans to mortgage farms.

Nowhere was the farm crisis worse than in the "dust bowl" across much of the Great Plains. In 1934, the National Resources Board reported that years of drought and erosion had largely destroyed 35 million acres of farmland and severely degraded an additional 100 million acres. From Texas to North Dakota, hundreds of thousands of people fled the dustbowl. In 1935, Roosevelt created the US Soil Conservation Service (SCS) within the Agriculture Department, which taught farmers how to preserve rather than destroy their soils, and provided subsidies for improvements. The SCS helped farmers manage their soil more effectively through crop rotation, contour planting, and the elimination of planting on marginal lands. To curb the destruction by ranchers of the nation's grasslands, the 1934 Taylor Grazing Act regulated grazing on public lands for the first time.

The Supreme Court continued its tradition of striking down progressive legislation. In 1936, the Supreme Court ruled the AAA unconstitutional in United States *v*. Bulter. Congress rewrote the AAA and passed it in February 1936 as the Soil Conservation and Domestic Allotment Act, then reinforced it with the 1938 Agricultural Adjustment Act. As important to the farm economy was the 1935 Rural Electrification Act which literally electrified rural America; 90 percent of farms had no electricity when the bill was passed; 90 percent did 15 years later.

The New Deal's most sweeping measures targeted industry for revival. In May 1933, Roosevelt submitted the National Industrial Recovery Act (NIRA) to Congress, which passed it on 16 June.

Never before, even during World War I, had the Federal government asserted greater powers over the economy. Under NIRA, the government and various industries acted as partners to promote both public and private goods. In return for the abolition of child labor, the establishment of minimum wages, and maximum work hours, industries were allowed to collude on price levels for their products – to be approved by the government. By May 1935, Washington had approved 557 basic and 189 supplemental "codes of fair competition" which affected 95 percent of all industrial workers.[7] The NIRA's legacy was mixed. It did boost production, and improve work conditions and wages, but at the price of higher prices and layoffs. In May 1935, the Supreme Court ruled the NIRA unconstitutional in Schechter Poultry Corp. *v.* United States.

The president also acted decisively on his campaign pledge to improve home ownership, work conditions, and wages. In June 1933, Congress passed the Home Owners Refinancing Act which created the Home Owners Loan Corporation, initially capitalized with $200 million and authorized to issue $2 billion in bonds to finance home mortgages. With a stroke of Roosevelt's pen millions of Americans who formerly could not afford a home were suddenly eligible. As the housing industry revived it became an engine of growth for related sectors. In 1935, Roosevelt addressed the needs of the retired by getting Congress to pass the Social Security Act which provided retirement money to those aged 65 years or older. That same year, Congress passed the National Labor Relations Act (Wagner Act) which included many of NIRA's progressive labor laws and a National Labor Relations Board to ensure that industry complied. Congress reinforced these measures in 1938 when it passed the Fair Labor Standard Act which granted labor unions full powers to organize, bargain, and strike, along with a 44-hour working week, child labor restrictions, and a minimum wage. These laws had a dramatic affect on union membership – between 1933 and 1941, the union's ranks rose from 2.5 million to 11 million. The new unions and their members were not necessarily united in goals or strategies. In 1938, the industrial unions broke away from the American Federation of Labor (AFL) to form the Congress of Industrial Organizations (CIO).[8]

Also of deep concern to Roosevelt was the plight of the nation's jobless and homeless, of which private charity succored only a few. Unlike Hoover, Roosevelt believed that the government must intervene when the private sector fails. He tried to save people from poverty and put them back to work through the 1933 Federal Emergency Relief Administration (FERA) and Public Works Administration (PWA) Acts. Other job and relief bills included the Civil Works Administration (CWA), Works Progress Administration (WPA), Civilian Conservation Corps (CCC), and National Youth Administration (NYA). The CCC mobilized an army of previously jobless men to build the nation's infrastructure and conserve its natural resources. Between 1933 and 1942, over 2 million men participated in CCC projects. FERA eventually transferred $500 million to states and cities to help the needy. The CWA provided work to the unemployed at the minimum wage of 40¢ an hour, and those workers built or improved more than 40 000 schools, 3500 playgrounds and athletic fields, 500 000 miles of roads, 40 000 schools, and 1000 airports. During its lifetime, the WPA spent $10 billion and employed 3.5 million workers to build or improve 5900 schools, 2500 hospitals, 1000 airports, and 13,000 playgrounds. By 1934, nearly 28 million people in 7.9 million homes were receiving some kind of government relief.[9]

Dams were the most important of Roosevelt's public works projects. He sought to achieve several objectives through his dam building. First, massive public works stimulate the economy by putting people to work directly on the project and, indirectly, through all the goods and services the project demands. Second, the dams create infrastructure such as electrical, transportation, and communiction grids that improve people's lives and provide greater economic opportunities. Third, the irrigation increases farm production. The centerpiece of this dam-building was the Tennessee Valley Authority (TVA) Act's passage on 18 May 1933. The TVA converted the Tennesee River watershed system into a series of hydroelectric dams, irrigation systems, navigation improvements, and flood controls that transformed that region from mass poverty to increased prosperity.

Applauding Roosevelt's conservation measures and urging him to do much more were a group of new environmental leaders such as Aldo Leopold, Ansel Adams, David Brower, Howard Zahniser, Robert Marshall, and Sigurd Olsen, and new national organizations such as the Izaak Walton League (1922) and the Wilderness Society (1935). Environmentalists steadily built up their philosophical foundations as well as their national organizations throughout the interwar era. Leopold, Marshall, and Adams in particular expanded the philosophy and proposals of environmentalism with lyrical writings and art. Through his haunting photographs and trenchant essays,

Adams popularized the perspectives of his fellow environmentalists. His book, *Sierra Nevada: The John Muir Trail* (1938) helped shift the Roosevelt White House's conception of national parks. When the Roosevelt White House pushed through a bill designating Kings Canyon National Park in 1940, no development, including roads, was allowed in the park itself. Adams could be just as eloquent with words as with photographs. When criticized for wanting to "lock up wilderness" as "elitist," Adams replied

> Is it a matter of snobbery that the priest does not permit the sale of peanuts in the aisles of the church? Is it snobbery that the Metropolitan Museum of Art objects to my playing my portable radio in the Egyptian Room?[10]

Despite this growth of environmental groups and eloquent leaders, their political power was dwarfed by more traditional Jeffersonian forces. Policy battles were largely the outcome of struggles between Jeffersonians and conservationists, with environmentalists fighting both on many issues. It would be decades before environmentalists began decisively shaping the policy agenda.

So what was the New Deal's legacy? How much did Roosevelt's programs alleviate the Great Depression in the short-term and squelch the chance of such a depression devastating the United States since then? Roosevelt's "bold, persistent experimentation" ultimately worked. In expanding government's role, Roosevelt succeeded in alleviating the vicious depressions that ravaged most Americans every decade or so. The socioeconomic safety net and countercyclical macroeconomic policies that Roosevelt pioneered have meant that today's recessions are relatively mild and brief. Roosevelt's policies of a half century ago today allow a greater percentage of the population to enjoy prosperous, healthy, freer lives. When Roosevelt took office, most people worked 10–12 hours, six days a week, 90 percent of rural homes lacked electricity, most of the elderly existed in poverty, many children worked, only about two-thirds of Americans graduated from high school, factory jobs were dangerous, and "Jim Crow" laws excluded blacks from voting. To varying extents, his New Deal policies alleviated these problems.

Yet, it was America's participation in World War II rather than the New Deal which was decisive in transforming the economy from depression to dynamism. The United States was little more prepared for World War II than it was World War I. Throughout the

1930s, Washington watched helplessly as Japan brutally conquered first Manchuria (1931), went to war against China (1937), and took over Indochina (1940–1), Italy attacked Ethiopia (1935), and Germany marched into the Rhineland (1936), Austria (1938), Czechoslovakia (1938–9), Poland (1939), and France and the Benelux countries (1940). Among the other industrial great powers, only Britain still held out, assailed constantly by German air and sea power. By the summer of 1940, the United States faced fascist, imperialist threats from across both the Pacific and Atlantic oceans.

Just as the United States had done little to allay and much to exacerbate the depresssion, it was similarly vacillating in the face of Japanese and German aggression. The Hoover White House's response to Japan's takeover of Manchuria was simply not to recognize it. Determined not to allow the country to be dragged into another world war, the isolationist majority in Congress passed a neutrality act in 1935 that prevented the United States from sending arms to any side in a war, even to victims of aggression. Though the neutrality act tied his diplomatic hands, Roosevelt refused to veto the bill for fear it would alienate his New Deal allies.

Even after 1939, as Germany overran most of Europe and beseiged Britain, Roosevelt had to be careful not to arouse congressional isolationists. In November 1939, he was able to have the neutrality act amended so that victims of aggression could pay cash for arms. Gradually he mobilized the United States for war. In May 1940, he reinstituted the National Defense Advisory Commision (NDAC); in August 1940, the Defense Plant Corporation (DPC); in December 1940, the Office of Production Management (OPM), in April 1941, the Office of Price Administration (OPA); and in August 1941, the Supply Priorities and Allocation Board (SPAB). The War and Navy departments wanted much more sweeping national controls over the economy, but Roosevelt rejected their repeated requests.[11] In January 1941, Roosevelt created the most powerful administration yet, the War Production Board (WPB), "delegating to it all the president's powers over industry, production, raw materials, factories, machine tools, priorities, allocations, and rationing."[12] The board included the production experts from the War, Navy, and Commerce departments, and the Board of Economic Warfare. Washington offered carrots as well as sticks to mobilize the economy behind the war, including an accelerated depreciation tax of 20 percent for defense industries, twice that of other industries. On 8 December 1941, when the United States finally declared war on

Japan the day after its attacks on Pearl Harbor and the Philippines, military spending composed 16 percent of America's economy and the bureaucratic infrastructure was in place to wage total war.

Yet despite such requests, incentives, and regulations, America's industrialists hesitated to invest heavily in equipment for fear that it would lead to overcapacity and depression after the war. Altogether, about $25 billion worth of new military plants and equipment was built during the war. Of this, the government supplied about 75 percent of all war production, and then leased it to private investors to run. The RFC supplied about $8 billion of the military industry, the DPC $7 billion, the War Department $5.4 billion, the Navy Department $2.9 billion, the Maritime Commission $600 million, and various other departments and agencies much lesser amounts. The government outright owned 90 percent of the aircraft, synthetic rubber, and magnesium industries, and 55 percent of the alumium and machine tool industries.[13] Washington built not just most of the factories, but most of the infrastructure as well, including a nation-wide web of natural gas and oil pipelines, refineries, and storage tanks, port facilities, warehouses, electricity plants, and military bases.

World War II brought the United States back to full employment. The jobless rate dropped from 14.5 percent in 1940 to 4.7 percent in 1942 and 1.9 percent in 1943. By the war's end, the Federal government employed about 2 million civilians and 10 million soldiers. The Selective Service System and War Manpower Commission mobilized most of this vast workforce. In addition, the civilian labor force increased by 5 million. As in World War I, women filled in the gaps in civilian employment, eventually contributing over 11 million of the workforce.[14]

Never before or since has the government managed the economy more carefully. The government not only built and ran entire industries, but imposed strict wage and price controls, and rationed many goods and services. Strikes were forbidden. Even the freedom to switch jobs was limited. The White House financed the war in several ways. As in World War I, it sold liberty bonds. In 1942, it increased the excess profit tax from 60 to 90 percent.

America's war effort further concentrated industry and agriculture. Between 1940 and 1945, 324 000 firms or about 10 percent of the nation's total disappeared either in bankruptcy or absorption by larger firms. Meanwhile, the military and industrial ranks were filled not just by the previously unemployed, but by 5.7 million people from the farm sector which increased its production through expanded use of tractors, cropland, and fertilizer. Farm income rose from $4.5 million in 1940 to $12.3 million in 1945, while farm debts fell from $6.6 million to $4.9 million. In all, the Great Depression and World War II were great socioeconomic levelers. The percentage of national wealth owned by the richest 1 percent of the population plunged from 19 percent in 1929 to 1 percent by 1945![15]

Throughout the Great Depression and World War II, Roosevelt had understood that American prosperity depended on global prosperity, and that only the United States had the economic power to convince other states to abandon protectionism for free trade. In 1934, Roosevelt got Congress to pass the Reciprocal Trade Act which empowered the president to negotiate trade treaties with other countries. But the most important step toward restoring the global trade system occurred at Bretton Woods, New Hampshire in 1944 when the representatives of 44 countries joined to negotiate two new international organizations, the International Monetary Fund (IMF) and the International Bank for Reconstruction and Development (IRBD, World Bank). The new global economy would be built on a gold standard in which the price of gold was fixed at $35 an ounce, and other currencies were tied to the dollar. Foreigners could convert their dollars into American gold. To keep their exchange rates fixed, central banks bought and sold currencies. By the time of Roosevelt death, the New Deal, World War II programs, and global economic initiatives had revolutionized America's political economy and its management.

POSTWAR PROSPERITY: 1945–73

For a quarter century after World War II until 1973, America's economy, middle class, and real wages expanded while inflation and unemployment remained mostly low. How did Washington contribute to this prosperous era? Roosevelt's "bold experimentation" resulted in macroeconomic tools powerful enough to smooth business cycles and a social safety net to help many of the needy. While presidents Truman, Eisenhower, and Kennedy did not appreciably add to America's nascent welfare state, they did not threaten Roosevelt's legacy. While each president tried, often unsuccessfully, to balance budgets, they adequately funded existing programs. President Johnson's "Great Society" programs did greatly expand the welfare state. America's economy never expanded in peacetime as vigorously as it did during the 1960s. These triumphs did not occur in isolation. American prosperity was intricately linked with a steadily expanding global economy. Although the United States continued to enjoy a trade surplus until 1971, its balance of payments continued to run in the red largely from the costs of America's foreign military and aid commitments. Unfortunately, by the late 1960s and early 1970s, America's economic dynamism was threatened by inflation unleashed by the Vietnam War's expenses and deteriorating trade power caused by the increasingly overvalued dollar. Then, in 1973, Washington watched in impotence as the Organization of Petroleum Exporting Countries (OPEC) quadrupled the price of oil. The result was a decade of economic stagnation and inflation.

In fall 1945, no one could have predicted that the United States was about to enjoy a quarter century of economic expansion. Amidst the war victory celebrations were worries that the United States would again slip into depression as Washington cut back spending and economic management. Despite these fears, as with America's previous wars, demobilization occurred hastily and somewhat haphazardly. On 18 August 1945, President Truman issued an executive order to the war bureaucracy that it

> move as rapidly as possible without endangering the stability of the economy toward the removal of price, wage, production, and other controls and toward the restoration of collective bargaining and the free market.[16]

By late 1945, virtually of these controls had been lifted and most of the $16 billion worth of government-owned facilities were being privatized. Government spending dropped from $83 billion in 1945 to $30 billion in 1946, and $25 billion in 1947. Meanwhile, revenues remained relatively high. A budget deficit of $20.7 billion in 1946 became an $8.4 billion surplus in 1948. When the postwar recession hit, it was mild and short. The war had pent up consumer demand; savings had accumulated. With the war over, Americans enjoyed an orgy of spending. Industries had trouble in first converting from war to civilian production and then keeping up with consumer demands. Inflation rather than employment was the problem. Prices rose an average 16.4 percent between June 1946 and August 1948.[17] Then, between 1948 and 1952, the economy grew at an average annual rate of 5.7 percent and productivity by 4.3 percent, the highest in American peacetime history.

Nonetheless, Washington tried to alleviate the anticipated economic problems of demobilization through the 1946 Employment Act which declared that

it is the continuing policy and responsibility of the federal Government to use all practical means consistent with its needs and obligations and other essential considerations of national policy with the assistance and cooperation of industry, agriculture, labor, and some state and local governments, to coordinate and utilize all its plants, functions, and resources for the purpose of creating and maintaining, in a manner calculated to foster and promote free enterprise and the general welfare, conditions under which there will be afforded useful employment, for those able, willing, and seeking to work, and to promote maximum employment, production, and purchasing power.

The bill created a Council of Economic Advisors (CEA) in the White House and a Joint Economic Committee in Congress, and required the president to submit annual economic reports to Congress.

Although most Americans and the Republican-controlled Senate wanted to return to isolationism, Truman struggled to build upon Roosevelt's Bretton Woods system. The White House negotiated treaties creating first the General Agreement on Tariffs and Trade (GATT) and the International Trade Organization (ITO). The Senate accepted the GATT in 1947 but rejected American participation in the ITO, fearing that to do so the United States would have to surrender its economic sovereignty.

Truman's efforts to rebuild the global economy were boosted by worsening relations with the Soviet Union. By early 1947, the wartime alliance with Moscow had disolved into bitter differences over the postwar world's fate. In March 1947, Truman declared Cold War against Moscow, promising that the United States would contain communist advances around the world. In June 1947, Secretary of State Marshall announced that the United States would aid Europe's reconstruction. The United States eventually gave $14 billion to western Europe and $2.2 billion to Japan to help them rebuild their shattered economies. That same year, the National Security Act created the Defense Department, Central Intelligence Agency, and National Security Advisor, the institutional core of what soon became a vast military–industrial complex. Washington reinforced the global economy with military relations by forming the North Atlantic Treaty Organization (NATO) in 1949.

In June 1950, communist North Korea invaded South Korea. The Truman adminstration responded by forging an alliance under United Nations auspices which went to South Korea's aid. The White House believed that the war could be quickly won and thus did not initially attempt to mobilize the economy. But after China intervened on North Korea's behalf and the war ground to a bloody stalemate, it was clear that America's economy had to be mobilized. In November 1950, Congress passed the Revenue and Defense Production Acts which provided accelerated depreciation allowances for investments in defense-related industries. The RFC provided low-interest loans for such investments. In December 1950, Truman created the National Production Authority and the Office of Defense Mobilization, the latter to which he subordinated the existing Economic Stabilization Agency, Wage Stabilization Board, Defense Production Administration, and Office of Price Stabilization. During the Korean War, the National Production Authority created over 550 industry advisory committees (IACs) composed of officials and industry representatives to coordinate investment, production, prices, and markets.[18]

The Korean War procurements along with the various incentives, cheap loans, and guidances offered by Washington spurred enormous investments in strategic industries across the economy and set off high growth rates that would, with minor recessions, continue until 1973. The Korean War also deepened and broadened the range of global American defense and aid commitments. Between 1950 and 1953, America's defense budget rose from $13 billion to $45 billion, and would stay around that level for another decade before soaring during the 1960s as the United States expanded its Indochina War. By the mid-1950s, the United States was allied with over 50 countries around the world to help contain the Soviet Union and communism. These foreign economic and military commitments around the world resulted in persistent balance of payments deficits, ever lower productivity and growth, and eventually trade deficits after 1970.

The Cold War split America's economic psyche, with the United

States engaging in "nation-building" economic initiatives abroad that it would not dare to do at home during peacetime. President Eisenhower argued in 1956 that

> no matter what we do in providing, through loans, for the urgent needs of other countries in investment capital, unless we simultaneously pursue a policy that permits them to make a living, we are doomed to eventual isolation and to the disappearance of our form of government.[19]

This apocalyptic warning did not apply to the United States. Ironically, Eisenhower refused to implement at home those policies which he claimed were so successful in developing foreign countries. The White House pursued an industrial policy double-standard. It advocated policies which developed foreign industries while denying American industries the benefits of those same policies. The excuse was that industrial policies – at home at least – were "socialistic." Those same policies overseas were lauded as strengthening democracy and stimulating economic development.

Despite their overseas commitments, presidents Truman and Eisenhower were fiscally conservative. Although Federal spending and deficits briefly rose during the Korean War (1950–3), they were quickly reduced afterwards. All along, both presidents resisted demands for tax cuts by lobby groups such as the Chamber of Commerce and National Association of Manufacturers. Eisenhower even refused to cut taxes or increase government spending during the recessions of 1957–8, and 1960–1. All along, the White House saw inflation rather than unemployment as the chief economic evil. Between 1948 and 1960, the economy lumbered along at an average annual rate of 2.9 percent, well below those of other industrial democracies except Britain. Eisenhower maintained that,

> Over the long term, a balanced budget is a sure index of thrifty management – in a home, in a business, or in the federal government. When achievement of a balanced budget is for long put off in a business or home, bankruptcy is the result.[20]

President John Kennedy broke with the fiscal conservatism and obsession with inflation. When he entered the White House, the unemployment rate was 6.7 percent. Determined to expand the economy, Kennedy succeeded by 1962 in convincing a congressional majority to approve a bill that liberalized the tax depreciation guidelines, reduced the top tax rate from 91 percent to 70 percent, lowered low-term interest rates, and cut corporate taxes. While cutting taxes, Kennedy increased government research, development, and procurement spending. Kennedy was the first president to try to stimulate economic growth by offering business a 7 percent investment tax credit on equipment purchases. As a result, corporate investments doubled from 1962 to 1964 while employment rose by 2.5 million, bringing the unemployment rate down to 5.6 percent. Kennedy wanted to bring unemployment down to no more than 4 percent. In late 1962, he asked Congress for 20 percent tax cuts for individuals and businesses. Congress rejected his appeal. Kennedy's policies resulted in average economic growth of 4.5 percent between 1960 and 1966, double the average 2.2 percent rate between 1953 and 1960. Real income increased by 20 percent and corporate profits doubled between 1960 and 1966, while inflation averaged only 1.3 percent a year.[21]

This extraordinary economic expansion continued under President Johnson's leadership. It was not until 1964, a year after Kennedy's death, that Johnson was able to sign into law Kennedy's proposed tax cuts with the Revenue Act, and the next year, he further cut taxes with the Excise Tax Reduction Act of 1965. Even before Johnson's Great Society programs, welfare expenditures for the poor and social security had risen steadily from $35.1 billion in 1950 to $108 billion in 1964.[22] Despite these measures, at least 16 percent of the American public remained mired in poverty. Determined to eliminate poverty altogether, Johnson pushed through Congress a dozen laws creating an array of welfare, health, education, and housing programs, known collectively as the Great Society. Johnson addressed health care with the passage of two bills in 1965, medicare for the elderly, and medicaid for the poor. The poverty rate did fall to 11 percent when Johnson left office. Finally, Johnson signed into law the voting rights acts of 1964 and 1965 which guaranteed civil rights protection for all Americans.

It was the unprecedented prosperity of the post-World-War-II era which gave environmentalists an opportunity to influence national, state, and local policies. When most people's material needs are satisfied, they begin to think more about quality of life needs, such as a clean environment and abundant natural recreation areas. Old and new environmental voices gave shape to these human yearnings.

In the postwar era, Aldo Leopold continued to develop his land ethic philosophy that he had originally conceived two decades earlier. According to Leopold, humanity's power to exploit the earth must be accompanied by responsibility. In his 1949 book, *A Sand Country Almanac*, Leopold argued that every ethical system in history rested

> upon a single premise: that the individual is a member of a community of interdependent parts. His instincts prompt him to compete for his place in that community, but his ethics prompt him also to co-operate.... A land ethic changes the role of *Homo sapiens* from conqueror of the land-community to plain member and citizen of it.[23]

William Vogt attempted to link American environmental concerns with worsening global problems. His 1948 book *Road to Survival* argued that unrestricted population and economic growth was unsustainable and would eventually wreck not just the United States but the planet. Humans are interdependent; what happens on one spot of earth drastically affects the lives of humans elsewhere.[24] During the 1950s, Sigurd Olsen expressed the ecological and spiritual value of Minnesota's north woods through books such as *The Singing Wilderness* and *Listening Point*.[25] One of the most eloquent and sophisticated voices for environmentalism was Wallace Stegner. All of Stegner's fiction and non-fiction writings explore the relationship between individuals and their various psychological, social, and natural environments.[26] But perhaps the most influential book of all was the 1962 publication of Rachel Carson's *Silent Spring*, which powerfully explored the impact that the unregulated spewing of chemicals into the environment was having on all animal and plant species, including humans.[27]

Of all the major politicians of those years, perhaps none was as openly an environmentalist as Adlai Stevenson, the Democratic challenger to Dwight Eisenhower in the 1952 and 1956 presidential elections. Stevenson expressed environmental sentiments even if he did not campaign for a specific agenda. He wrote:

> We travel together, passengers on a little spaceship, dependent on its vulnerable reserves of air and soil; all committed for our safety to its security and peace; preserved from annihilation only by the care, the work, and, I will say, the love we give our fragile craft.[28]

Stevenson was an exception. While the nation's mood was increasingly environmental, the politicians largely clung to Jeffersonian visions. Truman, Eisenhower, and Kennedy were unabashed Jeffersonians who reluctantly enacted some limited pollution control and conservation measures or halted major dams. Jeffersonian majorities blocked environmental proposals on congressional natural resource committees. For example, throughout this period, Wayne Aspinall, a Colorado Democrat, used his chair of the House Committee on Interior and Insular Affairs to derail scores of environmental initiatives.

President Lyndon Johnson swung between conservationist and environmentalist impulses. On 24 and 25 May 1965, President Johnson hosted the White House Conference on National Beauty which he likened to Teddy Roosevelt's 1908 conservation conference. His environmental side shined during his 8 February 1965 address to Congress on "Natural Beauty." Johnson promised that his public land policies would be based on

> not just the classic conservation of protection and development, but a creative conservation of restoration and innovation. Its concern is not with nature alone, but with the total relation between man and the world around him. Its object is not just man's welfare but the dignity of man's spirit.[29]

President Johnson's "Environmental Pollution Panel" of his Science Advisory Committee reported in 1965 that ever-worsening pollution threatened America's economic viability; only extensive government intervention could curb and perhaps reverse that threat.[30]

Before Johnson, despite the indifference or outright presidential hostility toward conservationism and environmentalism, some progress was made. Congress did not first attempt to address the nation's ever-worsening water pollution systematically until 1948, when it passed and Truman signed the Water Pollution Control Act. The new law merely asserted the Federal government's role in regulating interstate water pollution, and called for more extensive studies to reveal just how bad the problem was. The subsequent study, which was not completed until 1952, revealed that the problem was horrendous and getting worse. Nothing was done until 1956 when an amendment to the 1948 law was passed; the amendment was as toothless as the original law. Meanwhile, the nation's water pollution problem worsened. President Eisenhower expressed the attitude of most Americans when he called water pollution a "uniquely local blight," the concern of the state and local governments rather than Washington.[31] In this, of course, Eisenhower was profoundly wrong.

Like Eisenhower, most Americans ignored the problem until 1962 when Rachel Carson's book *Silent Spring* appeared, revealing the horrors silently being inflicted on America by the accumulated discharge of millions of tons of toxic wastes every year. Inspired by Carson, in the early 1960s, Senator Edward Muskie led the Senate fight for tough water pollution laws. President Johnson eventually backed the idea, along with a congressional majority. In 1965, President Johnson signed into law the Water Resources Planning Act which created the Water Resources Council with the duty of coordinating planning among different water basins and agencies. The Water Pollution Control Act of 1965 enhanced the Federal government's powers to clean up the nation's interstate waterways, and set a 30 June 1967 deadline for achieving it. In 1966, the Clean Water Restoration Act was the first to provide a significant amount of funding – $3.5 billion in grants – to help municipalities build sewage treatment plants and researchers to devise better waste treatment. Despite these laws, the power to regulate waterways remained largely with the states which could set their own standards. Federal and state laws alike remained toothless. Until 1972, the courts settled only one violation of the national water pollution regulations. Meanwhile, the problems worsened. The severity of water pollution was dramatically revealed in 1969 when the Cayahoga River caught fire in downtown Cleveland.

Man-made air pollution has been around since the first human mastered fire. Ever-expanding urbanization, suburbanization, and industrialization created increasingly severe air pollution problems just as it had water pollution. And, as with water pollution, the perception of just what air pollution is and does has changed dramatically over the last century. In the late nineteenth century, when some first voiced concern over the darkening skies over cities, suspended particulates such as soot and smoke were identified as the culprits, and diminished aesthetics were seen as the primary problem. Since then, using ever-more sophisticated measuring devices, scientists have been able to identify and determine the impact of the chemical cocktails filling the nation's lungs. Mercury, lead, carbon dioxide, ozone, sulfur oxides, particulates, and nitrogen oxides, to name some of the more prominent, not only sullied skies but diminished the length and quality of life itself. Prolonged exposure to chemicals can damage and sometimes kill.

Despite this growing awareness, as with water pollution, the fouling of air was considered a local concern and responsibility until recently. In 1881 Chicago became the first city to confront an ever-worsening air pollution problem by prohibiting particularly thick smoke emissions. As early as 1905, Los Angeles issued a similar ordinance. In 1947, California passed the Air Pollution Control Act which prohibited particularly dark emissions. But for most other states and municipalities, pollution was simply a sign of progress.

The nation's air quality worsened with industrialization, yet most politicians and people seemed oblivious to its effects. In 1948, a chemical fog settled over Donara, Pennsylvania, sickening 6000 people and killing 20. National outrage flared, then just as quickly faded, without a congressional response. In 1949, a study from the California Institute of Technology revealed that automobiles were the major cause of smog, while subsequent studies showed that automobiles contributed as much as 95 percent of smog. In 1953, a chemical fog killed 200 in New York City. Once again, national indifference followed horror.

In 1955, fearing that the chemical blanket that daily suffocates the Los Angeles basin could cause an even higher death toll, the city began negotiating with America's automobile manufacturers to reduce emissions. For the first time, Congress helped by targeting $5 million for research into emission reductions. California's pollution was certainly not just confined to Los Angeles. The air over all of California's cities was steadily worsening. In 1961, Sacramento passed a law requiring automobile manufacturers to install crankcase devices to curb emissions. Two years later, the state required exhaust control devices. And in 1966, California imposed state-wide auto emission standards.

The nation's first National Conference on Air Pollution was held in 1958. It spawned a series of studies which revealed that air pollution was not the local problem most believed, but instead that no place was immune from the drift and subsequent damage. Armed with these studies and heartened by California's efforts, four congressmen – Senator Edmund Muskie from Maine; former Health, Education, and Welfare Department (HEW) head, Abraham Ribicoff; Alabama Representative Kenneth Roberts; and Ohio Representative Paul Schenck – fought for national air pollution standards.

The result was the 1963 Clean Air Act which expanded modest

existing research programs, collected and systematized pollution data, and encouraged industry to develop pollution control equipment. As with most pioneering national environmental laws, the Act lacked teeth. In 1967, a second was passed with larger research grants. Although in 1968, the Federal government set national emissions standards, they were weak and compliance voluntary. Most in Washington still believed that the Federal government's role should be to assist rather than lead state and local efforts.

Those few environmental victories were limited or offset by defeats elsewhere. In 1950, Jackson Hole National Monument was made part of Grand Teton National Park, but only under provisions that allowed hunting and grazing. Environmentalists stopped the damming of Echo Canyon in the 1950s, but only by agreeing to allow Glen Canyon's destruction by damming. In 1964, after nearly seven years of struggle, environmentalists succeeded in pushing through Congress the Wilderness Protection Act which designated some lands as free from most development. Aspinall insisted that mining and grazing continue in designated wilderness areas. Nonetheless, the Wilderness Protection was a watershed in that for the first time the Federal government was required to hold public hearings on land use policy.

Despite or perhaps because of Johnson's social and environmental programs, the economy roared ahead during the 1960s at the fastest rate in peacetime American history. Since then, only the Clinton administration has come close to replicating that economic record. Unfortunately, these economic triumphs would be short-lived. By cutting taxes while he embarked on his Great Society welfare programs and deepening America's participation in the Vietnam War quagmire, Johnson expanded the Federal debt. Inflation rose rapidly as the government, businesses, and consumers all demanded ever more goods and services. Meanwhile, the American dollar became increasingly overvalued as Japan and Europe became increasingly competitive. America's payments balance slid deeper in the red while the trade surplus declined. Anti-war protests swelled in Washington and across the country. Johnson's inability to overcome these problems, which were largely of his own making, caused him to announce in March 1968 that he would not seek reelection.

In 1969, Richard Nixon entered the White House determined to restore America's economic dynamism and cut back its foreign commitments. To these ends, he pursued *détente* with the Soviet

Union and China, tried to negotiate peace with North Vietnam while withdrawing American forces from South Vietnam, and cut back military spending. Meanwhile, he confronted the Japanese and Europeans over their trade and investment barriers.

Despite these efforts, America's economic growth continued to slow while its inflation, unemployment, and payments balance worsened. By July 1971, the balance of payments deficit was deepening toward $23 billion for that year. The United States had only $10 billion worth of gold while foreign governments held $40 billion and foreign businesses and citizens $30 billion worth of dollars. The fear was that those holding dollars would demand American gold, thus overwhelming the Bretton Woods system of fixed exchange rates and convertibility into gold.

On 15 August 1971, Nixon announced his "New Economic Policy" in which he would suspend the conversion of dollars into gold, slap a 10 percent surcharge on tariffs, and impose a 90-day freeze on wages and prices. He followed up these measures in December 1971 by negotiating the dollar's 17 percent devaluation at the Smithsonian conference in Washington. As a result, economic growth and exports increased slightly while unemployment dropped, but inflation resumed its persistently high rate after controls were lifted.

President Richard Nixon is remembered for many things – favorably for his foreign and economic policies, notoriously for Watergate. Few people associate Nixon with environmentalism. Yet perhaps only Theodore Roosevelt pushed through more environmentally sound policies than Richard Nixon.[32] Congress passed and President Nixon signed the Environmental Policy Act (1969), the Clean Air Act (1970), the Alaska Native Claims Act (1971), the Coastal Zone Management Act (1972), the Insecticide, Fungicide, and Rodenticide Act (1972), the Endangered Species Act (1973), and the Safe Drinking Water Act (1974).

The symbolic transition of environmentalism from the political wilderness into the mainstream occurred in 1970 with the first Earth Day celebration (22 April) and passage of the Environmental Policy Act. There were several reasons for environmentalism's triumph. During the 1960s, environmentalism became a mass movement in the United States and in most other industrial democracies. For progressive Americans, environmentalism was a natural cause to champion after protesting against the Vietnam War and for civil rights. The technological devastation wrought by the Vietnam War and nuclear arms race, the fragility of the planet when seen from outer space, the ever-more sophisticated means of measuring environmental degradation, and the smog-choked urban and suburban areas all combined to foster among increasing numbers of people an environmental awareness and commitment. Science and environmentalism became increasingly interlinked from the late 1960s onward. An increasing number of studies by scientists such as Edward O. Wilson, Norman Myers, and Paul Erlich appeared which justified environmentalism's philosophical and political arguments.[33]

President Nixon created the Environmental Protection Agency (EPA) in 1970 as part of the National Environmental Policy Act of 1969. The EPA would act as a general staff for coordinating the nation's environmental policies. He also formed the Council on Environmental Quality (CEQ) as a three-member advisory group whose mission was to analyze environmental problems and recommend policies. Shortly after convening, the CEQ issued its first report.[34] It would have been a remarkable document for any administration, particularly a conservative one like Richard Nixon's. The CEQ blasted the historic relationship between Americans and their natural environment, asserting that the pervasive cornucopian attitudes had wasted and devastated American resources. America was a glutton, the CEQ argued; while its population accounted for only 6 percent of the world's people, it gobbled up 40 percent of the earth's exploited resources. The CEQ concluded that the United States had to abandon its Jeffersonian attitudes and practices and embrace environmentalism as the basis of its policies. To varying degrees, Nixon embraced these ideas.

He took the initiative in championing the cleanup of the nation's waterways. He first raised the issue in a Febuary 1970 speech to Congress and continued to press it for another two years. In 1972, Congress passed the Federal Water Pollution Control Act which finally asserted Washington's duty to protect waterways everywhere, whether they were interstate or not. The Act empowered the EPA to set tough regulations and specific deadlines for compliance. The National Discharge Elimination System (NDES) created by the Act required a Federal permit for any discharge. The Act sought the restoration of commercial fish and shellfish ecosystems by 1983 and the elimination of all pipeline discharges by 1985, thus making all navigable waters "swimmable and fishable." Strict standards for both water quality and effluents would be addressed by the best practical technology available. Cleanup would target both "point" and "non-point" pollution sources. The law required states to submit and enact comprehensive cleanup programs.

The 1974 Safe Drinking Water Act authorized the EPA to identify and eliminate those substances harming the nation's drinking water, and established the US Geological Survey's National Ambient Stream Quality Accounting Network (NASQUAN). Maintaining that it lacked the personnel, expertise, and funding to comply, the EPA refused to implement the law fully until 1976 when a court ruling forced it to regulate 24 of the over 50 categories it had neglected. The EPA then set tough standards through its National Primary Drinking Water Regulations which required the elimination of 83 contaminants within three years. A 1986 amendment banned lead piping and lead solder in public water systems. In 1991, the EPA imposed stricter lead regulations which reduced the amount allowed in tapwater from 50 parts per billion (p.p.b.) to 15 p.p.b. That same year, the EPA limited the amount of radon allowed in drinking water.

In 1970, Ralph Nader issued a massive report which blasted Washington for failing to systematically and seriously confront the air pollution problem. At once enlightened and chastised, a majority in Congress voted for the 1970 Clean Air Act, the first Federal effort with tough standards and enforcement powers. The Act required the EPA to develop standards for both stationary and vehicular pollution sources, and identified for cleanup seven pollutants – carbon monoxide, particulates, sulfur oxides, lead, hydrocarbons, nitrogen oxides, and ozone. Primary standards would be based on the health problems caused by those pollutants in the elderly and children; secondary standards on the pollutants' adverse effects on visibility, buildings, water, and crops. The Act targeted both existing and proposed new factories and vehicles.

The chemicals targeted by the Clean Air Act cause a range of health problems. Sulfur oxides spilling from oil and chemical refineries and utility boilers can accelerate lung and heart disease, and worsen colds and respiratory illnesses. Lead from gasoline and paint can hurt kidneys, reproductive and nervous systems, and cause brain damage, particularly in children. Carbon monoxide spewing from automobiles and trucks impairs the blood's ability to absorb oxygen and slow reflexes. Nitrogen oxides emanating from electric utility boilers and motor vehicles irritate lungs and lower immunity to viral infections. Ozone formed by the chemical reaction of hydrocarbons and nitrogen oxides impairs lungs, irritates the respiratory system, and worsens asthma. Particulate matter from vehicles, forest fires, dust, and industrial smokestacks can lodge carcinogenic chemicals in lungs and aggravate respiratory problems. The list of targeted chemicals has since expanded. Arsenic can cause cancer; asbestos, lung diseases including cancer; benzene, leukemia; beryllium, lung disease and the destruction of liver, kidney, spleen, and lymph glands; coke oven emissions, respiratory cancer; mercury, brain, kidney, and bowel cancer; radionuclides, cancer; vinyl chloride, lung and liver cancer.

The Act enlisted the states as allies in the fight against air pollution. After the EPA issued air standards, each state was required to create and enforce a State Implementation Plan (SIP) which first calculated the sources and amount of air pollution across the state, then devised a plan and timetable for reducing those emissions to reach Federal standards. EPA would approve each state's SIPs by 1979, and the states would implement their SIPs by 1982. The ideal SIP is composed quickly and comprehensively; it is enforced consistently with a variety of regulatory carrots and sticks. A combination of tax incentives backed by the threat of litigation can encourage industries to invest in pollution-control equipment. Unfortunately, the ideal SIP was rare. To further complicate matters, the Act divided the country into 247 Air Quality Control Regions (ACQRs), many of which encompassed two or more states. The EPA evaluated each region as either "attainment" or "nonattainment," of which the latter was broken down into five categories.

Although more sweeping than its mild predecessors, there were loopholes in the Clean Air Act. One allowed automakers to opt out of the standards if they made a "good faith effort" at compliance. The EPA in fact would continually roll back the year for compliance. Another problem was that Congress called for technologies that then did not exist, yet refused to allocate adequate funding for research and development. This helped Detroit claim that it lacked the money or technology to invest in control devices.

In 1972, General Motors, Ford, Chrysler, Volvo, and International Harvester used these loopholes when they applied for relief from the 1975 emission control deadline. EPA head William Ruckelshaus rejected their plea. The five automakers then took their case to Federal court. The judge ordered Ruckelshaus to review their application. Ruckelshaus did, and again rejected their application, then reversed himself and granted an extension.

Not just the automakers deplored Ruckelshaus' policies. In 1972, the Sierra Club sued the EPA, charging that Ruckelshaus had watered down the intent of Congress in the 1970 Clean Air Act. The Federal district court ruled in favor of the Sierra Club. The EPA appealed. In 1973, the Supreme Court upheld the lower court ruling. The following year, the EPA imposed tougher standards to comply with the court ruling.

THE STAGFLATION YEARS: 1974–80

Just when it seemed as if the United States was entering an unprecedented era of economic growth and environmental protection, disaster struck. The watershed in postwar economic history was OPEC's quadrupling of oil prices from $2.50 to $11 a barrel in 1973. After rising to about $17 a barrel in 1979, oil prices doubled to reach about $34 a barrel. As a result, from 1973 until oil prices collapsed in the mid-1980s, the United States and the entire global economy suffered low growth and high inflation. America's inflation increased from 3.3 percent in 1972 to 11 percent in 1974 while the economy contracted by 2 percent, the worst since 1946.[35] Although America's economic growth picked up thereafter, inflation, interest rates, and unemployment remained high.

Washington put environmentalism on the back burner well behind more pressing concerns of access to oil. In March 1974, President Nixon issued and Congress passed 14 amendments to the Clean Air Act which weakened many of its tougher measures, including postponing until 1982 the deadline for state compliance and extending indefinitely that for automakers. This was Nixon's last important industrial policy act. In August 1974, he resigned the presidency because the Watergate scandal was leading Congress to consider impeaching him on obstruction of justice charges.

As if the nation's economic and political crises were not debilitating enough, the United States suffered a series of geopolitical reverses during this decade. In 1975, Vietnam, Cambodia, and Laos fell to communism. In 1979, the pro-American Shah of Iran was overthrown by anti-American fundamentalists while the communist Sandanista movement came to power in Nicaragua. In December 1979, the Soviet Union invaded Afghanistan. Finally, Iranian militants took over America's embassy in Teheran and held the employees hostage for what would be 444 days.

Presidents Ford and Carter were no more able than Nixon to arrest the decline of American economic and geopolitical power. In his brief tenure (1974–5), Ford failed to launch any economic or foreign policy initiatives. Carter was more active. He started the deregulation of the airlines, trucking, and railroads, leading to great productivity and efficiency gains for those industries. He also vastly expanded funding for the Comprehensive Employment and Training Act (CETA), which had been created in 1973. Under Carter, CETA doubled in size to cover 725 000 hard-core unemployed.

Yet Carter's efforts did little to reverse American decline. America's trade deficit steadily worsened. By 1980, foreign goods competed with 70 percent of all American-made goods. An entire range of American industries such as automobiles, steel, television, machine tools, petrochemicals, shipbuilding, textiles, and even microelectronics began to crumble from the competition.[36]

Ford and Carter both expanded industrial policies that dealt with conservation and environmental issues. Though a Jeffersonian by inclination, President Ford succumbed to Hamiltonian pressures and expanded Nixon's conservation legacy. He signed the Insecticide, Fungicide, and Rodenticide Act Amendment in 1975, and the Toxic Substances Control Act, the Resource Conservation and Recovery Act, the Federal Land Policy and Management Act, and the Clean Water Act Admendments in 1976, all of which greatly expanded the Federal government's powers to regulate pollution.

The Toxic Substances Control Act (TSCA) was especially powerful. It requires the EPA to gather information on all chemicals from all private and public enterprises, assess the toxicity of those chemicals, screen new chemicals, and then control all those found to be toxic. Every year since, the EPA has issued its Toxic Release Inventory of the worst toxic chemicals. The 1976 National Forest Management Act required the Forest Service to follow an elaborate multiple-use formula for managing the nation's forests. The 1976 Resource Conservation and Recovery Act (RCRA) asserted Washington standards on solid waste problems on state and local governments. Even more sweeping was the 1976 Federal Land Policy and Management Act (FLPMA) which mandated not only multiple use but the protection of the nation's cultural and historical treasures.

In his four years in office (1977–81), President Carter won a string of environmental victories. In 1977, he succeeded in pushing through stronger water and air pollution standards, in 1978 stronger pesticide and endangered-species regulations, and in 1980 the Compensation and Liability Act that helped pollution victims. Carter's greatest environmental success was the 1980 Alaska Protection Act which preserved much of the state as wilderness.

The Carter White House's perspectives on the environment were exemplified by the publication of the *Global 2000 Report to the President* in 1980, the culmination of three years of research by the CEQ. They concluded that there would be

> global problems of alarming proportions by the year 2000. Environmental, resource, and population stresses are intensifying and will increasingly determine the quality of human life on our planet.... At the same time, the earth's carrying capacity... is eroding. The trends reflected in the Global 2000 Study suggest strongly a progressive degradation and impoverishment of the earth's natural resource base.[37]

These assumptions underlay most of the Carter administration's natural resource policies.

The White House had important interest groups as allies behind these visions and industrial policies. It was the Sierra Club rather than the Carter administraton that was primarily responsible for pushing through Congress the 1977 amendment to the Clean Air Act that required states to prove that any new pollution sources did not worsen conditions, thus effectively preventing them from permitting new sources unless offset by the reduction of old pollution sources. This approach, known as the "prevention of significant deterioration" (PSD), was accompanied by allowing polluters more flexibility in developing anti-pollution devices or the "best available control technology" (BACT). In 1979, Congress expanded the flexibility of the nation's environmental laws by allowing a "bubble policy" whereby polluters could reduce emissions from an entire complex rather than a specific source.

Jeffersonians fought back against these Hamiltonians intrusions into the marketplace. The Jeffersonian perspective was explicitly captured by a 1973 essay entitled: "What's Wrong with Plastic Trees?"[38] An article that honestly recounted the visceral pleasure that some Jeffersonians derive from bulldozing nature – the "adult" version of pulling wings off butterflies – was entitled "Speaking Out: Let's Spoil the Wilderness."[39] Many Jeffersonians see their struggle with conservationists and particularly environmentalists in biblical apocalyptic "good versus evil" terms. As *Wise Use Agenda* author Ron Arnold put it: "Our goal is to destroy, to eradicate the environmental movement."[40]

In the late-1970s, the spearhead of this Jeffersonian movement was the "sagebrush rebellion" among ranching, farming, mining, logging, and other industries in the 17 western states. "Sagebrushers" organized themselves into in a plethora of powerful organizations including the Alliance for America, Western States Public Coalition, and National Inholders Association, and tapped into the legal advice of the Mountain States Legal Foundation. Their ultimate aim is to deregulate all industries and sell off all public lands, including the national parks and wilderness areas, to private interests.

It was this resurgence of Jeffersonian zeal that put Ronald Reagan over the top in the 1980 election. Reagan's policies would simultaneously shift America's political alignment rightward and America's relative economic power downward.

6 Reaganomics versus Clintonomics, 1981–2000

In rhetoric if not reality, no modern president has personified Jeffersonianism better than Ronald Reagan. With its underlying assumption that "government is not the solution, it's the problem," "Reaganomics" was supposed to include massive cuts in taxes, government spending, regulations, and the national debt, massive increases in military spending, and a balanced budget. These policies would unleash the "magic of the marketplace" that would lead America into an era of unprecedented power and prosperity.

In words and deeds, few presidents have equaled Bill Clinton as a Hamiltonian. Clinton rejected the ideological choice between "bigger" or "smaller" government as intellectually vacuous. Instead, he promised to "reinvent" government so that it would do more with less. This involved reducing and reorganizing most Federal bureaucracies, and increasing the personnel, funding, and duties of others as was necessary to fulfill better their respective missions. In particular, Clinton promised to devote more financial, technological, and personnel resources to targeting industries and technologies that would be the powerhouses of America's economy and society in the twenty-first century. He also promised to enhance protection for medicare, medicaid, education, and the environment. Under "Clintonomics", government would not abdicate the widened array of responsibilities for national development that most Americans had come to support; indeed, it would renew its efforts toward that end by using much more cost-effective means.

How well did these two most explicit contemporary versions of Jeffersonianism and Hamiltonianism fare when their respective champions sat in the Oval Office? How far did politics compromise each vision from becoming reality?

REAGANOMICS

Like Jefferson, Reagan had a very simple approach to the problem of national development – eliminate government from the marketplace and the nation will reach new heights of wealth and well-being. During the 1980 presidential campaign, Reagan promised to revive American power and prosperity by cutting taxes and social spending, increasing military spending, and balancing the budget within four years.

Most informed observers called Reaganomics a recipe for economic disaster. George Bush, Reagan's chief rival in the Republican primaries, accused the former actor of peddling "voodoo economics" that would explode the national debt and lower national growth. Although Bush later recanted his warning after Reagan named him Vice-President, history proved him prescient. From 1981 when Ronald Reagan entered the White House until 1993 when George Bush left it, America's national debt tripled from $974 billion to $4.2 trillion, the United States went from being the world's greatest creditor to worst debtor nation; by 1987 the nation's trade deficit had soared to $178 billion while with Japan, America's fiercest rival, it reached $60 billion; average economic growth and the savings and investment rates slowed to the lowest level since the 1930s; real income for most Americans plunged while the gap between rich and poor widened; and a range of socioeconomic problems such as crime, drug abuse, unwed mothers, and environmental degradation worsened.[1]

What went wrong? In the 1989 film *Wall Street*, the character Gordon Gekko exclaimed: "Greed . . . is good. Greed is right. Greed clarifies, cuts through and captures the essence of the evolutionary spirit. . . . Greed – mark my words – will save America." In many ways, Mr. Gekko's ruminations captured the essence of what has become known as Reaganomics – those policies pushed by Presidents Ronald Reagan and George Bush between 1981 and 1992.

Reagan tried hard to fulfill his promises. But as one analyst remarked, "Seldom has an economic experiment been put into place with less conventional credentialing by professional economists."[2] America's vicious cycle of socioeconomic problems was exacerbated by the Reagan and Bush adminstrations' policies of tax cuts, spending hikes, promotion of a high dollar, support of military industries to the neglect of consumer industries, and, yes, the constant drumbeat that "greed is good." These ideologically driven policies unilaterally disarmed America. The nation's economic rivals, especially Japan, gleefully took advantage of Reaganomics to devastate American firms in American and foreign markets around the world.

Reaganomics' centerpiece was the Economic Recovery Tax Act

of 1981 which cut taxes on individuals by 23 percent over the next three years, reduced the top rate paid by the wealthiest from 70 percent to 50 percent, and indexed income tax rates to inflation by 1985. Business was boosted by a cut in the capital gains tax from 28 percent to 23 percent. Reagan's Office of Management and Budget predicted that these tax cuts would expand the economy 4.4 percent annually and generate a $28 billion budget surplus by 1986.

Lower inflation was the only clear economic success of the Reagan years, with average annual rate of 4.1 percent during his tenure, down from 8.7 percent from 1973 through 1980 when oil prices rose from $2.75 to $34 a barrel. There were two clear reasons for inflation's drop. The Federal Reserve maintained a tight monetary policy which kept interest rates high and thus business and household consumption low. This policy was perhaps the most important reason behind the 1981–2 recession which wrung considerable inflation out of the economy. As important was the global oil glut which caused oil prices to free-fall from about $34 a barrel during the early 1980s to $11 a barrel by the mid-1980s. Reagan's policies had a mixed effect on the inflation rate. His strong dollar policy subsidized a flood of imports that simultaneously kept prices lower than they otherwise might have been, but at the cost of lower economic growth and higher unemployment as foreign goods captured market share from American goods and profits flowed overseas instead of enriching Americans.

Reaganomics accomplished the administration's hidden agenda of redistributing wealth from the poor and middle classes to the rich. In fact, Reagan did not cut taxes as he promised – taxes actually went up during the Reagan years to 19.4 percent of GNP from 19.2 percent under Carter. What Reagan did was shift some of the tax burden from the rich to the middle class. Tax rates for the wealthiest 20 percent of the population dropped from 29 percent in 1980 to 26 percent while rates for the bottom fifth rose from 8 percent to 10 percent. The chief beneficiaries of Reagan's tax cuts were those people making over $200 000 a year – only 1 percent of all Americans. In all, Federal taxes cost the average middle-income American 18.2 percent of his earnings in 1980; 19.5 percent in 1992. Total Federal, state, and local taxes were 27.8 percent in 1980 and 28.0 percent in 1990. The Congressional Budget Office (CBO) estimates that the real effect has been that wealthy people pay 9 percent less in taxes every year, an enormous savings when compounded. Robert McIntyre, director of Citizens for Tax Justice, argues that those wealthy "are way undertaxed based on what they can afford, what they used to pay, and what they would pay in other countries."[3]

Nearly all of Reagan's other promises proved illusions. Real per-capita growth in the 1980s averaged 1.5 percent annually, actually lower than the 1970s' 1.8 percent rate or the 1960s' 2.5 percent rate. What little economic expansion that did occur was fueled by a consumer and government spending binge based on an ever-expanding debt. In 1986, the ratio of debt to disposable income reached 86.2 percent, the highest since 1945. Unemployment averaged 7.8 percent between 1980 and 1986. By 1986, the personal savings rate had fallen to 3.9 percent, the lowest rate since 1949.[4]

Although Reagan promised to decrease the government's size and deregulate the economy, he accomplished far less deregulation than the Carter White House. In fact, the Federal government's size increased rather than decreased under Ronald Reagan, from 24.6 percent of GNP to 25.7 percent. The Federal workforce increased 8 percent, with those employed in the White House increasing by 18 percent! In 1980, all Federal, state, and local government expenditures combined accounted for 32.6 percent of GNP; in 1985, it was 35.3 percent. Just as Reagan had shifted wealth from the poor and middle classe to the rich, his policies shifted more work from the Federal to the state and local governments. In order to make up for cutbacks in Federal subsidies, state and local governments had to expand their workforces by 20 percent during the 1980s.[5]

While Reagan cut some areas of government, he increased others such as defense and farm subsidies. Reagan did try to fulfill his promise to deregulate. If the White House could not eliminate or reduce an agency, it often simply ordered it to not comply with its own laws and duties. Among the more notorious examples of this were bureaucracies charged with protecting the environment such as the Interior Department and Environmental Protection Agency (EPA). The trouble with deregulation, of course, is that the regulations were enacted in the first place to curb various abuses and crimes. Contrary to popular belief, many regulations improve rather than erode market efficiency. In many cases, cutting back regulations proved to be penny wise and pound foolish; cutbacks and deregulation caused problems to fester and frequently become crises. Overall, the Federal government's unfunded liabilities such as hazardous waste cleanup, infrastructure maintenance, guaranteed loans which have defaulted or institutions which have bankrupted, health care, and so on surpassed $5 trillion in 1989.

Frederick Wolf, the General Accounting Office director, admitted in 1989 that Reagan's deregulation policies would actually cost the United States more than $300 billion, of which about half would be consumed by the savings and loan bailout. The annual losses to the government from defaulted loans and uncollected debts such as taxes owed by businesses and people increased from $40 billion in 1981 to $115 billion in 1988. According to Wolf, "budget cuts fell disproportionately on enforcement, oversight, management and accounting functions."[6]

The Reagan administration's loosening of regulations on leveraged buyouts encouraged corporations to engage in an orgy of buying and selling in pursuit of quick profits. The result was massive corporate debt. By the late 1980s, corporations paid out an average $1.6 billion in interest for every $1 billion they invested in manufacturing plants and equipment. That mounting debt was exceeded only by the soaring salaries for management. By 1987, businesses paid $2.3 billion in salaries for every $1 billion in taxes, the reverse of what it had been in 1953. By being allowed to deduct the interest payments on their debt, corporations withheld an annual average $92.2 billion from the Treasury during the 1980s and contributed only $67.5 billion. Hundreds of corporations paid no taxes at all. Corporations paid an average of only 17 percent during the 1980s, while individuals paid 83 percent; during the 1950s, corporations had paid 61 percent and individuals 39 percent of the tax bill.[7]

Rather than the $28 billion budget surplus in 1986 that Reagan promised, the White House racked up a $221 billion Federal budget deficit that year, the largest peacetime deficit as a percentage of GNP in the nation's history! From 1945 to 1980, the Federal debt as a percentage of GNP stayed relatively constant at around 25 percent. Reaganomics exploded the nation's debt. From 1981 to 1990, the Federal debt rose from $974 billion to $2.568 trillion, while state and local debt rose from $287 billion to $649 billion, average annual increases of 13.2 percent and 2.3 percent, respectively. The Federal debt rose from 27.2 percent to 47.0 percent of GNP, while state and local debt rose from 10.5 percent to 11.8 percent. During that decade, private debt rose from $2.868 trillion to $7.342 trillion, a 6.4 percent annual increase and rise from 105.5 percent to 134.3 percent of GNP. America's combined public and private debt rose from $3.898 trillion to $10.560 trillion, a 7.7 annual percent increase and rise from 142.7 percent to 193.2 percent of

GNP. By 1985, Reaganomics had transformed the United States from the world's largest creditor to the worst debtor nation. In other words, the United States owed foreigners more than foreigners owed the United States. By 1990, foreigners owned 17 percent of the national debt, up from 5 percent in 1969.[8]

To finance the Reagan administration's ever-growing debt mountain, the Federal Reserve had to keep interest rates high. During Reagan's first term, interest rates averaged 11.2 percent, only slightly below the 11.7 percent rate under Carter. Although interest rates dropped to an average 9.1 percent during Reagan's second term they were still the third highest for any president in American history. As interest rates rose, business investments and thus economic growth fell. Altogether, net business investments dropped from 3.2 percent of GNP to 1.9 percent by 1986. Meanwhile, household savings plummeted from 5 percent of income in 1981 to 2.5 percent throughout the 1980s.

Under Reaganomics, the rich indeed got even richer and the poor got poorer. The Congressional Budget Office reported in 1992 that between 1977 and 1989, 70 percent of the rise in the average after-tax income went to the wealthiest 1 percent of the population. Altogether, the wealthiest 20 percent of the population had their income increase by 116 percent, followed by the second highest quintile with an 8 percent gain, and the middle quintile a 2 percent rise. Meanwhile, the fourth and fifth lowest quintiles watched their incomes decline by 7 percent and 11 percent, respectively.[9]

How did Reaganomics leave so many Americans relatively worse off than before the "Gipper" took office? Reaganomics's personal and capital gains tax cuts for the wealthy exacerbated the trend toward an ever-more inegalitarian society. The cuts in capital gains taxes stimulated investments in real estate and stocks which paid enormous returns until the bubble burst in the late 1980s.

Although not only Democrats but moderate Republicans in Congress realized that Reaganomics was proving to be a disaster for the country, Reagan's carefully contrived all-American image and subsequent popularity with most Americans inhibited them from speaking out. Even some within the White House protested Reaganomics. Two of Reagan's CEA chairs, Murray Weidenbaum and Martin Feldstein, resigned when it was clear Reagan's policies were leading to economic disaster. OMB head, David Stockman admitted publicly that Reaganomics was simply "trickle-down economics" and the tax cuts a "Trojan horse to bring down the top [income tax] rates" for the very rich. Shortly after resigning in 1985, Stockman declared that, "We just can't live with these massive deficits without traumatic economic dislocation."[10]

In 1982 and 1984, however, realizing that they had committed a grievous economic mistake, a majority in Congress attempted to rectify it through slight tax increases and a raise in the social security payroll tax to save that system from bankruptcy. Even then, inequities abounded. Many of the nation's largest corporations took advantage of tax loopholes and contributed nothing to the Treasury. The 1986 Tax Reform Act attempted to restore some sanity to the system by closing many of the loopholes, while reducing the top rate for individuals to 28 percent from 50 percent and for corporations to 34 percent from 46 percent.

A 1985 White House personnel switch of Jim Baker with Don Regan from Chief of Staff to Treasury Secretary led to a policy switch. While Treasury Secretary, Reaganomics zealot Regan had pushed the strong dollar policy which devastated America's exports and economy. Upon taking the Treasury, the pragmatic Baker immediately tried to push down the dollar. His most important action occurred in September 1985 when he forged an agreement at the Plaza Hotel in New York among the finance ministers of Japan, West Germany, France, and Britain (Group of Five) to devalue the dollar. As the central banks of those countries began selling dollars and buying currencies from other industrial countries, the dollar fell. By 1987, the dollar's value against the yen had halved to around 120 yen compared to its 1985 height of 265 yen. In February 1987, the Group of Seven met at the Louvre in Paris to agree that the dollar had fallen far enough and to stabilize it at its current value.

Meanwhile, fiscal conservatives in Congress outraged by the ever swelling debt pushed through in 1986 the Gramm–Rudman–Hollings's bill which mandated reduced deficits until a balanced budget was reached in 1991. The bill was challenged in court on the constitutional grounds that it violated the separation of powers. A second deficit reduction bill known as Gramm–Rudman II passed in 1987 but lacked tough powers of enforcement. These revisions failed to arrest the harsh socioeconomic impact of Reagonomics.

The environment was another victim of Reaganomics. Ronald Reagan's public statements revealed his vast ignorance and *naïveté* about the world, perhaps no more glaringly than on environmental issues – Reagan once claimed "trees cause pollution." This statement seemed to set the tone for his administration; ideology rather than science, and special corporate interests rather than national interests shaped the Reagan White House's environmental policies.

In February 1981, one month after taking office, the Reagan administration ordered all regulatory agencies to produce Regulatory Impact Analyses (RIAs) for all new or revised regulations exceeding $100 000 in compliance costs, and forbade any regulatory changes unless the benefits exceeded the costs. The OMB annually conducted about 2000 RIAs. The General Accounting Office (GAO) captured the essential criticism of the RIA cost–benefit analysis when it argued:

> The EPA benefit–cost analyses cannot provide exact answers to regulating complex environmental problems largely because of gaps in underlying scientific data.... This data gap is troublesome in estimating physical improvements of the benefits of environmental regulation, such as improvements in water quality or better visibility. Problems also arise in calculating dollar values for these improvements... in estimating the costs of complying with environmental regulations. These data weaknesses... affect other federal agencies dealing with health and environmental regulations.[11]

Using this policy and the Federal budget, Reagan financially cut to the bone many praiseworthy programs into ineffectiveness or oblivion. For example, he killed a $2 million scientific study to determine the degree of human exposure to toxicity by measuring chemicals that accumulated in body fat.

The White House ordered appointed and professional officials alike to neglect or bend any laws designed to clean-up the environment. It also slashed funding and staff for virtually all those bureaucracies with environmental duties. For example, the Solid Waste Bureau's budget plummeted from $16 million in 1981 to $320 000 in 1982 and staff from 74 to one![12] Perhaps most destructively, Reagan brought in fervent anti-environmentalists James Watt as Interior Secretary and Anne Gorsuch (her name changed to Buford when she married after taking office) as EPA head.

Watt had founded the extreme right-wing Mountain States Legal Foundation in 1977. Shortly after taking office, Watt ordered a moratorium on any new national park land, opened up vast new public lands to mining and logging, and proposed leasing 1.3 million acres off California's coast for oil-drilling. He refused to touch the $1 billion in the Land and Water Conservation Fund which had been earmarked for buying new lands for the national park system, and used only half of the $1 billion Congress subsequently voted to aquire new park lands. Watt's rhetoric was as biting as his policies, with his frequent public distinctions between "liberals and Americans." Within months after he took office, a coalition of environmental groups began demanding his resignation. He was finally forced to resign in 1983 when he quipped that an Interior Department Coal Advisory Board included "a black, a woman, two Jews, and a cripple."

EPA head Buford's policies were just as regressive. Buford attempted to dismantle her agency and actually succeeded in carving away one-fifth of the budget and driving out many career officials. She then appointed anti-environmentalists to the EPA, while shunting aside the remaining professionals. Reagan's appointees went to some extraordinary lengths to avoid fulfilling their legal and adminstrative duties. Twenty of these Buford appointees were eventually forced to resign after investigators revealed corruption, conflict of interest, perjury, and other crimes. The most infamous was Rita Lavelle, the EPA Assistant for Hazardous Waste. Lavelle was convicted of perjury and obstruction of a congressional investigation over EPA mismanagement of the dioxin cleanup at Times Beach, Missouri. The penalty for Lavelle was a $10 000 fine and six months in jail.

Buford herself left under a heavy legal cloud. In 1983, Representative John Dingell, chairman of the Investigations and Oversight Committee of the Committee on Energy and Commerce, asked the EPA to submit documents on its enforcement of air pollution laws. Citing executive privilege, Buford refused. The House of Representatives voted Buford in contempt and ordered her arrest and incarceration in the Capitol jail by the Sergeant at Arms. Buford resigned instead.

The Reagan administration's stand on acid rain is an excellent example of how Reagonomics continually sacrificed hard science and national economic development on the altar of ideological purity and special interest groups. Although scientists had been studying the phenomena for decades, acid rain did not become an important issue until the early 1980s when several well-publicized reports excited public attention. A 1981 report revealed that acid rain was anywhere from 10 to 1000 times worse than would naturally occur across the north-east and was inflicting incalculable economic damage.

Pollution was the cause. By the early 1980s, American factories, power plants, and vehicles annually spewed into the atmosphere more than 30 million tons of sulfur dioxide and 20 million tons of nitrogen oxides.[13] When these chemicals combine with water vapor they fall to earth as acid rain, fog, or snow.

Acid rain inflicts enormous damage on America's economy. In 1983, the Interagency Task Force on Acid Precipitation, which represented 12 Federal agencies, reported that acid rain was the culprit in the destruction of lakes, forests, crops, and buildings across at least 17 states. In those states, acid rain annually caused at least $5 billion in property damage to buildings, while the 5 percent decline in softwood timber growth meant the annual loss of enough lumber to supply one-tenth of the new homes in the United States. And this was just the immediately measurable damage. The actual amount may have been many times greater.

Rather than promote the national economic interest in curbing such damage, the Reagan White House bowed to the polluters and their campaign contributions. The administration immediately rejected the report, claiming more information was necessary before any conclusion, let alone action, should be contemplated. A group of scientists from the White House Office of Science then took the bold step of denouncing the administration's position, arguing that "if we take the conservative point of view that we must wait until scientific knowledge is definitive, the accumulated deposit and damaged environment may reach the point of irreversibility."[14] Yet, even some utilities corporations have conceded that their emissions might contribute to the ever-worsening acid rain problem. In 1980, Edison Electric stated that acid rain not only existed and was a serious ecological problem, but that the "atmospheric emissions from utility plants may play a role in the occurance of acid rain."[15]

To scientists and environmentalists, the way to reduce the problem was as clear as the problem itself. The National Academy of Sciences released its own study in 1983 which asserted that the severe damage caused by acid rain could be reduced by imposing emissions controls on coal-burning power plants in both the United States and Canada.[16] In 1988, the National Acid Precipitation Assessment Program (NAPAP) found that acid rain had destroyed, among other things, over half the 2700 lakes in New York's Adirondack State Park, accounted for over one-quarter of all nitrogen oxides polluting Chesapeake Bay, and caused the massive die-off of red spruce in the Appalachian mountains.[17]

Although the Reagan White House's ideological presumptions withered throughout the 1980s beneath the objective analyses by the nation's leading scientists, it continued to deny the problem, and thus did nothing about acid rain. Annual reports of the White House Council on Environmental Quality either avoided mentioning acid rain at all or downplayed its effects, claiming more research was necessary before conclusions could be drawn. Domestic and international pressure built on the Reagan White House to do something.

Acid rain pits region against region and country against country. In 1984, New York, Maine, and Pennyslvania petitioned the EPA to force Illinois, Indiana, Kentucky, Michigan, Ohio, and Tennessee to reduce their sulfur emissions which were causing enormous damage to the north-east. The EPA rejected the petition, claiming it lacked the authority to act upon it. The following year, a larger coalition of north-eastern states again sued the EPA for relief. A Federal court ruled in their favor and ordered the EPA to enforce its own laws. But the Reagan appointees to the EPA continued to stonewall.

Acid rain born in the American industrial midwest damages Ontario and Quebec as severely as the north-east. It took the pleas of Canadian Prime Minister Brian Mulroney to spark Reagan White House action against acid rain. Ironically, Mulroney himself was a conservative and shared a contempt for environmental concerns. However, growing political pressures had forced him to act on a range of worsening environmental problems in Canada, some of which were caused by emissions blown in from the United States. Mulroney finally realized that pollution is not the freebie touted by economists but can devastate industries as well as ecosystems. Acid rain was destroying the salmon and maple sugar industries of eastern Canada. Estimates of the damage caused by American pollution sources ranged from 20 to 40 percent. Those businessmen were demanding that Ottawa act. In 1988, the Reagan White House grudgingly signed with 24 other nations a protocol in which signatories pledged to reduce their emissions of nitrogen oxides to 1987 levels by 1994. Reagan's diplomats did succeed in reducing the protocol's standards from the original proposal of a 30 percent cutback in nitrogen oxides by 1994.

The Reagan White House also dug in its heels against proposals to alleviate indoor pollution. For decades, scientists have been aware of the "sick building syndrome" (SBS) in which inside pollution can sometimes exceed that outside. Recent studies have revealed that as many as 30 percent of all buildings emit toxic chemicals which are harmful to the inhabitants. Indoor pollution can be as much as five times worse than the pollution blanketing the city streets outside. The thresholds for defining a sick building are high – 20 percent of the inhabitants must display syndromes such as dizziness, dry or itchy skin, sore throats, sinus congestion, nose irritation, fatigue, nausea, or headaches, before a building is so designated.[18] Here again, pollution diminished rather than enhanced American wealth and power by weakening its workers' productivity and swelling the health care bill. And once again ideology and special interests joined to thwart national interests. The Reagan White House marshalled support to kill any congressional proposals that addressed the issue. Nothing was done until the 1991 Indoor Air Quality Act imposed indoor pollution standards.

Asbestos is yet another severe indoor pollution problem. Asbestos has been mined and used for a variety of purposes since the Roman Empire. It was not until the early 1980s, however, that several studies revealed how dangerous asbestos is. A 1988 EPA study found 501 000 commercial and public buildings with crumbling (friable) asbestos which caused a health hazard.[19] With young lungs much more susceptible to asbestos, concern has mounted over its presence in the nation's schools. A 1983 Education Department survey reported that 14 000 schools had an asbestos problem which would cost $1.4 billion to repair. Three years later the Education Department revised its estimate to 35 000 schools whose asbestos would cost $3.1 billion to remove.[20] Fortunately, asbestos in only about one out of five of those schools requires immediate removal because it is "friable" or crumbling. Removal can worsen the problem by releasing the asbestos dust. The total bill for removal of friable asbestos may be anywhere from $30 billion to $150 billion.[21]

Since the 1970s, the Occupational Safety and Health Administration (OSHA) has pressured Congress to impose asbestos standards. In 1980, Congress finally passed the Asbestos School Hazard Detection and Control Act which helped state and local governments to evaluate the problem. By 1985, 16 insurance companies and 34 asbestos corporations set up a claims facility to deal with an explosion of litigation. Congress did not enact tough legislation until 1986 when its Asbestos Hazard Emergency Response Act allocated $600 million for removing asbestos. That same year, the EPA announced that in 1996 all asbestos products would be banned.

The Reagan White House did all it could to kill these bills.

Yet another indoor pollutant is radon-222, an invisible, odorless, radioactive gas that insidiously pollutes millions of homes and businesses across the country. Over 150 types of rocks and minerals emit radon. Radon accounts for about 55 percent of all radiation exposure, and perhaps as many as 13 000 lung cancer deaths a year.[22] The Reagan White House dismissed a series of studies revealing the danger posed by randon. The government has yet to impose radon emission standards.

The Reagan White House succeeded in delaying any action on the 1970 Clean Air Act, which was up for renewal in 1981. Although the old law stayed in effect, it had proved to be inadequate for reducing many of the nation's air pollutants. Some in Congress were just as obstructionist as the White House. Reagan and the Republican Party had allies in the Democratic Party camp, including such powerful leaders as Senate Majority leader Robert Byrd from West Virginia whose state was dependent on the coal industry, along with John Dingell, the Chair of the House Energy and Commerce Committee, whose district was dependent on the automobile industry.

The Reagan White House's bizarre belief that pollution was good since it reflected economic activity was attacked continuously by environmentalists. Although Reagan's White House had succeeded in packing the top ranks of the bureaucracies with anti-environmentalists, it could not completely muzzle lower-ranking officials. A series of alarming scientific reports issued throughout the 1980s, accompanied by public outrage, forced the White House grudgingly to respond. The Reagan administration tried to set back the policy clock to an era decades earlier before concepts such as greenhouse effect, toxic waste dump, population explosion, and environmental impact statement, became household words. Reality, however, continued to intrude on the White House.

The Reagan White House bowed to popular international efforts to slow the chemical destruction of the ozone layer. Under both powerful national and international pressure, in 1987 the Reagan White House reluctantly signed, with 24 other countries, the Montreal Protocol, whose signatories promised to freeze 1989 chlorofluorocarbon (CFC) production to 1986 levels and to halve CFC production by 2000. These efforts became even more urgent in 1988 when NASA's Ozone Trends Panel of scientists announced that chemicals had destroyed 3 percent of atmopheric ozone between 1969 and 1986. That 3 percent depletion would annually cause from 9 to 45 million new cases of skin cancer and 1.65 to 8.4 million cataract cases. Much more serious would be the effects on the food chain of continued ozone destruction. Crops and micro-organisms such as ocean plankton are vulnerable to ultraviolet radiation and increases could destroy vital food chain links. These "findings startled policymakers, industry representatives, and researchers around the world.... Within a matter of weeks the report's conclusions were widely accepted and public debate on the issue began to build. Suddenly ozone depletion was real."[23]

Later that year, the United States and 24 other countries signed the Montreal Protocol in which all signatories agreed to cut the production of CFCs. The potential costs of complying with the treaty were great – about $135 billion of American industrial, scientific, household, and government equipment depends on CFCs, while the United States manufactures about one-third of the world's CFC supply. Yet the benefits of eliminating ozone-destroying chemicals vastly outweigh the costs. The United States alone would save itself $6.5 trillion in health and food production costs by 2075, while the CFC and halon phase-out would only cost $27 billion.[24]

In 1988, James E. Hansen, director of NASA's Goddard Institute for Space Studies, announced that he was "99 percent certain" that global warming was occurring and would have a catastrophic effect on humanity. Hansen's Casandra-like warning crystalized the issue in Washington and across the nation. In August 1988, the EPA issued a warning to all relevant Federal and state agencies to prepare for the rising ocean waters and climate shifts spawned by the worsening greenhouse effect. Officials were bluntly told that the world's oceans would rise between 5 and 15 inches above sea level by 2025 and as much as 7 feet by 2100, leading to the loss of 80 percent of America's coastal wetlands. To slow global warming, the EPA recommended that the United States attempt to achieve an automobile fleet with a fuel efficiency of at least 40 miles per gallon, to reduce the average amount of fuel to heat a home to half what it took in 1980, and to impose taxes on coal, oil, and natural gas to encourage Americans to conserve and shift to renewable non-polluting sources such as solar and wind.[25]

Despite the Reagan White House's hostility to the environment, Congress was able to pass some measures that bettered rather worsened things. The Resource Conservation and Recovery Act (RCRA) of 1976 empowers the EPA to regulate the transport, storage, and treatment of hazardous and nonhazardous wastes. Amendments in 1980 and 1984 set even tougher cleanup standards and deadlines. The 1984 Hazardous and Solid Waste Amendment required double liners and leachable collection systems for all new landfills, and required the retrofitting of existing sites by 1988. In 1987, Congress finally enacted the Water Quality Act, after President Reagan vetoed two previous bills.

In all, Reaganomics was a socioeconomic, environmental, and moral disaster for the United States. Reaganomics locked America into a vicious socioeconomic cycle of lower economic growth, investments, savings, and higher interest rates, government spending, gap between rich and poor, poverty, and crime. During the 1980s, the economy actually grew less than in any decade since the Great Depression of the 1930s! Reaganomics did indeed make the rich richer and the poor poorer. The poverty rate rose from 11.4 percent in 1980 to 12.8 percent in 1989. Images frequently drown reality. Despite Reaganomic's disastrous impact, its sponsor left office with the highest popularity rating of any president since Franklin Roosevelt.[26]

Despite his promises to create a "kinder, gentler nation," President George Bush largely continued Reaganomics. On all policies, the Bush White House was split between ideologues such as the Office of Management and Budget (OMB) head Richard Darman, Council of Economic Advisors head Michael Boskin, and Chief of Staff John Sununu; and pragmatists such as Commerce Secretary Robert Mosbacher and Science Advisor Allan Bromley. The ideologues usually won. For example, on 11 November 1989, studies were simultaneously published by the National Advisory Committee on Semiconductors and the Economic Policy Institute warning that the United States was quickly falling behind in key high technology areas and that it could only regain the lead with comprehensive government policies. The ideologues dismissed the warning. John Sununu, the White House Chief of Staff, summed up Bush's economic outlook:

> The President feels very strongly that the free market system operates best when it does not have its hands tied by Government, is not shackled by a system that erroneously thinks it can improve it by command and control.[27]

During the 1988 election campaign, Bush had repeatedly faced the cameras and commanded, "Read my lips, no new taxes!" This was a remarkable statement from the man who had once been a fiscal conservative and had in the 1980 election campaign declared Reagan's promises "voodoo economics." His pledge to not raise taxes clearly helped Bush win the 1988 election but returned to haunt him four years later.

Although both the president and most in Congress wanted to reduce the deficit, Bush's insistence on a capital gains cut led to deadlock with Congress. Then, in 1990, Bush signed the Budget-Enforcement Act of 1990 which repealed the Gramm–Rudman deficit reduction bill and simply sought a reduction of $83 billion from the anticipated deficit over five years. To achieve the reduction, the bill raised the top rate for those Americans making over $80 000 from 28 percent to 31 percent, removed personal exemptions for those with incomes over $100 000, raised the gas tax by 5¢, and tightened other exemptions and deductions.

Aside from this tax bill, the centerpiece of Bush's economic policy was a banking reform bill that could have revamped the anachronistic and inefficient industry. But after he sent it to Congress, he lost interest and the bill died. Bush's only other significant economic initiative was to negotiate the North American Free Trade Association (NAFTA). NAFTA was signed on 17 December 1992. In all, Bush was disinterested in domestic policy and even national development, the "vision thing" as he dismissively called it. He largely concentrated on "foreign" policy issues, blind to the reality that all foreign and domestic policies are thoroughly meshed.

Although Bush continued most of Reagan's spend, tax, and borrow policies, he lacked his predecessor's luck and charisma. No postwar president has presided over slower economic growth than George Bush. Although the Federal Reserve did keep interest rates high, they averaged only 7.8 percent during the Bush administration compared to 10.1 percent during the Reagan years. Theoretically, those significantly lower rates should have boosted investment and thus economic growth. Instead, during Bush's four years the economy expanded by only 2.5 percent, disposable income by 1.2 percent, and jobs by 0.7 percent, while industrial production actually fell by 0.4 percent and the hourly wage fell by 1.7 percent. When confronted with such statistics, Bush and his staff disclaimed responsibility and instead pointed the finger at Congress, the Democrats, the Federal Reserve, and, somewhat heretically, the excesses of the 1980s.[28]

Bush supporters were certainly right to point to the 1980s' excesses as a source of the economic slowdown. Reaganomics quadrupled the national debt between 1980 and 1992. That immense increase in spending and borrowing stimulated an artificial expansion that will eventually have to be paid for. The prosperity of the 1980s was literally borrowed from the 1990s. Although Bush called his agreement to raise taxes in 1990 his greatest mistake, it would have been worse to sit by while the national debt continued to mount. In 1992, the Federal deficit was $368 billion and would have been much worse without the higher revenues.

Just as Bush, like Reagan, failed to understand the links between foreign and domestic policy, he was just as ignorant of how economic development and environmental protection enhance each other. Upon winning the White House in 1988, George Bush did pledge to be an "environmental president," adopt a "no net-loss of wetlands" policy, and strive for a "kinder, gentler America." While Bush's words were conservationist, his actions were thoroughly destructive. His choice for Interior Secretary, Manuel Lujan, followed his predecessor's policies of expanding access for corporations to public lands for minimal fees. Rather than protect wetlands, Bush promoted policies which would have opened for development nearly half of all currently designated wetlands. Although Bush did appoint former Conservation Foundation head William Reilly to lead the EPA, Reilly's efforts to enforce environmental law and address worsening problems were continually undercut by such White House conservatives as Vice-President Dan Quayle, Chief of Staff John Sununu, and OMB head Richard Darman. Quayle headed the White House Council on Competitiveness whose job was described by House Subcommittee on Health and the Environment Chair Representative Henry Waxman as "helping polluters block EPA efforts."[29]

Richly symbolic of the Bush administration's anti-environmentalism was its censorship of James Hansen, director of NASA's Goddard Institute for Space Studies, when he appeared before the Senate Subcommittee on Science, Technology, and Space on 8 May 1989. Hansen had previously stated he was 99 percent certain of the greenhouse effect's reality. Now he was ordered to express doubts over whether a greenhouse effect even existed or, if it did exist, whether it was primarily caused by people rather than Nature itself. Hansen later complained of his muzzling by the White House, arguing that,

I should be allowed to say what is my scientific position; there is no rationale by which OMB should be censuring scientific opinion. I can understand changing policy, but not science.[30]

In 1990, Congress passed and President Bush reluctantly signed the Clean Air Act. The new law established five categories for noncompliance – marginal, moderate, serious, severe, or extreme – and set new compliance deadlines for cities. While leaving the particulars to the cities, Washington asserted a strict framework in which the war against air pollution could be fought.

By its very toughness, the 1990 Clean Air Act created a very different set of problems from its weak predecessors. The Act required the EPA to write over 150 new rules within two years. Before then, the EPA had only enough personnel and budget to complete seven or eight new rulings annually. The EPA thus had to rely on councils of outside experts to help them write the new rules. Often these councils were packed with representatives from the very industries the EPA was charged with regulating. Conflicts of interests were rampant.

In all, a dozen years of Reaganomics was a national disaster. By nearly every interrelated measure of power, economic development, or social, environmental, and moral health, that latest version of Jeffersonianism left America worse rather than better off. During the 1992 presidential campaign, Reaganomics was challenged by a new version of Hamiltonianism, Clintonomics. Democratic candidate Bill Clinton, along with Reform Party leader Ross Perot, advocated comprehensive industrial policies to reverse America's decline, while George Bush waved the Jeffersonian anti-government banner. When the votes were tallied, Clinton had gotten 43 percent and Perot 19 percent of the vote while Bush mustered only 38 percent. Jeffersonianism was repudiated by nearly two-thirds of those Americans who voted; its eclipse, however, would prove to be brief.

CLINTONOMICS

Upon taking office in January 1993, the Clinton White House embarked on a range of macroeconomic initiatives such as reducing government spending and debt as a GNP percentage, devaluing the dollar, and forcing open protected foreign markets, along with new or enhanced industrial policies such as promoting the information super-highway, greater investments in high technology research and development, and expanding those industries targeted for development to include those that produced strategic consumer as well as military products.

The most successful of Clinton's macroeconomic initiatives was his reduction of the budget deficits. Clinton's 1993 budget passed by the narrowest of margins; every Republican voted against it. The plan will cut the expected deficit by $500 billion over five years by making $247 billion in spending cuts and $246 billion in new taxes. The plan also succeeded in raising taxes for the top 1.5 percent of income while lowering taxes for the poor and businesses. He did not, however, include in his plan his campaign promise for a middle-class tax cut. The policy had dramatic results. The budget deficit plunged from $340.5 billion in fiscal 1992 to $160 billion by 1995 and $112 billion in 1996. As Clinton pointed out, the budget would have been in surplus had it not been for the huge annual interest payments the United States must pay resulting from Reaganomic's quadrupling of the national debt.

Clinton swore to "reinvent government" by reorganizing and streamlining its functions and personnel, and assigned Vice President Gore to lead the task. The policy included many reforms. The current one-year budget was expanded to a two-year budget to extend the strategic outlook and reduce formulation costs and time. Each agency was asked to halve its regulations. Dozens of regional offices were closed. The ratio of supervisors to employees was increased from one for every seven to one for every 15. Private firms were allowed to take over many government printing and real estate management duties. Clinton's "reinvention of government" will take as long as a decade to complete, but will annually save tens of billions of dollars for the government, businesses, and households. From 1992 to 1996 alone, the Clinton White House reduced the Federal civilian payroll by 220 000 jobs, a remarkable savings.

This progressive reduction was somewhat offset by a White House cave-in to far-right Republican demands to raise defense spending to $264.3 billion in 1996, an amount $8 billion more than what the Pentagon itself proposed. The Republicans continued naively to believe that "national security" is synonymous with the amount of money tossed into the Pentagon's lap. Under Defense Secretary William Perry, however, the Pentagon did try to curb some of its bloated budget and wasteful spending. In November 1996, for example, the Pentagon chose models for a future Joint Strike Fighter developed by largely civilian aircraft producers Boeing and Lockheed over largely military producer McDonnell Douglas. The Joint Strike Fighter would be used by all four branches, an important departure from the policy of designing and producing different aircraft for each service. Boeing and Lockheed won the competition by cost as well as design. Lockheed, for example, had succeeded in cutting the production costs for its F-16 by 38 percent despite a 75 percent cut in production. Whether the Joint Strike Fighter succeeds in achieving the goal of costing only $30 million each remains to be seen. The Joint Fighter Project is estimated to generate $350 billion for its three decade run.[31]

Clinton was also successful in opening some foreign markets. Although the Bush administration had negotiated most of NAFTA, the Clinton White House renegotiated the treaty's environmental and labor clauses to enhance American interests in those areas. Even then, Congress barely passed NAFTA. The treaty took effect on 1 January 1994. NAFTA's passage was a major triumph for American interests. While the United States and Canada enjoy relatively free bilateral trade, NAFTA will require Mexico to cut drastically its web of import and investment barriers, and enforce strict environmental and labor protection laws. Mexico would have to open completely its banking and securities markets to American and Canadian firms by 2007 and 2004, respectively. In addition, NAFTA has domestic content rules for goods assembled in any one of those three countries from parts originating elsewhere. All three countries would eliminate all tariffs to each others' products over 15 years. Mexico's tariffs averaged 10 percent while America's were 3.5 percent. Any nationalization of another member's firms must be fully compensated.

Clinton has used NAFTA as a powerful economic bloc to pressure the two other blocs, the European Union and the informal but even more formidable Far East economy, to lower their trade and investment barriers. At an Asia Pacific Economic Cooperation (APEC) summit meeting at Seattle in November 1993, Clinton got the other 17 government leaders to agree in principle to creating a Pacific Basin free trade region among industrial nations by 2010 and all nations by 2020. The Clinton White House was also successful in concluding the Uruguay Round of GATT negotiations and converting that international organization into the more powerful World Trade Organization (WTO) in 1995. More recently, in November 1996 at APEC's Manila summit, Clinton convinced APEC's leaders to agree to eliminate tariffs on all computer products by 2000. These were important first steps that have yet to be codified by treaty.

While successful at liberalizing trade at the multilateral level, the Clinton administration had less success in fighting unfair traders such as Japan. In 1995, after months of tough negotiations the White House did get Tokyo to sign to an automobile agreement that slightly cracks open Japan's controlled market to American producers. In 1995, 142 000 cars were shipped from North America to Japan, of which 58 000 were from American producers and the rest from Japanese producers with plants in the United States. That figure must be offset by the 4 million Japanese cars sold in the United States, either from cars imported or manufactured in the United States. Nonetheless, this agreement along with a stronger yen from 1985 helped America regain its lead as the world's top automobile producer, which it had lost in 1979. In 1994, 12 million cars were produced in the United States compared to 11 million in Japan. If the figures are broken down into American versus Japanese producers, the latter continued to hold the lead.

Despite these and related efforts, America's trade deficit with Japan worsened to $59 billion in 1995, the worst in absolute terms since it suffered the same amount in 1987; in relative terms, the 1995 figure was less when adjusted for inflation. Although the trade deficit with Japan dropped to $50 billion in 1996, it could actually be twice that when exports from Japan's overseas factories are included. A major reason for Japan's persistent trade surplus, in addition to Tokyo's insidious trade and investment barriers, was the Clinton White House's decision to allow the dollar to strengthen against the yen from around 85 in 1994 to 115 in 1996. That yen devaluation gave an enormous advantage to Japanese producers and imposed an equally enormous disadvantage on American producers.

Here again, Reaganomic's legacy has been a dead weight on the promotion of American wealth and power. The quadrupling of America's national debt by the Reagan and Bush administrations put the United States in hock to foreign creditors, especially the Japanese. It was a Faustian bargain. In the short-term, American interest rates could remain lower by borrowing money from foreign rather than exclusively domestic creditors. Yet, by owning huge shares of American debt, Tokyo has asserted huge power over American policy. If any administration pushes too hard for "fair" and "equal" bilateral trade and investments with Japan, including a signficant devaluation of the dollar, Tokyo can simply threaten to dump its US Treasury bills. America's interest rates would soar, and its economy and stock market would freefall, along with the president's approval rating. Clinton's attempts to reduce the national debt will slowly wean the United States from its dependence on Japan. In the meanwhile, Japan will continue to enjoy its huge trade and investments surpluses that at once strengthen Japanese wealth and power and diminish America's.

The contradictory policies toward Japan reflected a White House split over international economic strategy. In June 1993, the Clinton White House announced that henceforth it would give higher priority to aiding foreign corporations expand their production in the United States than to aiding American firms expand their overseas production, although the first priority would continue to be American firms expanding production in the United States. The policy followed a debate between Council of Economic Advisors chief Laura Tyson and Labor Secretary Robert Reich. Tyson maintained that the ownership of production mattered because foreign owned corporations tend to keep their most value-added work at home while often bankrupting rival American businesses in the United States. Reich countered that production location and thus jobs for American workers was more important. Tyson lost.[32]

On 29 September 1993, President Clinton announced a 65-part plan to aid exports by cutting red tape, boosting export subsidies, and increasing lobbying in foreign capitals on behalf of American firms and industries. His goal was to increase American exports from $628 billion in 1992 to $1 trillion by 2000. By cutting red tape alone, Clinton estimated that exports would increase by $35 billion the following year and more thereafter. About 80 percent of Federal export financing goes to agriculture, which accounts for only 10 percent of American exports. Clinton promised to shift much of that money to support industrial good exports.[33]

Unfortunately, like previous administrations, the Clinton White House imposed unilateral economic sanctions which hurt American firms and had no effect on the targeted country. In April 1995, the White House announced that it was severing trade with Iran and Libya because both states supported international terrorism. The sanctions were a response to international and domestic criticism. In the months leading up to the announcement, the White House had tried to prevent Russia and China from selling nuclear technology to Iran. Those countries had pointed out that their sales were legal and that American firms conducted business with Iran. Meanwhile, Congressional Republicans meanwhile blasted the White House for being "soft" on Iran and offered even tougher measures.

The Clinton policy prevents American oil firms from handling any Iranian oil; previously they could sell it in third markets. Although Iran is banned from selling to the United States, it was allowed to buy non-lethal American products. The new policy cut off those sales. America's foreign rivals will rush to fill the trade gap left by American firms. Then in 1996, Clinton signed the Helms–Burton Act which would penalize foreign firms which lease property in Cuba formerly owned by Americans and nationalized by the communists. Once again, the sanctions will shoot America's economy in the foot by straining relations with its trade partners while having no discernible effect on Cuba's economy.

In other areas, Clinton's initiatives were stonewalled by Republicans and rebellious Democrats. During the 1992 campaign, he had repeatedly announced his determination to cut back spending on the two most voracious black holes in America's economy – defense and health. But these promises were economic as well as political gambles. He risked not only alienating entrenched special interests in the military and health care industrial complexes, but also the two biggest job creators of the 1980s. If other industries could not expand their job creation, the result would be a deep recession. In the end, the Pentagon succeeded in gaining Clinton's support for funding which would enable it to fight two wars at once, a highly unlikely senario, that boosted its budget. Meanwhile, Clinton's 1993 health care reform plan died in Congress, defeated by a coalition of powerful special interests.[34]

Environmentalists had hailed the 1992 victory of Bill Clinton and Al Gore as inaugurating a new progressive era after 12 years of policies that promoted environmental and thus economic destruction. While Clinton's environmental record as Arkansas governor was mixed, it was assumed that Gore, the author of a classic paen to environmentalism, *Earth in the Balance*, would pull the new president solidly on the environmental path.[35] Clinton packed his cabinet with such powerful environmentalists as Bruce Babbit as Interior Secretary, Carol Browner as EPA head, and Hazel O'Leary as Energy Secretary.

Disappointment soon followed as environmental issues took a back seat to other problems. Although the Democrats enjoyed majorities in both houses of Congress during his first two years, Clinton found his policy agenda obstructed by shifting coalitions of maverick Democrats and virtually all Republicans led by Senate Minority Leader Bob Dole and House Republican Minority Leader

Newt Gingrich. On one bill after another – deficit reduction, NAFTA, crime reduction – Clinton won by the thinnest of congressional margins. And Clinton paid a heavy price for each reluctant vote for his programs, particularly to those from Western states. To gain the votes of Western congressmen, Clinton backed away from mining and grazing reform. Congress voted down a measure to reform the Clean Water Act. To worsen matters, Clinton's ability to govern was also undermined by the most vicious mass-media criticism any modern president has yet endured.

Among Bill Clinton's many campaign promises was to raise fees for logging, mining, and grazing on public lands. Clinton had blasted the low-fee policy as a give-away to special interests at the taxpayer's expense. But less than two months after entering the White House, he caved in to pressure from western senators and announced he would no longer seek the fee increases in that year's budget. Although Clinton eventually succeeded in rounding up enough votes for his deficit reduction budget, he was severely criticized for allowing the subsidized exploitation of the nation's resources by special interests on public lands to continue. The timing of Clinton's retreat was particularly galling to environmentalists, since it occurred on the eve of his trip to Portland for the "Forest Summit" to resolve that region's logging controversy. At the summit, attended by environmentalists and cornucopians, Clinton forged a compromise whereby logging would be resumed at higher sustainable levels while, clear-cutting would be reduced and wildlife habitat preserved.

President Clinton did redeem some of his standing with environmentalists on 21 April 1993, when he announced that the United States would sign the Biodiversity Treaty and comply with the timetable for reducing carbon emmissions set by the Global Warming Treaty, both of which the Bush White House had rejected. Both treaties had been negotiated and signed by virtually all countries represented at the Rio de Janeiro Earth Summit in June 1992. In his annoucement, Clinton argued that the theoretical trade-off between economic growth and environmental protection did not exist; in fact, the opposite was true, economic development and environmental protection go hand-in-hand.

As if all of these problems were not bad enough, the Superfund program to clean up America's worst hazardous waste sites became politicized. On 6 October 1994, Republicans torpedoed a law proposed by President Clinton to reform Superfund. The Clinton measure would have cut Superfund costs and sped cleanup by reducing lawsuits, simplifying regulations, and lowering standards. While in principle, the Republican Party favored these goals, they killed the Superfund reform to deny Clinton a legislative victory on the eve of the mid-term elections. Their excuse was that the bill included retroactive liability for polluters before the original bill was passed in 1980. In addition to Clinton, the losers were, of course, taxpayers who must continue to pay the Superfund's huge annual costs, and even more so the one of four Americans who live within four miles of a toxic waste dump.

All told, during his first two years in office, Clinton's policies were largely successful. By most indicators, the economy and productivity grew faster, and the unemployment and inflation rates were lower than the mid-1960s. Some economic problems remained intractable, including the trade deficit, widening gap between rich and poor, and national pessimism. His environmental victories were limited – the 1993 logging agreement, 1993 signing of the Biodiversity and Global Warming treaties, and 1994 California Desert Protection Act protecting much of the Mohave Desert from development.

Most American voters are fickle, easily swayed by the prevailing winds of charisma, catchy slogans, and powerful images. A mere two years after two-thirds of voters embraced the industrial policy visions of Clinton and Perot, the Republican Party recaptured Congress with large majorities in both houses. The political tide shifted from a combination of Clinton's weak political skills and questions about his character, and the Republican Party's power to propound a new version of Reaganomics through a vast radio, newspaper (two of three newspapers are Republican), and direct mailing network. Republicans raised twice as many campaign donations from powerful interest groups and individuals alike. In all, the Republicans proved to be much more adept politicians than the Democrats. In concentrating on substance, the Clinton White House failed to win the media battle of images for the hearts and minds of American voters. While Clinton was discussing complex policy issues for which there are no easy answers, the Republican leaders spotlighted alleged scandals and promised to cut taxes. The average American may not respond to the vision of the information super-highway, but certainly understands the promise of a tax cut.

Leading the charge for a Republican Congress was Representative Newt Gingrich, the House Minority Leader, who got the Republican candidates for Congress to sign a "Contract with America" which included sweeping tax and spending cuts, a balanced budget amendment, and other measures. Although he once taught history at a community college, Gingrich apparently did not study the impact of Reaganomics on the United States. Much of his "Contract With America" was repackaged Reaganomics. Like Reagan, Gingrich promised that tax cuts would expand the economy and generate more revenues, thus paying for themselves. Those aware of the failures of Reaganomics warned that the result would be ever-worse national debt. Gingrich's promise to push through a balanced budget amendment received similar criticism. During a 1992 attempt by far-right Republicans to pass such an amendment, a group of 447 economists, which included seven Nobel Prize winners, signed a statement that concluded:

> When the private sector is in recession, a constitutional requirement that would force cuts in public spending or tax increases could worsen the economic turndown, causing greater loss of jobs, production, and income.[36]

Gingrich and his followers dismissed such criticism with their belief that the "magic of the marketplace" will solve all of the nation's ills.

Gingrich's "Contract" was bolstered by the Christian Coalition's "Contract with the American Family." The fundamentalist Christian Coalition forms the backbone of the radical right's political support and agenda, and presides over vast financial resources and a nation-wide, grass-roots level organizational empire. By the mid-1990s, fundamentalists had taken over more than 2200 school boards across the country, where they try to replace science with biblical notions of creation, impose prayers in the school day, and forbid sex education. Ironically, while the radicals condemn government, they have no qualms about government intervention in our bodies and bedrooms. The fundamentalists fight fiercely to outlaw abortion and homosexuality, among other currently legally accepted practices. They also want to eliminate public funding for family planning clinics and prevent biotechnology firms from genetic engineering, claiming that both practices violate "God's will."

After the Christian Coalition, perhaps no interest group has given the Republican Party more support than the National Rifle Association (NRA). In 1994, it had a war-chest of $29.3 million with which to buy congressional, statehouse, and local government votes and finance the campaigns of sympathetic politicians. Over the years, the NRA has managed to kill every significant gun-control measure that entered Congress. The NRA claims that American citizens have the unqualified right to own guns. In fact, the Constitution's Second Amendment states that, "A well regulated Militia, being necessary to the security of a free State, the right of the people to keep and bear Arms, shall not be infringed." In other words, there is no individual right to own guns; only members of a militia regulated by the state for the state's defense can do so. Even more troubling Republican allies are the so-called "citizens militias" which espouse the destruction of the Federal government. On 19 April 1995, militia members blew up the Federal building in Tulsa, Oklahoma, killing 164 people, wounding hundreds of others, and causing billions of dollars worth of damage.

On 8 November 1994, the power balance shifted from Hamiltonianism back toward Jeffersonianism when the Democratic Party lost both houses of Congress. Republicans Bob Dole and Newt Gingrich became Senate majority leader and House Speaker, respectively. The Republicans vowed to enact ten major bills during their first 100 days in office, including measures either to eliminate or reduce to the point of impotence the nation's environmental laws.

Despite its seemingly invincible power, the much balleyhooed "Gingrich Revolution" quickly sputtered to a halt. Defections by moderate Republicans sank the radicals' attempts to pass a balanced budget amendment. The President vetoed a Republican bill which would have eliminated most environmental, safety, and health regulations along with the entire Commerce Department. The Republican Congress and President Clinton split the difference on some issues such as welfare reform and the balanced budget timetable. Both Clinton and the Republicans side-stepped the future problem of funding social security.

Gingrichnomics seemed as concerned with protecting the rich as was Reaganomics. In April 1995, Congressional Republicans killed a clause in President Clinton's 1996 budget bill that would have raised about $3.6 billion from taxes over a decade from wealthy American expatriates worth over $5 million who had renounced their citizenship. In justifying the administration's policy, Treasury Department spokesperson Leslie Samuels declared: "If you've gotten your riches from America, you should pay your fair share of taxes. These expatriates are like economic Benedict Arnolds. They shouldn't have an unfair advantage over other citizens because they're superrich."[37] Republicans countered that Americans should be free to make money and even renounce their citizenship as they wished.

The Republicans also tried to push through a "tort reform" bill which would have made it much more difficult for fraud victims to sue those in whom they had entrusted their money. The bill would have sharply cut back the Securities and Exchange Commission's staff, budget, and powers. The bill was a blatant give-away to financial speculators. There is no litigation crisis. Securities suits are only 1 percent of all Federal civil cases and have not increased in over two decades. The stock market is booming. The only people the lawsuits harm are the criminals who annually defraud Americans of tens of billions of dollars. Although the Republicans claimed that the financial industry could regulate itself, as in all other economic sectors, the anti-fraud laws were written because, historically, anarchy had promoted criminality. Industries, like individuals, will not regulate themselves. That is why government exists.

In the summer of 1995, the Republicans and Clinton unveiled their respective plans to eliminate the budget deficit over time. The Republican proposal would have achieved a balanced budget by 2002 by cutting expected spending by $898 billion over those seven years, of which medicare would be cut by $270 billion, medicaid by $180 billion, welfare by $100.5 billion, agriculture by $13.4 billion, discretionary spending by $190 billion, and foreign aid by $23.4 billion. The Commerce Department would be completely eliminated and virtually all other government institutions severely reduced. The only significant spending increase would be $58.7 billion more for the Pentagon. During those years, the Republicans promised to cut taxes by $245 billion, which would include halving the current 28 percent capital gains tax, capping the corporate tax rate at 25 percent, and giving all Americans with annual incomes up to $200 000 a $500-a-child tax credit, with lesser credits going to those with incomes up to $250 000. The Republicans matched their proposal with incendiary rhetoric, with some congressmen going so far as to call government officials "Gestapo" and "jack-booted thugs." Clinton's plan also balanced the budget in seven years, but by moderate spending and tax cuts.

Either plan would drastically affect the economy. In the short term, the sharp cutbacks could push the economy into recession and retard a recovery. The Congressional Budget Office (CBO) predicted that the Republican budget cuts would diminish economic growth by 0.4 percent annually over the seven years. Over time, however, the lower spending and debt would allow interest rates to fall 1 or 2 percentage points as more capital is available for the private sector. Lower interest rates in turn would drive down the dollar's value, which could stimulate exports and inhibit imports, thus generating more growth.[38]

Ironically, in their idealogical zeal, the Republicans sought to destroy institutions such as the Council of Economic Advisors (CEA), Office of Technology Assessment, and Departments of Commerce, Education, and Energy, that had rendered enormous aid to their primary constituents, Big Business. Conservative economists have dominated the CEA since it was inaugurated in 1947. The CEA's budget in 1995 was $3.4 million. Over the years, the Office of Technology Assessment has funneled billions of dollars into private research and development projects. In 1994 alone, the Commerce Department helped American businesses win over $25 billion in contracts that would otherwise have gone to foreign firms, an excellent return on its $250 million budget. By eliminating the Energy Department and transferring its needed programs elsewhere, the Republicans would save no more than $3.5 million! In a bizarre rhetorical twist, radical Republicans claim that government institutions which promote the economy are "corporate welfare." Commerce Secretary Ronald Brown replied that, "Our global competitors are laughing at us. Just at that moment when we've finally learned that there is no way to win without a public–private partnership, without getting the government involved in promoting a nation's exports." the Republicans are trying to destroy those policies.[39]

By 1996, the political tide had again shifted. Radical Republican excesses had dampened the support for Jeffersonianism. Meanwhile, Clinton's policies of fiscal conservatism, strategic investments, administrative reforms, and environmental protection had successfully managed the economy into its best overall performance in three decades. Not since the mid-1960s had the nation's unemployment and inflation been so low, while the budget deficit was one-quarter its 1992 level, the gap between rich and poor that had been widening for decades was arrested and slightly reversed in 1996, and economic growth flowed at an average 2.5 percent rate over those four years. Clinton's version of Hamiltonianism had triumphed!

When Bob Dole retired from the Senate in June 1996 to run for president, Trent Lott took over his position as Senate Majority leader. Although a leading Jeffersonian, Lott realized he had to compromise or else risk the public's condemnation of the Republican Party as the king of gridlock and extremism. In the summer and fall 1996, Lott and Clinton hammered out compromises on welfare reform and the minimum wage that lessened the public's antagonism toward both parties.

These last minute deals allowed both sides to claim limited victories in the 5 November 1996 election. Bill Clinton was reelected in the 5 November 1996 election with 49 percent of the vote, defeating Bob Dole with 42 percent and Ross Perot with 9 percent. Yet the Republican Party retained both houses of Congress, expanding their hold over the Senate with a 55–45 lead and losing seats in the House of Representatives to a 229–206 margin. The Republicans in the Senate are considered more conservative than before the election and those in the House more moderate. That result probably reflected money more than ideology. In 1996 alone, the Republican Party raised and spent $398 million to the Democratic Party's $242 million.

What then is the future for Clintonomics and Reaganomics? Leaders in both parties pledged to make 1997 and beyond an era of bipartisanship. Will that be the reality? Although the Republican right wing has curbed some of its rhetorical excesses, it remains entrenched in the Party's leadership and committed to its Jeffersonian agenda. The ideological and political gulf will be difficult if not impossible to bridge on most issues. No matter whether cooperation or conflict prevails, one thing is certain. The unwinnable tug-of-war between those contemporary versions of Hamiltonianism and Jeffersonianism will shape the debate and policies.

7 The Industrial Policy Legacy

Policies shape more than the fate of industries, technologies, or firms. Directly or indirectly they can affect virtually every aspect of national development, including its growth rate and per-capita income; population growth rate; ethnic and racial mix; urban, suburban, and rural quality of life; environmental health; and class, racial, and regional disparities in wealth and dynamism. While Americans have much to cheer about in terms of their living standards and quality of life, there are several areas, such as the fall in real income, growing gap between rich and poor, and entrenched poverty, crime, illiteracy, and racial animosities, that call into question the efficacy of past, present, and future policies.

Misplaced and poorly implemented industrial policies – whether labeled macroeconomic, industrial, technology, or trade – are the most important reasons for such festering problems which a different set of policies could alleviate. Unfortunately, there are formidable political obstacles blocking the implemention of more progressive, far-sighted policies to manage those problems. Entrenched interest groups and partisan politics rather than planning determine America's industrial policies. Not surprisingly, the results are often contradictory, fall short of expectations, or actually provoke the opposite of what was intended.

What is the legacy of over two centuries of America's industrial policies? What kind of society have Washington's industrial policies created? What will the future hold?

AMERICAN DECLINE OR RENAISSANCE?

The perennial rivalry between Jeffersonians and Hamiltonians spills over into the debate over whether or not America is a declining power, and if so, what to do about it. Jeffersonians assert that America remains the world's greatest power and that only high taxes and regulations hobble the nation; cut those and America will soar on a "magic market ride" to unprecedented heights of prosperity and power.[1]

Hamiltonians counter that the real world is more complex. While America's economy has continued to surge upward in absolute terms, its geoeconomic rivals have caught up or even surpassed the United States by a range of financial, manufacturing, technological, trade, and socioeconomic indicators.[2] Policies, markets, power, and prosperity are thoroughly entwined – policies matter as much as markets in determining a nation's relative power and prosperity. America's relative decline can be partly attributed to its *ad hoc*, politically contrived, and ineffective industrial policies. To rebuild the nation's geoeconomic power, Washington must emulate its rivals and pursue comprehensive industrial policies that develop the economy.

Who is right? During the 1980s, the empirical if not political weight of the debate shifted decisively in favor of Hamiltonians. Although by most indicators, America's economy had been declining since 1973, Reaganomics grossly accelerated an array of socioeconomic problems. Perhaps the most startling of these problems was Reaganomics' quadrupling of America's national debt – between 1980 and 1992, it rose from $976 billion to $4.2 trillion. Other problems were just as troubling. In 1985, the United States was transformed from the world's greatest creditor to a debtor nation. During the 1980s, Japan surpassed the United States by manufacturing, technological, and financial indicators.[3] What caused America's relative geoeconomic decline? Among an array of interrelated reasons, America's irrational industrial policies were the most important.

Despite the growing importance of the information age and its highways, the manufacture of goods and services based on new or improved technologies must remain the backbone of national power. During the 1980s, American industries were bashed by an overvalued dollar, high interest rates, and misplaced and poorly executed industrial policies. Although manufacturing has rebounded in the 1990s, in the decades ahead it faces even worse challenges than its survivors have already overcome. A five-year study by the Office of Technology Assessment concluded in 1992 that American manufacturing in most industries had lost its competitive edge. It reported that America's share of world imports rose to 17.5 percent in 1986 from 12.9 percent in 1970, while its share of world exports fell from 13.8 percent to 10.3 percent. The result was an ever-worsening merchandise trade deficit that was draining American wealth, jobs, technologies, and finance. Manufacturing jobs numbered 20.2 million in 1981 and 18.4 million in 1991, a loss of 1.8 million jobs or a 9 percent reduction over a decade.[4]

Technology is yet another area where foreign rivals have equaled or leapfrogged the United States. In March 1991, the White House Council on Competitiveness released an intensive study of 94 technologies considered essential for industrial supremacy. The report concluded that the United States enjoyed a strong lead or remained competitive in about half and was weak or losing badly in the rest.[5]

The reasons for these declines are complex but include an ever-more competitive global market; the neomercantilist strategies of other countries; the high wages and health care costs of American labor; the decrease in research and development; the low savings rate; the nation's crumbling infrastructure; and the financial system which encourages short-term speculation rather than long-term investments. Federal policies have been partly responsible for either determining or tolerating all of these. The Council on Competitiveness urged that Washington help reverse this decline with a different set of policies that encouraged "patient" capital investments that look for long-term returns; upgraded education and training for workers, technicians, and scientists; the diffusion of appropriate technologies to entrepreneurs; the research and development of new technologies; and policies which nurture and promote "infant" cutting edge industries.

Such ideas, of course, are anathema to Jeffersonians. With no further comment, the Bush administration dismissed the report as advocating "industrial policy."[6] The Hamiltonian Clinton White House agreed that the report did indeed advocate a systematic industrial policy and warmly embraced the idea.

One of the most important advantages that America's toughest rivals enjoy is access to low-cost capital. For example, between 1987 and 1989, while American corporations raised $5.7 billion in equity, Japanese corporations raised $22 billion, or four times as much in an economy 60 percent America's size. One major reason why the Japanese can raise capital so easily is that stock prices regularly trade at 40 times a company's earnings, while for American stocks the trading rarely gets beyond ten times earnings. Thus, for Japanese firms it takes an average four times less stock to raise the same amount of capital as an American firm. Japanese firms also enjoy far lower interest rates than their American counterparts.

Why do Japanese firms enjoy such inexpensive and easy assess to equity and loans? The answer lies in Tokyo's rational, far-sighted, and systematic industrial policies which are designed constantly to expand the wealth, dynamism, and technological edge of Japan's economy at the expense of foreign rivals. Japan's stock markets are an insider's game; usually only 5–10 percent of the stock of Japan's industrial giants are for sale at any time. The demand for such stock is high because the supply is low, thus allowing Japanese firms to raise capital cheaply and quickly. Where are the other stocks? While American banks are forbidden from owning stocks in companies, Japanese banks, along with insurance firms and trading companies, are the financial cores of huge industrial groups known as *"keiretsu."*

The less money a corporation enjoys, the fewer investments it can make in the research, development, and marketing of new products. Here again, Japan's neomercantilist system surpassed in effectiveness that of the United States. In 1990, despite having an economy only two-thirds the size, Japan's $586 billion in capital investments surpassed America's $524 billion. The previous year, American industry contributed $71.77 billion on research and development while the government in Washington chipped in $68.73 billion. Meanwhile, Japanese industry spent $85.4 billion on research and development.[7]

Other factors frequently cited as reasons for the decline in manufacturing and technology are dubious at best. Since 1973, productivity has fallen seemingly in tandem with the drop in real income. Yet despite all that ails the United States, American workers are still the world's most productive. In 1990, the average full-time American employee annually produced $49 000 in goods and services, well above his counterparts in France of $47 000, Germany of $44 200, Japan of $38 200, and Britain of $37 100.[8] Over the past five decades, those countries either grew faster or as fast as the United States. During the 1980s, the per-capita incomes of Japan and Germany surpassed that of the United States. And yet America's productivity remains much higher. Wealth's distribution rather than its creation accounts for the differences.

High taxes are blamed for America's economic problems. American complaints about high taxes are not new. American Independence was fueled by a tax revolt, and ever since Americans have complained loudly about taxes – while denouncing any cutbacks in government services that affect them personally. All along, Americans have resisted tax increases, preferring to borrow against their children's future to spend today. Jeffersonians have led the tax revolt charge, claiming that the lower the taxes, the higher the savings and consumption, and thus the higher the economic growth.

Once again, reality is much more messy than the Jeffersonians would have us believe. Americans have relatively little reason to gripe about high rates. Among the 24 industrial countries of the Organization for Economic Cooperation and Development (OECD), only Turkey has a lower tax rate than the United States. While in 1989, tax revenues equaled 29.8 percent of America's gross domestic product (GDP), it was 31.3 percent in Japan, 34.0 percent in Canada, 37.1 percent in Italy, 37.3 percent in Britain, 37.4 percent in Germany, and 44.4 percent in France. Although America's lower tax rate leaves much more money in the pockets of households and businesses alike, it does not lead to higher saving rates, as Jeffersonians assert. Americans tend to spend rather than save their money. In fact, America's 4.7 percent savings rate was by far the lowest among leading democratic industrial countries; In contrast, French saved 12 percent of their household income, Germans 13.9 percent, Italians 15.6 percent, British 9.1 percent, Canadians 10.4 percent, and Japanese 14.3 percent. Nor did it lead to higher growth rates: in 1989, the United States grew 2.2 percent, Japan 3.4 percent, Germany 2.6 percent, France 2.8 percent, Italy 2.6 percent, and Britain 2.1 percent.[9] Although America's low savings are certainly a problem, that problem diminishes in global financial markets where American firms can borrow from the least expensive sources. The real problem is that foreign borrowing means that interest payments flow abroad rather than stay at home.

INDUSTRIAL POLICY PRIORITIES

The central problem behind America's relative decline is that politics rather than grand geoeconomic strategy shapes America's industrial policies. Not surprisingly, Washington's industrial policy priorities are starkly different from those of its economic rivals. A recent comparison of government subsidies to industry revealed that, not suprisingly, Washington spent the most on research and development for defense – 68.6 percent of total spending compared to London's 50.3 percent, Paris' 34.1 percent, Bonn's 12.5 percent, and Tokyo's tiny 4.5 percent. Washington's next largest percentage of money went to health – 11.9 percent compared to London's 4.3 percent, Paris' 3.6 percent, Bonn's 3.2 percent, and Tokyo's 2.4 percent. Spending on agriculture was roughly equal – while Washington spent 2.3 percent, London contributed 4.2 percent, Paris

3.6 percent, Bonn 2.0 percent, and Tokyo 4.0 percent. Surprisingly, there were similar percentages of R & D for civil space programs – 6.0 percent for Washington, 2.7 percent for London, 5.9 percent for Paris, 4.9 percent for Bonn, and 6.1 percent for Tokyo. To the glee of Jeffersonians everywhere, none of the countries devoted much to the environment – Washington and Tokyo tied with 0.5 percent, while Paris spent even less with 0.4 percent and London and Bonn weighed in at 1.0 percent and 3.3 percent, respectively. Nor were there significant differences in infrastructure R & D. Washington and Tokyo contributed 1.8 percent, Bonn 1.9 percent, Paris 3.2 percent, and London 1.5 percent. America's rivals grossly outspent the United States in two key categories – education and industry. While Washington spent a miserly 3.6 percent on education, London spent 20.2 percent, Paris 26.6 percent, Bonn 43.8 percent, and Tokyo 50.8 percent. And in industry, while Washington contributed a tragically paltry 0.2 percent of its R & D budget to industry, London spent 8.7 percent, Paris 10.6 percent, Bonn 15.3 percent, and Tokyo 4.8 percent.[10]

Although there are some clear winners, to varying extents, taxpayers pick up the tab and industrial policies shape every economic sector across the country. Some of the targets are of dubious importance at best. Its popularity aside, few would rate the sports industrial complex to be among America's strategic industries. Nonetheless, sports annually receive billions in tax dollars and other benefits. The popular perception is that sports teams bring wealth and tax revenues to the cities that harbor them, and thus justify any government handouts they receive along the way. That perception is grossly exaggerated; sports teams often cost their hosts a net loss. Economist Robert Noll admits that "opening a branch of Macy's has a greater economic impact."[11] Discretionary income is spent on sports events. If the sports events do not exist, then that income will go to other forms of entertainment. San Francisco, for example, got only a $3.1 million net gain from the Giants baseball team, a drop in a metropolitan economy worth $30 billion or 10 000 times larger.

Despite these realities, cities across the country compete to build immensely expensive sports palaces and then give them away to any club that deigns to use them. Toronto spent $580 million on its skydome, New York $100 million to refurbish Yankee Stadium. Some of the more extravagant city offers to attract a sports team include: St Petersburg's $138 million stadium with no team yet in sight;

Alexandria's $150 million stadium, sweetened by allowing the team owner to keep all ticket and concession sales; $135 million to refurbish the Baltimore stadium to keep the Orioles; $260 million for the St Louis dome; and $141 million for Coors' Field in Denver. And even after taking advantage of all that, owners are free to take their teams elsewhere. As sports writer Neil Sullivan puts it, "elected officials across the country have fallen all over themselves to open the public purse to build stadiums that by every reasonable standard should have been paid for by the ball clubs that use them."[12] After having enjoyed one city's facilities, an owner can take his or her franchise to an even better offer elsewhere.

Sports franchise owners are members of an exclusive oligopoly. In 1922, the Supreme Court ruled that baseball was exempt from antitrust laws. According to Noll, if a free market existed for baseball, there might well be 40 or 50 teams rather than the 26 today. Players would be paid much less; their salaries have increased 500 percent over the last decade. Team revenues increase 10–15 percent annually, boosted by TV income and merchandising. Cities would not "have to give away hundreds of millions of dollars to get one to relocate."[13] But such reforms are unlikely to happen any time soon; the sports industrial complex has too powerful a hold on Congress.

The restaurant business is yet another industrial complex that reaps enormous aid from public policies without being a strategic industry. The restaurant business is big business. Business-related meals represented a large chunk of the industry's sales. In 1989, 25 million Americans bought business meals at an average cost of $9.56. About 70 percent of those meals were purchased by people with annual incomes of less than $50 000.[14]

Washington's biggest boost for the restaurant industry is to allow businesses to deduct their meals and alcohol. Before 1986, businessmen could deduct 100 percent of their meals from Federal taxes. When Congress that year reduced the deductable rate to 80 percent, the National Restaurant Association protested that it would cost the industry jobs and profits. Those losses did not occur. In fact, the industry expanded 4 percent between 1986 and 1992.

Shortly after taking office, President Clinton proposed cutting the business tax deduction for meals from 80 percent to 50 percent of the cost, arguing that it would raise $16 billion more in annual revenues. His proposal ran into fierce opposition from the National Restaurant Association, which claimed it would cost the industry 160 000 jobs and $4 billion. The proposal died.[15]

The firearm industrial complex, led by the National Rifle Association (NRA) and comprising all those who manufacture or sell guns, is one of the nation's most powerful lobbies. In 1995, the NRA used its 3.5 million members and a $27 million war chest to continue to shoot down any gun-control measures. Americans overwhelmingly support far stronger regulation of firearms, with polls regularly indicating that 80–85 percent are in favor. Even gun owners support more restrictions. A 1995 *Time Magazine*/CNN Poll of 600 gun owners revealed that 47 percent opposed the NRA which claimed to speak on their behalf. Despite the fact that most Americans favor gun controls, the NRA has defeated nearly all attempts to institute them, even the most innocuous. Americans are required to register their marriages, children, and cars, but not their guns. In a bizzare twist of American values, until recently, the only guns banned anywhere in the United States were water pistols. In 1991, Boston's school board banned the Super Soaker water pistol.[16]

Americans have good reasons for wanting to restrict guns. The Center for Disease Control reports that firearm injuries and fatalities cost Americans $20 billion in 1992 alone. A handgun in the home is 64 times more likely to kill a family member than an intruder. The National Center For Health Statistics estimates that about 5 percent of male high school students carry guns to school. Gunfights in school classrooms are not uncommon.

In a narrow vote, President Clinton succeeded in pushing through Congress his 1994 Crime Bill which, among other things, supplied funding for 100 000 new police, banned 19 types of weapons out of 670 currently available in the United States, and required background checks for gun purchasers. All 19 of the banned guns were semiautomatic weapons. While fewer than 1 percent of all privately owned firearms in the United States are semiautomatic weapons, they are used for 8.4 percent of all crimes. The NRA shrilly opposed the bill. That bill has been an enormous success, especially its requirement that those who want to buy a gun must pass a background check. By 1997, the background checks had stopped over 100 000 felons and others from buying guns, thus checking the crimes that would have been committed with those guns. The 1994 Crime Bill combined with better police tactics, the diminishing crack epidemic, and a demographic contraction of teenagers to lower the crime rate dramatically across most of the United States by the mid-1990s. The lower the crime rate and its enormous costs, the higher the nation's economic development rate.[17]

While industrial complexes such as sports, restaurants, or guns receive enormous infusions of tax dollars and other government subsidies, many strategic sectors are starved of money. For example, studies reveal that for every dollar

> invested in 'core infrastructure' – streets and highways, water and sewer systems, airports and mass transit – corporations invest 25 cents in plant and equipment over the long-term. Thus does productivity increase 0.3 percent for every 1.0 percent increase in public investments in infrastructure.[18]

Politicians genuinely interested in creating wealth and jobs in their districts would logically fight for more public investments in infrastructure. Yet Congress continually shelves infrastructure and instead channels public funds into industries with much more political clout, even though they may have a much less positive impact on the nation's development.

During the 1980s, while hundreds of billions of dollars flowed into such things as junk bonds, glass skyscrapers, and the savings and loan bailout, America's infrastructure of bridges, roads, ports, pipelines, airports, and sewage systems crumbled. The ratio of public works to private capital fell from 54 percent in 1964 to 40 percent by 1989. It will cost an estimated $315 billion during the 1990s just to restore the nation's highways to their 1983 condition; an additional $72 billion will be necessary to shore up the nation's bridges; $15 billion just to modernize the nation's air-traffic control system. America's investments in infrastructure are abysmal compared to its economic rivals. In 1989–90, while the United States invested a minuscule 0.3 percent of its GNP in infrastructure, Japan invested 5.7 percent, Canada 1.8 percent, Britain 2.0 percent, Italy 4.8 percent, Germany 2.7 percent, and France 2.7 percent.[19]

Education is as important as infrastructure to the nation's economic development. Poorly educated people make poor workers. One of four Americans is functionally illiterate, a percentage which translates into 12 million illiterate workers. American firms spend $30 billion annually training and retraining their workers. Much of this training involves subjects that the workers should have learned in school. Small businesses, which can least afford these training programs, are the most likely to end up with poorly qualified workers.[20]

America is anything but number one in education. Here again,

Washington's policies are to blame. The result is an enormous drag on the nation's ability to compete in an ever-fiercer global economy. America's secondary education is a failure by most comparative measures. American kids regularly score among the lowest in international comparisons. In 1995, for example, American junior high school students ranked number 28 in math and number 17 in science compared to students from 41 countries.[21]

"American values" explains this dismal result. A deep and often acrimonious disregard for learning and thought has always characterized America's popular culture. This is partly reflected in how American and foreign students use their free time. Surveys revealed that while kids in other countries spent about as much time watching television (2.5 hours daily) as American kids (2.7), no nationality spent more time playing sports (2 hours daily). Here American kids simply follow the national religion of playing sports or worshipping one's local teams. How much more would American kids learn if the billions of dollars annually poured into school sports programs were invested in education instead? As if simple indifference to learning among most American kids were not bad enough, illegal drugs, tobacco, and guns have become endemic in the nation's schools.

More importantly, America's decentralized school system allows each of the nation's 7000 public school districts to determine their own standards and raise their own money. Jeffersonians applaud the decentralized system of local elected school boards as the next best thing to a completely private school system where the market determines standards. Hamiltonians dismiss a private system that only the wealthy or middle class could enjoy, and deplore the existing decentralized system as doomed to failure. With a neighborhood's tax base determining its level of spending on public schools, the schools in wealthy districts enjoy the finest facilities, teachers, and standards, while schools in poor districts go without. Class differences are thus perpetuated by the school system's funding inequities. Most countries, including all the other democratic industrial countries, have education ministries that impose national standards of education and redistribute money fairly among the districts.

Richly symbolic of many of education's ills was a controversy that arose from the Taveres, Florida school board in May 1994. The board voted three to two that in all classes, including biology, math, chemistry, and gymnastics as well as history and literature, teachers were required to teach that American culture "was superior to other foreign or historic cultures." Among the board's other policies were to refuse to accept government "Head Start" money for disadvantaged children, eliminate sex education, mandate creationism or a biblical view of biology and history, and censor certain politically incorrect books from the library. The school board's chair, Pat Hart, actually sends her own children to a private Christian school and admitted that she had never traveled outside of the United States, speaks no foreign language, and has never studied comparative culture, religion, or government. A dissident on the school board, Phyllis Patten, angrily asserted that,

> These are people with no experience and no education. You've got three people on that board with high school educations who want to wrap the Bible and the flag around themselves, who don't believe in public education and are trying to undermine the system.[22]

Such controversies over school board policies will become increasingly common. For decades fundamentalist Christian groups such as the "Moral Majority" and "Christian Coalition" have mounted a nation-wide, grass-roots struggle at the school board level for America's hearts and minds. By 1995, fundamental Christians controlled 2200 of the nation's 7000 school boards. They often got elected by hiding their radical Christian views until after they took office.

The ability to understand and appreciate the arts is an essential part of being educated. The arts are not only central to education but are also big business. In 1994, America's art world was a $37 billion industry employing 1.3 million people or 1.5 percent of the workforce, and generating tax revenues of $3.4 billion. Created in 1965, the National Endowment for the Humanities (NEH) contributes less than 2 percent of all arts patronage in the United States.[23] Yet, NEH grants are often the difference between success or failure for large arts complexes or projects. NEH recipients have an excellent chance of attracting private donations and loans.

Many of the same people who are determined to teach a biblical view of creation in the nation's public schools are also trying to destroy public support for the arts. Following their 1994 capture of Congress, the Republicans targeted for elimination the Federal budget for the arts and public broadcasting. In 1995, the National Endowment for the Humanities' budget was $167.4 million, down from the equivalent of $300 million in 1979 in constant dollar terms. New York artists received $26 million or 15 percent of the budget in 1994. Private donations exceeded $9 billion in 1994. The Lincoln Center for the Performing Arts alone spent $316 million that year. The entire Public Broadcasting Corporation had a budget of $285.6 million in 1995. Which cost America's taxpayers more – the National Endowment for the Arts or the Defense Department's 102 marching bands? In 1994, taxpayers shelled out $189.1 million for the bands and $170.2 million for the arts.[24] The 1995 Republican budget would have eliminated all arts spending by 1997. What do these spending priorities say about American values?

While the tiny sliver of remaining Federal funds as a percentage of total arts financing might be an argument for its elimination, Jane Alexander, who directs the National Endowment counters: "The Federal Role is small but very vital. We are a stimulus for leveraging state, local, and private money. We are a linchpin for the puzzle of arts funding."[25] Strings are attached to the Federal funds. Recipients must find anywhere from matching to three times the amount in private funds. Most artists far exceed these requirements. Each Endowment dollar attacts an average $11 dollars from state, local, and private sources. Former Endowment head John Frohnmayer reminds us that in 1990 the fund cost "each citizen 68 cents for everything we did, [compared with] the savings and loan scandal which will cost each of us at least $2,000."[26] Here again, Jeffersonians and Hamiltonians are at loggerheads.

INDUSTRIAL POLICIES AND SOCIOECONOMIC PROBLEMS

For the first time in American history, a generation entering the workforce will not do as well as the generation that bred them. Today's twenty-somethings, the so-called "Generation-X," will have fewer rather than more career opportunities and less wealth than their parents. Between 1977 and 1988, 60 percent of men joined the middle class before they were 30 years old; from 1989 to 1992, only 42 percent did so. Comparing those same blocks of years, the percentage becoming middle class before age 30 dropped from 74 percent to 56 percent among those with affluent parents, from 27 percent to 20 percent among those with poor parents, from 48 percent to 32 percent among those without a college education, from 69 percent to 55 percent among those with some college education,

from 65 percent to 47 percent among white men, and from 29 percent to 18 percent among black men.[27]

How can the economy continue to expand while real income for
most people falls? The answer is simple – the rich are getting more
money while most other people are getting less. Vast and growing
discrepancies between rich and poor characterize the United States.
The richest 1 percent enjoy more wealth than the poorest 90 percent. In 1989, the 834 000 wealthiest households owned $5.7 trillion
of net worth compared to the $4.8 trillion of 84 million other house-
holds. Between 1983 and 1989, the percentage of wealth held by
the richest 1 percent rose from 31 percent to 37 percent of the
nation's total, while the next richest 9 percent dropped from 35
percent to 31 percent, and the poorest 90 percent from 33 percent
to 32 percent. The leap in wealth for the richest 1 percent was
extraordinary given that the percentage hardly budged between 1961
and 1982. The largest previous rise in wealth for the nation's richest occurred during the 1920s before the Great Depression leveled
those gains.[28]

No country among the 24 OECD democratic industrial nations
suffers a greater gap between the rich and poor than the United
States. In 1993, the richest 1 percent of Americans owned 40 percent of the nation's wealth. Altogether, the richest 20 percent of
Americans, with incomes of $55 000 or more a year, owned 80 percent
of all wealth. The bottom 20 percent of households owned only 5.7
percent. In contrast, the richest 1 percent of Britons owned 18 percent
of their nation's wealth, down from 59 percent during the 1920s.[29]

Real income and hourly wages have decreased since 1973; those
annual decreases deepened during the 1980s. High school graduates in 1992 earned 26.5 percent less in entry-level wages than their
counterparts did in 1979; a 30-year-old man earned $3,000 a year
less in real wages (adjusted for inflation). The middle class has
shrunk over the past quarter century. In 1969, middle-income
Americans were 71.2 percent of the total; in 1989, they were only
63.3 percent. Meanwhile, the percentage of lower-income Americans
rose from 17.9 percent to 22.1 percent.[30]

Why has the nation's distribution of wealth become ever-more
inegalitarian? Nineteen seventy-three – the year of OPEC's quadrupling of oil prices – was the turning point. The subsequent dozen
years of low growth, and high interest rates, unemployment, and
inflation were a vicious economic cycle broken only when oil prices
halved during the mid-1980s. Nonetheless, as in any other era, some

people and businesses made enormous profits. The rich got richer and most others get poorer, not just in the United States, but in most other countries as well. Payroll increases lagged behind business profits – the threat of dismissal amidst high unemployment quelled demands for higher pay increases. And American workers increasingly competed not just with each other, but with cheaper overseas labor as well. Management was not only able to fend off demands for higher wages, but in turn demanded that the workers accept fewer benefits and even pay. The alternative, they warned, was to shut down the factory and move the production overseas to docile, cheaper workers. Management rarely shared the pain of such cutbacks.

What else explains the growing disparity in wealth? Some would attribute the decline in income for the working poor to laziness. Is this true? In fact, Americans are working more hours than at any time since World War II. Although in general, all Americans work more today than a decade ago, the poorest 40 percent are working more for less money. In 1989, the poorest fifth of Americans worked 4.6 percent more than they did a decade earlier, up to 850 hours a year. During the 1980s, their income dropped 4.1 percent in real terms. In contrast, the richest fifth worked 2.0 percent more, up to 3510 hours, but enjoyed income rises of 19.6 percent! Alarming as those statistics are in terms of fairness, they simply reflect the quantity rather than quality of work done. While the poor may be working more hours, the rich are not only working nearly four times more hours, but may be working more productively as well and thus can rightfully assert a claim to more pay.[31]

The New Deal policies of the 1930s and Great Society policies of the 1960s were supposed to alleviate such gaps between rich and poor by transferring some wealth from the former to the latter. Jeffersonians argue that such welfare destroys the incentive for the poor to work and instead makes them dependent like so many children on Federal largess. How much have welfare programs helped or hindered the nation's economic development?

If a welfare program is one that transfers wealth from others to a targeted group, then virtually every group in society is eligible for some form of welfare. Welfare for the rich and middle class exists alongside that for the poor. In 1993, Federal spending on social programs alone cost $762 billion, a figure which included the $302 billion in social security and $143 billion in medicare which went to the elderly, no matter how wealthy or poor they were.

Military retirees received $26 billion in retirement and disability benefits and $17 billion in veteran benefits, again regardless of their income. The subsidies for often quite wealthy farmers cost taxpayers $16 billion. In addition, Washington handed out over $400 billion in tax deductions which also went largely to middle- and upperclass Americans. Deductions for interest paid for mortgages cost $49 billion, an unabashed middle- and upper-income tax break. In all, most of the taxes paid by those with incomes of $20 000 or more a year come back to them in the form of entitlements. And what about the array of business subsidies? The Federal government's subsidies and tax advantages for industry – welfare if you will – rose from $77.1 billion in 1950 to $303.7 billion in 1980. In 1994, the Federal government spent $73 billion and pursued a vast range of research and development projects in over 700 laboratories under the auspices of the departments of Defense, Energy, Commerce, and Health and Welfare, NASA, and other agencies. The Energy Department alone spent $6 billion in its 21 laboratory complexes with their combined workforce of 60 000 employees. NASA has ten huge laboratories. The National Institute of Health invests $9 billion in various medical technologies, mostly through universities and other organizations. Private firms were the major beneficiaries of this research.[32]

Is all this welfare? Yes, of course it is. However, when most people think of welfare they imagine welfare for the poor. The cost of health care for the poor in the medicaid program was $76 billion, about 60 percent of the cost of medicare, which treats the elderly. Food stamps for the poor cost $25 billion, the child nutrition program $6 billion, the Aid to Families with Dependent Children (AFDC) $16 billion. Those four programs, specifically designed to alleviate poverty, cost only one of every four dollars in social welfare. Welfare payments differ greatly from state to state. For example, Mississipppi, Texas, New York, and California pay recipients $412, $476, $805, and $850 a month, respectively.

The AFDC program is central to the welfare system. Established under the Social Welfare Act of 1935, the program gives cash grants mostly to poor, single mothers. Although grants vary with family size, they diminish when income from other sources increases or the parents marry. Of the 1991 Federal budget, AFDC were 0.9 percent and food stamps 1.5 percent, or 2.4 percent altogether. States spent 2.2 percent of their budgets on AFDC. In the early 1990s, AFDC supported one of every seven American children.

For many Americans the word "welfare" may conjure up images of large black women with a half-dozen small children driving their Cadillacs to pick up their welfare checks. In fact, whites make up 38.1 percent of recipients, blacks 39.7 percent, hispanics (who can be any race) 16.6 percent, and others 5.6 percent. There is, however, a stark difference in the percentage of children from different races who become welfare recipients. Of those black children born between 1967 and 1969, 72 percent spent time on welfare, compared to only 16 percent of other children.

How have the Federal, state, and local welfare programs affected poverty? In 1965, the year President Lyndon Johnson began to enact his Great Society program, America's poverty rate was 17.3 percent. By 1974, the poverty rate had fallen to 11.2 percent. It rose after then to peak at 15.2 percent of Americans in 1983 and has hovered around that rate ever since. In 1991, 35.7 million Americans, or 14.2 percent of the population, lived in poverty. Forty percent of the poverty-stricken were children, 11 percent were elderly. With 16.0 percent, the south had the highest poverty rate followed by the west with 14.3 percent, the Midwest with 13.2 percent, and the north-east with 12.2 percent. Race, too, made a difference. The black poverty rate was 32.7 percent followed by hispanics with 28.7 percent, Asians and Pacific Islanders with 13.8 percent, and whites with 10.7 percent. That year, a family of four was considered poor if it had a cash income of less than $13 924.

Welfare as we know it clearly has not eliminated poverty, although it has certainly eased the lives of millions of recipients. But has it done more harm than good by making the recipient dependent on government largess, weakening his or her willingness to work, and encouraging the birth of children out of wedlock? The answer is unclear. Certainly, many recipients claim they want to work but would actually make less at low-wage jobs while child-care costs ate up most of their paychecks. The incentive is to remain on welfare rather than work for less income. The presence of adequate job training or child-care programs would undoubtedly free many from welfare. But those programs would cost far more in the short-term than the existing programs. And what of the claim that welfare encourages recipients to have more babies? Given that the rate of childbirths to unwed mothers has varied enormously since the programs were instituted, there is no apparent connection between assistance and single-parent children as some critics claim.

Americans are of two minds about welfare. As in other issues, attitudes toward welfare shift markedly depending on how the question is posed. For example, when a CBS/*New York Times* poll conducted on 6–8 May 1992 asked whether America spent too much, too little, or the right amount on "assistance for the poor," only 13 percent said too much, 64 percent said too little, and 16 percent said the right amount. When "assistance for the poor" was changed to "welfare," those saying the United States spent too much soarerd to 44 percent, while only 23 percent said too little, and 27 percent the right amount. Yet, regardless of which poll is used, a majority of Americans clearly prefer either the same amount or more spent in assisting the poor.[33]

The welfare system has changed enormously over the years since it was implemented. In real dollar terms, welfare has been declining for over two decades from a peak of nearly $10 000 in 1972 for a single parent with two children to about $7700 in 1991. Increasingly strapped for cash, states began reforming their welfare systems in the late 1980s.

During the mid-1990s, political pressure built up that eventually reformed the "welfare" system to "workfare." Among the many reasons Bill Clinton was elected president in 1992 was his promise to "end welfare as we know it." In 1993, he submitted a welfare reform bill to Congress that he promised would convert the existing system to workfare for most recipients; included in the bill was funding for job training, child-care, and transportation. Congress shelved Clinton's bill. In 1995, Congress again debated a welfare reform bill, this time one submitted by Republicans. The final bill encouraged an "up or out" program in which recipients would be cut off after several years whether or not they found jobs. Unlike Clinton's bill, the Republican versions failed to provide any significant job training, transportation, or child-care programs that would ease the recipient's integration into the workplace. The Republicans claimed that the market and private handouts would make up any short-falls; in all, charity would succor the homeless and hungry, while orphanges would take in children without parents or with "unfit" parents. Democrats countered that the Republican bill would actually drive current welfare receipients "out and down" rather than up. Clinton vetoed that bill and a similar one. In 1996, Clinton and the Congress passed a compromise bill that would end welfare to recipients after two years. It did not include funding for job training, transportation, or child-care. It remains to be seen whether the bill will increase or decrease poverty.

As a nation of immigrants, most Americans have traditionally supported the sentiments inscribed on the Statue of Liberty's pedestal: "Give me your huddled masses . . . " But as Americans become more aware of the problems of an increasingly overcrowded, culturally diverse and perhaps antagonistic population, the support for unlimited immigration decays. American attitudes toward immigrants have changed significantly over the past three decades. A nation-wide Gallop survey in June 1965 revealed that 39 percent thought immigration should remain the same, 28 percent that it should increase, and 33 percent that it should decrease. Subsequent polls indicated that increasing numbers of Americans wanted to reduce the number of immigrants. By June 1993, 61 percent said immigration should be reduced, only 27 percent that it should remain the same, and a mere 7 percent that it should be increased. In the latter poll, 68 percent agreed that most immigrants were here illegally and 55 percent said they would take jobs away from Americans. Blacks and whites had different attitudes toward immigrants. While blacks were nine percentage points more likely to fear that newcomers would take their jobs, they were also nine percentage points less likely to favor a decrease in immigration than whites.[34]

In the mid-1990s, immigration – legal as well as illegal – became an increasingly debated issue. Some critics asserted that immigrants came to America as much for its welfare programs as its job opportunities. Reform welfare and those who arrive will more likely be enterprising rather than lazy. Others argued that regardless of their motivation or means for coming, immigrants were failing to assimilate into American culture. The United States was becoming a checkerboard of different cultures rather than a melting pot of American culture. The answer to this problem was to limit the numbers and beef up assimilation programs. Yet another criticism of the present system was that the more people who live in the United States, the worse the environmental problems. The number of people allowed in should not excceed the number who leave the United States each year – about 200 000.

Here again, Jeffersonians and Hamiltonians are opposed, with the former adopting a "more the merrier" position on unrestricted immigration and population increases, while the latter argue that those allowed in should bring skills and wealth that enhance rather than diminish America's development. Hamiltonians are split over whether America's population should be allowed to rise forever;

some say the population increase can be accomodated if the newcomers are skilled and hardworking, while others call for a zero population growth policy.

Setting aside questions of the economic, cultural, and environmental impact of immigrants, there is no question that America's population is rapidly rising, and that immigrants are largely the cause. Although over the past several decades America's birth rate has declined toward a zero population growth level, immigration swelled the nation's population. The complexion as well as size of America's population changed considerably during this period. The 1965 Immigration Act removed nationality quotas and emphasized family ties and humanitarian needs. Black, Asian, and hispanic immigrants were the most numerous. And those numbers are increasing. In 1986, a Federal amnesty granted residency to 2.6 million illegal and mostly hispanic immigrants. Throughout the 1980s, 8.9 million people immigrated legally and about 3 million illegally to the United States, the highest level since comprehensive immigration laws were enacted in 1924 and the second highest since the great immigration waves that spanned the turn of the century. The 1990 Census recorded 19.7 million immigrants in the United States, or one in 12 Americans. Of those immigrants, an estimated 2.6 million were here illegally, a figure which rose to 3.2 million in 1992.[35]

If the nation's present immigration and birth rates hold steady, America's population will soar from 265 million in 1992 to 383 million by 2050, a 50.2 percent increase. The nation's complexion will change just as dramatically. Fertility and immigration rates vary considerably among racial and ethnic groups. While the white population will increase an estimated 29.4 percent between now and then, hispanics will increase 237.5 percent, blacks 93.8 percent, Native Americans 109.1 percent, and Asians and Pacific Islanders 412.5 percent.[36]

What are the benefits and costs of immigrants? Businesses benefit because the newcomers help keep labor rates low. Many immigrants are skilled and enterprising, thus expanding the nation's wealth. Yet, overall, immigrants are a net burden to taxpayers. The Carrying Capacity Network's nation-wide study revealed that every 100 unskilled immigrants put 25 native-born Americans out of jobs. The immigrants' poverty rate is 42.8 percent higher than that of native-born Americans, and immigrants receive 44.2 percent more welfare benefits. In 1992, the total public assistance bill at the Federal, state, and county levels was $42.5 billion for the 19.3 million legal and illegal immigrants who have arrived since 1970. This was the net cost after including public assistance for the 2.1 million displaced American workers and deducting $20.2 billion in taxes paid by the immigrants. The study estimated that 11.1 million legal and illegal immigrants would pour over America's borders within the next decade, generating $283.2 billion in revenue but costing taxpayers $951.7 billion. The net cost over the next decade is $668.5 billion of which illegal immigrants alone would cost $186.4 billion.[37]

In California alone, illegal immigrants and their US-born children, who automatically become citizens, cost California $2.9 billion a year in higher welfare, education, health care, and incarceration in 1992. The estimated 2.3 million legal and illegal immigrants who settled in Los Angeles County cost $808 million, while the 200 000 illegals alone in San Diego cost $145.9 million. While state and local governments bear the most costs, the Federal government benefits in additional revenue from the immigrants.

The reason for these net costs lies in the current immigration policy, which emphasizes family ties and refugees rather than wealth or skills. Skilled immigrants compose only 38 percent of the total. If immigration policy were changed to accept only skilled or professional immigrants, there would actually be a net revenue gain of $13.7 billion by 2002. Likewise, a crackdown on illegal immigrants would save taxpayers $186 billion by that year.

Industrialization and the policies which nurtured it has had an enormous impact on the relative wealth and economic dynamism among different regions. During the early nineteenth century, industrialization occurred first in New England and the mid-Atlantic states. By the early twentieth century, industrialization had spread to pockets across the midwest and Great Lakes states, as that region's population, entrepreneurships, and exploitation of natural resources expanded. During World War II, huge industrial complexes emerged on the Pacific coast, particularly in the Los Angeles, San Franciso, San Diego, Seattle, and Portland metropolises. American manufacturing reached a height during the 1960s. Then, during the 1970s, it experienced a relative decline as increasingly severe foreign competition helped convert the northern steel and automobile belt into the "rustbelt," and more and more industries began locating to the lower wages, regulations, living costs, and utility rates of the "sunbelt." Today, nearly every region and state has its own mix of industries.[38]

Still another socioeconomic change that has been stimulated by public policies is urbanization and then suburbanization that has shaped the United States over the past century. At the turn of the century, America was still a predominantly rural nation with three of four people living in the countryside or towns. In 1900, 19.7 percent of the population lived in cities, 5.8 percent in the suburbs, and 74.5 percent in the countryside. Throughout the early twentieth century, industrialization attracted ever-more people to cities and automobiles enabled their owners to commute to work from further away, thus swelling cities and suburbs alike. By 1950, 32.8 percent of Americans lived in cities, 23.3 percent in the suburbs, and 56.1 percent in rural areas. The postwar economic boom brought unprecedented wealth and mobility to the middle class. Increasing numbers of people fled the ever-worsening crime and expense of the cities for the suburbs. By 1990, the percentage of Americans living in cities had dropped to 31.3 percent and those in the countryside to 22.5 percent, while those in suburbia swelled to 46.2 percent of the population.[39]

INDUSTRIAL POLICIES AND THE ENVIRONMENT: JOBS VERSUS OWLS?

Jeffersonians assert that you can have more jobs or a cleaner environment, but you cannot have both; the more regulations, the lower the economic growth, and vice versa. In this assumed tradeoff between higher living standards and a higher quality of life, Jeffersonians called for "all-out growth." Hamiltonians were split on the issue, with some saying any tradeoff depended on circumstances and others calling for "no more growth."

In reality, the tradeoff does not exist. A recent study by Stephen M. Meyer proved conclusively that those states which invested the most in anti-pollution measures also enjoyed the highest living standards, while those states with fewer industrial regulations also had much lower living standards.[40] After analyzing and comparing the regulatory regimes of all 50 states, Myers divided them into 17 "strong," 15 "moderate," and 18 "weak" categories of environment regulation. The strong environmental states grew twice as fast as the weak ones throughout the 1970s and even the 1980s when Reaganomics stressed deregulation and minimal government. Myers concludes that at the very least, "the pursuit of environmental quality does not hinder economic growth and development," but found a positive correlation. Searching for an explanation of how regulation can actually spur rather than hinder growth, Myers suggests that regulations might have a Darwinian effect on competitiveness, weeding out the weak and promoting the more innovative businesses. At most, according to a Labor Department report, environmental regulations caused an insignificant 0.1 percent of job loss in the United States in 1988; in other words, 99.9 percent of all job loss resulted from non-regulatory reasons such as competition, poor business practices, and so on.

The positive relationship between a strong environment and economy was also found by another study sponsored by four groups – the Alliance to Save Energy, the American Council for Energy, the Natural Resources Defense Council, and the Union of Concerned Scientists. Their study, entitled "America's Energy Choices," calculated the numbers for three scenarios. The "Market Scenario" actually promoted the lowest gains in wealth; based on "least cost" energy, it would net the United States $1.8 trillion in additional growth over 20 years from $1.3 trillion in investments and $3.1 trillion in energy savings. The "Environmental Scenario" promoted much greater gains in wealth for Americans – $2.1 trillion in growth from $2.1 trillion in new investments in efficiency and conservation which would yield $4.2 trillion in savings. The "Climate Stabilization Scenario" attempts to cut greenhouse emissions sharply, and achieves the greatest surge in wealth – $2.3 trillion in growth from $2.7 trillion in investments and $5.0 trillion in savings.[41]

Given these realities, how do we explain the persistence of the view that Americans must choose between economic growth and environmental health, or "jobs versus owls" as it is framed in the Pacific north-west. Jeffersonians are to blame. Economic theorists treat pollution as an "externality" or freebie to the polluter. According to this mentality, any restrictions are evil because they sully pure market forces. The Jeffersonian "think tank" the Cato Institute, calls for abolishing all environmental regulations. Since the Republican Party's overwhelming congressional victory in November 1994, its members have made gutting America's environmental, safety, and health regulations a top priority.

Of course, people living in the real world know that there are no such things as "pure markets" – they are an abstraction. Regulations of any kind can either aid or hinder economic development – the net effects vary from one regulation to the next. A healthier society is beyond a doubt a wealthier society; however, exactly how much more so is extremely difficult to ascertain. The costs of installing pollution control equipment in factories and automobiles are relatively easy to calculate; those who bear the costs are even easier to determine. Far more difficult to estimate are the socioeconomic costs of doing nothing. The cleaner the environment, the greater the nation's savings in higher economic growth and tax receipts, lower taxes and government spending. Although recent restrictions on airborne toxic chemicals may cost industry $1 billion in 1995 and as much as $7 billion by 2005, this bill may be more than offset by tens of billions of dollars in annual savings to the entire nation.[42] Some values are impossible to calculate. How much, for example, is it worth to the nation to reduce the number of days in which the Smoky Mountains, Yosemite Valley, or Grand Canyon are obscured by smog?

In the nineteenth century, America's industrialization and urbanization expanded together, creating enormous wealth for a few and higher living standards for many. But industrialization and urbanization also contaminated soils, waters, and air with chemical cocktails of effluents. Today, chemical timebombs are ticking away in the backyards, faucets, and lungs of most Americans. America's factories, farms, businesses, and households annually spew 250 million tons of hazardous waste and 200 metric tonnes of municipal waste. Perhaps as many as 30 000 hazardous waste sites litter the nation.

Water pollution hurts the nation's economic health. When asked about the harmful effects of water pollution, many might envision images of dead fish, noxious smells, "no swimming" signs, and brownish drinking water. Of these, unsafe drinking water is probably the most worrisome to most people. "Don't drink the water," Americans admonish those who travel overseas. They may increasingly say that about their own drinking water.

In many regions across the country, the demand for usable water is exceeding the supply; the proliferation of homes, factories, farms, and other businesses have dried up aquifers and streams. As if this were not disaster enough, poisons are depriving people even of abundant water sources. Increasing millions of Americans have learned to their horror that various chemical and organic combinations have contaminated their drinking water.

According to the EPA, about 90 percent of the nation's 58 000 public drinking water systems meet its standards. In other words, about 10 percent of the population or 26 million people depend on drinking water which contains unacceptable levels of pollution. The EPA estimated in 1988 that over 9000 community water systems violated the health laws. The EPA figures may be overly optimistic. A 1988 study by consumer advocate Ralph Nader revealed that at least one-fifth of the nation's public water systems were plagued by some of over 2110 chemical compounds, of which 190 were known carcinogens.[43] It is not just carcinogenic chemicals which assail our bodies. Organisms such as parasites, bacteria, and viruses are found in surface and ground water alike. Parasites such as *Giardia* and *Cryptosporidium* cause gastrointestinal illnesses that cause severe discomfort but rarely death. Much more serious are diseases such as cholera, hepatitis, typhoid, and tuberculosis. Toxic heavy metals such as lead and mercury leach into the nation's water from countless sources, and inflict a range of diseases and damage to people including cancer, liver and brain damage, and birth defects.

Water pollution can be dangerous. No public system has pure water – all tolerate certain pollution levels. Particularly alarming is the ever-worsening threat to the nation's ground water. Once an aquifer is polluted, it could take nature thousands of years to cleanse it. Ground water provides for half the American population, 40 percent of irrigation, 25 percent of industries, and 95 percent of rural residents. Perhaps the worst water pollution threat is to the 19 million Americans who receive their drinking water from backyard wells whose quality is not monitored by the government. Many and perhaps most of those wells do not meet Federal standards.[44]

Streams and aquifers alike are contaminated by a broad range of less obvious sources including septic tanks, underground storage tanks, farm runoff, landfills, oil and gas brine sites, saltwater intrusion, road salting, mining, underground injection of wastes, stockyards, and construction. Among these actual or potential sources of water pollution, the EPA has identified millions of septic tanks and underground storage tanks; 180 000 surface impoundments such as ponds, lagoons, and pits which catch pollutants; 29 000 hazardous waste sites which may be eventually added to the "Superfund" list; 500 hazardous waste land disposal facilities; 16 000 municipal landfills; and millions of tons of herbicides and pesticides annually dumped in the nation's farm fields. All together there are over 20 million on-site waste disposal units scattered across the country, most of which are septic and underground storage tanks. And the poisons from most of those sites are leaking. Among the worst and most insidious culprits scattered across the country are from 5 to 6 million liquid underground storage tanks (LUSTs), of which most are in advanced states of decomposition and as many as 400 000 may currently be leaking.[45]

Contrary to their bucolic image, farms dump vast amounts of pollution into rural environments. Farmers pour hundreds of millions of tons of toxic pesticides and fertilizers on their crops each year. Most of these run off into America's waters. Organic pollutants such as parasites, bacteria, and viruses proliferate to dangerous levels in the uncontrolled discharges of human and livestock feces from feedlots, septic tanks, and untreated sewage. The more sediment in the water, the more easily these parasites and diseases fester. Erosion from farmlands, construction, and logged watersheds are the worst sediment sources. Farmlands are virulent sources of not only organic-born diseases, but also pesticides and herbicides.

Ironically, the chemicals dumped into water to kill harmful organisms can create their own hazards. Muncipalities first began adding chlorine to their drinking water at the turn of the century. By the 1930s, chlorine had reduced typhoid deaths to one-tenth their level a generation earlier. Unfortunately, chlorine itself can become hazardous if it combines with certain organisms in water, creating hundreds of carcinogenic chemical compounds.

Tailpipes and smokestacks are obvious sources of pollutants. Who, for example, has not crinkled his nose as he drove past a paper mill? Paper mills are among the worst polluters, annually discharging millions of tons of carcinogens. But there are many more subtle sources. In urban areas, dry cleaners are hot spots of such toxic wastes as tricholorethylene (TCE) and perchloroethylene (PCE).

Yet another problem related to water and air pollution is the solid and hazardous waste buildup. In March 1987, the barge *Mobro 400* embarked on what became a richly symbolic 6000 mile, 164 day odyssey. The barge was filled with Islip, Long Island garbage – garbage no muncipality or country wanted. The captain tried to dump his load in North Carolina, Florida, Louisiana, Mexico, Belize, and the Bahamas, but was everywhere ordered back to sea. A half year after leaving, the *Mobro 400* finally steamed back to New York where the trash was incinerated in Brooklyn, 40 miles from where its journey began.[46]

Americans are the world's most wasteful people, annually tossing out 1300 pounds, or twice as much trash as citizens of other democratic industrial countries. In 1990, households and businesses pitched 180 million tons of waste; the estimated amount in the year 2000 is 216 million tons. In 1990, this amounted to 4.2 pounds per person every day, and was expected to increase to 4.4 pounds by 2000 and 4.8 by 2010. What happens to all this trash? Nearly three of every four pounds or 73 percent of trash is landfilled, 14 percent is burned, and a mere 13 percent recycled.[47]

Why are Americans so wasteful? A frontier Jeffersonian outlook of endless resources to be used and discarded lingers in the national psyche. A "throw away" mentality is an integral part of the American cult of consumption. Goods that lose their cachet are easily tossed aside for the more stylish. The American obsession with packaging contributes to the problem. Much of what is dumped in landfills is the elaborate plastic, paper, cardboard, and glass containers of goods that will eventually follow. For several decades, disposable paper diapers have been a godsend for parents and bane for landfills. In one estimate, paper products composed 39.6 percent of a landfill; yard wastes 17.8 percent; rubber, leather, and wood 11.9 percent; metals 8.9 percent; plastics 7.9 percent; and food wastes and glass 6.9 percent each.[48] Virtually all of these materials are recyclable.

As if all these vast and ever-growing mountains of rotting, unsightly, and often toxic waste were not bad enough, Americans are running out of places to put it. Over 80 percent of all the landfills existing across the United States in 1986 will be filled by 2008. And as landfills dwindle, the price of dumping soars. An even worse problem than the growing scarcity of landfills is the seepage of poisonous wastes into aquifers, streams, and air. Wastedumps are cocktails of such hazardous chemicals as polychlorinated biphenyls (PCBs), lead, asbestos, mercury, and dioxin. Although these chemicals may be out of sight, they are literally not necessarily out of mind for humans. Toxic chemicals poison plants and animals up the food chain until they eventually seep into the bodies and brains of people.[49]

Just what, if anything, has the government done about these problems? The creation of the Environmental Protection Agency (EPA) in 1970 was supposed to represent a Federal watershed in the struggle against pollution. Although many Federal bureaucracies play a role, the EPA is chiefly responsible for developing and implementing comprehensive environmental policies. Unfortunately, with a budget of only $6 billion and 15 000 employees in 1994, the EPA has trouble fulfilling its sweeping duties. The EPA lacks not only the staff and funding to fulfill its ever-expanding range of missions, but has few legal teeth to force violators to obey the law. For example, in 1991 the EPA prosecuted 3109 cases but won penalties of only $28 million and 346 months of incarceration. Over 80 percent of the EPA regulations have been challenged by lawsuits. The EPA is partly responsible for all the hours and money lost in court. By continually retreating from enforcing its various laws, the EPA lost credibility with the industries it was supposed to regulate. The result was that "every major participant now knows that loopholes will always appear in the nick of time, thus obviating the need to impose sanctions in areas that fail to meet air quality standards."[50]

Bogged down in specific issues, the EPA failed to develop comprehensive policies. EPA policy shifts with each head and president. While most EPA heads have sincerely attempted to enforce the laws for which their agency is responsible, the agency succumbed to cornucopian policies during the Reagan and Bush years that frequently violated or evaded the law. Rosenbaum maintains that the

> EPA has no clearly mandated priorities, no way of allocating scarce resources between different statutes or between programs within a single law. Nor does the EPA have a congressional charter, common to most federal departments and agencies, defining its broad organizational mission and priorities. While the agency has had to make informal ad hoc decisions about program priorities to survive, these are much less satisfactory legally and politically than a clear mandated congressional agenda.[51]

Every government agency has its set of interest groups which it is charged with regulating or supporting. Sometimes the clients that one bureaucracy is charged with protecting will conflict with those of another. For example, the National Park Service (NPS) has been concerned for decades that worsening air pollution was gradually destroying Shenandoah National Park. In 1991, the NPS joined 15 environmental groups in fighting two proposed power plants in southwestern Virginia which would worsen the pollution at Shenandoah National Park. Virginia's government supported the plants to increase electricity and employment, and pressured the EPA and Virginia Department of Air Pollution to counter the NPS and environmentalist protests. The environmentalists lost.

The EPA has contributed only a portion of the direction and funding of the cleanup. Washington has passed scores of laws addressing various problems. Since 1970, Federal, state, and local governments have spent over $700 billion on cleaning the nation's air and waters. By the late 1980s, the United States was annually spending $90 billion on environmental safeguards.[52]

Although industries fought fiercely against the making and implemention of anti-pollution laws, compliance has not been the crushing burden that businesses claim it to be. First of all, business pays only about 60 percent of the cleanup bill for the messes they create; taxpayers are burdened with the rest. For example, it was estimated in 1995 that the chemical industry would only have to invest $95 million in order to achieve compliance with existing regulations that reduce such toxic carcinogens as benzene, methyl ethyl ketone, hexape, toluene, and hydrogen chlorine. The total bill for all businesses is only a sliver of its total investments – in 1987, businesses spent only 1.7 percent of all their investments on pollution control equipment. Overall, investments in anti-pollution equipment or cleanup efforts accounts for a minuscule 1.5 percent of GNP. And those investments create jobs and wealth.[53]

Ironically, although industries spewed the pollution, America's taxpayers not only pay for the medical bills and cleanups, in a variety of ways they subsidize the industries which vomit that pollution. Federal, state, and local governments develop industries by providing them tax incentives, infrastructure, below-market loans, protection from competitive imports, and other privileges. Labor Secretary Robert Reich estimated that in 1993, Washington alone granted corporations over $200 billion in "welfare." Perhaps the most expensive subsidy that taxpayers shovel into the coffers of industry is that which pays the ever-growing bill for pollution's ever-worsening effects. The American Lung Association estimates that the annual damage inflicted on the nation's 260 million pairs of lungs alone is $50 billion![54]

Over the past several decades, Hamiltonians of various types have made enormous progress in pushing laws through Congress and regulations through the bureaucracies that either clean up or slow the increases of water, land, and air pollution. Some of these laws or regulations have clearly been more effective than others. The relative effectiveness of two of these laws will be examined, one based on an American citizen's "right to know" and the other on an assumed "right to pollute."

In this public-relations-obsessed age, publicity is one of the most effective means of reducing pollution. Turning the spotlight on polluters – combined with the threat of suing them or boycotting their products – has led to considerable cleanup. The public currently can learn how much that neighborhood factory or business polluters because of the Federal requirement that polluters disclose that information. Currently, 286 chemicals are on the disclosure list. Twelve states use that information as the basis to levy fines on those polluters. The law has greatly succeeded. Between 1988 when the disclosure law was passed and 1993, the number of toxic chemical releases have plummeted by 43 percent. For example, after being forced to reveal how much toxic chemicals it spews, Monsanto Corporation announced plans to reduce the amount by 90 percent within three years. Other huge toxic polluters such as AT&T, Dow Chemical, Dupont, Merck, and 3M quickly announced similar clean up programs. The disclosure law affects over 23 000 factories.[55]

Far less effective has been the 1990 Clean Air Act tenet that established a market for the right to pollute. The Act halved the number of allowable sulfur emissions, but allowed those factories which reduced their pollution below those standards to sell the difference. The law theoretically gave firms an incentive to reduce pollution. Unfortunately, a polluters' market has yet to flourish. The current $140 price of a ton of legal pollution is one-tenth the amount economists had boldly predicted five years ago when the law was debated. The lower the price, the lower the incentive to reduce pollution in order to sell the difference to others. To preempt tougher standards, polluters grossly inflated the predicted prices. Congress accepted the polluters' predictions. The law backfired. The right-to-pollute market has actually worsened the acid rain and toxic chemical problem. It would have been far better for Congress to have simply imposed tough but obtainable standards and required all polluters to comply.[56]

The nation's accumulated Federal, state, and local air pollution laws have been effective in reducing – sometimes dramatically – some types of pollution. Between 1970 and 1988, particulates dropped 63 percent, lead emissions 90 percent, and sulfur oxides 27 percent, while nitrogen oxides increased by 7 percent. This is a remarkable achievement considering that since 1970 America's GNP and vehicle fleet have expanded by about 25 percent, with the number of cars rising from 147 million in 1970 to 187 million.[57]

Yet only one city – Minneapolis – has achieved the Clean Air Act standard. One in three Americans lives in air unfit to breathe. In 1994, about 350 counties consistently violated clean air standards. Meanwhile, the nation's factories, power plants, and vehicles are approaching the limits of effective emission controls. For example, the latest auto emissions controls remove about 96 percent of all pollutants. Further reductions are not technologically or economically feasible. Further emission reductions will have to come from more diverse sources such as dry cleaners, lawnmowers, paint producers, gasoline stations, fireplaces, backyard barbeques, and so on. Lawmakers have recently zeroed in on other significant pollution sources. On 1 October 1994, the EPA reached an agreement with pleasure boat manufacturers to cut emissions 75 percent by the year 2006. Recreational boats contribute about 3 percent of the nation's hydrocarbons. While policies have targeted point sources of pollution, about 65 percent of pollution flows from something other than a smokestack or drainage pipe. Of the remaining 35 percent of point pollution, industrial sources account for only 9 percent, municipal sources 17 percent, background 6 percent, and unknown sources 3 percent. About 350 toxic chemicals still foul the nation's air.[58]

No region has worse air pollution than southern California or has implemented tougher measures to deal with the problem. In 1977, Sacramento empowered the South Coast Air Quality Management District (which included the Los Angeles basin) to develop and enforce air quality standards from stationary sources. Two years later those responsible unveiled the Air Quality Management Plan (AQMP) for most of southern California. The plan was amended with even tougher standards in 1982. Yet compliance was spotty and it failed to meet 1970 Clean Air Act standards set for 1987. A 1989 amendment to AQMP overcame some objections but still fell short of the drastic measures necessary for compliance with national law. Revolutionary measures are essential for Los Angeles to comply with the Clean Air Acts. Proposals have included: banning the sale of backyard barbeques, gasoline-powered lawnmowers, and starter fluids; raising parking fees for cars conveying only one passenger; restricting all new tire sales to radials which shed fewer rubber particles; limiting the number of cars for each family; and reformulating paints and solvents.

An enormous amount has been spent trying to clean up water pollution. Before 1972, all Federal funds targeting water pollution amounted to only $2 billion; from 1972 to 1985, Congress appropriated $37 billion to assist local efforts at controlling water pollution. Tens of billions of dollars have been spent since then. How effective has that money been? How much more needs to be done?

Different reports have drawn different conclusions. Even that massive spending was not adequate enough to fulfill the law. Over

99 percent of these investments targeted point pollution such as sewage pipes – crop fields, feedlots, parking lots and other non-point sources were neglected. The 1985 deadline for a complete cleanup passed with water pollution still virulent. In 1987, the EPA estimated that $118 billion in investments would have to be made to bring the nation up to acceptable standards by the year 2000. Continuing cutbacks in Federal support for water treatment postpone the compliance of localities with Federal standards for the indefinite future. A year later in a 1988 report the EPA claimed that a successful cleanup had occurred, including the designation of 99 percent of those streams it had investigated as "fishable and swimmable." The EPA's survey, however, was limited to only 21 percent of the nation's total streams, 32 percent of its lake acres, and 55 percent of its estuarine miles. The credibility of the EPA's study was further weakened by the fact that it examined only six pollutants – fecal coliform bacteria, dissolved oxygen, total phosphorus, total mercury, total lead, and biochemical deposits. It neglected to measure a range of other heavy metals, synthetic organic compounds, and dissolved solids. Other studies indicated that at best the nation's waters were about as polluted as they were two decades earlier. While the EPA had succeeded in reducing pollution flowing from pipes it neglected "non-point" pollution from stockyards, farms, airport tarmacs, factory grounds, storm water runoffs, and so on. In all, the EPA's 1988 report seems to have been written by Reaganomics ideologues rather than scientists.[59]

All together, 24 Federal laws and a dozen agencies are responsible for regulating toxic chemicals and waste. Despite the seeming power, the task of identifying and controling carcingenic and toxic chemicals is nearly impossible to fulfill. Over 120 000 public and private enterprises produce and distribute chemicals, an activity which accounts for 8 percent of GNP. By the late 1980s, over 70 000 chemicals were actively used in the United States. Of those chemicals used, about 98 percent were considered harmless to humans; the EPA had banned or restricted about 500 chemicals it considered harmful. Scientists are annually creating from 500–1000 new chemicals. The EPA faces a backlog of 13 000 new chemicals to evaluate for approval. The toxicities of as many as 64 percent of pesticides, 70 percent of food additives, and 78 percent of common commercial chemicals have not been adequately tested.[60]

In 1980, Congress passed the Comprehensive Environmental Response, Compensation, and Liability Act (CERCLA), better known as "Superfund," and appropriated $1.6 billion to clean up the nation's hemorrhaging toxic waste dumps. EPA created a National Priorites List to target the nation's most dangerous sites. A 1984 congressional amendment to Superfund strengthened its enforcement power. Congress reauthorized Superfund in 1986 and 1990, giving it another $8.6 billion and $5.1 billion, respectively.

Despite the tens of billions of dollars spent, Superfund has cleaned up only a tiny fraction of the nation's toxic waste dumps. Altogether, between 1980 and 1994, the Superfund expended $22 billion to clean up 346 sites completely and removed the most dangerous chemicals from an additional 3300 sites on the Superfund National Priority List. The average cleanup cost $28 million and took a decade. Perhaps another 30 000 toxic waste dumps are scattered across the country. The reduced risk to local people, however, has been significant. Of the 41 million living within four miles of a toxic waste site before Superfund was created, about 23.5 million people no longer do.[61]

One of the few cleanup success stories involves PCBs. Between 1929 and 1976 when they were banned, over 1 billion pounds of PCBs were produced. Today about one-third or 312 million pounds of PCBs remain in use in electrical equipment such as transformers. Dangerous amounts of PCBs in humans have dropped from about 12 percent of Americans in 1979 to almost none in the 1980s, while trace amounts have declined from 62 percent of Americans to 9 percent. Encouraging as these statistics are, PCBs are stored in as many as 750 000 PCB sites, of which the EPA can identify only a fraction and regulate even fewer.[62]

Why has the cleanup taken so long and accomplished so little? It was much easier for Congress to devise tough standards than to get the EPA to enforce them. Senator George Mitchell was among many who blasted the "EPA's slow and timid implementation of the existing law. . . . The EPA has missed deadlines, proposed inadequate regulations, and even exacerbated the hazardous waste problem by suspending certain regulations."[63] The EPA publicly pleaded inadequate funding and personnel; privately, many EPA officials complained that the Reagan White House had ordered it to forgo its legal mandates.

Other problems impeded the implementation of the hazardous waste laws. Although businesses theoretically are responsible for cleaning up their own toxic dumps, in many cases the perpetrator has gone out of business leaving the mess to taxpayers. Another problem was that some states had so many toxic waste dumps that its cleanup crews were overwhelmed. Of the five top states on the EPA's Superfund National List, New Jersey had the most with 100, followed by Pennsylvania with 84, New York with 73, Michigan with 68, and California with 53. Each site requires a specific cleanup strategy but usually includes such methods as underground vacuum extraction, waste-eating microbes, chemical dechlorination, and soil washing. Regardless of the methods used, all are very time-consuming. Of the roughly 1200 dumps identified by the National Priorities List in the mid-1980s, about 41 percent are landfills, 37 percent industrial lagoons, and 33 percent industrial sites.[64]

While concentrating on the worst sites, Superfund neglected countless other bleeding toxic waste dumps. Mostly off the priorities lists are over 2 million underground petroleum and chemical storage tanks which are slowly rusting away. With a life of only 15–20 years, most of these died years ago and are leaking their toxic residues into the environment. The EPA was not authorized to address this toxic "sleeping giant" until 1984. Two years later, Congress appropriated $500 million to begin cleaning up the storage tanks, a task that may eventually cost as much as $50 billion to complete.[65]

No waste is more hazardous than radioactive waste. The United States has seventeen major and over one-hundred minor nuclear weapons factories. The cleanup of those sites alone will cost an estimated $200 billion.[66] In addition, America's nuclear energy industry has millions of tons of nuclear waste in temporary storage awaiting permanent disposal.

The responsibility for disposing of nuclear waste remained unsettled until Congress passed the 1982 Nuclear Waste Policy Act which authorized the Energy Department to oversee the worsening crisis. By 1998, the Energy Department must take over all nuclear waste sites and safely dispose of the growing mountain of radioactive materials. Although the Energy Department soon decided to store nuclear wastes deep underground, it still has not found a geologically stable and politically acceptable site. In 1986, the Energy Department proposed sites in Texas, Nebraska, and Washington. In a classic example of NIMBYism, the governors and legislatures of those states fiercely protested, despite the reality that over the decades each state had enjoyed billions of dollars and thousands of jobs from the nuclear industry setting up shop in their midst.

The Energy Department discarded its proposals and in 1987 selected Yucca Mountain in Nevada as the nuclear waste dump site, despite the vociferous protests of that state's government. In 1989, Nevada passed a bill forbidding the Federal government from storing nuclear wastes in the state. In 1991, the Energy Department announced that it would begin storing some nuclear wastes at a Waste Isolation Pilot Plant (WIPP) in salt caverns near Carlsbad, New Mexico. The plan faltered when a Federal judge declared that the Interior Department, which owns the land, could not legally transfer it to the Energy Department without congressional approval, nor could the Energy Department begin running WIPP without a state license to do so. To date, Congress has not authorized the land transfer between departments, nor has New Mexico's government issued a license to the Energy Department to operate the facility. Although it still holds no nuclear waste, the WIPP facility took ten years and $1.35 billion to plan and build, and $14 million each month to maintain.[67]

How successful have the nation's toxic waste laws been? Certainly the toxic wastes permeating our lives would be far more harmful had nothing been done. Yet, an enormous cleanup remains undone. The total cleanup costs of all hazardous waste sites, whether they are on the priorities lists or not, may be a staggering $750 billion! Meanwhile the problem worsens, as toxic waste destroys more ecosystems and human lives. The General Accounting Office (GAO) reported gloomily in 1986 that:

> Ten years after the Congress mandated the identification and control of hazardous wastes, EPA cannot say what portion of the universe of hazardous wastes it has identified and brought under regulation, or even if it is regulating the worst wastes in terms of potential impact on human health and the environment. Its waste identification activity has been hampered by low or changing priorities and changing approaches and strategies.[68]

How can the nation's waste disposal problem be better managed? At first glance, incineration may seem the best way to dispose of garbage. The first incinerator in the United States was built in New York City in 1895; soon municipalities across the country had built their own furnaces. Rather than eliminate trash, incinerators simply spread, in reduced form, often highly toxic soot across the landscape. Although the efficiency of incinerators has improved greatly over the last century, the problem of poisonous chemicals spreading with

the winds remains. While only about 14 percent of trash is incinerated in the United States, half that of Germany, Switzerland, Swe-
den, Denmark, and Japan goes up in smoke. With their dense
populations and limited space, the governments of those countries
have little choice but to incinerate.[69]

For coastal muncipalities, another "solution" to ever-growing trash
mountains was dump them in the deep blue sea. Barges hauled
trash miles out into the ocean and then flushed it. Unfortunately,
this trash disposal method also came back to haunt the public. Toxic
and unsightly wastes washed up on beaches. As early as 1933, New
Jersey sued New York City for ocean-dumping its trash. In 1934,
the Supreme Court ruled that New York had to desist from the
practice. While the Supreme Court ruling diverted municipal waste
back to landfills, it did not affect commercial and industrial waste.
Private businesses continued to dump wastes in the ocean for another
four decades until the 1972 Marine Protection, Research, and Sanc-
tuaries Act restricted it to 120 off-shore sites monitored by the US
Coast Guard. Tougher restrictions were imposed by the 1988 Ocean
Dumping Ban Act. Yet, ocean dumping continues.

The waste solution for many municipalities is to ship it abroad.
While properly disposing of hazardous wastes in the United States
may cost $250–300 per ton, many Third World countries eagerly
accept the waste for as little as $50 per ton. The practice whereby
rich countries dump their trash in poor countries has been called
"waste colonialism." The United States both exports and imports
hazardous wastes. In 1990, 1 percent or 139 000 tons of America's
hazardous wastes were exported to eight countries, of which the
bulk went to Canada and Mexico, and imported 110 000 tons. Many
American manufacturers have taken advantage of Mexico's
"Maquilladoras" which offer low taxes, cheap labor, and lax environmental regulations. Although a 1987 treaty required American firms
to ship back to the United States any wastes generated in the
Maquilladoras, it has not been enforced.[70]

There have been some attempts to regulate the international waste
trade. The 1972 UN Conference on the Human Environment raised
the issue, but did nothing about it. The UN Environment Program's
1984–5 Cairo Guidelines were the first attempt to suggest regulations. Exporting states were encouraged to notify and get the approval of the government of the importing country before shipping,
while the importing country should enact disposal methods as tough
as that of the exporting country. The guidelines are not legally binding

and depend on the participant's voluntary compliance. In 1989, 68 Third-World states in Africa, the Caribbean, and Pacific, known as the ACP group, joined with the European Community to sign the Lome Convention which outlaws the shipment of radioactive and other hazardous waste from the latter to the former. These groups also signed the Basel Convention on the Control of Transboundary Movements of Hazardous Wastes and their Disposal.[71] The United States supports but has not signed either treaty.

The most environmentally sound way to deal with trash (other than not creating it in the first place) is to recycle it. Northern Europeans and Japanese recyle as much as half of their trash, compared to only 13 percent for Americans. Unfortunately, various government subsidies and protection for the logging, mining, and petrochemical industries have made it more economical for businesses to buy virgin rather than recycled paper, plastic, metal, and other goods.

Some administrations have tried to encourage recycling. For years, the Nixon White House debated extending tax credits and subsidies for recyling programs. But in 1974, the EPA dismissed the idea because it believed a recycling industry was emerging on its own. The price for paper waste dropped from $60 a ton in 1974 to $5 a ton a year later. Then, during the 1990s, paper recyling increased steadily for several reasons. The Federal government and increasing numbers of states are requiring their bureaucracies to use recycled paper. Increasing numbers of cities are requiring residents to separate their garbarge into recyclables and non-recyclables. Finally, logging restrictions in the north-west forests and elsewhere have raised prices for virgin timber, thus making recycled paper more competitive.[72]

Just as the barge *Mobro 400* has become a symbol of, among other things, America's solid waste problem, the toxic ghost towns of Love Canal and Time Beach have become household words to the environmentally aware. The former residents who fled the toxic devastation lost not only their homes but may eventually lose their lives to cancer. But Love Canal and Time Beach are only the most dramatic examples of toxic spills that afflict thousands of neighborhoods across the country. Every day between 1988 and 1992 alone, 19 chemical accidents exploded somewhere in the country, releasing more than 680 million pounds of toxic wastes across the country. A ton of hazardous waste is annually created for every American. About 80 percent of all hazardous wastes are produced by 14 000 regulated producers such as chemical and related industries. Every year in the United States, over 360 million pounds of toxic wastes are dumped in streams and lakes, 1.22 billion pounds into underground wells, 2.4 billion pounds into the air, 560 million pounds into landfills, and 1.7 billion pounds into municipal treatment plants. By one GAO estimate, there may be as many as 425 000 hazardous waste sites scattered across the country.[73]

AMERICAN INDUSTRIAL POLICIES AND THE WORLD

America's industrial policies do not occur in isolation. Their relative effectiveness depends on how they compare to the industrial policies of America's rivals. And the impact of each nation's industrial and other policies is tempered by an ever-more interdependent global political economy.

Throughout the past half-century, revolutionary changes have transformed the nature of international relations and the power balance, changes for which American policies were largely the catalyst. The world's nations are drawn ever-more closely together in an ever-thickening web of trade, investment, cultural, communications, and environmental ties. Most nations share a common interest in developing and modernizing, however defined, as rapidly as possible. The world's political institutions such as the United Nations and economic institutions like the WTO, IMF, GATT, and IBRD, along with regional organizations such as the EC, NAFTA, Organization of American States (OAS), and APEC contribute to the modernization and development of its members. As Keohane and Nye put it,

> complex interdependence has three main characteristics: 1) state policy goals are not arranged in stable hierarchies, but are subject to trade offs; 2) the existence of multiple channels of contact among societies expands the range of policy instruments, thus limiting the ability of foreign offices tightly to control governments' foreign relations; and 3) military force is largely irrelevant.[74]

Conflict remains endemic in international relations and nations still assert their interests by wielding power. But governments increasingly assert their interests with economic rather than military power. In an ever-more interdependent world, the use of military power becomes ever-more irrelevant to achieving those interests. The financial, political, and moral costs of going to war rise ever higher, while the economic, strategic, and political benefits steadily diminish. Wars still devastate populations and ecosystems. Most wars, however, occur within rather than between states. Whether a conflict is geopolitical or geoeconomic, some states are much more adept at wielding power and have many more sources of power than others.[75]

Until recently, the Cold War prevented most Americans from fully appreciating the impact of an ever-thickening web of interdependence on international relations. Americans continued to cling to a conception of power rooted mostly in military terms long after West Europeans, East Asians, and others around the world adopted a much more sophisticated view, whose foundation was geoeconomic power.

The Cold War distorted more than Americans' conception of power; even more damaging, it warped American values. Evil the Soviet empire and communism certainly were, but they did not threaten American liberty or prosperity. The real threat came from within, from right-wing ideologues who convinced most Americans that, as Senator Barry Goldwater put it, "extremism in the defense of liberty is no vice." Or, in the words of the apocryphal American officer in Vietnam, "we had to destroy the village in order to save it." The "better Dead than Red" attitude might be ludicrous if it were not used as the justification for the erosion of civil liberties via the McCarthy hearings, blacklistings, domestic spying, ever-growing military and intelligence industrial complexes, and general garrison-state mentality. A majority of Americans truly believed they were the greatest nation on earth, God's chosen people, and that the American way should be the world's way. This hubris led to the jungles of Indochina and bank accounts of scores of dictators around the world. Literally trillions of dollars and tens of thousands of American lives were squandered in a crusade based on deep illusions about the world and America's place within it. Richard Berstein writes that the Cold War's legacy for American political culture is "insecurity, exaggerated self-love, polarization, and bitterness in political debates, as well as the nation's tendency to swing from moods of optimism and hope to darker days of anger and disillusionment."[76]

Not every American marched in lock-step to such slogans, demogogues, and repressions. A growing number saw through the hype and spoke out. The opposition peaked in the 1960s with the civil rights and anti-Vietnam-War movements, then dissipated in the 1970s into cynicism, apathy, and resignation. Increasing numbers of young people in particular are indifferent to the problems ravaging the nation and world. A survey of 333 703 college freshmen at 670 two- and four-year colleges and universities found that only 31.9 percent felt that "keeping up with political affairs" was important, the lowest percentage since the annual poll began in 1965. As recently as 1990, 42.4 percent thought keeping up was important, while 57.8 percent agreed in 1966. Even fewer actually discussed politics – 16.0 percent in 1994 compared to the height of 29.9 percent in 1968. Those who were willing to "participate in programs to help clean up the environment" dropped from one-third (33.6 percent) in 1992 to one-quarter (24.3 percent) in 1994.[77]

During the 1990s, even more disturbing and dangerous than a deep nihilism spreading across the population, was the rise of extreme right-wing "militia," Christian, and anarchist groups which directly attacked America's democratic values and institutions. In the post-Cold-War era, many Americans seem to have turned all the invective they used to focus on Reds, on themselves. Calls for hatred and violence spew from radio stations, newspapers, and even television stations across the nation. Paranoia and violence may be rooted among right-wing extremists, but increasingly afflict people along all points of the political spectrum. Without a trace of irony, the extreme right regularly compare government officials to "jack-booted thugs."[78]

All this has had an enormous impact on the traditional debate between Jeffersonians and Hamiltonians. That debate over government's proper role and power has raged since the nation's beginning. Although heated, the discourse has largely been civil until recently. Jeffersonians argue simply and perhaps simplistically that the weaker a government's duties and powers, the greater will be the nation's freedom and wealth. The market place supplies all needs and wants; the fewer the restraints on markets, the more efficiently it will do so. The government's role should be restricted to maintaining security from internal and foreign violence.

Hamiltonians counter that government should be as powerful as society's manifold problems. After all, problem-solving – doing what private citizens or businesses cannot or will not do on their own – is government's purpose. Government programs to address problems arise because the private sector is indifferent or incapable of ameliorating it, or frequently is the very cause of that problem. Still, Hamiltonians do acknowledge that policy is not the panacea for all of society's ills. Most problems may at best be manageable but not solvable. Crime, poverty, disease, discrimination, environmental destruction, ignorance, and so on can be alleviated but never truly eliminated. At some point, the spending to reduce such problems may well reach a point of diminishing returns. But what is that point?

Government programs directly or indirectly benefit virtually all in society. Everyone enjoys entitlements, including those who want to eliminate those of all others but their own. Republicans tend to set aside their anti-government rhetoric when programs that benefit themselves or their constituents are threatened. For instance, farmers voted in overwelming numbers for the Republican Party which claims it wants "small government." But those same farmers fight fiercely when anyone suggests eliminating the $9 billion in annual subsidies they enjoy. And the Republicans have discarded any suggestions that they reduce government's role in subverting a free market in agriculture.

Ultimately, politics shapes policies. In a liberal democracy, the shifting power balance among interest groups determines what government does or does not do. Relativists argue that the national interest equals those interest groups that are tough, wealthy, and savvy enough to convert their goals into national policy.

Which level of government is best able to manage a problem? Some demand that Federal programs be turned over to state and local government, arguing that because they are closer to the specific problems in their midst, they are better able to address them. Others argue that American government is too decentralized as it is, and that Americans could reap enormous savings and efficiencies by centralizing many government functions that are frequently duplicated in small, nearby communities across the nation.

Who is right? It depends. Whether a given problem is best managed by the Federal, state, or local government, or some combination, obviously varies from one to the next. What is undeniable is that state and local government dwarf the Federal government. Although Washington is popularly criticized for its immense workforce, in fact it represents only 16 percent of all government workers. State and local government employees account for 23 percent and a whopping 61 percent, respectively, of the total.

Comparisons of government size are usually based on its spending as a percentage of GNP. By that measure, the United States has one of the smallest governments among the democratic industrial countries. Washington has consumed around 22 percent of GNP and Federal employees have numbered around 2.9 million for the past 20 years. In fact, the 2.8 million civilian government jobs in 1995 was the lowest proportion (21 percent) of total employment than at any time since before World War II.[79] True, there was a time when the Federal government composed no more than an economic sliver – 3 percent of GNP back in 1932 before President Roosevelt's New Deal. Some may relish the idea of turning back the clock to that era of minimum government. But would America be better off? After all, real per-capita income has tripled since that time; people lead healthier, longer lives; social security and medicare have greatly reduced what was then endemic poverty among the elderly; laws segregating and discriminating against blacks have been eliminated; environmental destruction has been slowed and in some cases reversed; the number of national parks preserving American history and nature has increased; to name a few notable accomplishments. And America's problems have multiplied and deepened since the 1920s.

So what then is the Federal government's proper role? The relative successes and failures of industrial policies can be analysed. As any Hamiltonian will attest, some industrial policies work better than others, while some make things worse. The government is responsible for managing problems that markets either cannot solve or actually cause. Though the real world evidence tends to support the Hamiltonians, Jeffersonians value dogma above all else. Jeffersonians believe that less government is always better than more. What could be more simple?

Notes

Notes to the Introduction

1. Thomas Jefferson, *Notes on the State of Virginia* (Chapel Hill, NC: University of North Carolina Press, 1955), pp. 164–5.
2. Adam Smith, *An Inquiry into the Nature and Causes of the Wealth of Nations* (New York: Oxford University Press, 1993), pp. 220–1.
3. Alexander Hamilton, "Continentalist No. V" (18 April 1782), "Opinion on the Constitutionality of an Act to Establish a National Bank" (23 February 1791), "Report on the Subject of Manufactures" (5 December 1791), in Morton J. Frisch (ed.), *Sel.   1 Writings and Speeches of Alexander Hamilton* (Washington, DC: American Enterprise Institute, 1985), pp. 279, 312, 296, 294, 57, 299, 58–9, 311.
4. Aaron Wildavesky, "Industrial Policies," in Claude Barfield and William Schambra (eds), *The Politics of Industrial Policy* (Washington, DC: American Enterprise Institute for Public Policy Research, 1986), p. 15.
5. Thomas K. McCraw, "Mercantilism and the Market: Antecedants of American Industrial Policy," in Barfield and Schamba (eds), *Politics of Industrial Policy*, p. 33; James M. Swank, *The Industrial Policies of Great Britian and the United States* (Philadelphia, PA: American Iron and Steel Association, 1876).
6. Mancur Olson, "Supply-Side Economics, Industrial Policy, and Rational Ignorance," in Barfield and Schamba (eds), *Politics of Industrial Policy*, p. 266.
7. Robert B. Reich, "Small State, Big Lesson," *Boston Observer*, vol. 3 (July 1984), p. 32.
8. For the leading works on America's industrial policy debate, see: Michael and Susan Wachter, *Toward a New U.S. Industrial Policy?* (Philadelphia, PA: University of Pennsylvania Press, 1981); Barry Bluestone and Bennett Harrison, *The Deindustrialization of America: Plant Closings, Community Abandonment, and the Dismantling of Basic Industries* (New York: Basic Industries, 1982); Phyllis Levinson *et al.*, *The Federal Entrepreneur: The Nation's Implicit Industrial Policy* (Washington, DC: The Urban Institute, 1982); Robert Reich, "Making Industrial Policy," *Foreign Affairs*, Spring 1982; Congressional Budget Office, *The Industrial Policy Debate* (Washington, DC: Government Printing Office, 1983); US International Trade Commission, *Foreign Industrial Targeting and its Effects on US Industries, Phase I, Japan* (Washington, DC: USITC Publication 1437, 1983); Richard B. McKenzie, "National Industrial Policy: An Overview of the Debate," Heritage Foundation, *Backgrounder*, no. 275, 12 July 1983; Chalmers Johnson (ed.), *The Industrial Policy Debate* (San Francisco, CA: Institute for Contemporary Studies, 1984); Steven Schlosstein, *Trade War: Greed, Power, and Industrial Policy on Opposite Sides of the Pacific* (New York: Congdon & Weed, 1984);

William Cline, "US Trade and Industrial Policy: The Experience of Textiles, Steel, and Automobiles," in Paul Krugman (ed.), *Strategic Trade Policy and the New International Economics* (Cambridge, MA: MIT Press, 1986); Claude E. Barfield and William A. Schambra (eds), *The Politics of Industrial Policy* (Washington, DC: American Enterprise Institute for Public Policy Research, 1986);

For the mercantilist foundation of most industrial policies, see, Friedrich List, *The National System of Political Economy* (London: Longmans, Green, 1885); Eli F. Heckscher, *Mercantilism*, 2 vols (London: Allen & Unwin, 1955); Jacob Viner, "Mercantilist Thought," in *International Encyclopedia of the Social Sciences* (New York: Macmillan, 1968), pp. 435–43; Chalmers Johnson, *MITI and the Japanese Miracle* (Stanford, CA: Stanford University Press, 1982); Paul Krugman, "The US Response to Foreign Industrial Targeting," *Brookings Papers on Economic Activity*, vol. 15, no. 1 (1984); Richard Harris, *Trade, Industrial Policy, and International Competition* (Toronto: University of Toronto Press, 1985); Donald McFetridge, "The Economics of Industrial Policy," in D.G. McFetridge (ed.), *Canadian Industrial Policy in Action* (Toronto: University of Toronto Press, 1985); Avinash K. Dixit and Albert S. Kyle, "The Use of Protection and Subsidies for Entry Promotion and Deterrence," *American Economic Review*, vol. 75, March 1985); Jonathan Eaton and Gene M. Grossman, "Optimal Trade and Industrial Policy under Oligopoly," *Quarterly Journal of Economics*, vol. 101 (May 1986), pp. 383–406; James A. Brander, "Shaping Comparative Advantage: Trade Policy, Industrial Policy, and Economic Performance," in R.G. Lipsey and W. Dobson (eds), *Shaping Comparative Advantage*, Policy Study No. 2 (Toronto: C.D. Howe Institute, 1987); Joan Pearce and John Sutton, *Protection and Industrial Policy in Europe* (London: Routledge & Kegan Paul, 1986); C.T. Saunders (ed.), *Industrial Policies and Structural Change* (London: Macmillan, 1987); James A. Brander, "Rationales for Strategic Trade and Industrial Policy," in Paul Krugman (ed.), *Strategic Trade Policy and the New International Economics* (Cambridge, MA: MIT Press, 1986);

Although every analysis of the subject notes the strengths and weaknesses of specific industrial policies, for ideological critiques see, Charles L. Schultze, "Industrial Policy: A Dissent," *Brookings Review*, vol. 2, no. 1 (Fall 1983), pp. 3–12; Charles L. Schultze, "Cars, Quotas, and Inflation," *Brookings Bulletin*, vol. 17, no. 3 (1983), pp. 3–4; Herbert Stein, *Presidential Economics* (New York: Simon and Schuster, 1984).

9. "President Bush's Press Conference," *New York Times*, 25 June 1992.
10. Atack and Passell, *A New Economic View of American History*, p. 651.
11. Laura D'Andrea Tyson, *Who's Bashing Whom? Trade Conflict in High-Technology Industries* (Washington, DC: Institute for International Economics, 1992), p. 1.
12. US Bureau of the Census, *Statistical Abstract of the United States*, 1990, 110th edn (Washington, DC: Government Printing Office, 1990).
13. Ikenberry, "Institutional Approach," p. 230; See also, Charles Tilly (ed.), *The Formation of National States in Western Europe* (Princeton,

NJ: Princeton University Press, 1975); Gianfranco Poggi, *The Development of the Modern State* (Stanford, CT: Stanford University Press, 1978); Reinhard Bendix, *Kings and People: Power and the Mandate to Rule* (Berkeley, CA: University of California Press, 1978); Peter Evans, Dietrich Rusechemeyer, and Theda Skocpol (eds), *Bringing the State Back In* (New York: Cambridge University Press, 1985).

Notes to Chapter 1: Policymaking

1. Hugh Heclo, "Issue Networks and the Executive Establishment," in Anthony King (ed.) *The New American Political System*, (Washington, DC: American Enterprise Institute, 1979), p. 89.
2. Graham Allison, *Essence of Decision* (Boston, MA: Little, Brown, 1971), p. 163.
3. For an excellent article which explores these different ways of analyzing foreign economic policy, see G. John Ikenberry, "Conclusion: An Institutional Approach to American Foreign Economic Policy, *International Organization*, vol. 42, no. 1 (Winter 1988), pp. 219–43.

System-centered approaches include, Charles Kindleberger, *The World in Depression* (Berkeley, CA: University of California, 1973); Immanuel Wallerstein, *The Modern World System*, vols 1 and 2 (New York: Academic Press, 1974 and 1976); Robert Keohane and Joseph Nye, *Power and Interdependence* (Boston, MA: Little, Brown, 1977); Robert Keohane, "The Theory of Hegemonic Stability and Changes in International Economic Regimes," in Ole Hosti, R. Siverson, and Alexander George (eds), *Change in the International System* (Boulder, CO: Westview Press, 1980); Stephen Krasner, *International Regimes* (Ithaca, NY: Cornell University Press, 1982); David A. Lake, "International Economic Structures and American Foreign Economic Policy, 1887–1934," *World Politics*, vol. 28 (April 1976), pp. 317–43; Bruce Russett, "The Mysterious Case of Vanishing Hegemony; Or Is Mark Twain Really Dead?," *International Organization*, vol. 39 (Spring 1985); Duncan Snidal, "The Limits of Hegemonic Stability Theory," *International Organization*, vol. 39 (Autumn 1985), pp. 579–614; Robert Gilpin, *The Political Economy of International Relations* (Princeton, NJ: Princeton, 1987);

Society-centered approaches include, E.E. Schattschneider, *Politics, Pressures, and the Tariff* (New York: Prentice Hall, 1935); David Truman, *The Government Process: Political Interests and Public Opinion* (New York: Knopf, 1951); Robert Dahl, *Who Governs?* (New Haven, CT: Yale University Press, 1963); Theodore Lowi, *The End of Liberalism* (New York: Norton, 1969); Jonathan J. Pincus, *Pressure Groups and Politics in Antebellum Tariffs* (New York: Columbia University Press, 1977); Timothy McKeown, "Firms and Tariff Regime Change: Explaining the Demand for Protection," *World Politics*, vol. 36 (January 1984), pp. 215–33;

State–centered approaches include, Peter Katzenstein, "Conclusion: Domestic Structures and Strategies of Foreign Economic Policy," in

Peter Katzenstein (ed.), *Between Power and Plenty* (Madison, WI: University of Wisconsin, 1978); Peter Katzenstein, *Small States in World Markets* (Ithaca, NY: Cornell University Press, 1986); Stephen Krasner, *Defending the National Interest* (Princeton, NJ: Princeton University, 1978); Peter Evans, *Dependent Development* (Princeton, NJ: Princeton University Press, 1979); Peter B. Evans, Dietrich Rueschemeyer, and Theda Skocpol (eds), *Bringing the State Back In* (Cambridge: Cambridge University Press, 1985).

4. Aaron Wildavesky, "Industrial Policies in American Political Culture," in Claude Barfield and William Schambra (eds), *The Politics of Industrial Policy* (Washington, DC: American Enterprise Institute for Public Policy Research, 1986), p. 17.

    See also, Lucian Pye, *Politics, Personality, and Nation Building* (New Haven, CT: Yale University Press, 1962); Lucian Pye (ed.), *Political Culture and Political Development* (Princeton, NJ: Princeton University Press, 1965); Gabriel Almond and Sidney Verba, *The Civic Culture* (Boston, MA: Little, Brown, 1965); Paul Egon Rohrlich, "Economic Culture and Foreign Policy: the Cognitive Analysis of Economic Policy Making," *International Organization*, vol. 41, no. I (Winter 1987), pp. 61–91.

5. Louis Hartz, *The Liberal Tradition in America* (New York: Harcourt Brace, 1955); Lloyd A. Free and Hadley Cantril, *The Political Beliefs of Americans* (New York: Simon and Schuster, 1968); Richard Hofstadter, *The American Political Tradition* (New York: Vintage, 1972).

6. Hugh Heclo, "Industrial Policy and the Executive Capacities of Government," in Claude Barfield and William Schambra (eds), *The Politics of Industrial Policy* (Washington, DC: American Enterprise Institute for Public Policy Research, 1986), p. 303.

7. Hugh S. Norton, *The Employment Act and the Council of Economic Advisors, 1946–1976* (Columbia, SC: University of South Carolina Press, 1977).

8. Quoted in Richard Neustadt, *Presidential Power* (New York: John Wiley & Sons, 1960), p. 18; see also, Clinton Rossiter, *The American Presidency* (New York: Harcourt, Brace, Jovanovich, 1984); James Barber, *Presidential Character* (Englewood Cliffs, NJ: Prentice Hall, 1985); Thomas Cronin, *The State of the Presidency* (Chicago, IL: Scott, Foresman, & Co., 1980); Bert Rockman, *The Leadership Question: The Presidency and the American System* (New York: Praeger, 1984).

9. Ikenberry, "Institutional Approach," p. 224.

10. George C. Edwards and Ira Sharkansky, *The Policy Predicament* (San Francisco, CA: W.H. Freeman & Co., 1978), p. 293.

11. Walter A. Rosembaum, *Environmental Politics and Policy* (Washington, DC: Congressional Quarterly, 1991), p. 9.

12. Quoted in Margaret E. Kriz, "Pesticidal Pressures," *National Journal*, (12 December 1988), pp. 3125–6.

13. Walter Rosenbaum, Environmental Politics and Policy, 2nd edn (Washington, DC: Congressional Quarterly Press, 1991), p. 83.

14. See Keith Schneider, "Environment Laws Face a Stiff Test from Landowners," *New York Times*, (20 January 1992), p. A-1.

15. Robert H. Boyle, "Activists at Risk of Being SLAPPed," *Sports Illustrated* (25 March 1991), pp. 20–3.
16. Martin and Susan Tolchin, *Buying into America: How Foreign Money is Changing the Face of our Nation* (New York: Berkley Books, 1988); James Lester, "A New Federalism?," in Norman J. Vig and Michael E. Kraft (eds), *Environmental Policy in the 1990s*, (Washington, DC: Congressional Quarterly Press, 1990), pp. 59–79.
17. Michael S. Greve, "Environmentalism and Bounty Hunting," *Public Interest*, vol. 97 (Fall 1989), p. 24.
18. Marianne Lavelle and Marcia Coyle, "Unequal Protection: The Racial Divide in Environmental Law," *National Law Journal*, (21 September 1992), p. S-2.
19. William Glaberson, "Coping in the Age of 'Nimby,'" *New York Times* (19 June 1988), Section 3, p. 1.
20. Theodore W. Lowi, *The End of Liberalism* (New York: W.W. Norton & Co., 1969), p. 95.
21. John Kingdom, *Agendas, Alternatives, and Public Policy* (Boston, MA: Little, Brown, & Co., 1984).
22. Leslie Wayne, "Lobbyists' Gifts to Politicians Reap Benefits, Study Shows," *New York Times*, (23 January 1997).
23. Walter Lippman, *The Phantom Public* (New York: Macmillan, 1925), p. 4.
24. V.O. Key, *Public Opinion and American Democracy* (New York: Alfred Knopf, 1961), p. 38.
    See also, Everett Carl Ladd, "The Polls: Taxing and Spending," *Public Opinion Quarterly*, vol. 43 (Spring 1979); Robert S. Erikson, "Economic Conditions and the Presidential Vote," *American Political Science Review*, vol. 83 (Spring 1989), pp. 567–73; Gregory B. Markus, "The Impact of Personal and National Economic Conditions on Presidential Voting, 1956–1988," *American Journal of Political Science*, vol. 36 (1992), pp. 829–34; Michael B. MacKuen, Robert S. Erikson, and James A. Stimson, "Peasants or Bankers," *American Political Science Review*, vol. 86 (September 1992), pp. 597–611; Leo Bogart, *Silent Politics* (New York: John Wiley & Sons, 1972); Karlyn Keene and Everett Ladd, "Government as Villain," *Government Executive* vol. 11 (January 1988) pp. 13–16.
25. Walter A. Rosenbaum, *Environmental Politics and Policy* (Washington, DC: Congressional Quarterly, 1991), p. 77.
26. Rosenbaum, *Environmental Politics and Policy*, p. 73.
27. James G. March and Johan P. Olsen, "The New Institutionalism: Organizational Factors in Political Life," *American Political Science Review*, vol. 78 (September 1984), p. 735. See also, Theodore Lowi, *The End of Liberalism* (New York: W.W. Norton & Co., 1979); Andrew McFarland, "Public Interest Lobbies vs. Minority Faction," in Cigler and Loomis, (eds), *Interest Group Politics* (Washington, DC: Congressional Quarterly Press, 1983).

Notes to Chapter 2: Policies

1. Steven Greenhouse, "Lessons Across Six Decades as Clinton Tries to Make Jobs," *New York Times* (23 November 1992).
2. Howard Shuman, *Politics and the Budget: The Struggle Between the President and the Congress* (Englewood Cliffs, NJ: Prentice Hall, 1992); Aaron Wildavesky, *The New Politics of the Budgetary Process* (Glenview, IL: Scott, Foresman, 1988).
3. For a concise discussion of monetary policy from which much information of the following section derives, see Robert C. Puth, *American Economic History* (Chicago, IL: Dryden Press, 1982), p. 175; John P. Frendreis and Raymond Tatalovich, *The Modern Presidency and Economic Policy* (Itasca, IL: F.E. Peacock, 1994), ch. 5.
4. Richard H. Timberlake, *The Origins of Central Banking in the United States* (Cambridge, MA: Harvard University Press, 1978).
5. Paul Studenski and Herman Krooss, *Financial History of the United States* (New York: McGraw-Hill, 1965), p. 104.
6. John Odell, *US International Monetary Policy: Markets, Power, and Ideas as Sources of Change* (Princeton, NJ: Princeton University, 1982; William Greider, *Secrets of the Temple: How the Federal Reserve Runs the Country* (New York: Simon & Schuster, 1988).
7. Fred Shapiro, "Last Words on Taxes," *New York Times* (16 April 1993).
8. Mancur Olson, "Supply-Side Economics, Industrial Policy, and Rational Ignorance," in Claude E. Barfield and William A. Schambra (eds), *The Politics of Industrial Policy* (Washington, DC: American Enterprise Institute, 1986), p. 265.
9. Ibid.
10. Alan Bromley, "US Technology Policy: The Path to Competitiveness," Address to the Technology 2000 Meeting (Washington, DC: 27 November 1990).
11. Edmund Andrews, "Swords to Plowshares: The Bureaucratic Snags," *New York Times* (15 February 1993); Office of Technology Assessment, *Competing Economies: America, Europe, and the Pacific Rim* (Washington, DC: GPO, October 1991).
12. Robert Reinhold, "Los Angeles Cancels Huge Contract With a Japanese Maker of Rail Cars," *New York Times* (23 January 1992).
13. William Broad, "Vast Sums for New Discoveries Pose a Threat to Basic Science," *New York Times* (27 May 1990).
14. Philip Hilts, "Energy Chief says Accounting Problems snag Supercollider Project," *New York Times* (30 June 1993).
15. William Broad, "Small-scale Science Feels the Pinch from Big Projects," *New York Times* (4 September 1990); William Broad, "Ridden With Debt, US Companies Cut Funds for Research," *New York Times* (30 June 1992).
16. Martin Tolchin, "A Debate Over Access to American Research," *New York Times* (17 December 1989); Anthony DePalma, "Universities Reliance on Companies raises Vexing Questions on Research," *New York Times* (17 March 1993).
17. William Broad, "Clinton to Promote High Technology, With Gore in Charge," *New York Times* (10 November 1992).

18. Edmund Andrews, "Clinton's Technology Plan would Redirect Billions from Military Research," *New York Times* (23 February 1993).
19. Edmund Andrews, "Washington Growing as a Financial Angel to Industry," *New York Times* (1 May 1994).
20. E.E. Schattschneider, *Politics, Pressures and the Tariff* (New York: Prentice Hall, 1935); Jonathan Pincus, *Pressure Groups and Politics in Antebellum Tariffs* (New York: Columbia University Press, 1977); Peter Gourevitch, "International Trade, Domestic Coalitions, and Liberty: Comparative Responses to the Crisis of 1873–1896," *Journal of Interdisciplinary Studies*, vol. 8 (Autumn 1977); Robert Baldwin, *The Political Economy of US Import Policy* (Cambridge, MA: MIT Press, 1986); Real P. Laverge, *The Political Economy of US Tariffs* (New York: Academic Press, 1983).
21. David A. Lake, "The State and American Trade Strategy in the Prehegemonic Era," *International Organization*, vol. 42, no. 1 (Winter 1988), pp. 51, 52.
22. Charles P. Kindleberger, *The World in Depression, 1929–39* (Berkeley, CA: University of California Press, 1973).
23. Frendreis and Tatalovich, *The Modern Presidency and Economic Policy*, pp. 150, 157; Judith Goldstein, "Ideas, Institutions, and American Trade Policy," *International Organization*, vol. 42, no. I (Winter 1988), pp. 179–217.
24. For explorations of the relationship between geopolitical and geoeconomic power, see: William Kennedy, *Rise and Fall of the Great Powers* (New York: Random House, 1987); Charles H. Ferguson, "America's High Tech Decline," *Foreign Policy*, vol. 74 (Spring 1989), pp. 123–44; B.R. Inman and Daniel F. Burton, "Technology and Competitiveness: The New Policy Frontier," *Foreign Affairs*, vol. 69, no. 2 (Spring 1990), pp. 116–34; Wayne Sandholtz, Michael Borrus, and John Zysman (eds), *The Highest Stakes: The Economic Foundations of the Next Security System* (London: Oxford University Press, 1992); Jeffrey Garten, *A Cold Peace: America, Japan, Germany and the Struggle for Supremacy* (New York: Times Books, 1992); Lester Thurow, *Head to Head: The Coming Economic Battle Among Japan, Europe, and America* (New York: Morrow, 1992); William Nester, *American Power, the New World Order, and the Japanese Challenge* (New York: St Martin's Press, 1993;

For the views of strategic trade theorists, see James Brander and Barbara Spencer, "Export Subsidies and International Market Share Rivalry," *Journal of International Economics*, vol. 18, nos 1–2 (February 1985), pp. 85–100; Paul Krugman (ed.), *Strategic Trade Policy and the New International Economics* (Cambridge, MA: MIT Press, 1986); William Dickens and Kevin Lang, "Why it Matters what we Trade: A Case for an Active Trade Policy," in William Dickens, Laura D'Andrea Tyson, and John Zysman (eds), *The Dynamics of Trade and Employment* (Cambridge, MA: Ballinger, 1988) pp. 87–112; Paul Krugman, *The Age of Diminished Expectations: US Economic Policy in the 1990s* (Cambridge, MA: MIT Press, 1990); David J. Richardson, "The Political Economy of Strategic Trade Policy," *International Organization*, vol. 44 (Winter 1990), pp. 107–35; Michael Porter, *The Competitive Advantage of Nations* (New York: Free Press, 1990).

25. Gary Horlick, "The United States Anti-Dumping System," in John H. Jackson and Edwin A. Vermulst (eds), *Anti-dumping Law and Practice: A Comparative Study* (Ann Arbor, MI: University of Michigan Press, 1989); Richard Boltuck and Robert Litan (eds), *Down in the Dumps: Administration of Unfair Trade Laws* (Washington, DC: Brookings Institute, 1991).
26. Michael Porter, "The Structure within Industries and Companies' Performance," *Review of Economics and Statistics*, vol. 61 (May 1979), p. 215.
27. Helen V. Milner and David B. Yoffie, "Between Free Trade and Protectionism: Strategic Trade Policy and a Theory of Corporate Trade Demands," *International Organization*, vol. 43, no. 2 (Spring 1989), p. 247.
28. Robert Keohane, "Reciprocity in International Relations," *International Organization*, vol. 40 (Winter 1986), pp. 1–28; Robert E. Baldwin, *The Political Economy of US Import Policy* (Cambridge, MA: MIT Press, 1985).
29. Keith Bradsher, "Trade Panel Approves Canada-Lumber Duty," *New York Times* (26 June 1992); Thomas O. Bayard and Kimberly Ann Elliott, *Reciprocity and Retaliation: an Evaluation of Aggressive Trade Policies* (Washington, DC: Institute of International Economics, 1992).
30. Keith Bradsher, "As US Urges Free Markets, its Trade Barriers are Many," *New York Times* (7 February 1992).
31. Sylvia Nasar, "The High Price of Protectionism," *New York Times* (13 November 1993), "Government Says Federal Tariffs Cost Shoppers $19 billion Yearly," *New York Times* (28 November 1993).
32. Keith Bradsher, "Level of Government Assistance for American Exporters is Debated," *New York Times* (3 March 1992).
33. Laura D'Andrea Tyson, "They Are Not US: Why American Ownership still Matters," *The American Prospect*, vol. 4 (Winter 1991), pp. 37–48; Edward M. Graham and Paul R. Krugman, *Foreign Direct Investment in the United States* (Washington, DC: Institute for International Economics, 1991); Gene Koretz, "Will Direct Foreign Investment Help on the Trade Front," *Businessweek* (16 December 1991).
34. John Cushman, "Clinton Seeks Taxes on Hidden Profits," *New York Times* (23 October 1992).
35. Keith Bradsher, "Foreign Interests find their Best Lobbyist in American Business," *New York Times* (2 November 1993); Pat Choate, *Agents of Influence: How Japan's Lobbyists in the United States Manipulate America's Political and Economic System* (New York: Knopf, 1990).
36. Tyson, *Who's Bashing Whom?*, p. 57.
37. Fred C. Bergsten and William R. Cline, *The United States–Japan Economic Problem* (Washington, DC: Institute for International Economics," 1987), p. 55.
38. Frendreis and Tatalovich, *The Modern Presidency and Economic Policy*, ch. 12.
39. Stuart Bruchey, *Enterprise*, p. 194.
40. Tyson, *Who's Bashing Whom?*, p. 292.

Notes to Chapter 3: Industrialization Roots, 1607–1860

1. For prominent works on America's colonial political economy, see: Oliver P. Chitwod, *A History of Colonial America* (New York: Harper & Bros, 1961); Curtis P. Nettels, *The Roots of American Civilization* (New York: Appleton, Century, Crofts, 1963); Max Savelle and Robert Middlekauff, *A History of Colonial America* (New York: Holt, Rinehart & Winston, 1964); Stuart Bruchey, *The Colonial Merchant: Sources and Readings* (New York: Harcourt, Brace, & World, 1966); James T. Shepherd and Gary M. Walton, *Shipping, Maritime Trade, and the Economic Development of Colonial America* (Cambridge: Cambridge University Press, 1972); Edwin J. Perkins, *The Economy of Colonial America* (New York: Columbia University Press, 1980).

   For prominent works on both the colonial and the early Republic's political economy, see: Joseph S. Davis, *Essays in the Earlier History of American Corporations*, 2 vols (Cambridge, MA: Harvard University Press, 1917); Victor S. Clark, *History of Manufacturing in the United States, 1607–1860*, 3 vols (Washington, DC: Carnegie Foundation, 1929); J. Russell Smith, *North America: Its People and the Resources, Development, and Prospects of the Continent as an Agricultural, Individual, and Commercial Area* (New York: Harcourt, Brace, 1925); Douglass C. North, *The Economic Growth of the United States, 1790 to 1860* (Englewood Cliffs, NJ: Prentice Hall, 1961); Stuart Bruchey, *Roots of American Economic Growth, 1607–1861* (London: Hutchinson, 1965).

2. See J.H. Elliott, *The Old World and the New, 1492–1650* (Cambridge: Cambridge University Press, 1970); Robert-Henri Bautier, *The Economic Development of Medieval Europe* (New York: Harcourt, Brace, Jovanovich, 1971); Douglass C. North and Robert Paul Thomas, *The Rise of the Western World: A New Economic History* (Cambridge: Cambridge University Press, 1973); Lynn White, *Medieval Technology and Social Change* (Oxford: Clarendon Press, 1962).

3. A.C. Littleton and Basil C. Yamcy (eds), *Studies in the History of Accounting* (Homewood, IL: Richard D. Irwin, 1956).

4. Mary Dewar (ed.), *A Discourse of the Commonweal of this Realm of England, Attributed to Sir Thomas Smith* (Charlottesville, VA: University Press of Virginia), p. 122.

5. J.H. Parry, "Colonial Development and International Rivalries Outside Europe," in *The New Cambridge Modern History*, vol. III, p. 521.

6. Immanuel Wallerstein, *The Modern World System* (New York: Academic Press, 1974), p. 96.

7. John Winthrop, "Sermon on the Arbella," in Stuart Bruchey (ed.), *The Colonial Merchant: Sources and Reading* (New York: Harcourt, Brace, & World, 1966), p. 95.

8. James M. Cassady, *Demography in Early America* (Cambridge, MA: Harvard University Press, 1969), p. 133; Richard Morris, *Government and Labor in Early America* (New York: Columbia University Press, 1946), p. 45; Alice Hanson Jones, *Wealth of a Nation to be: The American Colonies on the Eve of the Revolution* (New York: Columbia

University Press, 1980), pp. 34–7; James Henretta, *The Evolution of American Society, 1700–1815: An Interdisciplinary Analysis* (Lexington: D.C. Heath, 1973); Gary Walton and James F. Shepherd, *The Economic Rise of Early America* (New York: Cambridge University Press, 1979); Edwin Perkins, *The Economy of Colonial America* (New York: Columbia University Press, 1988).

9. Bernard Bailyn, *Voyagers to the West: A Passage in the Peopling of America on the Eve of the Revolution* (New York: Alfred A. Knopf, 1986), pp. 199–200.

10. David W. Galenson, *White Servitude in Colonial America: An Economic Analysis* (Cambridge: Cambridge University Press, 1981), p. 38; see also, Abbott Emerson Smith, *Colonists in Bondage: White Servitude and Convict Labor in America, 1607–1776* (Chapel Hill, NC: University of North Carolina Press, 1968).

11. Winthrop D. Jordan, *White Over Black* (Chapel Hill, NC: University of North Carolina Press, 1968), p. 66; Peter Coclanis, "Economy and Society in Colonial Charleston: The Early Years, 1670 to 1719," PhD dissertation, Columbia University, 1983, p. 36; James Porter, "The Growth of Population in America, 1700–1860," in D.V. Glass and D.E.C. Eversley (eds), *Population in History* (London: Edward Arnold, 1965), p. 641.

12. Peter Wells Bidwell and John I. Falconer, *History of Agriculture in the Northern United States, 1620–1860* (Washington, DC: Carnegie Institute, 1925); Lewis C. Gray, *History of Agriculture in the Southern United States to 1860* (Washington, DC: Carnegie Institute, 1933); Gavin Wright, *The Political Economy of the Cotton South* (New York: W.W. Norton & Co., 1978).

13. Quoted in Bruchey, *Enterprise*, p. 99.

14. Jared Eliot, *Essays upon Field Husbandry in New England, and Other Papers, 1748–1762*, eds Harry J. Carman and Rexford G. Tugwell (New York: Columbia University Press, 1934), pp. 112–13, 134. See also Harry Carman (ed.), *American Husbandry* (Port Washington, NY: Kennikat Press, 1964).

15. Stevenson W. Fletcher, *Pennsylvania Agriculture and Country Life, 1640–1840* (Harrisonburg, PA: Pennsylvania Historical and Museum Commission, 1950), p. 3.

16. Morris, *Studies in American Law*, pp. 62–3; Bruchey, *Enterprise*, pp. 129–30.

17. James T. Shepherd and Gary Walton, *Shipping, Maritime Trade, and the Economic Development of Colonial North America* (Cambridge: Cambridge University Press, 1972); James Henretta, *The Evolution of American Society, 1700–1815, An Interdisciplinary Analysis* (Lexington, MA: D.C. Heath, 1973), p. 78.

18. Bruchey, *Enterprise*, p. 132.

19. Jensen, *Maritime Commerce*, p. 89.

20. Lewis C. Gray, *History of Agriculture in the Southern United States to 1860* (New York: Peter Smith, 1941).

21. Bruchey, *Enterprise*, p. 80.

22. Bruchey, *Enterprise*, p. 82.

23. Henretta, *Evolution of American Society*, pp. 78–79; See also, Max G. Schumacher, *The Northern Farmer and his Markets during the Late Colonial Period* (New York: Arno Press, 1975).

24. Jacob M. Price, "Economic Function and the Growth of American Port Towns in the 18th Century," *Perspectives in American History*, vol. 8 (1974), p. 176; See also, Leilla Sellers, *Charleston Business on the Eve of the American Revolution* (Chapel Hill, NC: University of North Carolina Press, 1934; Converse D. Clowse, *Economic Beginnings in Colonial South Carolina, 1670–1730* (Columbia, SC: University of South Carolina Press, 1971).

25. Shepherd and Walton, Shipping, Maritime Trade, pp. 101, 94–5. Robert Thomas, "A Quantitative Approach to the Study of the Effects of British Imperial Policy on Colonial Welfare: Some Preliminary Findings," *Journal of Economic History*, vol. 25 (1965), pp. 615–38; Peter McClelland, "The Cost to America of British Imperial Policy," *American Economic Review*, vol. 59 (1969), pp. 370–81; Peter McClelland, "The New Economic History and the Burdens of the Navigation Acts: A Comment," *Economic History Review*, vol. 26 (1973), pp. 679–86; Lawrence Harper, "Mercantilism and the American Revolution," *Canadian Historical Review*, vol. 23 (1942), pp. 1–15; Lawrence Harper, "The Effect of the Navigation Acts on the Thirteen Colonies," in Harry Scheiber (ed.), *The United States Economic History* (New York: Knopf, 1964), pp. 42–78; Roger Ransom, "British Policy and Colonial Growth: Some Implications of the Burden from the Navigation Acts," *Journal of Economic History*, vol. 28 (1968), pp. 427–35; Larry Neal, "Interpreting Power and Profit in Economic History: A Case Study of the Seven Years' War," *Journal of Economic History*, vol. 37 (1977), pp. 20–35; Gary Walton, "The New Economic History and the Burdens of the Navigation Acts," *Economic History Review*, vol. 24 (1971), pp. 533–42.

26. Leslie Brock, *The Currency of the American Colonies, 1700–64* (New York: Arno Press, 1975), p. 17; see also Richard A. Lester, *Monetary Experiments: Early American and Recent Scandanivian* (New York: Augustus Kelly, 1939).

27. Bruchey, *Enterprise*, p. 92.

28. Bruchey, *Enterprise*, p. 91.

29. Joseph Albert Ernst, *Money and Politics in America, 1755–75: A Study in the Currency Act of 1764 and the Political Economy of Revolution* (Chapel Hill, NC: University of North Carolina Press, 1973), pp. 8–10; Richard Lester, "Currency Issues to Overcome Depression in Delaware, New Jersey, New York, and Maryland, 1715–1737," *Journal of Political Economy*, vol. 47 (1939); F. James Ferguson, *The Power of the Purse* (Chapel Hill, NC: University of North Carolina Press, 1961), pp. 5–6.

30. Jackson Turner Main, *The Social Structure of Revolutionary America* (Princeton, NJ: Princeton University Press, 1965); Bernard Bailyn, *Ideological Origins of the American Revolution* (Cambridge, MA: Harvard University Press, 1967); J. Franklin Jameson, *The American Revolution Considered as a Social Movement* (Princeton, NJ: Princeton

University Press, 1967); Edwin Burrows and Michael Wallace, "The American Revolution: the Ideology and Psychology of National Liberation," *Perspectives in American History*, vol. 6 (1972), pp. 208–215; Joseph Ernst, *Money and Politics in America, 1755–1775: A Study in the Currency Act of 1764 and the Political Economy of Revolution* (Chapel Hill, NC: University of North Carolina Press, 1973); Jack P. Greene, "An Uneasy Connection: An Analysis of the Preconditions of the American Revolution," in Stephen G. Kurtz and James H. Hutson (eds), *Essays on the American Revolution* (Chapel Hill, NC: University of North Carolina Press, 1973); Robert A. Gross, *The Minute Men and their World* (New York: Hill & Wang, 1976); Edmund Morgan, *Birth of the Republic, 1763–1789* (Chicago, IL: University of Chicago Press, 1977); Oliver M. Dickerson, *The Navigation Acts and the American Revolution* (New York: Octagon, 1978); Gary B. Nash, *The Urban Crucible: Social Change, Political Consciousness, and the Origin of the American Revolution* (Cambridge, MA: Harvard University Press, 1979). F. James Ferguson, *The American Revolution: A General History, 1763–1790* (Homewood, IL: Dorsey Press, 1979).
31. Gerald A. Gunderson, *A New Economic History of America* (New York: McGraw-Hill, 1976), p. 89.
32. *Hamilton Papers*, vol. XII, p. 362 (September 1792).
33. Charles Calomiris, "Institutional Failure, Monetary Scarcity, and the Depreciation of the Continental," *Journal of Economic History*, vol. 48 (1988), pp. 47–68; Curtis P. Nettels, *The Emergence of a National Economy, 1775–1815* (New York: Holt, Rinehart & Winston, 1962), pp. 76–7.
34. Quoted in Bruchey, *Enterprise*, p. 114.
35. *Letters and other Writings of James Madison*, 4 vols (Philadelphia, PA: J.B. Lippincott), vol. I, pp. 226–7.
36. *The Federalist Number 11* (24 November 1787), *Hamilton Papers*, vol. IV, p. 340.
37. Catherine Drinker Bowen, *Miracle at Philadelphia* (Boston, MA: Little, Brown, & Co., 1966).
   In 1913 there appeared "An Economic Interpretation of the Constitution" in which the author Charles Beard argued that the American Constitution was devised to protect the economic interests of its authors rather than democracy for Americans. Beard's book stimulated a debate which has continued loudly through today. Some historians like Forrest McDonald have carefully reexamined the evidence and found little basis for Beard's claim, while others such as Robert McGuire and Robert Ohsfeldt have pointed out that indeed the delegates voted more for their pocketbooks than their constituents. Charles Beard, *An Economic Interpretation of the Constitution* (New York: Macmillan, 1913); Forrest McDonald, *We the People: The Economic Origins of the Constitution* (Chicago, IL: University of Chicago Press, 1958); Robert McQuire and Robert L. Ohsfeldt, "Economic Interests and the American Constitution: A Quantitative Rehabilitation of Charles A. Beard," *Journal of Economic History*, vol. 44 (1984), pp. 509–20; Robert McQuire and Robert L. Ohsfeldt, "An Economic Model

of Voting Behavior over Specific Issues at the Constitutional Convention of 1787," *Journal of Economic History*, vol. 46 (1986), pp. 79–112.

38. James Savage, "Balanced Budgets and American Politics," dissertation in progress, University of California, Berkeley, 1984, quoted by Wildavesky, in *The Politics of Industrial Policy*, p. 23.

39. Alexander Hamilton, "Report on a National Bank," in *Hamilton Papers*, vol. VII, pp. 305–42.

40. J. Van Fenstermaker, *The Development of American Commercial Banking: 1782–1837* (Kent, OH: Bureau of Economic and Business Research, 1965), p. 13; Bruchey, *Enterprise*, pp. 165–92; see also, Bray Hammond, *Banks and Politics in America from the Revolution to the Civil War* (Princeton, NJ: Princeton University Press, 1957); Lance E. Davis, "Banks and Their Economic Effects," in Lance E. Davis *et al.* (eds), *American Economic Growth: An Economist's History of the United States* (New York: Harper & Row, 1972); Paul B. Trescott, *Financing American Enterprise: The Story of Commercial Banking* (New York: Harper & Row, 1963).

41. Leon M. Schur, "The Second Bank of the United States and the Inflation After the War of 1812," *Journal of Political Economy*, vol. 68 (1960), pp. 119–20; Bruchey, *Enterprise*, p. 175.

42. Alexander Hamilton, "Report on Manufactures, December 5, 1791," in Jacob Cooke (ed.), *The Reports of Alexander Hamilton* (New York: Harper & Row, 1964).

43. Bruchey, *Enterprise*, p. 47.

44. John C. Fitzpatrick (ed.), *The Writings of George Washington, 1745–1799* (Washington, DC: Government Printing Office, 1934–44), vol. 35, pp. 233–5.

45. Bruchey, *Enterprise*, p. 149.

46. Quoted in Jacob Viner, *Dumping: A Problem in International Trade* (Chicago, IL: University of Chicago Press, 1923), p. 38.

47. Quoted in Lebergott, *The Americans* (1984), p. 129; Donald Adams, "American Neutrality and Prosperity, 1793–1808: A Reconsideration," *Journal of Economic History*, vol. 40 (1980), pp. 713–38; Bennett Baack and Edward Ray, "The Political Economy of Tariff Policy: A Case Study of the United States," *Explorations in Economic History*, vol. 44 (1984), pp. 73–93; Jonathan Pincus, *Pressure Groups and Politics in Antebellum Tariffs* (New York: Columbia University Press, 1977).

48. Douglass C. North, "The United States Balance of Payments, 1790–1860," in National Bureau of Economic Research (eds), *Trends in the American Economy in the 19th Century*, Studies in Income and Wealth, vol. 24 (Princeton, NJ: Princeton University Press, 1960), pp. 573–627; Claudia Goldin and Frank Lewis, "The Role of Exports in American Economic Growth during the Napoleonic Wars, 1793–1807," *Explorations in American History*, vol. 17 (1980), pp. 291–308;

49. Thomas Jefferson to Thomas Lomax, 12 March 1799, in Paul Leiscester Ford (ed.), *The Writings of Thomas Jefferson* (New York: G.P. Putnam's Sons, 1892–99), vol. 7, p. 373; Robert W. Tucker and David C.

Hendrickson, "Thomas Jefferson and American Foreign Policy," *Foreign Affairs*, vol. 69, no. 2 (Spring 1990).

50. Stanley Lebergott, *The Americans* (New York: W.W. Norton & Co., 1984), p. 128. Jeffrey Frankel, "The 1807–1809 Embargo Against Great Britain," *Journal of Economic History*, vol. 42 (1982), pp. 291–308.

51. All quotes from Carter Goodrich, *Government Promotion of American Canals and Railroads* (New York: Columbia University Press, 1960).

52. Bureau of the Census, *Historical Statistics of the United States, Colonial Times to 1970* (Washington, DC: Government Printing Office, 1976), vol. I, pp. 22–3.

53. Paul Gates, *History of Public Land Law Development* (Washington, DC: Government Printing Office, 1968), pp. 130–31,; Edward S. Rastatter, "Nineteenth Century Public Land Policy: The Case for the Speculator," in David C. Klingaman and Richard K. Vedder (eds), *Essays in Nineteenth Century Economic History: The Old Northwest* (Athens, OH: Ohio University Press, 1975).

54. Shanks, *This Land is Your Land*, p. 51; Harry N. Scheiber, *Ohio Canal Era: A Case Study of Government and the Economy* (Athens, OH: Ohio University Press, 1969); Bruchey, *Enterprise*, p. 210.

55. Harvey Seagal, "Canals and Economic Development," in Carter Goodrich (ed.), *Canals and American Economic Development* (New York: Columbia University Press, 1961), pp. 216–48.

56. Carter Goodrich, *Canals and American Economic Development* (New York: Columbia University Press, 1961), pp. 184–5.

57. Hugh G.J. Aitken (ed.), *The State and Economic Growth* (New York: Social Science Research Council, 1959); Bruchey, *Enterprise*, pp. 205–6.

58. Quoted in Carl B. Swisher, *Roger B. Taney* (Hamden, CT: Archon Books, 1935), p. 367; See also, Carter Goodrich, "The Revulsion against Internal Improvements," *Journal of Economic History*, vol. 10 (1950), pp. 145–69.

59. Bruchey, *Enterprise*, p. 132; see also, Guy S. Callender, "The Early Transportation and Banking Enterprises of the States in Relation to the Growth of Corporations," *Quarterly Journal of Economics*, vol. 17 (1902); Oscar and Mary F. Handlin, "Origins of the American Business Corporation," *Journal of Economic History*, vol. 5 (1945).

60. Bruchey, *Enterprise*, pp. 216–17.

61. First quote from F.W. Taussig (ed.), *State Papers and Speeches on the Tariff* (Cambridge, MA: Harvard University Press, 1892), pp. 258, 265; second quote from William Letwin (ed.), *A Documentary History of American Economic Policy Since 1789* (New York: W.W. Norton & Co., 1972), p. 63; see also, Robert A. Lively, "The American System: A Review Article," *Business History Review*, vol. 29 (1955).

62. Robert Remini, *Andrew Jackson and the Bank War* (New York: W.W. Norton & Co., 1967), p. 44.

63. Nathan Rosenberg, "Innovative Responses to Materials Shortages," in Rosenberg (ed.), *Perspectives on Technology* (Cambridge: Cambridge University Press, 1976); Nathan Rosenberg, *The American System of Manufactures* (Edinburgh: Edinburgh University Press, 1969); Alfred

Chandler, *The Visible Hand: The Managerial Revolution in American Business* (Cambridge, MA: Belknap Press in Harvard University Press, 1977); David Houndshell, *From American System to Mass Production* (Baltimore, MD: Johns Hopkins Press, 1986).

64. Bruchey, *Enterprise*, pp. 154, 258; North, *Economic Growth*, pp. 133; see also, Leo Rogin, *The Introduction of Farm Machinery and its Relation to the Productivity of Labor in the Agriculture of the United States during the Nineteenth Century* (Berkeley, CA: University of California Press, 1931); Paul W. Gates, *The Farmer's Age: Agriculture, 1815–1860* (New York: Holt, Rinehart & Winston, 1960); Paul A. David, *Technical Choice, Innovation and Economic Growth; Essays on American and British Experience in the Nineteenth Century* (Cambridge: Cambridge University Press, 1975). Lewis C. Gray, *History of Agriculture in the Southern United States to 1860*, 2 vols (Glouster, MA: Peter Smith, 1958), pp. 610–11; Stuart Bruchey, *Cotton and the Growth of the American Economy* (New York: Harcourt, Brace, & World, 1967); Susan Previant Lee, *The Westward Movement of the Cotton Economy, 1840–1860: Perceived Interests and Economic Realities* (New York: Arno Press, 1977); Eric Kerridge, *The Agricultural Revolution* (London: Allen & Unwin, 1967); E.L. Jones, *Agriculture and the Industrial Revolution* (New York: John Wiley, 1974); for works on the industrial revolution, see Arnold Toynbee, *The Industrial Revolution* (Boston, MA: Beacon Press, 1956); Phyllis Deane, *The First Industrial Revolution* (Cambridge: Cambridge University Press, 1965); David S. Landes, *The Unbound Prometheus* (Cambridge: Cambridge University Press, 1969); Peter Mathias, *The First Industrial Nation* (New York: Charles Scribner's Sons, 1969).

65. Susan Lee, "Antebellum Southern Land Expansion: A Second View," *Agricultural History*, vol. 52 (1978), pp. 488–502; Jeremy Atack and Fred Bateman, *To Their own Soil: Agriculture in the Antebellum North* (Ames, IA: Iowa State University Press, 1987).

66. Paul Monroe, *The Founding of the American Public School System: A History of Education in the United States* (New York: Macmillan, 1940), vol. 1; H.G. Good, *A History of American Education* (New York: Macmillan, 1956); Lawrence A. Cremin, *American Education: The National Experience, 1783–1876* (New York: Harper & Row, 1980).

67. Rosenberg, *The American System*, p. 17.

68. Bruchey, *Enterprise*, p. 149; see also, George Rogers Taylor (ed.), *The Early Development of the American Cotton Textile Industry* (New York: Harper & Row, 1969); Paul A. Davis, "Learning by Doing and Tariff Protection: A Reconsideration of the Case of the Ante-Bellum United States Cotton Textile Industry," *Journal of Economic History*, vol. 30 (1970), pp. 521–601; Fred Bateman and Thomas Weiss, "Comparative Regional Development in Antebellum Manufacturing," *Journal of Economic History*, vol. 35 (1975), pp. 182–208.

69. Mark Bils, "Tariff Protection and Production in the Early US Cotton Textile Industry," *Journal of Economic History*, vol. 44 (1984), pp. 1033–46; Paul A. Davis, "Learning by Doing and Tariff Protection: A Reconsideration of the Case of the Ante-Bellum United States

Cotton Industry," *Journal of Economic History*, vol. 30 (1970), pp. 521–601; Gordon Bjork, "The Weaning of the American Economy: Independence, Market Changes, and Economic Development," *Journal of Economic History*, vol. 24 (1964), pp. 541–60.

70. Albert Field, "The Magnetic Telegraph, Price, and Quantity Data, and the New Management of Capital," *Journal of Economic History*, vol. 52 (1992), pp. 401–13.

71. Louis C. Hunter, *Steamboats on the Western Rivers* (Cambridge, MA: Harvard University Press), p. 36; Mak Walton and Gary Walton, "Steamboats and the Great Productivity Surge in River Transportation," *Journal of Economic History*, vol. 32 (1972), pp. 619–40.

72. Albert Fishlow, *American Railroads and the Transformation of the Antebellum Economy* (Cambridge, MA: Harvard University Press, 1965); George Rogers Taylor, *The Transportation Revolution, 1815–1860* (New York: Western Holt, Rinehart, & Winston, 1951); Robert W. Fogel, *Railroads and American Economic Growth: Essays in Econometric History* (Baltimore, MD: Johns Hopkins Press, 1964); Erik Haites and Gary Walton, *Western River Transportation: The Era of Early Internal Development*, 1810–1860 (Baltimore, MD: Johns Hopkins University Press, 1975).

73. Bruchey, *Enterprise*, p. 152.

74. Van Fenstermaker, *American Commercial Banking*, p. 94.

75. Hugh Rockoff, "The Free Banking Era: A Reexamination," *Journal of Money, Credit, and Banking*, vol. 6, no. 2 (May 1974), p. 150; Margaret Myers, *A Financial History of the United States* (New York: Columbia University Press, 1970), p. 129; Bray Hammond, *Banks and Politics in America from the Revolution to the Civil War* (Princeton, NJ: Princeton University Press, 1957).

76. Quotes from Bruchey, *Enterprise*, pp. 178–80; see also, Walter B. Smith, *Economic Aspects of the Second Bank of the United States* (Cambridge, MA: Harvard University Press, 1953); Thomas P. Govan, *Nicholas Biddle, Nationalist and Public Banker, 1786– 1844* (Chicago, IL: University of Chicago Press, 1959); Jean Wilburn, *Biddle's Bank, the Crucial Years* (New York: Columbia University Press, 1967).

77. Quoted in Arthur M. Schlesinger, *The Age of Jackson* (Boston, MA: Little, Brown, 1946), p. 109.

78. Bruchey, *Enterprise*, p. 188.

79. Quotes from Govan, *Nicholas Biddle*, p. 112.

80. Quoted in Schlesinger, *Age of Jackson*, p. 89.

81. Quoted in Govan, *Nicholas Biddle*, p. 115.

82. Bruchey, *Enterprise*, p. 183.

83. Fogel and Engerman, *Time on the Cross*, p. 25; Gavin Wright, *Political Economy of the Cotton South: Households, Markets, and Wealth in the Nineteenth Century* (New York: W.W. Norton & Co., 1978), pp. 27–8; Eugene Genovese, *The Political Economy of Slavery: Studies in the Economy and Society of the Slave South* (New York: Pantheon, 1965), p. 3; Wright, *Political Economy of the American South*, p. 35; see also, Kenneth Stampp, *The Peculiar Institution* (New York: Alfred A. Knopf, 1956); Alfred H. Conrad and John Meyer, "The Econom-

ics of Slavery in the Ante-bellum South," *Journal of Political Economy*, vol. 66 (1958), pp. 95–122; William N. Parker, "Slavery and Southern Economic Development: An Hypothesis and Some Evidence," *Agricultural History*, vol. 44 (1970), pp. 115–25; Hugh Atkins, *Did Slavery Pay? Readings in the Economics of Black Slavery in the United States* (Boston, MA: Houghton Mifflin, 1971); Gavin Wright, "New and Old Views on the Economics of Slavery," *Journal of Economic History*, vol. 33 (1973), pp. 452–66; Eugene Genovese, *Roll, Jordan, Roll: The World the Slaves Made* (New York: Pantheon, 1974); Robert Fogel and Stanley Engerman, *Time on the Cross: The Economics of American Negro Slavery* (New York: Little, Brown, 1974); Paul A. David *et al.*, *Reckoning with Slavery: A Critical Study of the Quantitative History of American Negro Slavery* (New York: Oxford University Press, 1976); Willie Lee Rose (ed.), *A Documentary History of Slavery in North America* (New York: Oxford University Press, 1976); Claudia Goldin, *Urban Slavery in the American South, 1820–1860* (Chicago, IL: University of Chicago Press, 1976).

84. Robert Gallman, "The Pace and Pattern of American Economic Growth," in Lance Davis, Richard Easterlin, and William Parker (eds), *American Economic Growth* (New York: Harper & Row, 1972), p. 35.

85. Robert E. Gallman, "The Pace and Pattern of American Economic Growth," in Lance E. Davis *et al.* (eds), *American Economic Growth* (New York: Harper & Row, 1972), p. 53; quote from Bruchey, *Enterprise*, p. 161.

86. Quoted in Carl N. Degler, *Out of Our Past: The Forces that Shaped America* (New York: Harper & Row, 1959), p. 47.

87. Quotation by Irwin G. Wyllie, *The Self-made Man in America: The Myth of Rags to Riches* (New Brunswick, NJ: Rutgers University Press, 1954), pp. 12–13. Both quotes found in Bruchey, *Enterprise*, pp. 194–5.

88. Quoted in Wyllie, *The Self-made Man in America*, p. 66.

89. Alexis de Tocqueville, *Democracy in America*, ed. Phillips Bradley, 2 vols (New York, 1945), vol. 2, pp. 54, 74, 298.

90. Standing Bear, *Land of the Spotted Eagle* (Boston, 1933), pp. 38, 196.

91. Quoted in John Mack Faragher, *Daniel Boone: The Life and Legend of an American Pioneer* (New York: Henry Holt & Co., 1992), pp. 67, 301.

92. Both quotes from Nash, *Wilderness and the American Mind*, pp. 69, 70.

93. Both quotes from ibid., pp. 58, 44.

94. Lord George Gordon Byron, *Manfred: A Dramatic Poem* (London, 1817), pp. 33–4.

95. Ralph Waldo Emerson, *Self-reliance: The Wisdom of Ralph Waldo Emerson*, ed. Richard Welan (New York: Bell Tower, 1991), p. 43.

96. Quoted in Nash, *Wilderness and the American Mind*, p. 97.

97. Henry David Thoreau, "Walking," in *Excursions, The Writings of Henry David Thoreau*, vol. IX, Riverside edn, 11 vols (Boston, MA: Houghton Mifflin, 1893), pp. 251, 280.

98. Thoreau, *Maine Woods, Writings*, pp. 3, 82, 85–6, 94–5, 107.

99. Taylor, *Transportation Revolution*, pp. 133–5.

100. Bruchey, *Enterprise*, pp. 220–1; see also, Ronald E. Shaw, *Erie Water*

West: A History of the Erie Canal, 1792–1854 (Lexington, KT: University of Kentucky Press, 1966); Harry N. Scheiber, *Ohio Canal Era: A Case Study of Government and the Economy, 1820–1861* (Athens, OH: University of Ohio Press, 1969); Carter Goodrich, "Internal Improvements Reconsidered," *Journal of Economic History*, vol. 30 (1970).

Notes to Chapter 4: Industrialization Unbound, 1860–1932

1. Robert E. Gallman and Edward S. Howle, "Trends in the Structure of the American Economy since 1840," in Robert W. Fogel and Stanley L. Engerman (eds), *The Reinterpretation of American Economic History* (New York: Harper & Row, 1971), p. 26; Stanley Lebergott, "Labor Force and Employment, 1800–1960," in Dorothy Bradley, National Bureau of Economic Research (eds), *Output, Employment, and Productivity in the United States after 1800*, vol. 30 *Studies in Income and Wealth* (New York: Columbia University Press, 1966), p. 119; Moses Abramovitz and Paul A. David, "Reinterpreting Economic Growth: Parables and Realities," *American Economic Review*, vol. 63 (1973), p. 429; Lance E. Davis, "Capital Formation in the United States during the Nineteenth Century," in *The Cambridge Economic History of Europe*, vol. 7, p. 368.

   See also, Edward C. Kirkland, *Industry Comes of Age: Business, Labor, and Public Policy* (New York: Holt, Rinehart & Winston, 1961); Robert Higgs, *The Transformation of the American Economy, 1865–1914* (New York: John Wiley, 1971); Jeffrey G. Williamson, *Late Nineteenth Century American Development: A General Equilibrium History* (Cambridge: Cambridge University Press, 1974).

2. Folke Hilgerdt, *Industrialization and Foreign Trade* (Geneva: League of Nations, 1945), tables 7, 8, 9, 13; Mary Locke Eyenbach, *American Manufactured Exports, 1879–1914* (New York: Arno Press, 1976), pp. 2, 7. Robert E. Lipsey, "Foreign Trade," in Lance Davis *et al.* (ed.), *American Economic Growth* (New York: Harper & Row, 1972), pp. 898–9; Bureau of the Census, *Historical Statistics of the United States, Colonial Times to 1970* (Washington, DC: Government Printing Office, 1976), vol. II, p. 903; John G.B. Hutchins, *The American Maritime Industries and Public Policy, 1789–1914: An Economic History* (Cambridge, MA: Harvard University Press, 1941).

3. Stanley Lebergott, "The Return to US Imperialism, 1890–1929," *Journal of Economic History*, vol. 32 (1972), p. 231; Mira Wilkins, *The Emergence of Multinational Enterprise: American Business Abroad from the Colonial Era to 1914* (Cambridge, MA: Harvard University Press, 1970), pp. 67–9, 97, 103.

4. Quotation from Thomas McCraw, "Mercantilism and the Market: Antecedents of American Industrial Policy," in Claude Barfield and William Schambra (eds), *The Politics of Industrial Policy* (Washington, DC: American Enterprise Institute, 1986), pp. 37, 39.

5. Charles and Mary Beard, *The Rise of American Civilization* (New York:

Macmillan, 1927), p. 99; Louis Hacker, *The Triumph of American Capitalism* (New York: Columbia University Press, 1940).

6. Thomas C. Cochran, "Did the Civil War Retard Industrialization?," in Ralph Andreano (ed.), *The Economic Impact of the Civil War* (Cambridge, MA: Schenkman, 1862); Stanley L. Engerman, "The Economic Impact of the Civil War," *Explorations in Economic History*, vol. 3 (1955), pp. 176–99; Jeffrey G. Williamson, *Late Nineteenth Century American Development: A General Equilibrium Analysis* (London: Cambridge University Press, 1974).

7. Bruchey, *Enterprise*, pp. 255–6.

8. Stephen J. DeCanio and Joel Mokyr, "Inflation and the Wage Lag during the American Civil War," *Explorations in Economic History*, vol. 14 (1977), pp. 311–36; Bruchey, *Enterprise*, p. 256; Robert W. Fogel, *Without Consent or Contract: The Rise and Fall of American Slavery*, vol. 1 (New York: W.W. Norton & Co., 1989); James Sellers, "The Economic Incidence of the Civil War on the South," in Ralph Andreano (ed.), *The Economic Impact of the Civil War* (Cambridge, MA: Shenkman, 1962), pp. 57–62; Claudia Goldin and Frank Lewis, "The Economic Cost of the American Civil War: Estimates and Implications," *Journal of Economic History*, vol. 35 (1975), pp. 294–326; Richard Watch, "A Note on the Cochran Thesis and Small Arms Industry in the Civil War," *Explorations in Entrepreneurial History*, vol. 4 (1966), pp. 57–62; Roger Ransom, *Conflict and Compromise: The Political Economy of Slavery, Emancipation, and the American Civil War* (New York: Cambridge University Press, 1989).

9. US Bureau of the Census, *Historical Statistics of the United States* (Washington, DC: Government Printing Office, 1975); Jeffrey Williamson, "Watersheds and Turning Points: Conjectures on the Long-term Impact of Civil War Financing," *Journal of Economic History*, vol. 34 (1974), pp. 631–61; John A. James, "Public Debt Management Policy and Nineteenth Century American Economic Growth," *Explorations in Economic History*, vol. 21 (1984), pp. 192–217.

10. Peter Lindert, "Long-run Trends in American Farmland Values," *Agricultural History*, vol. 62 (1988), pp. 45–86; Anne Mayhew, "A Reappraisal of the Causes of Farm Protest in the United States, 1879–1900," *Journal of Economic History*, vol. 32 (1972), pp. 464–75; Gavin Wright, "American Agriculture and the Labor Market: What Happened to Proletarization?," *Agricultural History*, vol. 62 (1988), pp. 182–209; Robert Higgs, "Railroad Rates and the Populist Uprising," *Agricultural History*, vol. 44 (1970), p. 295.

11. Bruchey, *Enterprise*, p. 314.

12. Bruchey, *Enterprise*, p. 312; John A. James, *Money and Capital Markets in Postbellum America* (Princeton, NJ: Princeton University Press, 1978).

13. Bruchey, *Enterprise*, p. 152.

14. Peter Temin, *Iron and Steel in Nineteenth Century America* (Cambridge, MA: MIT Press, 1964), appendix C, table c4; see also, Joseph Frazier Well, *Andrew Carnegie* (New York: Oxford University Press, 1970); W. Paul Strassmann, *Risk and Technological Innovation: American*

Manufacturing Methods during the Nineteenth Century (Ithaca, NY: Cornell University, 1959); Nathan Rosenberg, *Technology and American Economic Growth* (New York: Harper & Row, 1972); Nathan Rosenberg, "Selection and Adaptation in the Transfer of Technology: Steam and Iron in America, 1800–1870," in Nathan Rosenberg (ed.), *Perspectives on Technology* (Cambridge: Cambridge University Press, 1976).

15. Nathan Rosenberg, "Technological Change in the Machine Tool Industry, 1840–1910," *Journal of Economic History*, vol. 23 (1963), p. 423.

16. Daniel Nelson, *Managers and Workers, Origins of the New Factory System in the United States, 1880–1920* (Madison, WI: University of Wisconsin Press, 1975); Alfred Chandler, *The Visible Hand: The Managerial Revolution in American Business* (Cambridge, MA: Harvard University Press, 1977); David Hounshell, *From the American System to Mass Production: The Development of Manufacturing in the United States, 1800–1932* (Baltimore, MD: Johns Hopkins Press, 1984).

17. Robert W. Fogel, *Railroads and American Economic Growth: Essays in Econometric History* (Baltimore, MD: Johns Hopkins Press, 1964); Aldred D. Chandler, *The Railroads: The Nation's First Big Business* (New York: Harcourt, Brace & World, 1965).

18. C. Knick Harley, "Transportation, the World Wheat Trade, and the Kuznets Cycle, 1850–1913," *Explorations in Economic History*, vol. 17 (1980), pp. 224–5.

19. Robert Fogel, *Railroads and American Economic Growth: Essays in Econometric History* (Baltimore, MD: Johns Hopkins University Press, 1964); Bruchey, Enterprise, pp. 270–1; W.W. Rostow, *The Stages of Economic Growth: A Non-Communist Manifesto* (Cambridge: Cambridge University Press, 1960); Louis Hacker, *The Triumph of American Capitalism* (New York: Columbia University Press, 1940); Jeremy Atack and Jan Brueckner, "Steel Rails and American Railroads, 1867–1880, A Reply to Harley," *Explorations in American History*, vol. 20 (1983), pp. 258–62.

20. Albert Fishlow, "Internal Transportation," in Lance Davis *et al.* (eds), *American Economic Growth* (New York: Harper & Sons, 1972), pp. 468–547.

21. Bruchey, *Enterprise*, p. 310; see also, Charles M. McCurdy, "American Law and the Marketing Structure of the Large Corporation, 1875–1890," *Journal of Economic History*, vol. 38 (1978), pp. 631–49.

22. Quoted in George W. Rollins, *The Struggle of the Cattlemen, Sheepmen, and Settler's for Control of Lands in Wyoming* (New York: Arno Press, 1979), p. 169; see also, Walter P. Webb, *The Great Plains* (Boston, MA: Ginn, 1931); Gilbert C. Fite, *The Farmers Frontier, 1865–1900* (New York: Holt, Rinehart, & Winston, 1966).

23. Rodman Paul, *Mining Frontiers of the Far West: 1848–1880* (New York: Holt, Rinehart & Winston, 1963); Gary D. Lipcap, *The Evolution of Private Mineral Rights: Nevada's Comstock Lode* (New York: Arno Press, 1978).

24. Rollins, *Struggle of the Cattlemen, Sheepmen, and Settlers*, pp. 43, 65;

Louis Pelzer, *The Cattlemen's Frontier: A Record of the Trans-Missis-sippi Cattle Industry from Open Times to Pooling Companies, 1850–1890* (New York: Russell & Russell, 1969).

25. Fred Shannon, *The Farmer's Last Frontier: Agriculture, 1860–1897* (New York: Farrar & Rinehart, 1945); Martin L. Primack, *Farm formed Capital in Agriculture, 1850 to 1910* (New York: Arno Press, 1977).

26. Quoted in Victor S. Clark, *History of Manufacturers in the United States*, 3 vols (New York: Peter Smith, 1949), p. 174; see also, Donald Dewey, *Monopoly in Economics and Law* (Chicago, IL: Rand McNally, 1959).

27. Bruchey, *Enterprise*, pp. 340–1; Atack and Passell, *A New Economic View of American History*, pp. 485, 487; Henry R. Seager and Charles A. Gulick, *Trust and Corporation Problems* (New York: Harper & Bros, 1929); Ralph L. Nelson, *Merger Movements in American Industry, 1895–1956*, National Bureau of Economic Research, General Series, no. 66 (Princeton, NJ: Princeton University Press, 1959).

28. Bruchey, *Enterprise*, p. 343.

29. Quoted in Vincent P. Carosso, *The Morgans: Private International Bankers, 1854–1913* (Cambridge, MA: Harvard University Press, 1987), p. 258.

30. William Z. Ripley, *Railroads, Finance, and Organization* (New York: Longman, Green, 1915); Thomas C. Cochran, *Railroad Leaders, 1845–1890: The Business Mind in Action* (Cambridge, MA: Harvard University Press, 1953); John F. Stover, *American Railroads* (Chicago, IL: University of Chicago Press, 1961); Alfred D. Chandler, *The Railroads, America's First Big Business* (New York: Harcourt, Brace, and World, 1965).

31. Lee Benson, *Merchants, Farmers, and Railroads: Railroad Regulation and New York Politics, 1850–1887* (Cambridge, MA: Harvard University Press, 1955); John D. Hicks, *The Populist Revolt* (Minneapolis, MN: University of Minnesota Press, 1934).

32. Hans B. Thorelli, *The Federal Antitrust Policy: Origination of an American Tradition* (Baltimore, MD: Johns Hopkins Press, 1955); William Letwin, *Law and Economic Policy in America* (New York: Random House, 1965); Albro Martin, *Enterprise Denied: Origin of the Decline of American Railroads* (New York: Columbia University Press, 1971).

33. Bureau of the Census, *Historical Statistics of the United States, Colonial Times to 1970*, 2 vols (Washington DC: Government Printing Office, 1976), vol. I, p. 129; see also, Stanley Lebergott, *Manpower in Economic Growth: The American Record Since 1800* (New York: McGraw-Hill, 1964); Melvyn Dubovsky, *Industrialism and the American Worker, 1865–1920* (New York: Thomas Crowell, 1975).

34. Bruchey, *Enterprise*, p. 264; Ansley J. Coale and Melvin Zelink, *New Estimates of Fertility and Population in the United States: A Study of Annual White Births from 1855 to 1960 and of Completeness of Ennumeration of Censuses from 1880 to 1960* (Princeton, NJ: Princeton University Press, 1963); Hope T. Eldridge and Dorothy Swain Thomas, *Population Redistribution and Economic Growth*, 3 vols (Philadelphia, PA: American Philosophical Society, 1964); Richard A. Easterlin, *Population, Labor Force, and Long Swings in Economic Growth: The*

American Experience (New York: Columbia University Press, 1968); Peter Jensen Hill, *The Economic Impact of Immigration into the United States* (New York: Arno Press, 1975); Jacob Riis, *How the Other Half Lives* (New York: Scribner's, 1890).

35. Bureau of the Census, *Historical Statistics, 1976*, vol. I, p. 129; W. Elliot Brownlee and Mary M. Brownlee (eds), *Women in the American Economy: A Documentary History, 1675–1929* (New Haven, CT: Yale University Press, 1976); Bruchey, *Enterprise*, p. 355.

36. Dubovsky, *Industrialization and the American Worker*, p. 19.

37. Henry David, *The History of the Haymarket Affair* (New York: Russell & Russell, 1958).

38. John I. Griffin, *Strikes: A Study in Quantitative Economics* (New York: Columbia University Press, 1939), pp. 38, 44, 73; Bureau of the Census, *Historical Statistics*, vol. II, pp. 177, 126, 127; see also, Henry Pelling, *American Labor* (Chicago, IL: University of Chicago Press, 1960); Edward Kirkland, *Industry Comes of Age: Business, Labor, and Public Policy* (New York: Holt, Rinehart, & Winston, 1961).

39. Bureau of the Census, *Historical Statistics, 1976*, vol. I, p. 168; Clarence D. Long, *Wages and Earnings in the United States, 1860–90* (Princeton, NJ: Princeton University Press, 1960); Albert Rees, *Real Wages in Manufacturing, 1890–1914* (Princeton, NJ: Princeton University Press, 1961).

40. Bruchey, *Enterprise*, p. 322. Bureau of Census, *Historical Statistics to 1970*, pp. 1, 76; Lawrence A. Cremin, *The Transformation of the School: Progressivism in American Education, 1876–1957* (New York: Alfred A. Knopf, 1961); Alexandra Oleson and John Voss (eds), *The Organization of Knowledge in the United States* (Baltimore, MD: Johns Hopkins University Press, 1979).

41. Roger Ransom and Richard Sutch, *One Kind of Freedom: The Economic Consequences of Emancipation* (Cambridge: Cambridge University Press, 1977), p. 53; see also, E. Merton Coulter, *The South during Reconstruction, 1865–1877* (Baton Rouge, LA: Louisiana State University, 1947); C. Van Woodward, *Origins of the New South, 1877–1913* (Baton Rouge, LA: Louisiana State University, 1951); C. Vann Woodward, *The Burden of Southern History* (Baton Rouge, LA: Louisiana State University Press, 1960); Ralph Andreano, (ed.), *The Economic Impact of the American Civil War* (Boston, MA: Schenkman, 1967); Paul W. Gates, *Agriculture and the Civil War* (New York: Alfred A. Knopf, 1965); Gavin Wright, "The Strange Career of the New Southern Economic History," in Stanley I. Kutler and Stanley N. Katz (eds), *The Promise of American History: Progress and Prospects* (Baltimore, MD: Johns Hopkins Press, 1982).

42. Wilkins, *Multinational Enterprise*, pp. 74–5; Jules David, *American Political and Economic Penetration of Mexico, 1877–1920* (New York: Arno Press, 1976); Walter Lafeber, *The New Empire: American Expansion, 1860–1898* (Ithaca, NY: Cornell University Press, 1963); Richard Easterlin, *Population, Labor Force, and Long Swings in Economic Growth: The American Experience* (New York: Columbia University Press, 1968).

43. George P. Marsh, *Man and Nature, or Physical Geography as Modified by Human Action* (New York: Charles Scribner, 1864), p. 328.

44. John Wesley Powell, *Report on the Lands of the Arid Regions of the United States*, US House of Representatives, Executive Document 73, 45th Congress, 2nd Session (Washington, DC: US Government Printing Office, 3 April 1878).
45. John F. Reiger, *American Sportsmen and the Origins of Conservation* (Norman, OK: University of Oklahoma Press, 1986), p. 20.
46. Samuel P. Hays, *Conservation and the Gospel of Efficiency: The Progressive Conservation Movement, 1890–1920* (Cambridge, MA: Harvard University Press, 1959), p. 266; see also J. Leonard Bates, "Fulfilling American Democracy: The Conservation Movement, 1907–1921," *Mississippi Valley Historical Review*, vol. XLIV (1957), pp. 29–57.
47. Muir, *A Thousand Mile Walk to the Gulf*, ed. William F. Bade (Boston, MA: 1816), p. 212.
48. Ibid., 98.
49. Emerson to Muir, 5 February 1872, Bade (ed.), *Life and Letters of Ralph Waldo Emerson*, vol. I, pp. 259–60.
50. Muir, "The Wild Parks and Forest Reservations of the West," *Atlantic Monthly*, vol. 81 (1898), p. 15.
51. Frederick Jackson Turner, *The Frontier in American History* (New York: Dover Publications, 1996).
52. Theodore Roosevelt, "The Pioneer Spirit and the American Problem," *Works*, pp. 18, 23.
53. Theodore Roosevelt, "Wilderness Reserves: The Yellowstone Park," *Works*, pp. 3, 311–12.
54. Theodore Roosevelt, "Opening Address by the President," in Newton C. Blanchard (ed.), *Proceedings of a Conference of Governors in the White House* (Washington, DC: US Government Printing Office, 1909), p. 12.
55. William E. Leuchtenberg, "The New Deal and the Analogue of War," in John Braeman *et al.* (eds), *Change and Continuity in Twentieth Century America* (Athens, OH: Ohio University Press, 1966), p. 85; see also, Robert D. Cuff, *The War Industries Board: Business–Government Relations during World War I* (Baltimore, MD: Johns Hopkins Press, 1973); (Paul A.C. Koistinin, "The 'Industrial–Military Complex' in Historical Perspective: World War I," *Business History Review*, vol. 41 (1967); Grosvenor B. Clarkson, *Industrial America in the World War: The Strategy behind the Line, 1917–1918* (Boston, MA: Houghton Mifflin, 1923).
56. Charles Gilbert, *American Financing of World War I* (Westport, CT: Greenwood Press, 1970), pp. 205, 211; Stanley Lebergott, *Manpower in American Economic Growth: The American Record Since 1800* (New York: McGraw Hill, 1964), pp. 512, 525; Soule, *Prosperity Decade*, p. 252.
57. Maurine Weiner Greenwald, *Women, Work, and War: The Impact of World War I on Women Workers in the United States* (Westport, CT: Greenwood Press, 1980); Bureau of the Census, *Historical Statistics to 1970*, vol. I, p. 126; John Maurice Clark, *The Cost of the World War to the American People* (New Haven, CT: Yale University Press, 1931), pp. 1332–3.
58. Paul Samuelson and Everett E. Hagen, *After the War, 1918–1920 Military*

and Economic Demobilization of the United States, its Effect on Employment and Income (Washington, DC: National Resources Planning Board, 1943).

59. Elmus L. Wicker, "A Reconsideration of Federal Reserve Policy during the 1920–21 Depression," *Journal of Economic History*, vol. 26 (1966); George Soule, *The Prosperity Decade, 1917–1929* (New York: Holt, Rinehart, and Winston, 1947).

60. Alfred A. Chandler, *The Visible Hand: The Managerial Revolution in American Business* (Cambridge, MA: Harvard University Press, 1977); John Herman Lorant, *The Role of Capital Improving Innovations in American Manufacturing during the 1920s* (New York: Arno Press, 1975); George Soule, *Prosperity Decade, From War to Depression, 1917–29* (New York: Holt, Rinehart, & Wilson, 1962).

61. Daniel Pope, *The Making of Modern Advertizing* (New York: Basic Books, 1983).

62. Bruchey, *Enterprise*, pp. 443–4.

63. Bureau of the Census, *Historical Statistics to 1970*, vol. II, p. 864.

64. Robert A. Gordon, *Economic Instability and Growth: The American Record* (New York: Harper & Row, 1974), p. 22; Bureau of the Census, *Historical Statistics*, vol. II, pp. 379, 383, 386–7.

65. Kindleberger, *World Depression*, p. 56.

66. Robert M. Coen, "Labor Force and Unemployment in the 1920s and 1930s," *Review of Economics and Statistics*, vol. 55 (1973), pp. 40–55; Stuart D. Brandes, *American Welfare Capitalism, 1880–1940* (Chicago, IL: University of Chicago Press, 1976); Simon Kuznets, *Shares of Upper Income Groups in Income and Saving* (New York: National Bureau of Economic Research, 1953), p. 132.

67. H. Thomas Johnson, "Postwar Optimism and the Rural Financial Crisis of the 1920's," *Explorations in Economic History*, vol. 11 (1973), pp. 178, 179n. Frederick Strauss and Louis H. Bean, *Gross Farm Income and Indices of Farm Production and Prices in the United States, 1869–1937*, US Department of Agriculture, Technical Bulletin no. 703 (Washington, DC: Government Printing Office, 1940); Brownlee, *Dynamics*, pp. 398–9. Lawrence A. Jones and David Durand, *Mortgage Lending Experience in Agriculture* (Princeton, NJ: Princeton University Press, 1954).

68. Soule, *Prosperity Decade*, p. 162; Charles P. Kindleberger, *The World in Depression* (London: Penguin Books, 1973), p. 117.

69. William E. Leuchtenburg, *The Perils of Prosperity* (Chicago, IL: University of Chicago Press, 1959), p. 242; Ralph Nelson, *Merger Movements in American Industry, 1895–1956* (Princeton, NJ: Princeton University Press, 1959); John Kenneth Galbraith, *The Great Crash: 1929* (Boston, MA: Houghton Mifflin, 1954), pp. 73, 83.

70. Milton Friedman and Anna Schwartz, *A Monetary History of the United States, 1869–1960* (Princeton, NJ: Princeton University Press, 1963), p. 257; Robert J. Gordon and James A. Wilcox, "Monetary Interpretations: An Evaluation and Critique," in Karl Brunner (ed.), *The Great Depression Revisited* (Boston, MA: Martinus Nijhoff, 1980).

71. Friedman and Schwartz, *Monetary History*, p. 317.

72. Ellis W. Hawley, "Herbert Hoover, the Commerce Secretariat, and the Vision of an 'Associative State,' 1921–1928," *Journal of American History*, vol. 61 (1974), pp. 116–40; Albert U. Romasco, "Herbert Hoover's Policies for Dealing with the Great Depression: The End of the Old Order or the Beginning of the New?" in Martin L. Fausol and George T. Mazuzam (eds), *The Hoover Presidency: A Reappraisal* (Albany, NY: State University of New York Press, 1974); David Burner, *Herbert Hoover, A Public Life* (New York: Alfred A. Knopf, 1979).
73. Ellis W. Hawley, "Herbert Hoover and American Corporatism, 1929–1933," in Fausold and Mazuzam (eds), *Hoover Presidency*, pp. 101–19; James Olson, *Herbert Hoover and the Reconstruction Finance Corporation, 1931–33* (Ames, IO: University of Iowa Press, 1977).
74. Albert U. Romasco, *The Poverty of Abundance: Hoover, the Nation, the Depression* (New York: Oxford University Press, 1965); John A. Garraty, *The Great Depression: An Inquiry into the Causes, Course, and Consequences of the Worldwide Depression of the Nineteen-Thirties, as seen by Contemporaries in the Light of History* (New York: Harcourt, Brace, Jovanovich, 1986); Freidman and Schwartz, *Monetary History*, pp. 317–20; Lester V. Chandler, *American Monetary Policies, 1928–41* (New York: Harper & Row, 1971); Heywood W. Flisig, *Long-term Capital Flows and the Great Depression: The Role of the United States, 1927–33* (Ithaca, NY: Cornell University Press, 1975); Barry Eichengreen, *Golden Fetters: The Gold Standard and the Great Depression, 1919–1939* (New York: Oxford University Press, 1992).
75. Bruchey, *Enterprise*, p. 437.

Notes to Chapter 5: Industrialization Bound, 1933–80

1. Ellis W. Hawley, "The New Deal and Business," in *The New Deal, The National Level*, 2 vols, ed. John Braeman *et al.* (Columbus, OH: Ohio State University Press, 1975), vol. I, p. 57; see also, William E. Leuchtenburg, *Franklin D. Roosevelt and the New Deal, 1932–1940* (New York: Harper & Row, 1963); Albert U. Romasco, *The Politics of Recovery: Roosevelt's New Deal* (New York: Oxford University Press, 1983); Michael Bernstein, *The Great Depression: Delayed Recovery and Economic Change in America, 1929–1939* (New York: Cambridge University Press, 1987.
2. Bruchey, *Enterprise*, p. 472.
3. Ibid.
4. Quoted in Kevin Baker, "FDR: A Democracy-Builder, Eager to Try," *International Herald Tribune*, (13 April 1995).
5. Quoted in Lewis H. Kimmel, *Federal Budget and Fiscal Policy, 1789–1958* (Washington, DC: Brookings Institute, 1959), p. 176.
6. Bruchey, *Enterprise*, p. 466; Roy Lubove, *The Struggle for Social Security, 1900–1935* (Cambridge, MA: Harvard University Press, 1968).
7. Chandler, *American Monetary Policy*, p. 221; Susan Estabrook Kennedy, *The Banking Crisis of 1933* (Lexington, KY: University Press of Kentucky, 1973).

8. Walter Lippman, "The Permanent New Deal," *Yale Review*, New Series, vol. 24 (1935), p. 230.

9. Bruchey, *Enterprise*, pp. 453–4; Lester Chandler, *America's Greatest Depression, 1929–1941* (New York: Harper and Row, 1970), p. 194.

10. Robert Turnage, "Ansel Adams: the Role of the Artist in the Environmental Movement," *Living Wilderness*, vol. 43 (1980), pp. 8–9.

11. Harold G. Vatter, *The US Economy in World War II* (New York: Columbia University Press, 1985); Richard Polenberg, *War and Society: The United States, 1941–1945* (Philadelphia, PA: J.B. Lippincott, 1972); John Morton Blum, *V was for Victory: Politics and American Culture during World War II* (New York: Harcourt, Brace, and Jovanovich, 1976); Donald M. Nelson, *Arsenal of Democracy* (New York: Harcourt, Brace, 1946); Bruchey, *Enterprise*, p. 475.

12. R. Elberton Smith, *The Army and Economic Mobilization* (Washington, DC: Government Printing Office, 1959), p. 77.

13. Gerald T. White, *Billions for Defense: Government Financing by the Defense Plant Corporation during World War II* (Tuscaloosa: University of Alabama Press, 1980), pp. 6, 10.

14. Vatter, *US Economy*, pp. 14–19; Bureau of the Census *Historical Statistics*, vol. I, pp. 466–7, 483.

15. Bureau of the Census, *Historical Statistics*, vol. II, p. 914; Federal Trade Commission, *Report on Wartime Costs and Profits for Manufacturing Corporations, 1941 to 1945* (Washington, DC: Government Printing Office, 1947); Walter W. Wilcox, *The Farmer in the Second World War* (Ames, IO: Iowa State University Press, 1947); Kuznet, *Shares of Upper Income Groups*, p. 132.

16. Executive Order no. 9599, 19 August 1945, *Federal Register*, vol. X, pp. 10155–8.

17. Bruchey, *Enterprise*, p. 487.

18. Paul A. Tiffany, *The Decline of American Steel: How Management, Labor, and Government went Wrong* (New York: Oxford University Press, 1988), p. 113.

19. Eisenhower to E.E. Hazlett, 3 August 1956, Paper of Dwight D. Eisenhower, Name Series, Box 18, Hazlett (January 1956–November 1958) Folder, DDE Library. See also, Robert A. Divine, *Eisenhower and the Cold War* (New York: Oxford University Press, 1981); Herbert S. Parmet, *Eisenhower and the American Crusades* (New York: Macmillan, 1972).

20. Quoted in Lewis Kimmel, *Federal Budget and Fiscal Policy, 1789–1958* (Washington, DC: Brookings Institute, 1958), p. 250; Herbert Stein, *The Fiscal Revolution in America* (Chicago, IL: University of Chicago Press, 1969), p. 368.

21. Walter E. Heller, *New Dimensions of Political Economy* (Cambridge, MA: Harvard University Press, 1966), pp. 76–7.

22. Bruchey, *Enterprise*, p. 520.

23. Aldo Leopold, *A Sand Country Almanac and Sketches Here and There* (New York: Oxford University Press, 1949), p. 209.

24. William Vogt, *Road to Survival* (New York: William Sloane, 1948).

25. Sigurd Olson, *Listening Point* (New York, 1958); Sigurd Olson, *The Singing Wilderness* (New York).

26. Wallace Stegner, *Beyond the Hundredth Meridian: John Wesley Powell and the Second Coming of the West* (Boston, MA: Houghton Mifflin, 1954); Wallace Stegner, *This is Dinosaur* (New York: Knopf, 1955).
27. Rachel Carson, *Silent Spring* (Boston, MA: Houghton Mifflin, 1962).
28. Quoted in Roderick Nash, *American Environmentalism: Readings in Conservation History* (New York: McGraw-Hill, 1990), p. 187.
29. Lyndon B. Johnson, "Natural Beauty – Message from the President of the United States," *Congressional Record*, 89th Congress, 1st Session, vol. 111, pt. 2 (8 February 1965), p. 2086.
30. Environmental Pollution Panel, President's Science Advisory Committee, *Restoring the Quality of our Environment* (Washington, DC: US Government Printing Office, 1965).
31. James Ridgeway, *The Politics of Ecology* (New York: E.P. Dutton, 1970), p. 51.
32. For President Nixon's environmental policies, see: John C. Whitaker, *Striking a Balance: Environment and Natural Resources Policy in the Nixon–Ford Years* (Washington, DC: American Enterprise Institute, 1976).
33. Edward O. Wilson, *Sociobiology: The New Synthesis* (Cambridge, MA: Harvard University Press, 1975); Norman Myers, *The Sinking Ark: A New Look at the Problem of Disappearing Species* (Oxford: Oxford University Press, 1979); Paul and Anne Erlich, *Extinction: The Cause and Consequences of the Disappearing Species* (New York: 1981).
34. Council on Environmental Quality, *Environmental Quality: The First Annual Report of the Council on Enrivonmental Quality* (Washington, DC: US Government Printing Office, 1970).
35. David Calleo, *The Imperious Economy* (Cambridge, MA: Harvard University Press, 1982).
36. Robert Reich, *The Next American Frontier* (New York: Basic Books, 1983), p. 121.
37. President's Council on Environmental Quality and US Department of State, *The Global 2000 Report*, vol. 1, *Summary* (Washington, DC: GPO, 1980), p. iii.
38. Martin Kreiger, "What's Wrong with Plastic Trees?," *Science*, vol. 179 (1973).
39. Robert Wernick, "Speaking Out: Let's Spoil the Wilderness," *Saturday Evening Post*, vol. 238 (6 November 1965). Other prominent cornucopian perspectives include: Eric Hoffer, *The Temper of Time* (New York: 1967); Rene Dubos, "Symbiosis Between the Earth and Mankind," *Science*, vol. 193 (1976); Rene Dubos, *A God Within* (New York: 1972); Rene Dubos, *The Resilience of Ecosystems* (Boulder, CO: 1978); Rene Dubos, *The Wooing of Earth* (New York: 1980); Eric Julber, "Let's Open Up Our Wilderness Areas," *Reader's Digest*, vol. 100 (1972), pp. 125–8; Eric Julber, "The Wilderness: Just How Wild Should It Be?" *Trends*, vol. 9 (1972), pp. 15–18; William Tucker, "Is Nature Too Good For Us?" *Harper's* (March 1982), pp. 27–35.
40. Ron Arnold.

Notes to Chapter 6: Reaganomics versus Clintonomics

1. For critical accounts of Reaganomics, see John L. Palmer and Isabel V. Sawhill (eds), *The Reagan Experiment, An Examination of Economic and Social Policies under the Reagan Administration* (Washington, DC: Urban Institute, 1982); William Greider, *The Education of David Stockman and other Americans* (New York: E.P. Dutton, 1986); Benjamin Friedman, *Day of Reckoning: The Consequences of American Economic Policy under Reagan and After* (New York: Random House, 1988); Robert Heilbroner and Peter Bernstein, *The Debt and the Deficit: False Alarms Real Possibilities* (New York: W.W. Norton & Co., 1989); Kevin Phillips, *Boiling Point: Republicans, Democrats, and the Decline of the Middle-Class* (New York: Random House, 1993).

   For laudatory accounts of Reaganomics, see Paul Craig Roberts, *The Supply-side Revolution: An Insider's Account of Policymaking in Washington* (Cambridge, MA: Harvard University Press, 1984); Robert Eisner, *How Real is the Federal Deficit?* (New York: Free Press, 1986); Robert Bartley, *The Seven Fat Years* (New York: The Free Press, 1992).

2. F. Thomas Juster, "The Economics and Politics of the Supply-side View," *Economic Outlook USA* (Autumn 1981), University of Michigan, Survey Research Center, p. 81.

3. David Rosenbaum, "The Push and Pull over Taxes," (7 December 1992).

4. Bruchey, *Enterprise*, p. 536.

5. Paul Peretz, "Economic Policy in the 1980s," in Paul Peretz (ed.), *The Politics of American Economy Policy Making* (Armonk, NY: M.E. Sharpe, 1986), p. 444; "Where the Jobs Are: Government," *US News & World Report* (17 August 1992).

6. Quoted in Jeff Gerth, "Regulators Say 80's Budget Cuts May Cost US Billions in 1990's," *New York Times* (19 December 1989).

7. Donald Bartlett and James B. Steele, *America: What Went Wrong?* (Kansas City: Universal Press Syndicate Company, 1992), pp. 40–65.

8. Ed Rubenstein, "A Decade of Debt," *National Review* (12 August 1991); Steel and Bartlett, *What Went Wrong?*, p. 50.

9. Sylvia Nasar, "The Richest Getting Richer: Now It's a Political Issue," *New York Times* (11 May 1992).

10. Quoted in William Greider, "The Education of David Stockman," *Atlantic Monthly* (December 1981), p. 46; quoted in Warren Weaver, "$100 Billion Tax Rise Is Urged by Stockman," *New York Times* (30 September 1985).

11. US General Accounting Office, "Cost–Benefit Analysis can be Useful in Assessing Environmental Regulations, despite Limitations," Report no. GAO/RCED 84–62 (April 1984), p. 7.

12. Cynthia Pollock, *Mining Urban Wastes: The Potential for Recycling* (Washington, DC: Worldwatch Institute, April 1987), p. 15.

13. US General Accounting Office, "The Debate over Acid Precipation: Opposing Views, Status of Research," Report no. EMD-81-131 (September 1981), p. 28.

14. *New York Times* (28 June 1983).

15. Quoted in the General Accounting Office, "The Debate over Acid Precipitation: Opposing Views, Status of Research," EMD-81-131 (Washington, DC: GPO, 1981), p. 16.
16. National Research Council, *Acid Deposition Atmospheric Processes in Eastern North America: A Review of Current Scientific Understanding* (Washington, DC: National Academy Press, 1983).
17. *New York Times* (24 July 1988, 7 July 1989, 25 April 1988).
18. R.W. Bell *et al.*, *The 1990 Toronto Personal Exposure Pilot Study* (Toronto: Ontario Ministry of the Environment, 1991), p. 18.
19. "Damaged Material in 510,000 Buildings, Potential Work Hazard, Seen in EPA Report," *Occupational Safety and Health Reporter* (9 March 1988).
20. Barry I. Castleman, *Asbestos: Medical and Legal Aspects* (Englewood Cliffs, NJ: Prentice Hall Law and Business, 1990), p. 66.
21. Brooke T. Mossman *et al.*, "Asbestos: Scientific Developments and Implications for Public Policy," *Science*, vol. 247 (19 January 1990), p. 294.
22. US Environmental Protection Agency, *A Citizen's Guide to Radon: What it is and What to do About it*, Pamphlet no. OPA 86-004 (Washington, DC: GPO, August 1986).
23. Cynthea Pollock Shea, *Protecting Life on Earth: Steps to Save the Ozone Layer* (Washington, DC: Worldwatch Institute, 1988), p. 14.
24. *New York Times*, 7 March 1989; *New York Times*, 21 September 1988.
25. *New York Times*, 4 March 1989; Flavin, *Slowing Global Warming*, pp. 49–74.
26. *The Gallup Report 280* (January 1989), pp. 12–13.
27. David Rosenbaum, "On the Economy, Bush followed Reagan's Lead, Not His Success," *New York Times* (29 June 1992).
28. Ibid.
29. Henry Waxman, "Quailing over Clean Air," *Environment*, vol. 33, no. 6 (July–August 1991), p. 24.
30. *New York Times* (8 May 1989).
31. Keith Bradsher, "In Shift, White House will Stress Aiding Foreign Concerns in US," *New York Times* (2 June 1993).
32. Jeff Cole *et al.*, "The Sky's the Limit: Do Lean Times Mean Fighting Machines will be Built for Less?" *Wall Street Journal* (18 November 1996).
33. Keith Bradsher, "US Plans more Aid to Exports," *New York Times* (30 September 1993).
34. Steven Greenhouse, "Changes in Military and Health Spending Would Slow Job Growth," *New York Times* (26 April 1993).
35. Al Gore, *Earth in the Balance: Ecology and the Human Spirit* (New York: Plume, 1993).
36. David Hage and Robert Blackman, "The Repackaging of Reaganomics: Republican Tax Cuts could well Boost the Deficit," *US News and World Report* (12–18 December 1994); Adam Clymer, "Balanced-budget Amendment Fails to Gain House Approval," *New York Times*, (12 June 1992).
37. Karen De Witt, "Ultrarich Expatriates Live in Luxury, and US Loses,"

International Herald Tribune (16 April 1995); Robert Hershey, "Closing a Tax Loophole and Opening Another," *New York Times* (10 July 1995).

38. John M. Berry, "To Wipe out Budget Deficit, It's Pain Before Gain," *International Herald Tribune* (11 May 1995).

39. David Sanger, "Republicans take Aim at Programs Designed to Promote Exports," *International Herald Tribune* (24 May 1995); David Sanger, "An Odd Target for Republicans," *International Herald Tribune* (11 May 1995); David Boaz, "Budget Cuts: Less Than Meets the Eye," *New York Times* (6 July 1995).

Notes to Chapter 7: The Industrial Policy Legacy

1. For some prominent recent Jeffersonian books on this debate, see Joseph Nye, *Bound to Lead: The Changing Nature of American Power* (New York: Basic Books, 1990); Henry Nau, *The Myth of American Decline: Leading the World Economy into the 1990s* (Oxford: Oxford University Press, 1990).

2. For some prominent recent Hamiltonian books on this debate, see Paul Kennedy, *The Rise and Fall of the Great Powers* (New York: Random House, 1987); Robert Kuttner, *The End of Laissez-Faire* (New York: Alfred A. Knopf, 1991); Paul Kennedy, "Fin de Siecle America," *New York Review of Books* (28 June 1990); Steven Schlosstein, *The End of the American Century* (New York: Congdon & Weed, 1989).

3. See William Nester, *American Power, The New World Order, and the Japanese Challenge* (New York: St Martin's Press, 1993); William Nester, *Power Across the Pacific: A Diplomatic History of American Relations with Japan* (New York: New York University Press, 1996).

4. "Study Finds US Behind in Key Fields," *New York Times* (20 March 1991).

5. Ibid.

6. Martin Tolchin, "Report Says US Industry in a Decline," *New York Times*, (13 November 1992).

7. William Broad, "Japan Seen Passing US in Research by Industry," *New York Times* (25 February 1992).

8. Sylvia Nasar, "US Output per Worker Called Best," *New York Times* (13 October 1992).

9. Peter Passell, "Taxes, Deficits, and the American Way," *New York Times* (1 March 1992); "Taxes, Savings, and Investment: An International Comparison," *New York Times* (27 January 1992). In 1990, America's total tax revenues as a GNP percentage were 29.4 percent compared to Japan's 31.3 percent, Canada's 34.0 percent, Italy's 37.1 percent, Britain's 37.3 percent, Germany's 37.4 percent, and France's 44.4 percent. In 1990, while Americans saved only 4.7 percent of their income, Japanese saved 14.3 percent, Canadians 10.4 percent, Britains 9.1 percent, Italians 15.6 percent, Germans 13.9 percent, and French 12.0 percent. Peter Passell, "Taxes, Savings, and Investment: An International Comparison," *New York Times* (27 January 1992).

10. Peter Passell, "High-Tech Industry is Hard to Help," *New York Times* (2 February 1993).
11. "If They Build it They Might Come," *Time* (24 August 1992).
12. Ibid.
13. Ibid.
14. Florence Fabricant, "Will a Lower Tax Break be Bad for the Appetite?" *New York Times* (26 June 1993).
15. Ibid.
16. John Liscio, "It's Time for a National Yahoo Tax," *US News & World Report* (27 July 1992).
17. B. Drummond Ayres, "Rifle Association is Under Fire (and is Returning it," *New York Times* (22 May 1995).
18. Louis Uchitelle, "Shifting Spending to Public Works," *New York Times* (29 November 1989); Robert Reich, "US Neglect of Public Investment is Real Villain," *Japanese Economic Journal* (30 September 1989).
19. Otto Friedrich, "Freed from Greed?" *Time* (1 January 1990); "Taxes, Saving and Investment: An International Comparison," *New York Times* (27 January 1992).
20. "Study: Basic Literacy Woes Dog Workers," *Omaha Herald Tribune* (5 June 1992).
21. Peter Applebome, "Americans Straddle the Average Mark in Math and Science," *New York Times* (21 November 1996).
22. Larry Rohter, "Battle Over Patriotism Curriculum," *New York Times* (15 May 1994).
23. Robert Pear, "A Hostile House Trains its Sights on Funds for Arts," *New York Times* (9 January 1995).
24. Paul Goldberger, "Clinton's Arts Dinner Whetted Appetites still Unsatisfied," *New York Times*.
25. Ralph Blumenthal, "Cultural Groups Mobilize to take on the New Congress," *New York Times* (10 January 1995).
26. John Frohnmayer, "The Sayings of Chairman John," *New York Times* (16 April 1993).
27. "Young face Tougher Times," *New York Times* (4 June 1995).
28. Sylvia Nasar, "Fed Gives New Evidence of 80's Gains by Richest," *New York Times* (30 May 1992).
29. Keith Bradsher, "US Ranks First in Economic Inequality," *International Herald Tribune* (16 April 1995).
30. Steven Greenhouse, "Income Data show Years of Erosion for US Workers," *New York Times* (7 September 1992); "US Says Middle Class Shrinking," *New York Times* (21 February 1992).
31. Jason DeParle, "House Data on US Incomes sets off Debate on Fairness," *New York Times* (21 May).
32. Reich, *New American Frontier,* p. 178; Michael Wines, "Taxpayers are Angry: They're Expensive, too," *New York Times* (20 November 1994); Robin Toner, "New Politics of Welfare Focuses on Its Flaws," *New York Times* (5 July 1992). Unless otherwise indicated, the following poverty statistics come from the last two articles.
33. Robin Toner, "New Politics of Welfare Focuses on Its Flaws," *New York Times* (5 July 1992).

34. Robert Pear, "A New Tide of Immigration Brings Hostility to the Surface, Poll Finds," *New York Times* (27 June 1993).
35. Rebecca Clark and Jeffry Passel, "Studies Are Deceptive," *New York Times* (3 September 1993).
36. Robert Pear, "Population Growth outstrips Earlier US Census Estimates," *New York Times* (4 December 1992).
37. Unless otherwise indicated, the statistics for this and the following two paragraphs come from, Donald Huddle, "A Growing Burden," *New York Times* (3 September 1993).
38. Ann Markusen *et al.*, *The Rise of the Gunbelt: The Military Remapping of Industrial America* (New York: Oxford University Press, 1991); James C. Cobb, *The Selling of the South: The Southern Crusade for Industrial Development, 1936–1980* (Baton Rouge, LA: Louisiana State University Press, 1982).
39. "Moving to the Suburbs," *New York Times* (1 June 1992).
40. Stephen M. Meyer, "Aint Necessarily So: The Myth of Jobs Versus the Environment," SIERRA (March/April 1993), p. 45.
41. Fred Elmer, "Saving the the Economy by Saving the Environment," SIERRA ATLANTIC, vol. 20, no. 1, p. 15.
42. Lydia Wegman, "Air Toxics: The Strategy," *EPA Journal*, vol. 17, no. 1 (January–February 1991), pp. 32–3.
43. Edward Calabrese and Charles E. Gilbert, "Drinking Water Quality and Water Treatment Practices: Charting the Future," in Edward J. Calabrese, Charles E. Gilbert and Harris Pastides (eds), *Safe Drinking Water Act: Amendments, Regulations, and Standards* (Chelsea, MI: Lewis, 1989); *New York Times* (6 January 1988).
44. US General Accounting Office, "Ground Water Overdrafting must be Controlled," Report no. CED-80-96 (12 September 1980).
45. US Environmental Protection Agency, *Environmental Progress and Policies: EPA'S Update* (Washington, DC: EPA, August 1988), p. 52.
46. See Shirley E. Perlman, "In the Barge's Wake," *Rush to Burn: Solving America's Garbage Crisis?* (Washington, DC: Island Press, 1989), pp. 243–8.
47. Switzer, *Environmental Politics*, p. 103; US Environmental Protection Agency, *Characterization of Municipal Solid Waste in the United States: 1990 Update*, EPA/530-SW-90-042 (Washington, DC: GPO, June 1990), p. ES-3.
48. Switzer, *Environmental Politics*, p. 104.
49. Cynthia Pollock, *Mining Urban Wastes: The Potential for Recycling* (Washington, DC: Worldwatch Institute, April 1987), p. 15.
50. R. Shep Melnick, *Regulation and the Courts* (Washington, DC: Brookings Institute, 1983), p. 378; Switzer, *Environmental Politics*, p. 179; Marianne Lavelle, "Taking About Air," *The National Law Journal* (10 June 1991), p. 30.
51. Rosenbaum, *Environmental Politics and Policies*, p. 123.
52. "Paper Recycling Growth Shows Solid Progress toward 1995 Goal," *Journal of the Air Waste Management Association*, vol. 42, no. 6 (June 1992); Louis Blumberg and Robert Gottlieb, *War on Waste: Cam America win its Battle with Garbage* (Washington, DC: Island Press, 1989), pp. 66–7; "Chemical Hazards Prompt Safety Alert," *Omaha World Herald* (18 August 1994); Walter Rosenbaum, *Environmental Politics and Policy*

(Washington, DC: Congressional Quarterly, 1991), pp. 47–8; US General Accounting Office, "Efforts to Cleanup DOD Owned Inactive Hazardous Waste Disposal Sites," Report no. GAO/NSIAD-85-41 (12 April 1985), pp. i–ii.

53. US Department of Commerce, Bureau of the Census, *Statistical Abstract of the United States, 1989* (Washington, DC: GPO, 1989), pp. 204–5; Paul Portney, "EPA and the Evolution of Federal Regulation," in Paul R. Portney (ed.), *Public Policies for Environmental Protection* (Washington, DC: Resources for the Future, 1990), p. 11; John Cushmen, "House Bill Would Block New EPA Pollution Rules," *New York Times* (27 June 1995).

54. John Garrison, "Will the New Law Protect Public Health," *EPA Journal*, vol. 17, no. 1 (January–February 1991), p. 58. The estimate includes both direct health costs and the costs of lost work days.

55. John H. Cushmann, "Efficient Pollution Rule under Attack: Requirement to Disclose Toxic Emissions led to Big Reduction," *New York Times* (28 June 1995).

56. Matthew Wald, "Acid-rain Pollution Credits are not Enticing Utilities," *New York Times* (5 June 1995).

57. "Air", *EPA Journal*, vol. 16, no. 5 (September–October 1990), p. 16.

58. US Environmental Protection Agency, *Environmental Progress and Challenges: EPA's Update* (Washington, DC: EPA, August 1988), p. 46; Sandra Postel, *Altering the Earth's Chemistry: Assessing the Risks* (Washington, DC: Worldwatch Institute, 1986).

59. Kenneth Frederick, "Water Resources: Increasing Demand and Scarce Supplies," in Kenneth Frederick and Roger Sedjo (eds.), *America's Renewable Resources: Historical Trends and Current Challenges* (Washington, DC: Resources for the Future, 1991), pp. 50–2; Rosenbaum, *Environmental Politics and Policy*, p. 199.

60. Environmental Protection Agency, *Environmental Progress and Challenges: EPA's Update* (Washington, DC: EPA, August 1988), p. 126; World Resources Institute, *World Resources, 1987* (New York: Basic Books, 1987), p. 204.

61. Keith Schneider, "The Superfund, Present and Proposed," *New York Times* (6 October 1994); Jack Lewis, "Superfund, RCRA, and UST: The Clean-up Threesome," *EPA Journal*, vol. 17, no. 3 (July–August 1991), pp. 7–14.

62. US General Accounting Office, "Toxic Substances: EPA Has Made Limited Progress in Identifying PCB Users," Report no. GAO/RCED 88-127 (April 1988), p. 3; Council on Environmental Quality, *Environmental Quality, 1986*, tables 9–9, 9–6.

63. Quoted in Christopher Harris, William L. Want, and Morris A. Ward, *Hazardous Waste: Confronting the Challenge* (New York: Quorum Books, 1987), p. 87.

64. Mary Devine Worobec, *Toxic Substances Controls Guide* (Washington, DC: Bureau of National Affairs, 1989); see also Richard C. Fortuna and David J. Lennett, *Hazardous Waste Regulation, the New Era: An Analysis and Guide to RCRA and the 1984 Amendments* (New York: McGraw-Hill, 1987).

65. "Questions the Public is Asking: An Interview with Don Clay," *EPA*

Journal, vol. 17, no. 3 (July–August 1991), p. 18.

66. Douglas Pasternbak, with Peter Cary, "A $200 billion Scandal," *US News & World Report* (14 December 1992), pp. 34–7.

67. Good articles assessing the politics and ecology behind the Yucca Mountain choice include, Paul Slovic, Mark Layman, and James H. Flynn, "Risk Perception, Trust, and Nuclear Waste: Lessons from Yucca Mountain," *Environment*, vol. 33, no. 3 (April 1991), pp. 6–7; William J. Broad, "Experts Clash on Risk of Nuclear Waste Site," *New York Times* (3 December 1991), p. B-10; Charles R. Malone, "National Energy Strategy and High Level Nuclear Waste," *Bioscience*, vol. 41, no. 11 (December 1991), p. 729; Eliot Marshall, "The Geopolitics of Nuclear Waste," *Science* (22 February 1991), pp. 864–7; Switzer, *Environmental Politics*, p. 117.

68. US General Accounting Office, "Toxic Substances," p. 23; Milton Russell, E. William Colglazier, and Bruce E. Tonn, "The US Hazardous Waste Legacy," *Environment*, vol. 34, no. 6 (July–August 1992), pp. 12–15.

69. Michael Spector, "Incinerators: Unwanted and Politically Dangerous," *New York Times* (12 December 1991), p. B-1; Pollock, *Mining Urban Wastes*, pp. 16–17.

70. Switzer, *Environmental Politics*, pp. 118, 119.

71. C. Russell Shearer, "Comparative Analysis of the Basel and Bamako Conventions on Hazardous Waste," *Environmental Law*, vol. 23, no. 1 (1993), p. 141.

72. John C. Whitaker, *Striking a Balance: Environment and Natural Resources Policy in the Nixon–Ford Years* (Washington, DC: American Enterprise Institute, 1976), pp. 113–16; Richard L. Hembra, director, Environmental Protection Issues, Resources, Community, and Economic Development Division, US General Accounting Office, in "Observations on the Environmental Protection Agency's Budget and Public Works, US Senate" (7 March 1990).

73. US Department of Commerce, Bureau of the Census, *Statistical Abstract of the United States* (Washington, DC: GPO, 1989), table 353, p. 204.

74. Robert Keohane and Joseph Nye, "Power and Interdependence Revisited," *International Organization*, vol. 41, no. 4 (Autumn 1987), pp. 737–8; for an in-depth exploration of these themes, see William R. Nester, *International Relations: Geopolitical and Geoeconomic Continuities and Changes* (New York: HarperCollins, 1995).

75. Albert Hirschman, *National Power and the Structure of Foreign Trade* (Berkeley, CA: University of California Press, 1945); Charles Kindleberger (ed.), *The International Corporation* (Cambridge, MA: MIT Press, 1970); William Nester, *American Power, the New World Order, and the Japanese Challenge* (New York: St Martin's Press, 1993).

76. Richard Berstein, "Long Conflict deeply marked the Self-image of Americans," *New York Times* (2 February 1992).

77. "College Freshmen Less Political," *New York Times* (9 January 1995).

78. John Kenneth Galbraith, *The Culture of Contentment* (Boston, MA: Houghton Mifflin, 1992).

79. Sylvia Nasar, "The Bureaucracy: What's Left to Shrink?," *New York Times* (11 June 1995).

Bibliography

Abramovitz, Moses and Paul A. David, "Reinterpreting Economic Growth: Parables and Realities," *American Economic Review,* **63** (1973).

Adams, Donald, "American Neutrality and Prosperity, 1793–1808: A Reconsideration," *Journal of Economic History,* **40** (1980), pp. 713–38.

Adams, Gordon, *The Iron Triangle: The Politics of Defense Contracting* (New York: Council of Economic Priorities, 1981).

Adams, Gordon, "The B-1: Bomber for all Seasons?," *Council on Economic Priorities Newsletter* (February 1982).

Adams, Walter and J.B. Dirlam, "Big Steel, Invention and Innovation," *Quarterly Journal of Economics,* **80** (May 1966), pp. 167–89.

Adams, Walter, "The Steel Industry," in Walter Adams (ed.), *The Structure of American Industry,* 5th edn (New York: Macmillan, 1977).

Aitken, Hugh G.J. (ed.), *The State and Economic Growth* (New York: Social Science Research Council, 1959).

Albro, Martin, *Enterprise Denied: Origin of the Decline of American Railroads* (New York: Columbia University Press, 1971).

Almond, Gabriel and Sidney Verba, *The Civic Culture* (Boston, MA: Little, Brown, 1965).

Anchordoguy, Marie, "Mastering the Market: Japanese Government Targeting of the Computer Industry," *International Organization,* **42**, no. 3 (Summer 1988), pp. 509–43.

Anchordoguy, Marie, *Computers Inc.: Japan's Challenge to IBM* (Cambridge, MA: Harvard University Press, 1989).

Anderson, Marion, Jeb Brugmann and George Erickcek, *The Price of the Pentagon: The Industrial and Commercial Impact of the 1981 Military Budget* (Lansing, MI: Employment Research Associates, 1982).

Anderson, Odin and Jacob Feldman, *Family Medical Costs and Voluntary Health Insurance: A Nationwide Survey* (New York: McGraw-Hill, 1956).

Anderson, Odin, Patricia Collette, and Jacob Feldman, *Changes in Family Medical Expenditures and Voluntary Health Insurance: A Five-Year Survey* (Cambridge, MA: Harvard University, 1963).

Andreano, Ralph (ed.), *The Economic Impact of the American Civil War* (Boston, MA: Schenkman, 1967).

Asher, Norman and Leland D. Strom, "The Role of the Department of Defense in the Development of Integrated Circuits," *IDA Paper P-1271* (Arlington, VA: Institute for Defense Analyses, 1977).

Ashley, Jo Ann, *Hospitals, Paternalism, and the Role of the Nurse* (New York: Teachers College Press, 1976).

Atack, Jeremy and Jan Brueckner, "Steel Rails and American Railroads, 1867–1880: A Reply to Harley," *Explorations in American History,* **20** (1983), pp. 258–62.

Atack, Jeremy and Fred Bateman, *To their own Soil: Agriculture in the Antebellum North* (Ames, IO: Iowa State University Press, 1987).

Atkins, Hugh, *Did Slavery Pay? Readings in the Economics of Black Slavery in the United States* (Boston, MA: Houghton Mifflin, 1971).

Baack, Bennett and Edward Ray, "The Political Economy of Tariff Policy: A Case Study of the United States," *Explorations in Economic History*, **44** (1984), pp. 73–93.

Bailey, Stephen, *Congress makes a Law* (New York: Columbia University Press, 1950).

Bailyn, Bernard, *Ideological Origins of the American Revolution* (Cambridge, MA: Harvard University Press, 1967).

Bailyn, Bernard, *Voyagers to the West: A Passage in the Peopling of America on the Eve of the Revolution* (New York: Alfred A. Knopf, 1986).

Baldwin, David A., *Foreign Aid and American Foreign Policy* (New York: Praeger, 1966).

Baldwin, Robert, *The Political Economy of US Import Policy* (Cambridge, MA: MIT Press, 1986).

Baldwin, Robert and Paul Krugman, "Market Access and International Competition: A Simulation Study of 16K Random Access Memories," in Robert C. Feenstra (ed.), *Empirical Methods for International Trade* (Cambridge, MA: MIT Press, 1988), pp. 171–197.

Barber, James, *Presidential Character* (Englewood Cliffs, NJ: Prentice Hall, 1985).

Barfield, Claude E. and William A. Schambra (eds), *The Politics of Industrial Policy* (Washington, DC: American Enterprise Institute for Public Policy Research, 1986).

Barlow, William and David O. Powell, "To Find a Stand: New England Physicians on the Western and Southern Frontier, 1790–1840," *Bulletin of the History of Medicine*, **54** (Fall 1980).

Barnett, Donald F. and Louis Schorsch, *Steel: Upheaval in a Basic Industry* (Cambridge, MA: Ballinger, 1983).

Bartlett, Donald, and James B. Steele, *America: What Went Wrong?* (Kansas City: Universal Press Syndicate Company, 1992).

Bartley, Robert, *The Seven Fat Years* (New York: The Free Press, 1992).

Bateman, Fred and Thomas Weiss, "Comparative Regional Development in Antebellum Manufacturing," *Journal of Economic History*, **35** (1975), pp. 182–208.

Baum, Claude, *The System Builders* (Santa Monica: Systems Development Corporation, 1981).

Bautier, Robert-Henri, *The Economic Development of Medieval Europe* (New York: Harcourt, Brace, Jovanovich, 1971).

Bayard, Thomas O. and Kimberly Ann Elliott, *Reciprocity and Retaliation: An Evaluation of Aggressive Trade Policies* (Washington, DC: Institute of International Economics, 1992).

Beard, Charles, *A Economic Interpretation of the Constitution* (New York: Macmillan, 1913).

Beard, Charles and Mary, *The Rise of American Civilization* (New York: Macmillan, 1927).

Beaty, Jack, "The Exorbitant Anachronism," *Atlantic Monthly* (June 1989).

Beltz, Cynthia, *High-tech Maneuvers: Industrial Policy Lessons of HDTV* (Washington, DC: AEI Press, 1991).

Bendix, Reinhard, *Kings and People: Power and the Mandate to Rule* (Berkeley, CA: University of California Press, 1978).

Benson, Lee, *Merchants, Farmers, and Railroads: Railroad Regulation and New York Politics, 1850–1887* (Cambridge, MA: Harvard University Press, 1955).

Bergsten, Fred C. and William R. Cline, *The United States–Japan Economic Problem* (Washington, DC: Institute for International Economics, 1987).

Bernstein, Michael, *The Great Depression: Delayed Recovery and Economic Change in America, 1929–1939* (New York: Cambridge University Press, 1987).

Bhagwati, Jagdish, *Lectures in International Trade* (Cambridge, MA: MIT Press, 1983).

Bhagwati, Jagdish, *Protectionism* (Cambridge, MA: MIT Press, 1988).

Bhagwati, Jagdish and Hugh Patrick (eds), *Aggressive Unilateralism* (Ann Arbor, MI: University of Michigan Press, 1990).

Bhagwati, Jagdish, *The World Trading System at Risk* (Princeton, NJ: Princeton University Press, 1991).

Bidwell, Peter, and John I. Falconer, *History of Agriculture in the Northern United States, 1620–1860* (Washington, DC: Carnegie Institute, 1925).

Bils, Mark, "Tariff Protection and Production in the Early US Cotton Textile Industry," *Journal of Economic History*, **44** (1984), pp. 1033–46.

Bjork, Gordon, "The Weaning of the American Economy: Independence, Market Changes, and Economic Development," *Journal of Economic History*, **24** (1964), pp. 541–60.

Blendon, R.J. and D.E. Altman, "Public Attitudes about Health Care Costs: A Lesson in National Schizophrenia," *New England Journal of Medicine*, **311** (1984), pp. 613–16.

Blendon, Robert, *et al.*, "Satisfaction with Health Care in Ten Nations," *Health Affairs*, **9**, no. 2 (1990).

Bluestone, Barry, and Bennett Harrison, *The Deindustrialization America: Plant Closings, Community Abandonment, and the Dismantling of Basic Industries* (New York: Basic Industries, 1982).

Blum, John Morton, *V Was for Victory: Politics and American Culture during World War II* (New York: Harcourt, Brace, and Jovanovich, 1976).

Bogart, Leo, *Silent Politics* (New York: John Wiley & Sons, 1972).

Boltuck, Richard, and Robert Litan (eds), *Down in the DUMPS: Administration of Unfair Trade Laws* (Washington, DC: Brookings Institute, 1991).

Borden, William S., *The Pacific Alliance: United States Foreign Economic Policy and Trade Recovery, 1947–1955* (Madison: University of Wisconsin Press, 1984).

Borrus, Michael, James Millstein, and John Zysman, "US–Japanese Competition in the Semiconductor Industry," *Policy Papers in International Affairs*, **17** (Berkeley: Institute for International Studies, University of California, 1983).

Borrus, Michael, *Competing for Control: America's Stake in Microelectronics* (Cambridge, MA: Ballinger, 1988).

Borrus, Michael and Jeffrey Hart, "Display's the Thing: The Real Stakes in the Conflict Over High-resolution Display," *BRIE Working Papers*, **52**

(Berkeley, CA: Berkeley Roundtable on the International Economy, 1992).

Bowen, Catherine Drinker, *Miracle at Philadephia* (Boston, MA: Little, Brown, & Co. 1966).

Brander, James, and Barbara Spencer, "Export Subsidies and International Market Share Rivalry," *Journal of International Economics*, **18**, nos 1–2 (February 1985), pp. 85–100.

Brander, James A., "Rationales for Strategic Trade and Industrial Policy," in Paul Krugman (ed.), *Strategic Trade Policy and the New International Economics* (Cambridge, MA: MIT Press, 1986).

Brander, James A., "Shaping Comparative Advantage: Trade Policy, Industrial Policy, and Economic Performance," in R.G. Lipsey and W. Dobson (eds), *Shaping Comparative Advantage*, Policy Study no. 2 (Toronto: C.D. Howe Institute, 1987).

Brandes, Stuart D., *American Welfare Capitalism, 1880–1940* (Chicago, IL: University of Chicago Press, 1976).

Brock, Leslie, *The Currency of the American Colonies, 1700–64* (New York: Arno Press, 1975).

Bromley, Alan, "US Technology Policy: The Path to Competitiveness," Address to the Technology 2000 Meeting (Washington, DC: 27 November 1990).

Brownlee, W. Elliot and Mary M. Brownlee (eds), *Women in the American Economy: A Documentary History, 1675–1929* (New Haven, CT: Yale University Press, 1976).

Bruchey, Stuart, *Roots of American Economic Growth, 1607–1861* (London: Hutchinson, 1965).

Bruchey, Stuart, *The Colonial Merchant: Sources and Readings* (New York: Harcourt, Brace, & World, 1966).

Bruchey, Stuart, *Cotton and the Growth of the American Economy* (New York: Harcourt, Brace, & World, 1967).

Bureau of Labor Statistics, "US Congress, JEC, 88th Congr., 1st Sess., Hearings," *Steel Prices, Unit Costs, and Foreign Competition* (Washington, DC: GPO, 1963).

Burner, David, *Herbert Hoover, A Public Life* (New York: Alfred A. Knopf, 1979).

Burrows, Edwin and Michael Wallace, "The American Revolution: the Ideology and Psychology of National Liberation," *Perspectives in American History*, **6** (1972), pp. 208–15.

Callender, Guy S., "The Early Transportation and Banking Enterprises of the States in Relation to the Growth of Corporations," *Quarterly Journal of Economics*, **17** (1902).

Calleo, David, *The Imperious Economy* (Cambridge, MA: Harvard University Press, 1982).

Calomiris, Charles, "Institutional Failure, Monetary Scarcity, and the Depreciation of the Continental," *Journal of Economic History*, **48** (1988), pp. 47–68.

Carman, Harry (ed.), *American Husbandry* (Port Washington, NY: Kennikat Press, 1964).

Carosso, Vincent P., *The Morgans: Private International Bankers, 1854–1913* (Cambridge, MA: Harvard University Press, 1987).

Carrol, S.L., "The Market for Commercial Aircraft," in R.E. Caves and M.J. Roberts (eds), *Regulating the Market* (Cambridge, MA: Ballinger, 1975), pp. 145–69

Cassady, James M., *Demography in Early America* (Cambridge, MA: Harvard University Press, 1969).

Cathell, D.W., *The Physician Himself* (Philadephia, PA: F.A. Davis, 1890).

Chandler, Alfred, *The Railroads: The Nation's First Big Business* (New York: Harcourt, Brace & World, 1965).

Chandler, Alfred, *The Visible Hand: The Managerial Revolution in American Business* (Cambridge, MA: Belknap Press in Harvard University Press, 1977).

Chandler, Alfred A. and Stuart Bruchey (eds), *Giant Enterprise: Ford, General Motors, and the Automobile Industry* (New York: Arno Press, 1980).

Chandler, Lester, *America's Greatest Depression, 1929–1941* (New York: Harper & Row, 1970).

Chandler, Lester V., *American Monetary Policies, 1928–41* (New York: Harper & Row, 1971).

Chitwood, Oliver P., *A History of Colonial America* (New York: Harper & Bros., 1961).

Choate, Pat, *Agents of Influence: How Japan's Lobbyists in the United States Manipulate America's Political and Economic System* (New York: Knopf, 1990).

Clark, John Maurice, *The Cost of the World War to the American People* (New Haven, CT: Yale University Press, 1931).

Clark, Victor S., *History of Manufacturers in the United States*, 3 vols (New York: Peter Smith, 1949).

Clarkson, Grosvenor B., *Industrial America in the World War: The Strategy Behind the Line, 1917–1918* (Boston, MA: Houghton Mifflin, 1923).

Cline, William, "US Trade and Industrial Policy: The Experience of Textiles, Steel, and Automobiles," in Paul Krugman (ed.), *Strategic Trade Policy and the New International Economics* (Cambridge, MA: MIT Press, 1986).

Clowse, Converse D., *Economics Beginnings in Colonial South Carolina, 1670–1730* (Columbia: University of South Carolina Press, 1971).

Coale, Ansley and Melvin Zelink, *New Estimates of Fertility and Population in the United States: A Study of Annual White Births from 1855 to 1960 and of Completeness of Ennumeration of Censuses from 1880 to 1960* (Princeton, NJ: Princeton University Press, 1963).

Cobb, James C., *The Selling of the South: The Southern Crusade for Industrial Development, 1936–1980* (Baton Rouge, LA: Louisiana State University Press, 1982).

Cochran, Thomas C., *Railroad Leaders, 1845–1890: The Business Mind in Action* (Cambridge, MA: Harvard University Press, 1953).

Cochran, Thomas, "Did the Civil War Retard Industrialization?" in Ralph Andreano (ed.), *The Economic Impact of the Civil War* (Cambridge, MA: Schenkman, 1862).

Cochrance, Rexmond C., *Measures for Progress: A History of the National Bureau of Standards* (Washington, DC: US Department of Commerce, GPO, 1966).

Coen, Robert M., "Labor Force and Unemployment in the 1920s and 1930s," *Review of Economics and Statistics*, **55** (1973), 40–55.

Congressional Budget Office, *The Industrial Policy Debate* (Washington, D.C.: Government Printing Office, 1983).

Conrad, Alfred H. and John Meyer, "The Economics of Slavery in the Ante-bellum South," *Journal of Political Economy*, **66** (1958), pp. 95–122.

Cordtz, Dan, "Change Begins in the Doctor's Office," *Fortune*, **81** (January 1970).

Coulter, E. Merton, *The South during Reconstruction, 1865–1877* (Baton Rouge, LA: Louisiana State University, 1947).

Crandall, Robert W., *The US Steel Industry in Recurrent Crisis* (Washington, DC: Brookings, 1981).

Crandall, Robert, "Investment and Productivity Growth in the Steel Industry: Some Implications for Industrial Policy," in Walter H. Goldberg (ed.), *Ailing Steel: The Transatlantic Quarrel* (New York: St Martin's Press, 1986).

Cremin, Lawrence A., *The Transformation of the School: Progressivism in American Education, 1876–1957* (New York: Alfred A. Knopf, 1961).

Cremin, Lawrence A., *American Education: The National Experience, 1783–1876* (New York: Harper & Row, 1980).

Cronin, Thomas, *The State of the Presidency* (Chicago, IL: Scott, Foresman & Co., 1980).

Cuff, Robert D., *The War Industries Board: Business–Government Relations During World War I* (Baltimore, MD: Johns Hopkins Press, 1973).

Dahl, Robert, *Who Governs?* (New Haven, CT: Yale University Press, 1963).

David, Jules, *American Political and Economic Penetration of Mexico, 1877–1920* (New York: Arno Press, 1976).

David, Paul A., "Learning by Doing and Tariff Protection: A Reconsideration of the Case of the Antebellum United States Cotton Textile Industry," *Journal of Economic History*, **30** (1970), pp. 521–601.

David, Paul A., *Technical Choice, Innovation and Economic Growth; Essays on American and British Experience in the Nineteenth Century* (Cambridge: Cambridge University Press, 1975).

David, Paul A. et al., *Reckoning with Slavery: A Critical Study of the Quantitative History of American Negro Slavery* (New York: Oxford University Press, 1976).

David, Henry, *The History of the Haymarket Affair* (New York: Russell & Russell, 1958).

Davis, Lance E., "Capital Formation in the United States during the Nineteenth Century," in *The Cambridge Economic History of Europe*, vol. 7.

Davis, Joseph S., *Essays in the Earlier History of American Corporations*, 2 vols (Cambridge, MA: Harvard University Press, 1917).

Davis, K. and D. Rowland, *Medicare Policy: New Directions for Health and Long-Term Care* (Baltimore, MD: Johns Hopkins University Press, 1986).

Davis, Lance E. "Banks and Their Economic Effects," in Lance E. Davis et al. (eds), *American Economic Growth: An Economist's History of the United States* (New York: Harper & Row, 1972).

Deane, Phyllis, *The First Industrial Revolution* (Cambridge: Cambridge University Press, 1965).

DeCanio, Stephen J. and Joel Mokyr, "Inflation and the Wage Lag during the American Civil War," *Explorations in Economic History*, **14** (1977), pp. 311–36.

Defense Science Board Task Force, *Foreign Ownership and Control of US Industry* (Washington, DC: Defense Science Board, June 1990).

Defense Science Board Task Force, *Foreign Ownership and Control of US Industry*, released by the Office of Congressman Mel Levine (D-CA), 13 May 1991.

Degler, Carl N., *Out of Our Past: The Forces that Shaped America* (New York: Harper & Row, 1959).

DeGrasses, Robert W., *Military Expansions, Economic Decline: The Impact of Military Spending on US Economic Performance* (New York: M.E. Sharpe, 1983).

Derian, Jean-Claude, *America's Struggle for Leadership in Technology* (Cambridge, MA: MIT Press, 1990).

Dewar, Mary (ed.), *A Discourse of the Commonweal of this Realm of England, Attributed to Sir Thomas Smith* (Charlottesville, VA: University Press of Virginia, 1973).

Dewey, Donald, *Monopoly in Economics and Law* (Chicago, IL: Rand McNally, 1959).

Dickens, William and Kevin Lang, "Why it Matters what we Trade: A Case for an Active Trade Policy," in William Dickens, Laura D'Andrea Tyson, and John Zysman, (eds), *The Dynamics of Trade and Employment* (Cambridge, MA: Ballinger, 1988), pp. 87–112.

Dickerson, Oliver M., *The Navigation Acts and the American Revolution* (New York: Octagon, 1978).

Divine, Robert A., *Eisenhower and the Cold War* (New York: Oxford University Press, 1981).

Dixit, Avinash K. and Albert S. Kyle, "The Use of Protection and Subsidies for Entry Promotion and Deterrence," *American Economic Review*, **75** (March 1985).

Dixit, Avinash, "Optimal Trade and Industrial Policy for the US Automobile Industry, in Robert Feenstra (ed.), *Empirical Methods for International Trade* (Cambridge, MA: MIT Press, 1988), pp. 141–65.

Donaldson, S.M., *Hold On, Mr. President!* (New York: Random House, 1987).

Dubovsky, Melvyn, *Industrialism and the American Worker, 1865–1920* (New York: Thomas Crowell, 1975).

Dyer, Davis, Malcom Salter and Alan Webber, *Changing Alliances* (Boston, MA: Harvard Business School Press, 1987).

Easterlin, Richard A., *Population, Labor Force, and Long Swings in Economic Growth: The American Experience* (New York: Columbia University Press, 1968).

Eaton, Jonathan and Gene M. Grossman, "Optimal Trade and Industrial Policy under Oligopoly," *Quarterly Journal of Economics*, **101** (May 1986), pp. 383–406.

Eckstein, Otto and Gary Fromm, "Steel and Postwar Inflation," Study Paper no. 2, US Congress, JEC, 86th Congr., 1st Sess., *Materials Prepared in Connection with the Study of Employment, Growth, and Prices Levels* (Washington, DC: GPO, 1959).

Eichengreen, Barry, *Golden Fetters: The Gold Standard and the Great Depression, 1919–1939* (New York: Oxford University Press, 1992).

Eisner, Robert, *How Real is the Federal Deficit?* (New York: Free Press, 1986).

Eldridge, Hope T. and Dorothy Swain Thomas, *Population Redistribution and Economic Growth*, 3 vols (Philadelphia, PA: American Philosophical Society, 1964).

Eliot, Jared, *Essays upon Field Husbandry in New England, and other Papers, 1748–1762*, ed. Harry J. Carman and Rexford G. Tugwell (New York: Columbia University Press, 1934).

Elliott, J.H., *The Old World and the New, 1492–1650* (Cambridge: Cambridge University Press, 1970).

Endicott, Kenneth M. and Ernest M. Allen, "The Growth of Medical Research 1941–1953 and the Role of the Public Health Service Research Grants," *Science*, **118** (25 September 1953).

Engerman, Stanley L., "The Economic Impact of the Civil War," *Explorations in Economic History*, **3** (1955), pp. 176–99.

Erikson, Robert S., "Economic Conditions and the Presidential Vote," *American Political Science Review*, **83** (Spring 1989), pp. 567–73.

Ernst, Dieter and David O'Connor, *Competing in the Electronics Industry – The Experience of Newly Industrializing Economies* (London: Pinter, 1992).

Ernst, Joseph Albert, *Money and Politics in America, 1755–75: A Study in the Currency Act of 1764 and the Political Economy of Revolution* (Chapel Hill, NC: University of North Carolina Press, 1973).

Evans, Peter B., Dietrich Rueschemeyer, and Theda Skocpol (eds), *Bringing the State Back In* (Cambridge: Cambridge University Press, 1985).

Evans, Robert G. and Morris L. Barer, "The American Predicament," in *Health Care Systems in Transition* (Paris: OECD, 1990).

Evans, Stephen Peter, *Dependent Development* (Princeton, NJ: Princeton University Press, 1979).

Eyenbach, Mary Locke, *American Manufactured Exports, 1879–1914* (New York: Arno Press, 1976).

Federal Trade Commission, *Report on Wartime Costs and Profits for Manufacturing Corporations, 1941 to 1945* (Washington, DC: Government Printing Office, 1947).

Feigenbaum, Susan, "Risk Bearing in Health Care Finance," in Carl Schramm (ed.), *Health Care and its Costs: Can the US Afford Adequate Health Care?* (New York: W.W. Norton & Co., 1987).

Fenstermaker, J. Van, *The Development of American Commercial Banking: 1782–1837* (Kent, OH: Bureau of Economic and Business Research, 1965).

Ferguson, Charles H., "America's High Tech Decline," *Foreign Policy*, **74** (Spring 1989), pp. 123–44.

Ferguson, Charles H. and Charles R. Morris, *Computer Wars: How the West can win in a Post-IBM World* (New York: Times Books, 1993).

Ferguson, F. James, *The Power of the Purse* (Chapel Hill, NC: University of North Carolina Press, 1961).

Ferguson, F. James, *The American Revolution: A General History, 1763–1790* (Homewood, IL: Dorsey Press, 1979).

Field, Albert, "The Magnetic Telegraph, Price, and Quantity Data, and the New Management of Capital," *Journal of Economic History*, **52** (1992), pp. 401–13.

Fine, Sydney, *The Automobile under the Blue Label* (Ann Arbor, MI: University of Michigan Press, 1963).

Fisher, Franklin M., James W. McKie, and Richard B. Mancke, *IBM and the US Data Processing Industry: An Economic History* (New York: Praeger, 1983).

Fishlow, Albert, *American Railroads and the Transformation of the Antebellum Economy* (Cambridge, MA: Harvard University Press, 1965).

Fishlow, Albert, "Internal Transportation," in Lance Davis *et al.* (eds), *American Economic Growth* (New York: Harper & Sons, 1972), pp. 468–547.

Fite, Gilbert C., *The Farmers Frontier, 1865–1900* (New York: Holt, Rinehart & Winston, 1966).

Fitzpatrick, John C. (ed.), *The Writings of George Washington, 1745–1799* (Washington, DC: Government Printing Office, 1934–44).

Flamm, Kenneth, *Targeting the Computer: Government Support and International Competition* (Washington, DC: Brookings, 1987).

Flamm, Kenneth, *Creating the Computer: Government, Industry, and High Technology* (Washington, DC: The Brookings Institute, 1988).

Fletcher, Stevenson W., *Pennsylvania Agriculture and Country Life, 1640–1840* (Harrisonburg, PA: Pennsylvania Historical and Museum Commission, 1950).

Flisig, Heywood W., *Long-term Capital Flows and the Great Depression: The Role of the United States, 1927–33* (Ithaca, NY: Cornell University Press, 1975).

Fogel, Robert W., *Railroads and American Economic Growth: Essays in Econometric History* (Baltimore, MD: Johns Hopkins Press, 1964).

Fogel, Robert and Stanley Engerman, *Time on the Cross: The Economics of American Negro Slavery* (New York: Little, Brown 1974).

Fogel, Robert W., *Without Consent or Contract: The Rise and Fall of American Slavery*, vol. 1 (New York: W.W. Norton & Co. 1989).

Ford, Paul Leiscester (ed.), *The Writings of Thomas Jefferson* (New York: G.P. Putnam's Sons, 1892–99).

Frankel, Jeffrey, "The 1807–1809 Embargo Against Great Britain," *Journal of Economic History*, **42** (1982), pp. 291–308.

Free, Lloyd and Hadley Cantril, *The Political Beliefs of Americans* (New York: Simon & Schuster, 1968).

Frendreis, John and Raymond Tatalovich, *The Modern Presidency and Economic Policy* (Itasca, IL: F.E. Peacock Press, 1994).

Freshnock, L.J., *Physicians and Public Attitudes on Health Care Issues* (Chicago, IL: American Medical Association, 1984).

Friedman, Benjamin, *Day of Reckoning: The Consequences of American Economic Policy under Reagan and After* (New York: Random House, 1988).

Friedman, Milton and Anna Schwartz, *A Monetary History of the United States, 1869–1960* (Princeton, NJ: Princeton University Press, 1963).

Fuchs, Victor, *Who Shall Live?* (New York: Basic Books, 1974).

Galbraith, John Kenneth, *The Great Crash: 1929* (Boston, MA: Houghton Mifflin, 1954).

Galbraith, John Kenneth, *The Culture of Contentment* (Boston, MA: Houghton Mifflin, 1992).

Galenson, David W., *White Servitude in Colonial America: An Economic Analysis* (Cambridge: Cambridge University Press, 1981).

Gallman, Robert E. and Edward S. Howle, "Trends in the Structure of the American Economy since 1840," in Robert W. Fogel and Stanley L. Engerman (eds), *The Reinterpretation of American Economic History* (New York: Harper & Row, 1971).

Gallman, Robert, "The Pace and Pattern of American Economic Growth," in Lance Davis, Richard Easterlin, and William Parker (eds), *American Economic Growth* (New York: Harper & Row, 1972).

Garraty, John A., *The Great Depression: An Inquiry into the Causes, Course, and Consequences of the Worldwide Depression of the Nineteen-Thirties, as seen by Contemporaries in the Light of History* (New York: Harcourt, Brace, Jovanovich, 1986).

Garten, Jeffrey, *A Cold Peace: America, Japan, Germany and the Struggle for Supremacy* (New York: Times Books, 1992).

Gates, Paul W., *The Farmer's Age: Agriculture, 1815–1860* (New York: Holt, Rinehart & Winston, 1960).

Gates, Paul W., *Agriculture and the Civil War* (New York: Alfred A. Knopf, 1965).

Gates, Paul, *History of Public Land Law Development* (Washington, DC: Government Printing Office, 1968).

Genovese, Eugene, *The Political Economy of Slavery: Studies in the Economy and Socity of the Slave South* (New York: Pantheon, 1965).

Genovese, Eugene, *Roll, Jordan, Roll: The World the Slaves Made* (New York: Pantheon, 1974).

Gerster, Arpad, *Recollections of a New York Surgeon* (New York: Paul B. Hoeber, 1929).

Gervasi, Tom, *The Myth of Soviet Military Supremacy* (New York: Harper & Row, 1987).

Gilbert, Charles, *American Financing of World War I* (Westport, CT: Greenwood Press, 1970).

Gilpin, Robert, *The Political Economy of International Relations* (Princeton, NJ: Princeton, 1987).

Goldin, Claudia and Frank Lewis, "The Economic Cost of the American Civil War: Estimates and Implications," *Journal of Economic History*, **35** (1975), pp. 294–326.

Goldin, Claudia, *Urban Slavery in the American South, 1820–1860* (Chicago, IL: University of Chicago Press, 1976).

Goldin, Claudia and Frank Lewis, "The Role of Exports in American Economic Growth During the Napoleonic Wars, 1793–1807," *Explorations in American History*, **17** (1980), pp. 291–308.

Goldstein, Judith, "Ideas, Institutions, and American Trade Policy," *International Organization*, **42** (Winter 1988), pp. 179–217.

Good, H.G., *A History of American Education* (New York: Macmillan, 1956).

Goodrich, Carter, "The Revulsion against Internal Improvements," *Journal of Economic History*, **10** (1950), pp. 145–69.

Goodrich, Carter, *Government Promotion of American Canals and Railroads* (New York: Columbia University Press, 1960).

Goodrich, Carter, "Internal Improvements Reconsidered," *Journal of Economic History*, **30** (1970).

Gordon, Robert A., *Economic Instability and Growth: The American Record* (New York: Harper & Row, 1974).

Gordon, Robert J. and James A.Wilcox, "Monetary Interpretations: An Evaluation and Critique," in Karl Brunner (ed.), *The Great Depression Revisited* (Boston, MA: Martinus Nijhoff, 1980).

Goven, Thomas P., *Nicholas Biddle, Nationalist and Public Banker, 1786–1844* (Chicago, IL: University of Chicago Press, 1959).

Graham, Edward M. and Paul R. Krugman, *Foreign Direct Investment in the United States* (Washington, DC: Institute for International Economics, 1991).

Gray, Lewis C., *History of Agriculture in the Southern United States to 1860* (Washington, DC: Carnegie Institute, 1933).

Greene, Jack P. "An Uneasy Connection: An Analysis of the Preconditions of the American Revolution," in Stephen G. Kurtz and James H. Hutson (eds), *Essays on the American Revolution* (Chapel Hill, NC: University of North Carolina Press, 1973).

Greenwald, Maurine Weiner, *Women, Work, and War: The Impact of World War I on Women Workers in the United States* (Westport, CT: Greenwood Press, 1980).

Greider, William, "The Education of David Stockman," *Atlantic Monthly* (December 1981).

Greider, William, *The Education of David Stockman and Other Americans* (New York: E.P. Dutton, 1986).

Greider, William, *Secrets of the Temple: How the Federal Reserve runs the Country* (New York: Simon & Schuster, 1988).

Griffin, John I., *Strikes: A Study in Quantitative Economics* (New York: Columbia University Press, 1939).

Griffith, Robert K., *The Military–Industrial Complex: A Historical Perspective* (New York: Praeger, 1980).

Gross, Robert A., *The Minute Men and their World* (New York: Hill & Wang, 1976).

Gourevitch, Peter, "International Trade, Domestic Coalitions, and Liberty: Comparative Responses to the Crisis of 1873–1896," *Journal of Interdisciplinary Studies*, **8** (Autumn 1977).

Gunderson, Gerald A., *A New Economic History of America* (New York: McGraw-Hill, 1976).

Haber, Samuel, "The Professions and Higher Education in America," in Margaret Gordon (ed.), *Higher Education and the Labor Market* (New York: McGraw-Hill, 1974).

Hacker, Louis, *The Triumph of American Capitalism* (New York: Columbia University Press, 1940).

Haites, Erik and Gary Walton, *Western River Transportation: The Era of Early Internal Development, 1810–1860* (Baltimore, MD: Johns Hopkins University Press, 1975).

Hammond, Bray, *Banks and Politics in America from the Revolution to the Civil War* (Princeton, NJ: Princeton University Press, 1957).

Hamilton, Alexander, "Report on a National Bank" (1790), in Jacob Cooke (ed.), *The Reports of Alexander Hamilton* (New York: Harper & Row, 1964).

Hamilton, Alexander, "Continentalist Number 5" (1790), in Jacob Cooke (ed.), *The Reports of Alexander Hamilton* (New York: Harper & Row, 1964).

Hamilton, Alexander, "Report on Manufactures, December 5, 1791," in Jacob Cooke, (ed.), *The Reports of Alexander Hamilton* (New York: Harper & Row, 1964).

Hamilton, Alexander, "Report on the Subject of Manufactures," (1791) in H.C. Syrett (ed.), *The Papers of Alexander Hamilton*, vol. 10 (New York: Columbia University Press, 1966).

Handlin, Oscar and Mary F., "Origins of the American Business Corporation," *Journal of Economic History*, **5** (1945).

Harley, C. Knick,"Transportation, the World Wheat Trade, and the Kuznets Cycle, 1850–1913," *Explorations in Economic History*, **17** (1980), pp. 224–5.

Harper, Lawrence, "Mercantilism and the American Revolution," *Canadian Historican Review*, **23** (1942), pp. 1–15.

Harper, Lawrence, "The Effect of the Navigation Acts on the Thirteen Colonies," in Harry Scheiber (ed.), *The United States Economic History* (New York: Knopf, 1964), pp. 42–78.

Harris, Richard, *Trade, Industrial Policy, and International Competition* (Toronto: University of Toronto Press, 1985).

Hart, Jeffrey, and Laura D'Andrea Tyson, "Responding to the Challenge of HDTV," *California Management Review*, **31** (Summer 1989), pp. 132–45.

Hartung, William D., *And Weapons for all: How America's Multi-billion Dollar Arms Trade Warps our Foreign Policy and Subverts Democracy at Home* (New York: Harper-Collins, 1994).

Hartz, Louis, *The Liberal Tradition in America* (New York: Harcourt Brace, 1955).

Hawley, Ellis, "Herbert Hoover, the Commerce Secretariat, and the Vision of an 'Associative State,' 1921–1928," *Journal of American History*, **61** (1974), pp. 116–140.

Heckscher, Eli F., *Mercantilism*, 2 vols (London: Allen & Unwin, 1955).

Heclo, Hugh, "Industrial Policy and the Executive Capacities of Government," in Claude Barfield and William Schambra (eds), *The Politics of Industrial Policy* (Washington, DC: American Enterprise Institute for Public Policy Research, 1986).

Heilbroner, Robert, and Peter Bernstein, *The Debt and the Deficit: False Alarms/Real Possibilities* (New York: W.W. Norton, 1989).

Heller, Walter, *New Dimensions of Political Economy* (Cambridge, MA: Harvard University Press, 1966).

Henretta, James, *The Evolution of American Society 1700–1815: An Interdisciplinary Analysis* (Lexington, MA: D.C. Heath, 1973).

Hicks, John D., *The Populist Revolt* (Minneapolis, MN: University of Minnesota Press, 1934).

Higgs, Robert, "Railroad Rates and the Populist Uprising," *Agricultural History*, **44** (1970).

Higgs, Robert, *The Transformation of the American Economy, 1865–1914* (New York: John Wiley, 1971).

Hill, Peter Jensen, *The Economic Impact of Immigration into the United States* (New York: Arno Press, 1975).

Hippel, Eric von, *The Sources of Innovation* (New York: Oxford University Press, 1988).

Hirschman, Albert, *National Power and the Structure of Foreign Trade* (Berkeley, CA: University of California Press, 1945).

Hofstadter, Richard, *The American Political Tradition* (New York: Vintage, 1972).

Hogan, William T., *Economic History of the Iron and Steel Industry in the United States*, 5 vols (Lexington, MA: Lexington Books, 1971).

Holman, Mary, *The Political Economy of the Space Program* (Palo Alto, CA: Pacific Books, 1974).

Horlick, Gary, "The United States Anti-Dumping System," in John H. Jackson and Edwin A. Vermulst (eds), *Anti-Dumping Law and Practice: A Comparative Study* (Ann Arbor, MI: University of Michigan Press, 1989).

Houndshell, David, *From the American System to Mass Production: The Development of Manufacturing in the United States, 1800–1932* (Baltimore, MD: Johns Hopkins Press, 1984).

Howell, Thomas R. *et al.*, *Steel and the State: Government's Intervention and Steel's Structural Crisis* (Boulder, CO.: Westview Press, 1988).

Howell, Thomas *et al.*, *The Microelectronics Race: The Impact of Government Policy on International Competition* (Boulder, CO: Westview Press, 1988).

Howell, Thomas, Brent L. Bartlett, and Warren Davis, *Creating Advantage: Semiconductors and Government Industrial Policy in the 1990s* (Santa Clara: Semiconductor Industry Association, 1992).

Hunter, Louis C., *Steamboats on the Western Rivers* (Cambridge, MA: Harvard University Press, 1936).

Huntington, Samuel, The Soldier and State: *The Theory and Practice of Civil-Military Relations* (Cambridge, MA: The Belknap Press, 1957).

Hutchins, John G.B., *The American Maritime Industries and Public Policy, 1789–1914: An Economic History* (Cambridge, MA: Harvard University Press, 1941).

Ikenberry, G. John, "Conclusion: An Institutional Approach to American Foreign Economic Policy, *International Organization*, **42** (Winter 1988), pp. 219–43.

Inman, B.R. and Daniel F. Burton, "Technology and Competitiveness: The New Policy Frontier," *Foreign Affairs*, **69** (Spring 1990), pp. 116–34.

James, John A., *Money and Capital Markets in Postbellum America* (Princeton, NJ: Princeton University Press, 1978).

James, John A., "Public Debt Management Policy and Nineteenth Century American Economic Growth," *Explorations in Economic History*, **21** (1984), pp. 192–217.

Jameson, J. Franklin, *The American Revolution Considered as a Social Movement* (Princeton, NJ: Princeton University Press, 1967).

Janowitz, Morris, *The Professional Soldier: A Social and Political Portrait* (New York: Putnam, 1960).

Johnson, Chalmers, *MITI and the Japanese Miracle* (Stanford, CA: Stanford University, 1982).

Johnson, Chalmers (ed.), *The Industrial Policy Debate* (San Francisco, CA: Institute for Contemporary Studies, 1984).

Johnson, H. Thomas, "Postwar Optimism and the Rural Financial Crisis of the 1920's," *Explorations in Economic History*, **11** (1973).

Jones, Alice Hanson, *Wealth of a Nation to be: The American Colonies on the Eve of the Revolution* (New York: Columbia University Press, 1980).

Jones, E.L., *Agriculture and the Industrial Revolution* (New York: John Wiley, 1974).

Jones, Lawrence A. and David Durand, *Mortgage Lending Experience in Agriculture* (Princeton, NJ: Princeton University Press, 1954).

Jordan, Winthrop D., *White over Black* (Chapel Hill, NC: University of North Carolina Press, 1968).

Katz, Harold C., *The Decline of Competition in the Automobile Industry, 1920–1940* (New York: Arno Press, 1977).

Katz, Harold C., *Shifting Gears: Changing Labor Relations in the US Automobile Industry* (Cambridge, MA: MIT Press, 1985).

Katzenstein, Peter, "Conclusion: Domestic Structures and Strategies of Foreign Economic Policy," in Peter Katzenstein (ed.), *Between Power and Plenty* (Madison, WI: University of Wisconsin, 1978).

Katzenstein, Peter, *Small States in World Markets* (Ithaca, NY: Cornell University Press, 1986).

Keene, Karyn and Everett Ladd, "Government as Villain," *Government Executive*, (January 1988), 11, pp. 13–16.

Kennedy, Susan Estabrook, *The Banking Crisis of 1933* (Lexington, PA: University Press of Kentucky, 1973).

Kennedy, William, *Rise and Fall of the Great Powers* (New York: Random House, 1987).

Keohane, Robert, "The theory of Hegemonic Stability and Changes in International Economic Regimes," in Ole Hosti, R. Siverson, and Alexander George (eds), *Change in the International System* (Boulder, CO: Westview Press, 1980).

Keohane, Robert, "Reciprocity in International Relations," *International Organization*, **40** (Winter 1986), pp. 1–28.

Keohane, Robert and Joseph Nye, *Power and Interdependence* (Boston, MA: Little, Brown, 1977).

Keohane, Robert, and Joseph Nye, "Power and Interdependence Revisited," *International Organization*, **41** (Autumn 1987), pp. 737–8.

Kerridge, Eric, *The Agricultural Revolution* (London: Allen & Unwin, 1967).

Key, V.O., *Public Opinion and American Democracy* (New York: Alfred Knopf, 1961).

Keynes, John Maynard, *The General Theory of Employment, Interest, and Money* (New York: Harcourt, Brace & Co., 1936).

Kimmel, Lewis H., *Federal Budget and Fiscal Policy, 1789–1958* (Washington, DC: Brookings Institute, 1959).

Kindleberger, Charles (ed.), *The International Corporation* (Cambridge, MA: MIT Press, 1970).

Kindleberger, Charles P., *The World in Depression* (London: Penguin Books, 1973).

Kirkland, Edward C., *Industry Comes of Age: Business, Labor, and Public Policy* (New York: Holt, Rinehart & Winston, 1961).

Koistinin, Paul A.C. "The 'Industrial–Military Complex' in Historical Perspective: World War I," *Business History Review*, **41** (1967).

Krasner, Stephen, *Depending the National Interest* (Princeton, NJ: Princeton University, 1978).

Krasner, Stephen, *International Regimes* (Ithaca, NY: Cornell University Press, 1982).

Krueger, Anne, "Theory and Practice of Commercial Policy, 1945–1990, *NBER Working Papers 3569* (Cambridge, MA: National Bureau of Economic Research, 1991).

Krugman, Paul, "The US Response to Foreign Industrial Targeting," *Brookings Papers on Economic Activity*, **15** (1984).

Krugman, Paul (ed.), *Strategic Trade Policy and the New International Economics* (Cambridge, MA: MIT Press, 1986).

Krugman, Paul, *The Age of Diminished Expectations: US Economic Policy in the 1990s* (Cambridge, MA: MIT Press, 1990).

Kuttner, Robert, "Economists Really Should Get Out More Often," *Business Week* (24 April 1989).

Kuznets, Simon, *Shares of Upper Income Groups in Income and Saving* (New York: National Bureau of Economic Research, 1953).

Ladd, Everett Carl, "The Polls: Taxing and Spending," *Public Opinion Quarterly*, **43** (Spring 1979).

Lafeber, Walter, *The New Empire: American Expansion, 1860–1898* (Ithaca, NY: Cornell University Press, 1963).

Lake, David A., "International Economic Structures and American Foreign Economic Policy, 1887–1934," *World Politics*, **28** (April 1976), pp. 317–43.

Lake, David A. "The State and American Trade Strategy in the Pre-Hegemonic Era, *International Organization*, **42** (Winter 1988), pp. 51, 52.

Landes, David S., *The Unbound Prometheus* (Cambridge: Cambridge University Press, 1969).

Lauderbaugh, Richard A., *American Steel Makers and the Coming of the Second World War* (Ann Arbor, MI: University of Michigan Research Press, 1980).

Lave, Judith and Lester, *The Hospital Construction Act: An Evaluation of the Hill–Burton Program, 1948–1973* (Washington, DC: American Enterprise Institute, 1974).

Laverge, Real P., *The Political Economy of US Tariffs* (New York: Academic Press, 1983).

Lebergott, Stanley, *Manpower in Economic Growth: The American Record Since 1800* (New York: McGraw-Hill, 1964).

Lebergott, Stanley, "Labor Force and Employment, 1800–1960," in Dorothy Bradley (ed.), *Output, Employment, and Productivity in the United States after 1800* National Bureau of Economic Research, vol. 30 *Studies in Income and Wealth* (New York: Columbia University Press, 1966).

Lebergott, Stanley, "The Return to US Imperialism, 1890–1929," *Journal of Economic History*, **32** (1972).

Lebergott, Stanley, *The Americans* (New York: W.W. Norton & Co., 1984).

Lee, Susan Previant, *The Westward Movement of the Cotton Economy, 1840–1860: Perceived Interests and Economic Realities* (New York: Arno Press, 1977).

Lee, Susan, "Antebellum Southern Land Expansion: A Second View," *Agricultural History*, **52** (1978), pp. 488–502.

Lester, Richard A., *Monetary Experiments: Early American and Recent Scandinavian* (New York: Augustus Kelly, 1939).

Lester, Richard, "Currency Issues to Overcome Depression in Delaware, New Jersey, New York, and Maryland, 1715–1737," *Journal of Political Economy*, **47** (1939).

Letwin, William, *Law and Economic Policy in America* (New York: Random House, 1965).

Letwin, William (ed.), *A Documentary History of American Economic Policy Since 1789* (New York: W.W. Norton & Co., 1972).

Leuchtenburg, William E., *The Perils of Prosperity* (Chicago, IL: University of Chicago Press, 1959).

Leuchtenburg, William E., *Franklin D. Roosevelt and the New Deal, 1932–1940* (New York: Harper & Row, 1963).

Leuchtenberg, William E. "The New Deal and the Analogue of War," in John Braeman *et al.* (eds), *Change and Continuity in Twentieth Century America* (Athens, OH: Ohio University Press, 1966).

Levin, Richard, "The Semiconductor Industry," in Richard R. Nelson (ed.), *Government and Technical Progress: A Cross-Industry Analysis* (New York: Pergamon, 1982).

Levinson, Phyllis *et al.*, *The Federal Entrepreneur: The Nation's Implicit Industrial Policy* (Washington, DC: The Urban Institute, 1982).

Levit, Katherine R. and Cathy A. Cowan, "Businesses, Households, and Governments: Health Care Costs, 1990," *Health Care Financing Review*, **13** (1991).

Lindert, Peter, "Long-Run Trends in American Farmland Values," *Agricultural History*, **62** (1988), pp. 45–86.

Lipcap, Gary P., *The Evolution of Private Mineral Rights: Nevada's Comstock Lode* (New York: Arno Press, 1978).

Lippman, Walter, *The Phantom Public* (New York: Macmillan, 1925).

Lipsey, Robert E. "Foreign Trade," in Lance Davis *et al.* (eds), *American Economic Growth* (New York: Harper & Row, 1972), pp. 898–9.

List, Freidrich, *The National System of Political Economy* (London: Longmans, Green, 1885).

Littleton, A.C. and Basil C. Yamcy (eds), *Studies in the History of Accounting* (Homewood, ILL: Richard D. Irwin, 1956).

Lively, Robert A., "The American System: A Review Article," *Business History Review*, **29** (1955).

Lockwood, William, *The Economic Developnment of Japan* (Princeton, NJ: Princeton University Press, 1954).

Long, Clarence B., *Wages and Earnings in the United States, 1860–90* (Princeton, NJ: Princeton University Press, 1960).

Loory, Stuart H., *Defeated: Inside America's Military Machine* (New York: Random House, 1973).

Lorant, John Herman, *The Role of Capital Improving Innovations in American Manufacturing during the 1920s* (New York: Arno Press, 1975).

Lowi, Theodore, *The End of Liberalism* (New York: Norton, 1969).

Lubove, Roy, *The Struggle for Social Security, 1900–1935* (Cambridge, MA: Harvard University Press, 1968).

MacKuen, Michael B., Robert S. Erikson, and James A. Stimson, "Peasants or Bankers," *American Political Science Review*, 86 (September 1992), pp. 597–611.

Main, Jackson Turner, *The Social Structure of Revolutionary America* (Princeton, NJ: Princeton University Press, 1965).

Manners, Gerald, *The Changing World Market for Iron Ore, 1950–1980* (Baltimore, MD: Johns Hopkins Press, 1971).

Mansfield, Edwin, *Industrial Research and Technological Innovation* (New York: W.W. Norton & Co., 1968).

March, James G. and Johan P. Olsen, "The New Institutionalism: Organizational Factors in Political Life," *American Political Science Review*, 78 (September 1984).

Markus, Gregory B., "The Impact of Personal and National Economic Conditions on Presidential Voting, 1956–1988," *American Journal of Political Science*, 36 (1992), pp. 829–34.

Markusen, Ann *et al.*, *The Rise of the Gunbelt: The Military Remapping of Industrial America* (New York: Oxford University Press, 1991).

Mathias, Peter, *The First Industrial Nation* (New York: Charles Scribner's Sons, 1969).

Matsushita, Mitsuo and Lawrence Repeta, "Restricting the Supply of Japanese Automobiles: Sovereign Collusion?" *Case Western Reserve Journal of International Law*, 14 (Winter 1982).

Mayhew, Anne, "A Reappraisal of the Causes of Farm Protest in the United States, 1879–1900," *Journal of Economic History*, 32 (1972), pp. 464–75.

McClelland, Peter, "The Cost to America of British Imperial Policy," *American Economic Review*, 59 (1969), pp. 370–81.

McClelland, Peter, "The New Economic History and the Burdens of the Navigation Acts: A Comment," *Economic History Review*, 26 (1973), pp. 679–86.

McCurdy, Charles M., "American Law and the Marketing Structure of the Large Corporation, 1875–1890," *Journal of Economic History*, 38 (1978), pp. 631–49.

McDonald, Forrest, *We The People: The Economic Origins of the Constitution* (Chicago, IL: University of Chicago Press, 1958).

McCraw, Thomas, "Mercantilism and the Market: Antecedents of American Industrial Policy," in Claude Barfield and William Schambra (eds), *The Politics of Industrial Policy* (Washington, DC: American Enterprise Institute, 1986).

McFarland, Andrew, "Public Intrest Lobbies vs. Minority Faction," in Cigler and Loomis (eds), *Interest Group Politics* (Washington, DC: Congressional Quarterly Press, 1983).

McFetridge, Donald, "The Economics of Industrial Policy," in D.G. McFetridge (ed.), *Canadian Industrial Policy in Action* (Toronto: University of Toronto Press, 1985).

McKenzie, Richard B., "National Industrial Policy: An Overview of the Debate," Heritage Foundation, *Backgrounder*, no. 275 (12 July 1983).

McKeown, Timothy, "Firms and Tariff Regime Change: Explaining the Demand for Protection," *World Politics*, **36** (January 1984), pp. 215–33.

McQuire, Robert and Robert L. Ohsfeldt, "Economic Interests and the American Constitution: A Quantitative Rehabilitation of Charles A. Beard," *Journal of Economic History*, **44** (1984), pp. 509–20.

McQuire, Robert and Robert L. Ohsfeldt, "An Economic Model of Voting Behavior over Specific Issues at the Constitutional Convention of 1787," *Journal of Economic History*, **46** (1986), pp. 79–112.

Millis, Walter, *Arms and Men: A Study in American Military History* (New York: Putnam, 1956).

Mills, C. Wright, *The Power Elite* (New York: Oxford University Press, 1956).

Milner, Helen V. and David B. Yoffie, "Between Free Trade and Protectionism: Strategic Trade Policy and a theory of Corporate Trade Demands," *International Organization*, **43** (Spring 1989), pp. 239–73.

Mingos, Harry, "Birth of an Industry," in G.R. Simonson (ed.), *The History of the American Aircraft Industry* (Cambridge, MA: MIT Press, 1968), pp. 43–44.

Monroe, Paul, *The Founding of the American Public School System: A History of Education in the United States*, vol. 1 (New York: Macmillan, 1940).

Morgan, Edmund, *Birth of the Republic, 1763–1789* (Chicago, IL: University of Chicago Press, 1977).

Morris, Richard, *Government and Labor in Early America* (New York: Columbia University Press, 1946).

Mowery, David, and Nathan Rosenberg, "The Commercial Aircraft Industry," in Richard Nelson (ed.), *Government and Technical Progress: A Cross-Industry Analysis* (New York: Pergamon Press, 1982), pp. 101–61.

Mowery, David, and Nathan Rosenberg, "New Developments in US Technology Policy: Implications of Competitiveness and International Trade Policy," *California Management Review*, **32** (Fall 1989), pp. 107–24.

Myers, Margaret, *A Financial History of the United States* (New York: Columbia University Press, 1970).

Nash, Gary B., *The Urban Crucible: Social Change, Political Conciousness, and the Origin of the American Revolution* (Cambridge: MA: Harvard University Press, 1979).

National Advisory Committee on Semiconductors, *Toward a National Semiconductor Strategy: Regaining Markets in High-volume Electronics* (Washington, DC: National Advisory Committee on Electronics, 1991).

Neal, Larry, "Interpreting Power and Profit in Economic History: A Case Study of the Seven Years' War," *Journal of Economic History*, **37** (1977), pp. 20–35.

Nelson, Daniel, *Managers and Workers, Origins of the New Factory System in the United States, 1880–1920* (Madison, WI: University of Wisconsin Press, 1975).

Nelson, Donald M., *Arsenal of Democracy* (New York: Harcourt, Brace, 1946).

Nelson, Ralph, *Merger Movements in American Industry, 1895–1956*, National Bureau of Economic Research, General Series, no. 66 (Princeton, NJ: Princeton University Press, 1959).

Nelson, Richard, "US Technological Leadership: Where did it Come From and Where did it Go?," *Research Policy*, **19**, pp. 117–32.

Nester, William, *Japanese Industrial Targeting: The Neomercantilist Path to Economic Superpower* (New York: St Martin's Press, 1991).

Nester, William, *American Power, The New World Order, and the Japanese Challenge* (New York: St Martin's Press, 1993).

Nester, William R., *International Relations: Geopolitical and Geoeconomic Continuities and Changes* (New York: Harper Collins, 1995).

Neustadt, Richard, *Presidential Power* (New York: John Wiley & Sons, 1960).

Nettels, Curtis P., *The Emergence of a National Economy, 1775–1815* (New York: Holt, Rinehart & Winston, 1962).

Nettels, Curtis P., *The Roots of American Civilization* (New York: Appleton, Century, Crofts, 1963).

Nocera, Joseph, *A Piece of the Action: How the Middle Class Joined the Money Class* (New York: Simon & Schuster, 1994).

North, Douglass C., "The United States Balance of Payments, 1790–1860," in National Bureau of Economic Research, *Trends in the American Economy in the 19th Century*, Studies in Income and Wealth, vol. 24 (Princeton, NJ: Princeton University Press, 1960), pp. 573–627.

North, Douglass C., *The Economic Growth of the United States, 1790 to 1860* (Englewood Cliffs, NJ: Prentice Hall, 1961).

North, Douglass C. and Robert Paul Thomas, *The Rise of the Western World: A New Economic History* (Cambridge: Cambridge University Press, 1973).

Norton, Hugh S., *The Employment Act and the Council of Economic Advisors, 1946–1976* (Columbia, SC: University of South Carolina Press, 1977).

Odell, John, *US International Monetary Policy: Markets, Power, and Ideas as Sources of Change* (Princeton, NJ: Princeton University, 1982).

Office of Technology Assessment, *Competing Economies: America, Europe, and the Pacific Rim* (Washington, DC: GPO, October 1991).

Office of the US Trade Representative, *Procedures to Introduce Supercomputers* (Washington, DC: GPO, 1990).

Oleson, Alexandra and John Voss (eds), *The Organization of Knowledge in the United States* (Baltimore, MD: Johns Hopkins University Press, 1979).

Olson, James, *Herbert Hoover and the Reconstruction Finance Corporation, 1931–33* (Ames, IA: University of Iowa Press, 1977).

Olson, Mancur, "Supply-side Economics, Industrial Policy, and Rational Ignorance," in Claude E. Barfield and William A. Schambra (eds), *The Politics of Industrial Policy* (Washington, DC: American Enterprise Institute, 1986).

Palmer, John L. and Isabel V. Sawhill (eds), *The Reagan Experiment, An Examination of Economic and Social Policies under the Reagan Administration* (Washington, DC: Urban Institute, 1982).

Parker, William M., "Slavery and Southern Economic Development: An Hypothesis and Some Evidence," *Agricultural History*, **44** (1970), pp. 115–25.

Parmet, Herbert S., *Eisenhower and the American Crusades* (New York: Macmillan, 1972).

Parry, J.H., "Colonial Development and International Rivalries Outside Europe," in *The New Cambridge Modern History*.

Pearce, Joan and John Sutton, *Protection and Industrial Policy in Europe* (London: Routledge & Kegan Paul, 1986).

Pelzer, Louis, *The Cattlemen's Frontier: A Record of the Trans-Mississippi Cattle Industry from Open Times to Pooling Companies, 1850–1890* (New York: Russell & Russell, 1969).

Pennick, James *et al.*, *The Politics of American Science: 1939 to the Present* (Cambridge, MA: MIT Press, 1972).

Peretz, Paul, "Economic Policy in the 1980s," in Paul Peretz (ed.), *The Politics of American Economic Policy Making* (Armonk, NY: M.E. Sharpe, 1986).

Perkins, Edwin J., *The Economy of Colonial America* (New York: Columbia University Press, 1980).

Peters, B. Guy, *American Public Policy: Promise and Performance* (Chatham, NJ: Chatham House, 1993).

Phillips, Robert Kevin, *Boiling Point: Republicans, Democrats, and the Decline of the Middle-class* (New York: Random House, 1993).

Pincus, Jonathan, *Pressure Groups and Politics in Antebellum Tariffs* (New York: Columbia University Press, 1977).

Poggi, Gianfranco, *The Development of the Modern State* (Stanford, CA: Stanford University Press, 1978).

Polenberg, Richard, *War and Society: The United States, 1941–1945* (Philadephia, PA: J.B. Lippincott, 1972).

Pollard, Robert A., *European Security and the Origins of the Cold War, 1945–1950* (New York: Columbia University Press, 1985).

Pope, Daniel, *The Making of Modern Advertizing* (New York: Basic Books, 1983).

Porter, James, "The Growth of Population in America, 1700–1860," in D.V. Glass and D.E.C. Eversley (eds), *Population in History* (London: Edward Arnold, 1965).

Porter, Michael, "The Structure within Industries and Companies' Performance," *Review of Economics and Statistics*, **61** (May 1979).

Porter, Michael, *The Competitive Advantage of Nations* (New York: Free Press, 1990).

"Preliminary Report of the Special Committee on Investigation of the Munitions Industry," *Senate Report*, 74 Congr., 1 Sess., No. 944, Part I (Serial 9881).

Prestowitz, Clyde, Alan Tonelson, and Robert Jerome, "The Last Gasp of GATTism," *Harvard Business Review* (March–April 1991).

Price, Jacob M., "Economic Function and the Growth of American Port Towns in the 18th Century," *Perspectives in American History*, **8** (1974).

Primack, Martin, *Farm Formed Capital in Agriculture, 1850 to 1910* (New York: Arno Press, 1977).

Pursell, Carroll W. (ed.), *The Military–Industrial Complex* (New York: Harper & Row, 1972).

Puth, Robert C., *American Economic History* (Chicago, IL: Dryden Press, 1982).

Pye, Lucian, Politics, Personality, and Nation Building (New Haven, CT: Yale University Press, 1962).

Pye, Lucian (ed.), *Political Culture and Political Development* (Princeton, NJ: Princeton University Press, 1965).

Rae, John, *The American Automobile Industry* (Boston, MA: Twyane Publishers, 1984).

Ransom, Roger, "British Policy and Colonial Growth: Some Implications of the Burden from the Navigation Acts," *Journal of Economic History*, **28** (1968), pp. 427–35.

Ransom, Roger and Richard Sutch, *One Kind of Freedom: The Economic Consequences of Emancipation* (Cambridge: Cambridge University Press, 1977).

Ransom, Roger, *Conflict and Compromise: The Political Economy of Slavery, Emancipation, and the American Civil War* (New York: Cambridge University Press, 1989).

Rastatter, Edward S., "Nineteenth Century Public Land Policy: The Case for the Speculator," in David C. Klingaman and Richard K. Vedder (ed.), *Essays in Nineteenth Century Economic History: The Old Northwest*, (Athens, OH: Ohio University Press, 1975).

Rees, Albert, *Real Wages in Manufacturing, 1890–1914* (Princeton, NJ: Princeton University Press, 1961).

Reich, Robert, "Making Industrial Policy," *Foreign Affairs* (Spring 1982).

Reich, Robert B., *The Next American Frontier* (New York: Times Books, 1983).

Relman, Arnold S., "The New Medical–Industrial Complex," *New England Journal of Medicine*, **303** (23 October 1980), pp. 963–70.

Remini, Robert, *Andrew Jackson and the Bank War* (New York: W.W. Norton, 1967).

Renn, Steven, "The Structure and Financing of the Health Care Delivery System of the 1980s," in Carl J. Schramm (ed.), *Health Care and its Costs: Can the US Afford Adequate Health Care?* (New York: W.W. Norton & Co., 1987).

"Report and Recommendations of the Senate Republican Task Force on Industrial Competitiveness and International Trade," (16 March 1983), p. 1.

Rettig, Richard A., *Cancer Crusade: The Story of the National Cancer Act of 1971* (Princeton, NJ: Princeton University Press, 1977).

Rice, John R., *HDTV: The Politics, Policies, and Economics of Tomorrow's Television* (New York: Union Square Press, 1990).

Richardson, David J., "The Political Economy of Strategic Trade Policy, *International Organization*, **44** (Winter 1990), pp. 107–35.

Riis, Jacob, *How the Other Half Lives* (New York: Scribner's, 1890).

Ripley, William Z., *Railroads, Finance and Organization* (New York: Longman, Green, 1915).

Roberts, Paul Craig, *The Supply-side Revolution: An Insider's Account of Policymaking in Washington* (Cambridge, MA: Harvard University Press, 1984).

Rockman, Bert, *The Leadership Question: The Presidency and the American System* (New York: Praeger, 1984).

Rockoff, Hugh, "The Free Banking Era: A Reexamination," *Journal of Money, Credit, and Banking*, **6** (May 1974).

Rodman, Paul, *Mining Frontiers of the Far West: 1848–1880* (New York: Holt, Rinehart & Winston, 1963).

Rogin, Leo, *The Introduction of Farm Machinery and its Relation to the Productivity of Labor in the Agriculture of the United States during the Nineteenth Century* (Berkeley, CA: University of California Press, 1931).

Rohrlich, Paul Egon, "Economic Culture and Foreign Policy: the Cognitive Analysis of Economic Policy Making," *International Organization*, **41** (Winter 1987), pp. 61–91.

Rollins, George W., *The Struggle of the Cattlemen, Sheepmen, and Settlers for Control of Lands in Wyoming* (New York: Arno Press, 1979).

Romasco, Albert U., *The Poverty of Abundance: Hoover, The Nation, The Depression* (New York: Oxford University Press, 1965).

Romasco, Albert U., "Herbert Hoover's Policies for Dealing with the Great Depression: The End of the Old Order or the Beginning of the New?" in Martin L. Fausol and George T. Mazuzam (eds), *The Hoover Presidency: A Reappraisal* (Albany, NY: State University of New York Press, 1974).

Romasco, Albert U., *The Politics of Recovery: Roosevelt's New Deal* (New York: Oxford University Press, 1983).

Rose, Willie Lee (ed.), *A Documentary History of Slavery in North America* (New York: Oxford University Press, 1976).

Rosen, Steven (ed.), *Testing the Theory of the Military–Industrial Complex* (Lexington, MA: D.C. Heath, 1973).

Rosenberg, Nathan, "Technological Change in the Machine Tool Industry, 1840–1910," *Journal of Economic History*, **23** (1963).

Rosenberg, Nathan, *The American System of Manufactures* (Edinburgh: Edinburgh University Press, 1969).

Rosenberg, Nathan, *Technology and American Economic Growth* (New York: Harper & Row, 1972).

Rosenberg, Nathan, "Selection and Adaptation in the Transfer of Technology: Steam and Iron in America, 1800–1870," in ed. Nathan Rosenberg, (ed.), *Perspectives on Technology* (Cambridge: Cambridge University Press, 1976).

Rosenberg, Nathan, "Innovative Responses to Materials Shortages," in Nathan Rosenberg (ed.), *Perspective on Technology* (Cambridge: Cambridge University Press, 1976).

Rosenbloom, Richard and Michael Cusamano, "Technological Pioneering and Competitive Advantage: The Birth of the VCR Industry," *California Management Review*, **29** (Summer 1987), pp. 51–76.

Rossiter, Clinton, *The American Presidency* (New York: Harcourt, Brace, Jovanovich, 1984).

Rostow, W.W., *The Stages of Economic Growth: A Non-Communist Manifesto* (Cambridge: Cambridge University Press, 1960).

Russett, Bruce, "The Mysterious Case of Vanishing Hegemony; Or Is Mark Twain Really Dead?," *International Organization*, **39** (Spring 1985).

Russell, Robert W., "Congress and the Proposed Industrial Policy Structures," in Claude Barfield and William Schambra (eds), *The Politics of Industrial Policy*(Washington, DC: American Enterprise Institute, 1986).

Salisbury, Harrison E., *A Time of Change* (New York: Harpers & Row, 1988).

Samuelson, Paul, and Everett E. Hagen, *After the War, 1918–1920 Military and Economic Demobilization of the United States, Its Effect on Employment and Income* (Washington, DC: National Resources Planning Board, 1943).

Sandholtz, Wayne, Michael Borrus, and John Zysman (eds), *The Highest Stakes: The Economic Foundations of the Next Security System* (London: Oxford University Press, 1992).

Sarkesian, Sam C. (ed.), *The Military–Industrial Complex: A Reassessment* (Beverly Hills, CA: Sage, 1972).

Saunders, C.T. (ed.), *Industrial Policies and Structural Change* (London: Macmillan, 1987).

Savelle, Max and Robert Middlekauff, *A History of Colonial America* (New York: Holt, Rinehart & Winston, 1964).

Schattschneider, E.E., *Politics, Pressures, and the Tariff* (New York: Prentice Hall, 1935).

Schieber, George, Jean-Pierre Poullier, and Leslie Greenwald, "Health Care Systems in Twenty-four Countries," *Health Affairs*, 10 (1991).

Scheiber, Harry N., *Ohio Canal Era: A Case Study of Government and the Economy, 1821–1861* (Athens, OH: Ohio University Press, 1969),

Scheurman, William, *The Steel Crisis: The Economics and Politics of a Declining Industry* (Westport, CT: Greenwood Press, 1986).

Schiltz, Michael, *Public Attitudes Toward a Social Security, 1935–1965* (Washington, DC: US Government Printing Office, 1970).

Schlosstein, Barry Stephen, *Trade War: Greed, Power, and Industrial Policy on Opposite Sides of the Pacific* (New York: Congdon & Weed, 1984).

Scholten, Catherine M., "On the Importance of the Obstetrick Art: Changing Customs of Childbirth in America, 1760 to 1825," *William and Mary Quarterly* (Summer 1977), pp. 427–45.

Schumacher, Max G., *The Northern Farmer and his Markets during the Late Colonial Period* (New York: Arno Press, 1975).

Schur, Leon M., "The Second Bank of the United States and the Inflation after the War of 1812," *Journal of Political Economy*, 68 (1960), pp. 119–120.

Schultze, Charles L., "Industrial Policy: A Dissent," *Brookings Review*, 2 (Fall 1983), pp. 3–12.

Schultze, Charles L. "Cars, Quotas, and Inflation," *Brookings Bulletin*, 17 (1983), pp. 3–4.

Seagal, Harvey, "Canals and Economic Development," in Carter Goodrich (ed.), *Canals and American Economic Development* (New York: Columbia University Press, 1961), pp. 216–48.

Seager, Henry R. and Charles A. Gulick, *Trust and Corporation Problems* (New York: Harper & Bros, 1929).

Sellers, Leilla, *Charleston Business on the Eve of the American Revolution* (Chapel Hill, NC: University of North Carolina Press, 1934).

Sellers, James, "The Economic Incidence of the Civil War on the South," Ralph Andreano (ed.), in *The Economic Impact of the Civil War* (Cambridge, MA: Shenkman, 1962), pp. 57–62.

Shannon, Fred, *The Farmer's Last Frontier: Agriculture, 1860–1897* (New York: Farrar & Rinehart, 1945).

Shaw, Ronald E., *Erie Water West: A History of the Erie Canal, 1792–1854* (Lexington, PA: University of Kentucky Press, 1966).

Shear, Jeff, *The Keys to the Kingdom: The FSX Deal and the Selling of America's Future* (New York: Doubleday, 1994).

Shepherd, James T. and Gary M. Walton, *Shipping, Maritime Trade, and the Economic Development of Colonial America* (Cambridge: Cambridge University Press, 1972).

Shryock, Richard, *American Medical Research* (New York: Commonwealth Fund, 1947).

Shuman, Howard, *Politics and the Budget: The Struggle between the President and the Congress* (Englewood Cliffs, NJ: Prentice-Hall, 1992).

Smaller War Plants Corporation, "Economic Concentration and World War II," 79 Congrs., 2 Sess., S. Doc. 206 (1946), pp. 21, 54.

Smith, Adam, *The Wealth of Nations* (New York: Modern Library, 1937).

Smith, Abbott Emerson, *Colonists in Bondage: White Servitude and Convict Labor in America, 1607–1776* (Chapel Hill, NC: University of North Carolina Press, 1968).

Smith, R. Elberton, *The Army and Economic Mobilization* (Washington, DC: Government Printing Office, 1959).

Smith, J. Russell, *North America: Its People and the Resources, Development, and Prospects of the Continent as an Agricultural, Individual, and Commercial Area* (New York: Harcourt, Brace, 1925).

Smith, Walter B., *Economic Aspects of the Second Bank of the United States* (Cambridge, MA: Harvard University Press, 1953).

Snidal, Duncan, "The Limits of Hegemonic Stability Theory," *International Organization*, **39** (Autumn 1985), pp. 579–614.

Somers, Herman and Anne, *Doctors, Patients, and Health Insurance* (Washington, DC: Brookings Institute, 1961).

Spar, Deborah and Ray Vernon, *Beyond Globalism: Remaking American Foreign Economic Policy* (New York: Free Press, 1989).

Spencer, Linda, *Foreign Investment in the United States: Unemcumbered Access* (Washington, DC: Economic Strategy Institute, 1991).

Spencer, Linda, "High Technology Acquistions: Summary Charts, October 1988–April 1992, Washington, DC: Economic Strategy Institute, 1992.

Sonnefeld, Sally *et al.*, "Projections of National Health Expenditures through the Year 2000," *Health Care Financing Review*, **13** (1991).

Soule, George, *The Prosperity Decade, 1917–1929* (New York: Holt, Rinehart & Winston, 1947).

Speakes, Larry, with Robert Pack, *Speaking Out* (New York: Scribner's & Sons, 1988).

Stampp, Kenneth, *The Peculiar Institution* (New York: Alfred A. Knopf, 1956).

Starr, Paul, *The Social Transformation of American Medicine* (New York: Basic Books, 1982).

Starr, Paul, *The Logic of Health Care Reform: Why and How the President's Plan Will Work* (New York: Whittle Books, 1994).

Stegemann, Klaus, "Policy Rivalry Among Industrial States: What Can We Learn From Models of Strategic Trade Policy," *International Organization*, **43** (Winter 1989).

Stein, Herbert, *The Fiscal Revolution in America* (Chicago, IL: University of Chicago Press, 1969).

Stein, Herbert, *Presidential Economics: The Making of Economic Policy from Roosevelt to Reagan and Beyond* (New York: Simon & Schuster, 1984).

Stockfish, J.A., *Plowshares into Swords: Managing the Defense Establishment* (New York: Mason and Lipscomb, 1973).

Stover, John F., *American Railroads* (Chicago, IL: University of Chicago Press, 1961).

Strassmann, W. Paul, *Risk and Technological Innovation: American Manufacturing Methods during the Nineteenth Century* (Ithaca, NY: Cornell University, 1959).

Strauss, Frederick and Louis H. Bean, *Gross Farm Income and Indices of Farm Production and Prices in the United States, 1869–1937* (US Department of Agriculture, Technical Bulletin no. 703 (Washington, DC: Government Printing Office, 1940).

Strickland, Stephen, *Politics, Science, and Dread Disease: A Short History of United States Medical Research Policy* (Cambridge, MA: Harvard University Press, 1972).

Stubbing, Richard and Richard Mendel, "How to Save $50 Billion a Year," *Atlantic Monthly* (June 1989).

Studenski, Paul, and Herman Krooss, *Financial History of the United States* (New York: McGraw-Hill, 1965).

Summers, Colonel Harry, "A Bankrupt Military Strategy: Our Military Assets no longer Cover our Foreign Policy Liabilities," *Atlantic Monthly* (June 1989).

Swank, James S., *The Industrial Policies of Great Britain and the United States* (Philadelphia, PA: American Iron and Steel Foundation, 1876).

Swisher, Carl B., *Roger B. Taney* (Hamden, CT: Archon Books, 1935).

Talbott, Strobe, "Rethinking the Red Menace," *Time* (1 January 1990).

Taussig, F.W. (ed.), *State Papers and Speeches on the Tariff* (Cambridge, MA: Harvard University Press, 1892).

Taylor, George Rogers, *The Transportation Revolution, 1815–1860* (New York: Western Holt, Rinehart, & Winston, 1951).

Taylor, George Rogers (ed.), *The Early Development of the American Cotton Textile Industry* (New York: Harper & Row, 1969).

Taylor, Roger and Bonnie Newton, "Can Managed Care Reduce Employers' Retiree Medical Liability," *Benefits Quarterly*, 7 (1991).

Temin, Peter, *Iron and Steel in Nineteenth Century America* (Cambridge, MA: MIT Press, 1964).

Thomas, Keith, *Religion and the Decline of Magic* (New York: Scribner, 1971).

Thomas, Robert, "A Quantitative Approach to the Study of the Effects of British Imperial Policy on Colonial Welfare: Some Preliminary Findings," *Journal of Economic History*, 25 (1965), pp. 615–38.

Thomas, Robert, *An Analysis of the Pattern of Growth in the Automobile Industry* (New York: Ayer, 1977).

Thorelli, Hans B., *The Federal Antitrust Policy: Origination of an American Tradition* (Baltimore, MD: Johns Hopkins Press, 1955).

Thurow, Lester, *Head to Head: The Coming Economic Battle among Japan, Europe, and America* (New York: Morrow, 1992).

Tiffany, Paul A., *The Decline of American Steel: How Management, Labor, and Government went wrong* (New York: Oxford University Press, 1988).

Timberlake, Richard H., *The Origins of Central Banking in the United States* (Cambridge, MA: Harvard University Press, 1978).

Tolchin, Martin and Susan, *Selling our Security: The Erosion of America's Assets* (New York: Alfred Knopf, 1992).

Toynbee, Arnold, *The Industrial Revolution* (Boston, MA: Beacon Press, 1956).

Trescott, Paul B., *Financing American Enterprise: The Story of Commercial Banking* (New York: Harper & Row, 1963).

Truman, David, *The Government Process: Political Interests and Public Opinion* (New York: Alfred A. Knopf, 1951).

Tucker, Robert W. and David C. Hendrickson, "Thomas Jefferson and American Foreign Policy," *Foreign Affairs*, **69** (Spring 1990).

Tyson, Laura D'Andrea, "They Are Not US: Why American Ownership Still Matters," *The American Prospect*, **4** (Winter 1991), pp. 37–48.

Tyson, Laura D'Andrea, *Who's Bashing Whom? Trade Conflict in High-technology Industries* (Washington, DC: Institute for International Economics, 1992).

Ullman, Harlan, *In Irons: US Military Might in the New Century* (Washington, DC: National Defense University Press, 1995).

US Bureau of the Census, *Historical Statistics of the United States, Colonial Times to 1970* (Washington, DC: Department of Commerce, 1975).

US Congress, House Energy and Commerce Committee," Report on HR 4360,

Index